ADA

THE LIFE AND TIMES

OF

THE EMPRESS PULCHERIA

A.D. 399-A.D. 452

Elibron Classics
www.elibron.com

Elibron Classics series.

© 2005 Adamant Media Corporation.

ISBN 1-4021-7086-6 (paperback)
ISBN 1-4021-0720-X (hardcover)

This Elibron Classics Replica Edition is an unabridged facsimile
of the edition published in 1907 by Swan Sonnenschein & Co.,
London.

THE LIFE AND TIMES OF THE
EMPRESS PULCHERIA A.D. 399—A.D. 452

THE LIFE AND TIMES

OF

THE EMPRESS PULCHERIA

A.D. 399—A.D. 452

BY

ADA B. TEETGEN

WITH NINE ILLUSTRATIONS AND MAP

LONDON
SWAN SONNENSCHEIN & CO., Lim.
25 HIGH STREET, BLOOMSBURY, W.C.
1907

To
My Mother

FOREWORD

Some word of explanation should be offered for that rarity of references in the following pages which may be held to detract from their worth. The writer dares not claim for her book any value save that arising from the freshness of her subject. In the whole range of literature dealing with the later Roman Empire, there is no history of the Augusta Pulcheria apart from such incidental attention as she receives at the hands of modern historians, and apart from brief notices in the old Chronicles and in fragments of lost works. The period in which she lived has, however, been much studied, and in attempting to arrange an historical background whereby to throw into relief this shadowy Empress, the writer has been content to draw upon the common, obvious and well-accredited sources of information. It is because the pretensions of the book are modest that its pages are not strewn with references, and other evidences of original research. It has, in these respects, been built upon the labours of historians like Tillemont, Finlay, Hefele and others. The object of the work has been not to contribute anything fresh to history, but to rescue the personality of Saint Pulcheria.

The writer has to record her gratitude to the friends who have encouraged her to go through with her task; first and foremost to the Rev. Father Elphege Power,

O.S.B., for his scholarly translation of the Augusta's letters, for unflagging interest and ever-ready help; to the Rev. Father Thomas Smith for similar kindnesses; to Mr. and Mrs. Okey, and to the Rev. Father Sydney Smith, S.J., for having read the book in the weary stage of manuscript, and offered the writer many useful suggestions; to Mr. Campbell of the South Kensington Museum for his assistance in the matter of the illustrations; to the authorities in the numismatic department of the British Museum for permission to photograph the coins; to M. Jean Paul Laurens, the great French painter, for most kindly according permission to reproduce his magnificent picture, "St. Jean Chrysostôme," (Salon, 1893) in the book; and last, but not least, to her father for his broad-minded sympathy and interest, and for much invaluable criticism.

CONTENTS

CONTENTS—*Continued*

LIST OF ILLUSTRATIONS

ÆLIA PULCHERIA AUGUSTA.
Enlarged from a Coin.

[*Face p.* 1. *Introduction.*

The Empress Pulcheria.

INTRODUCTION

IT has been the fashion of late years to rescue the minor characters of history from the natural perspective of their times, and to write of them with disproportionate emphasis. Lest it should be thought that the present book is another effort of this kind, it is desirable to introduce the subject of it as befits her imperial rank. The fact that oblivion has fallen upon one character rather than upon another, in any given epoch, does not necessarily settle the question of importance. St. Pulcheria is forgotten in comparison with many personalities of her day, but as virtual Empress of the East Roman world from A.D. 414 to A.D. 453, she can scarcely be called a minor character.

She was the eldest sister of the Emperor Theodosius II., Regent during his minority, first among his counsellors during his entire reign, and Empress in her own right on his death, she should occupy some niche in the temple of history. She was unanimously proclaimed Empress of the East in the year 450, and " the Romans for the first time submitted to a female reign." *

A record of the life of the Augusta should be doubly interesting, since, in virtue of her supreme position, it brings us into contact with all the great men and events of a day singularly rich in historical import. It would be impossible to appreciate her, either as saint or sovereign, without a knowledge of the times in which she lived, and her biography necessarily becomes a chapter in the history of the East Roman Empire. It touches life in the fifth century at every point. Queen as well as nun, St. Pulcheria not only had the world to conquer but to rule. As final arbitress of the destinies of half the Empire, and of the fortunes of the Catholic faith within its borders, affairs of state, ecclesiastical, and lay, were

---

* Gibbon, Ch. xxxiv.

the materials out of which her perfection had to be wrought, as the quiet duties of the cloister are those of the Religious, and the domestic cares of private life, those of other Christian women. In a state and in an age when all were theologians, even a woman could merit praises befitting a bishop. The Byzantine Emperors were ever tending to some state between that of laymen and of prelates, and even so early as the fifth century St. Leo could praise in St. Pulcheria the zeal and spirit of a priest. Thus to write of her without surrounding her with the world in which she lived would be but adding to the panegyrics of those hagiographers whose concern is less the story than the moral.

The fifth century, however, is such a fertile period that its history has been written and re-written from every point of view by numberless scholars, any one of whose works would form a background for the life and reign of St. Pulcheria. Its dramatic happenings, its characteristics, its tendencies, its figures, its monuments are all sufficiently familiar. But there remains a certain novelty in viewing history and the Empire from any spot save Rome. The Byzantine aspect of the story is a new aspect. St. Pulcheria cannot, strictly, be called a Byzantine princess, for even those writers who date the transition from things Roman to Byzantine so early as the fifth century, do not consider that the old Empire came to an end before its very close. The Byzantine Empire, as distinct from the Roman, was really inaugurated by the social and administrative changes which came about between the years A.D. 610 and A.D. 717. Thus Finlay dates its commencement from the period when these alterations, united with the new policies of the Emperor Leo III, produced a visible new effect on the Empire. This was more than two and a half centuries after the reign of Theodosius II. But "it is inevitable to speak of Byzantine history, or art, or civilisation when we refer to that which had its seat on the Bosphorus," * and in this sense it should be no anachronism to call the Augusta Pulcheria a Byzantine, and to refer to her times as such.

It is not through any discoveries we may make about the imperial lady's private life that her significance becomes apparent. It is rather in the character she stamped upon her reign, in the part she played behind the scenes of the world in that day, in the guiding influence she exercised over the Emperor, in her loyal co-operation with St. Leo the Great, that we find the things revealing her to us as saint.

She is a unique figure in Byzantine history, for the fifty years during which the daughter of Arcadius was the dominant power in the Empire and in society, form an interregnum, if one may so call it, of uprightness and morality in a state whose record is often described as the most disgraceful and decadent the world has ever

---

* F. Harrison. Note 1 to the Rede Lecture of 1900 " Byzantine History in the Early Middle Ages."

known. Every act of injustice, every disastrous consequence, every crime of Theodosius' reign, every indignity put upon the Church in those years, was the result of some temporary absence of Pulcheria from court, or of the momentary ascendancy of an influence antagonistic to hers. It was beyond her power to mend the weakness of her brother's character, but the Augusta did all that a woman possessed of capacity just short of genius could do, to hold the reins of government and yet let it appear that another did so. As her Bollandist historian insists "...... she governed the Roman world most ably, but referred everything praiseworthy to her brother." * Under her administration able generals were entrusted with the conduct of prudent campaigns; upright ambassadors chosen to negotiate honourable treaties; and orthodox priests appointed to the Churches it was her delight to multiply. She had something of the English Elizabeth's instinct for character, and might indeed be described as a masculine-minded woman, did not that term rob her of the nun-like grace and humility with which all her actions were stamped.

As it has been already remarked, no life of the Augusta, either as Empress or Saint, ever seems to have been written. The materials for it are too scanty. The various contemporary correspondences like those of Theodoret, St. Isidore of Pelusium, St. Cyril, St. Simeon Stylites and even of St. Leo the Great, which might be supposed to include and preserve a few letters of the Empress, are disappointing in this respect. The writer has only been able to find about three or four. Beside the compilations of literary antiquarians like the laborious Tillemont, and the Bollandists, it is to be doubted whether the necessary data for such a biography have been collected or even indicated. Some few of the Byzantine historians, such as Socrates, Sozomen, Evagrius, refer to the Augusta in the progress of their annals, but not to any full or satisfactory extent

Among modern writers however, M. Amédée Thierry has made the fourth and fifth centuries peculiarly his own, and has treated the salient features and events of the reign of Theodosius II. with his accustomed erudition and charm. He entertains the highest esteem for St. Pulcheria. The learned monograph on "Athenais" by F. Gregorovius gives some account of the Augusta, especially of her childhood, but outside the general and well-known Church and secular histories, she finds no place in literature.

For a glimpse into the private or even into the ceremonial life of the Imperial Palace we are indebted to the works † of an Emperor who lived in it five centuries later than St. Pulcheria, and who was only concerned to elaborate and confirm the etiquette of his

* Acta Sanctorum, Sept. 15.

† Byzantinae Historiae Scriptorum Corpus. Bonnae 1828-70 Constantinus Porphyrogenetus.

own imposing court. How far the scenes he depicts may be taken as descriptive also of the marriages of the first Eudoxias, the installation of the earlier Bishops, is a question for antiquarians. Perhaps Dr. Paspates himself could hardly settle it.

St. Pulcheria stood in the Eastern Empire for the supremacy of the Church of Rome at a time when the hydra-headed heresies of the age had survived the onslaughts even of St. Augustine, and when the jealousy of Alexandria seemed to threaten the authority of the Holy See. She was hailed, during her lifetime, by the members of an Œcumenical Council, as a second St. Helena. The moment in which she was raised up to illuminate the annals of the Church was one of darkness, peril and disastrous presage. Throughout the fourth century the Fathers, east and west, had warred for the integrity of the truth ; in many a forgotten desert cell a devoted man or woman had striven for it in prayer and penitence ; and a host of saintly ladies at Rome, Constantinople, and Jerusalem, had begun to draw down upon their cause the benediction of the poor and suffering. As a woman, St. Pulcheria may have been no more remarkable than any of St. Jerome's disciples in the western capital, but her position as Empress was everything to the example her steadfast faith and goodness set the world.

Speaking of the state of the Empire, after the Peace of the Church, and describing the condition of Christendom before the advent of St. Benedict, the great historian of the monks remarks that often as the Church "has passed through trials, been persecuted, compromised, betrayed and dishonoured I doubt if at any time she stood nearer than now to the brink of that precipice down which God has promised she shall never fall. I doubt if she ever endured a sadder lot than under that long series of monarchs who believed themselves her benefactors and protectors, and who at the same time refused her liberty, peace, and honour." * St. Pulcheria stood comparatively near the beginning of this history, but already she had the devastating blight of Arianism to repair, the martyrdom of S. Chrysostom to expiate, and the corruption of incredible worldliness to withstand.

In the fourth century Christianity presented a picture of violent contrasts. On the one hand its political victory under Constantine "provoked a revival of all those pagan vices which the faith ought to have annihilated," † the world, in its utmost depravity, invaded even the highest ranks of the priesthood, and pagan vice and atheistic thought seemed to claim society for their own. "Christianity did not succeed in transforming the ancient world." ‡ Not a sentiment opposed to the old methods of violence, injustice, and trickery obtained amongst the relationships of men, and life went

---

* Montalembert " Monks of the West." Vol. 1, p. 196.

† Ibid, p. 191.

‡ Ibid, p. 204.

on in the great cities of the Empire as voluptuously, as wickedly, as luxuriously, as if the ideal of Christian living had never been displayed. Persecutions broke out between Christians as bloody and as barbarous as any they ever suffered under Diocletian, and the purity of the faith was everywhere undermined by proud and persistent heresy. Emperors took upon themselves to define dogmas and coerce Popes. The wonderful monasticism of the Egyptian deserts had given place to langour, sterility, and often to brutality. " The monks," wrote Newman, " were a very rude and excitable set of men . . . . they were not under the strict discipline which afterwards prevailed. . . . Moreover there was a vast number of fanatical monks at that day whom the Church did not recognise." * St. Benedict had not yet arisen to mould the order, as no man had done before him, to beneficial ends for souls and nations, and without his inspired rule, monks had much degenerated from the type of S. Anthony.

At the end of the fourth century, there occurred an extraordinary phenomenon in the world's history. One whole era had come to an end—and there was a pause, pending the next. Civilisation had overreached itself; the inspiration of Christianity had apparently failed, and even in the West where life never became quite so corrupt as in the effete East, monasticism—the highest expression of the Church's ideal—had become warped and fanatical. " The Roman Empire before the advent of the barbarians was an abyss of servitude and corruption. The barbarians without the monks [Benedictines] were chaos. The barbarians and the Benedictines united, recreated the world which was to be called Christendom." † With the Goth master of Rome, and Benedict master of Goth, a new and vigorous era dawned for humanity.

It was in the dark hour immediately preceding the dawn that St. Pulcheria's lot was cast. She was Empress in the East when Rome fell. A Catholic on the throne of the Arian Emperors, and of the Apostate, a nun in the Palace of Eudoxia, without the setting of history the whole significance of her life would be lost. Without the drama the world was witnessing in the West, without the movement and stir of the passionate lives of the men and women who surrounded this crowned nun, the contrast would be pointless. Upon this crowd history fastens for the material of a strange and stirring tale through which the theme of St. Pulcheria runs, like a golden thread in the variegated woof. It is a throng of intensely dramatic interest.

The adventures of the Empress Placidia alone, or the miseries of her daughter Honoria, form a romance by themselves, but they come into contact at many points with the life of St. Pulcheria. Indeed the story of the Roman world during the first half of the

---

* " The Arians of the Fourth Century."
† Montalembert " Monks of the West," Vol. I. p. 210.

fifth century reads like one of those full and "leisurely" novels of the mid-Victorian era in which four or five plots, each of compelling interest, are intertwined, while out of every situution fresh developments arise.

It is said that St. Jeanne de Chantal had an original devotion in praying for those in high places. She used every means in her power to communicate it to her nuns. She balanced the cares, responsibilities, opportunities and circumstances of kings and princes against those of people safe in the obscurity of humbler life, and felt they needed the assistance and support of prayer as greatly as did any other class of souls. If St. Jeanne had ever heard of the Augusta Pulcheria, she would have reflected with consolation, that the throne can yield Saints to God equally with the cloister; that positions beaten upon most fiercely by the dazzle of the world can nevertheless help the soul to so much the more glorious a triumph. The Church has numbered many Kings and Queens among her Saints, and this is one of the general lessons of their lives, but St. Pulcheria as an Empress of Byzantium may point it most clearly of all. When we remember the women who came after her on that throne—the Theodoras, the Irenes of fearful interest, it seems a pity that hitherto the opposite fame of Pulcheria has not been as loudly proclaimed.

If the trials of the Saints bear a proportion to their holiness, even in the judgment of men, the sufferings Pulcheria was called upon to endure, raise her in sanctity to the level of some of the greatest women the Church has delighted to honour. Apart from the vicious atmosphere of the city, apart from the jealousy of Athenais, (Theodosius' wife,) apart from the enmity naturally borne towards her by all whose motives with her brother could have no comparison with her own, the Augusta was called upon to bear what must ever be the heaviest of all crosses to a good woman. She was grossly slandered by the Nestorians, and by the fast and fashionable cliques of Constantinopolitan society. The crime imputed to her was the blacker for her religious profession. The fidelity of her mother to Arcadius had been impeached, and wicked minds harboured suspicions as to the legitimacy of Theodosius, but this was nothing to the calumnies secretly cherished and circulated about his sister. She was supposed to commit sins whose very mention is forbidden by St. Paul. It were absurd to pause a moment to refute the imputation. As Gibbon somewhere observes, "a prudent historian will refuse to examine the propriety until he has ascertained the truth" of a statement. The truth about Pulcheria lay probably in exactly the reverse of the assertions of those who were not only her personal enemies, but the enemies of religion itself.

The age of St. Pulcheria is known to ecclesiastical students as one of councils and controversies, to historians as the period of decline in the Empire, and the struggle into being of the barbarian nations around it. Biographers are confronted with a host of monumental personalities, but for all that, two causes have contributed to belittle her reign. It was preceded by that of Theodosius the Great, a man of scarcely less significance in history than Constantine himself, and succeeded seventy years afterwards, by the famous Justinian epoch. These reigns constitute all that is generally remembered of late Roman history, and the personality of Theodosius II. was in no way calculated to make a landmark in it. But St. Pulcheria, as the only one of the great Spaniard's descendants upon whom the least portion of his mantle fell, as the only woman who had ever ruled the Roman Empire in her own right, has a claim upon the remembrance of posterity. A far greater claim she has upon the affection of the Church, and if the Greeks still continue to celebrate her festival, it should not be overlooked that she belongs far more to Rome. It will be shown, later, how the eastern half of the Empire began to lose its distinctively Roman characteristics under Theodosius I., and how with the gradual reassertion of the Greek national spirit the foundations of the great schism between the western and eastern Churches were already laid when Pulcheria, honoured now by both alike, was Empress in Byzantium. Roman only in name, since she came from a Spanish family and was born of a Frankish mother, the Augusta was profoundly Catholic, and her unwavering loyalty to the Pope did much to promote the final supremacy of the western See over its great rivals in her own dominion.

Last of all she was a great Religious. She turned the Imperial Palace of Constantinople into a convent, and at a time when St. Jerome and St. Augustine were writing letters of delighted approbation to a noble maiden who, after the flight of her family from Rome, resolved to live a life of simplicity, chastity, and retirement in Africa,—herself made the vow that, in Demetrias, astonished all the world. Christian virtue was all but suffocating in the atmosphere of society in the fourth century. When the ideal of asceticism was first preached to the western world by St. Athanasius and St. Jerome, it was eagerly appreciated by the earnest in all classes of men. The days were past, however, when the desert offered itself an asylum for the persecuted; a place of penitence for the sinful, and a refuge for those who would dare the devil sooner than the world. Now that the mere profession of Christianity had become a less decided mark of separation than it was in earlier times, devout people longed for some manner of life which would help them to the heroism no longer attainable through martyrdom, and to a holiness which had ceased to be the common characteristic of a Christian.

To the sister of St. Ambrose, to the noble ladies of Rome who gathered together in the Aventine Palace of St. Proba, to Demetrias, to Melania, to that galaxy of devout women among whom the name of Monica is conspicuous—and to Pulcheria herself, the religious life was no more than the exercise of their faith. They became nuns, not as Euphrosyne, Thais and Pelagia had become penitents, but as the women of Galilee and Judæa had become Christians.

Up to this time monasticism had made but little provision for such vocations. These ladies were drawn together from the rich and influential ranks of life. Their wealth and prestige imposed upon them duties not incompatible with the renunciation of pomp and marriage, and in the counsel, encouragement, and friendship of such men as Ambrose, Augustine, Hilarius, Jerome, Chrysostom, Cyril, they found sanction and guidance for their aspirations. Inasmuch however as a vow of virginity does not make a nun, nor a life of retirement and prayer entitle a woman to be called a Religious, the Augusta Pulcheria and her sisters were not nuns in the modern strict meaning of the word. They were bound by no vow of obedience. They were not even enrolled among the deaconesses and it seems as if the most intelligible parallel to their profession is to be found in the plan of life designed by S. Francis for the tertiaries, or secular associates, of his order, in the thirteenth century. St. Pulcheria had the aspirations of a St. Eustochium, and was yet denied the sphere of St. Nicareta. She might not indeed retire to the convents of Jerusalem or Bethlehem, like St. Jerome's disciples, nor could she busy herself among the byeways and noisome purlieus of her own great city, tending the sick and poor, like St. Chrysostom's devoted assistants. Her place was at the Emperor's side. She took her vow of virginity to safeguard his throne from the pretensions of possible rivals. When the flight of time made it clear to her that she was no less needful to the Empire and to him, as a man, than she had been when he was a child, she put the opportunity of realising her private wishes aside, and refused to become a deaconess in 447, as she had denied herself in 414. But for all this it is not misleading to call her a nun. She was truly nunlike in her life, and no contrast could be greater than that between the moral and religious atmosphere of the Imperial Palace under the regime of Eudoxia and under that of her daughter.

Pulcheria's claim also to the title Saint, is founded on the esteem of her own contemporaries rather than on a modern bull of canonisation. For centuries there was no need of any scrupulous process to elevate an individual to this rank. The inscribing of his or her name on the local calendar by the bishop of the place, as one held in veneration by the people, was quite sufficient. Not until the year 1153 did the Pope assume his right to control the entries on the dyptichs of the various Churches, and to add to such lists only at his own discretion. The Augusta was looked upon as a Saint, for her prudence, her charity, her goodness, during her lifetime, and the Emperor Marcian always referred to her as such.

This was enough to give her the title in her own age, and succeeding times have confirmed it.

It would be beyond the scope of such a work as this, to do more, in dealing with the religious controversies of the time, than treat them as historical incidents. The popular ferment in Constantinople during the sittings of the Councils of Ephesus or Chalcedon, the anxieties and cares of the Augusta, the conflict between affection and duty in the Emperor's unreliable will, the vicissitudes of the great actors in those tumultuous scenes—all these things are not theology but history. As such they are essential to the story. The truths they confirmed, and the heresies they exposed, endure to the present day and are constantly being argued afresh. The Church renews her patience with the perversity of men from age to age: in the most modern of controversies, which the faithful are only too grateful and content to leave in the hands of their theologians, the Arianism, Pelagianism, Nestorianism—what you will—of the early centuries are constantly reappearing. It is no more fitting or necessary in a sketch of St. Pulcheria, champion of the faith though she was, to venture on the subtleties of these religious questions, than it would be, in writing an account of the Oxonians of 1840, to engage upon a doctrinal history of the Tractarian movement.

A coin, above all other contemporary relics, has the power of making the age that produced it, a reality to the twentieth century imagination. The miniature, the carving, the inscription, the ornament, the weapon, the vase, even the precious MS. has less power to impress with a sense of actuality than has the coin which passed from hand to hand among historic peoples, and circulated through Empires like their very blood. The thrill with which the historian takes up a coin is worth volumes of his history. That little object has fallen into his hand at last across an immense gulf of time! From the age when it was in request and use, to the present curious moment, whole eras, dynasties, nations have come and passed. The sense of touch, so rarely gratified in a museum, brings him into something like contact with the hands that wrought this or fashioned that, and in the case of a coin the impulse to handle the thing is peculiarly appropriate. Nothing however, quenches the dreamer and causes him to subside into the antiquarian more abruptly than that most deadening of all environments, the numismatic department of a great museum. After a moment or two he drops the little coin back into its dreary slot, and makes a note of the inscription. He remembers only that it is a valuable exhibit; the daylight of the present causes all the past to fade; the jargon of Greek, Punic or Latin bartering dies out of his ears, the glint of the sun on the gold is gone, the brown hands that exchanged the moneys are less now than dust, and the days of old can never come again.

The Imperial coinage of St. Pulcheria's reign has a further interest

than this imaginative one.   It has preserved for us the only means
whereby we might hope to reconstruct her protrait.   One of those
small gold discs, in size hardly as large as a Victorian sixpence, is an
immediate link with the Augusta 'whose image and superscription'
it bears.   " Ælia Pulcheria Augusta," this was the imperial legend,
and the sign, that if the Emperor's sister were not actually the first
lady in the Empire (according to his wife) she had, at least, the
rank and privileges of an Empress.

CHAPTER I

The Empress celebrated in history as the enemy of St. Chrysostom, should, according to the evidence of the contemporary coinage, be called Eudocia and not Eudoxia. Writers seem to have conspired to reverse the names of the wives of Arcadius and Theodosius II. Neither in this Chapter nor in Chapter IX, have I presumed to correct so trivial, and so obstinate a mistake.

THE story of the Byzantine Princess Pulcheria opens with the comedy of her father's marriage on April 27th in the year of Our Lord three hundred and ninety five.

The people of Constantinople had not enjoyed so rare a piece of fun since the late Emperor had allowed the shadow of a hated minister to fall upon the throne. Theodosius the Great was much mistaken in the character of the man to whom, at the close of his reign, he largely entrusted the administration of the Empire, and in whom he reposed all confidence. Rufinus was nothing but an upstart, whose diligence and capacity for business blinded his master to the baseness of his principles. At the death of the Emperor this man, who had risen from the practice of the law to the Prefecture of the East, was all powerful in the State and in the Imperial Palace. But he was hated by the Byzantines, a volatile and irresponsible people, who could resent his oppression and discuss his crimes even if they had no power to overthrow him. And the young Arcadius, elder son and successor of the Emperor, was no more fitted personally to shake off this malicious domination than was the Empire to withstand it.

A year or so previously Rufinus had built a magnificent residence for his wife and daughter in the suburb of the Oak at Chalcedon. To this he added a monastery and a church. It was generally supposed that he would confirm this great establishment and secure his influence over the youthful Emperor Arcadius by bestowing his daughter Maria upon that prince in marriage. The project was universally detested, although in the Byzantine State public opinion had no weight against it. Thus the boyish escapade by which this lady was unceremoniously rejected delighted Constantinople and shattered the ambition of Rufinus' lifetime.

In the year 391 Promotus, Master General of Theodosius' infantry, quarrelled with Rufinus. His consequent disgrace and banishment were quickly followed by his death. This man had done great service to the Empire, and a common sentiment of justice demanded that some reparation should be made to his memory. He left a widow, the notorious Marsa, and two boys. The Emperor accordingly allowed the latter to be brought up in the Imperial Palace with Arcadius and Honorius. The honour was sufficient, if not singular.

In after years these sons of Promotus took under their protection a cousin of their mother, Eudoxia, the lovely daughter of Bauto, a Frankish general who like their father had also been a soldier of the Empire. In the year of Arcadius' succession this wild and winsome beauty had reached the age of twenty-one.

Great was the astonishment throughout the capital when one day, shortly after the return of Rufinus from his vengeful journey to Antioch, the Emperor proclaimed his immediate intention to marry. He was then about eighteen years of age.

The edict went forth for the decoration of streets and palaces, for the preparation of a gala programme in the Hippodrome, and for all to be done that officialdom could do to gladden the heart of an unloved bride. Deputations from the circus factions waited on the Prefect to elaborate the plans of civil functions; the imperial 'dromoi'* displayed their silken bunting on the blue waters of the Bosphorus; the Patriarch Nectarius gave orders for a sumptuous banquet in his Palace; the 'sacred' horses of the Emperor's chariot went down to meet the convoy from Chalcedon, and all Constantinople lined the anticipated route of the bridal procession. In the Palace of the lady Sylvania, all was haste and confusion. Wondering not a little at the unseemly haste of these impulsive nuptials, Rufinus must have awaited the coming of the escort with some degree of indignation. Despite the habit of self-confidence which a long time of domination had engendered, some faint misgiving had attended his return to court. Time had hardly sufficed for him to detect whence this arose, when it smote him unmistakably on the Emperor's wedding-day. Arcadius' independence was unprecedented—sinister.

The proud Maria stood in the great hall of her father's palace longing for the supreme moment when she should feel the weight of the imperial mantle on her shoulders, and feast her eyes on the rich regalia of an Empress. The lady Sylvania strained her gaze across the dancing straits to catch the starting of the gala fleet.

And the appointed hour struck. A splendid procession issued from the gates of the Imperial enclosure and took its imposing way through the servilely acclaiming city. In the midst of it were borne the diadem, buskins, jewels and royal robes destined for the empress elect. The eyes of the people feasted on the glittering throng, and the wrinkled face of the shrivelled eunuch enthroned amidst it, twitched with malicious enjoyment as if at some enigmatic jest.

Great was the astonishment again, as the pageant took an

* Galleys and vessels of war.

The Theodosian Dynasty.

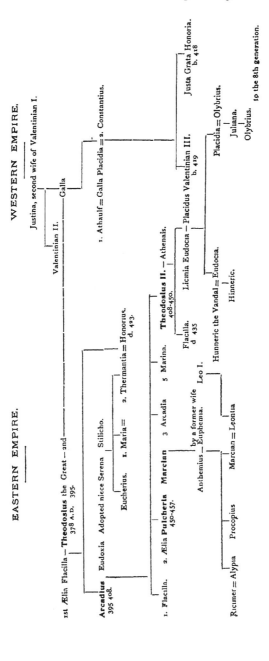

unforeseen direction. Great was the stress and crush as the crowds of sight-seers strove to readjust themselves. A murmur like that of the sea went through the streets and died into the silence of mystified expectancy as Eutropius directed the course further and further away from the shore. When at length the procession came to an unexpected standstill before the palace of Promotus, and the Chamberlain entering there, respectfully invested —not Maria—but Eudoxia with the imperial insignia, the populace broke into hearty appreciation of the coup.

The daughter of Bauto had been chosen over her rival's haughty and unconscious head, amid every circumstance of insult to Rufinus.

The beautiful Frank was straightway conducted to the Palace, and the dignified ceremonies of the marriage were immediately begun. The festivities lasted for days. Never had the ' euripos '* of the Hippodrome so overflowed with the herbs and cakes dear to its pampered audiences, never had the largesses of fish done such honour to the faction who provided them, never had the charioteers received such ovations. All Constantinople laughed and congratulated itself over Rufinus' bitter humiliation.

The two men responsible for Arcadius' revolt were Arsenius, his tutor, and Eutropius, the eunuch Chamberlain. Both the one and the other had pressed Eudoxia upon his notice. Doubtless Promotus' sons had lauded their protégée to Arcadius with the freedom of brothers. The Emperor's boyish fancy was caught by her beautiful picture, and the intrigue against Rufinus met with instant success.

Henceforth Eudoxia's impetuous caprice was Arcadius' only law. He loved her with the devotion of a sleepy lap-dog, and gave way to her imperious moods at the constant expense of his conscience. After the fall of Rufinus, favourite succeeded favourite in ascendancy over the Emperor, but Eudoxia, did she care, could always assert her paramount influence with success. She contrived the further ruin of Rufinus ; and a few years later, Eutropius himself, to whom she owed her elevation, fell from the pinnacle of his glory at the instance of her tears.

A long time afterward an abbot, bowed and venerable, wept over the palm baskets he was making in the solitude of an Egyptian laura to think how he had been of the world and in it. The saint of unknown name mourned the worldly wisdom of Arsenius, and it may be, breathed many a prayer for the repose of the soul of the woman he had helped to the diadem of a queen.

Eudoxia was full of "the pride of life." Her upbringing in the house of Marsa, a notoriously gay and unprincipled woman, must have been responsible for her undisciplined character. Inconsistent and impulsive, steeped in the flattery and luxury of the corruptest city in the Empire, and intoxicated with her sudden eminence, she led a vain and passionate existence. Her religion was nothing but

---

* A sort of trench before the seats of the spectators.

the veneer of circumstance. Until the coming of St. John from Antioch her conscience never stirred. After that event, however, it seems as if some appreciation of better things was aroused within her. She could feel a real regret at not being able to win the countenance of a man she recognised as holy. But her impulsive acts of piety and theatrical expressions of humility or reverence, deceived the Patriarch less than her own soul. St. John soon understood the Empress. High as his love for his mother had raised the ascetic's estimate of womanhood, he had no toleration for its sins and despicabilities. The more roughly perhaps, he dealt with them. He would have none of Eudoxia's insincerity. She, with her high spirit, would brook none of his reproofs. Her scruples were easily forgotten when her pride was touched, and in the end the paganism of her race would out. Yet the worst harm the famous Empress wrought—in all fairness be it said—was the outcome of lesser faults than those of calculation and depravity. Surrounded by the gayest and most fashionable ladies of Constantinopolitan society, she queened it in a world entirely to her liking. She ignored and despised her husband, but incidentally became the mother of some saints. The story of her great struggle against St. Chrysostom, and against the leaven he sowed in her life, is one of the best known in history. The remorse and misery of her last months give a final touch to as pitiable a tale as ever roused indignation.

Of St. Pulcheria's father it is impossible to say much. He more resembles the invertebrate sea anemone to which Synesius likened him, than a man. Arcadius' marriage was his single act of self-assertion. It was a rare instance of initiative, but at least it brought him a certain meed of happiness. Too indolent to resent Eudoxia's disdain, he was yet complacent enough to reciprocate whatever kindness she found it expedient to show him. His love for her was the keenest emotion he was capable of feeling, and he asked little of life save the peace which for one in his position was only a form of indolence and weakness. Throughout his reign he was astonishingly impotent and inactive. In the Imperial Palace at Constantinople he led a life as supine and insignificant as that of his brother at Ravenna. Owing something to their utter lack of fraternal affection, as well as either's incapacity to grasp the affairs of his own or the other's half of Empire, the Roman world drifted widely asunder under Arcadius and Honorius. It was generally admitted that any man of character and initiative stood for more in East or West than the occupant of the throne. The disasters that befel the Empire after the death of Theodosius were generally the result of his sons' inexperience and languor.

One thing Arcadius did for the Empire worthy of all praise. At the approach of death he provided it, in the person of Anthemius, with a guardian whose integrity and ability might be trusted to repair the harm of his own reign.

The entire family of this Emperor and Empress was born between the years 395 and 405.

Historians differ as to whether there were three daughters or four, and as to their respective ages. Nothing can come of a fresh survey of the arguments.

Were the Princess Flacilla the eldest child and not identical with Arcadia, as one writer suggests, she may have died in infancy. Or she may have retired into religious life still more obscure than that to which her sisters dedicated themselves in 414, for the tablet erected in St. Sophia to commemorate the vow of virginity taken in that year by the imperial sisters, makes no mention of Flacilla. Nor does a princess of that name appear to have owned any palace in the city, like Pulcheria and the others. The historian of " The Decline and Fall " makes a further suggestion that she may have been prevented by some bodily or mental imperfection from assuming the honours of her rank.

However this may have been, all are agreed that Pulcheria herself was born in the year 399 A.D. ; we even have the date, January 19th.

St. John had then been Patriarch of Constantinople eleven months, and Eutropius had worn the "palmata vestis" of his disgraceful consulate since the first kalends of the new year. He was still intoxicated with the vanity of his monstrous success, and while Rome writhed under the ignominy of it, and Claudian filled his verse with satire, the eunuch was ready with that insolence to the Empress which was shortly to bring about the dramatic dénouement of his wierd career.

St. Pulcheria was baptised by the great St. Chrysostom in the baptistry of St. Sophia, and the first of those memorable scenes was witnessed which were to identify her with the pre-Justinian basilica.

In the fourth century baptism was frequently delayed that the grace of so momentous a sacrament might attend the catechumen's deathbed, but the Great Theodosius who had only been baptised after the alarm of an illness, secured it early for his children, and so also did Arcadius. Theodosius II. and his sisters were all baptised in infancy. The vain and beautiful Eudoxia made the occasion one of display and self-aggrandisement, and it was celebrated by holiday festivities in the city.

Pulcheria was ushered into a world that glittered for her truly, but the glance of St. Chrysostom was the fairest thing the child encountered.

The only glimpse we catch of her babyhood is in connection with the downfall of Eutropius. One day in the autumn of that same year the minister had the hardihood to bid Eudoxia remember that as she owed her position to him so too could he cast her from it. The imperious beauty flushed into angry tears at the insult. Snatching her child in her arms she rushed from the "purple chamber" to Arcadius' presence, to demand would he brook such insolence to its mother! The Emperor fretted at his wife's impetuosity. He had had experience of her variable moods. But he was as weak in defending his favourites as in defying them.

In a moment Eutropius was flying through the Palace for the sanctuary of St. Sophia. He had fallen, at a word, from the summit of prosperity to the gutter of disgrace and execration. The city howled him down, the people baited him around the altar. The story of St. Chrysostom's grand intercession, standing between the grovelling wretch and the bloodthirsty populace, of the eunuch's respite, and of the Empress's perfidious revenge needs no retelling here.

In the following year Eudocia gave birth to another daughter, Arcadia, and in 401 her little son was born.

Meanwhile the tragedy of St. Chrysostom's end drew on. Within a year or two of his advent to the capital, this great Savonarola of the fifth century, found himself committed to an uncompromising course of denunciation and reform. He was now in the full torrent of his indignation against the worldliness and vice around him.

Some traits in his character, some contradictions in his lot, remind us of his great contemporary Theodoret. Father Newman's sympathetic sketch of the historian Bishop shows the suffering of a noble nature in uncongenial surroundings. The man in whom sincerity found it so difficult to strike a balance with humility, was under a double disadvantage. Keenly conscious of powers and sympathies for which he had no scope, Theodoret was restive as a captured thing. He longed for such a sphere as Chrysostom's. He did his utmost not to hate the stagnant provincial See from which he was condemned to look on at the doings of the world. So strenuous was the struggle between ambition and resignation in his large, capable soul that he fell short of the sainthood such a cross might have conferred upon him.

St. Chrysostom, on the other hand, wrested the trials of his Patriarchate to his eternal glory. His priest's heart broke itself on the barriers of vice and folly everywhere upreared against him, he may indeed have sighed for a more congenial lot. Right man in the right place as he undoubtedly was, St. John set about his great task doomed for tragedy. He scorned to make use of the world, its maxims and conventions, even to overcome the world. His passionate zeal for purity and earnestness, pressed in every quarter with the tactlessness of a man who had no respect for persons, set him in a very short time at variance with every class of society. The simplicity of his manner of life disappointed the poor, who looked for pomp and circumstance, and no less displeased the wealthy who accused him of being remiss in the duties of his station. They had been accustomed to the lavish hospitality of the Patriarcheon, and to the courtly presence of its host at their

2

own sumptuous boards   The clergy as a body felt unequal to the
expectations of their Archbishop.   They were an idle, pleasure-
seeking class.   They opposed at first a mere *vis inertiæ* to the
vigorous demand made upon their religious energies.   As time
went on and Chrysostom's discipline began to winnow their ranks,
opposition deepened into mutiny among them.

Society at large was wrought rather to fury than to repentance
by the Patriarch's crusade against its sins.   The gay and fashionable seceded from his following as soon as the discovery was
made that these startling sermons were designed for more than
novel effect.   Rage succeeded to the Empress's astonishment at
this intrepid speech.   It served the interests of the courtiers to
inflame her anger by reporting every censure calculated to reflect
upon her.   Her outraged pride was quick to take offence, even
when it was not directly given, but the Patriarch did not pause to
make exception for the first lady in the realm.   Eudoxia hated
Chrysostom the more madly as she had hoped to master him.

All the gentleness and sweetness of his nature had to be
repressed in favour of its sternness.   The priest whose craving for
solitude with Almighty God had been set aside at the prayer of his
lonely and loving mother, had now to smother gentle impulses and
present that aspect to his people which cost him such bursting
tears in secret.   If Theodoret suffered intellectual starvation,
chained to an outlandish spot, Chrysostom, forced into the hottest
of the strife, endured a crucifixion of heart.

He drew down upon himself the hatred of the powerful.   His
apostolic carelessness of favour and position rendered him
unassailable.   Years ago he had defied the devil and the flesh, now
he was in mortal combat with the world.   The impotence of his
enemies came from their sense of his altitude, from their perception
that to persecute him was but to betray their own baseness.   The
whole population of the city, clerical and lay, was quickly winnowed
by the saint.   Eudoxia found herself identified with the chaff.
Only such women as Olympia, Salvina, Nicareta, Patrocla, only
the poor and despised, only the sick and helpless knew Chrysostom
for what he was.

The Empress and her court were pitted in venomous indignation
against him.   Arcadius drifted.   Meantime the Patriarch feared
no more from their resentment than from the machinations of
unworthy ecclesiastics and the enmity of his peers.

The year of Theodosius II.'s birth saw the disaffection of the
capital thicken into plots against the Patriarch.   While he was away
in the winter months on a visitation at Ephesus, Severian, Bishop
of Gabala, to whom he had delegated his authority, endeavoured
to weaken St. John's influence in every direction.   A conspiracy
was formed against him, headed by the Empress and the ladies of
her court, among them Marsa, Castricia, Eugraphia and others.

The storm was all but precipitated on the saint's devoted head

RAGE SUCCEEDED TO THE EMPRESS'S ASTONISHMENT AT THIS INTREPID SPEECH.—*Page* 18.

[*Face p.* 18.

by a sermon he preached shortly after his return to his cathedral church. He was supposed to have alluded to Eudoxia as Jezebel, and the insult rankled. For a time however the Empress could do little but nurse her anger. Her son was born in April, and the great occasion of his baptism required a show of cordiality.

By an unprecedented favour the infant Theodosius was declared at the same time Cæsar and Augustus. "All the city," says the secretary of a contemporary Bishop, "was crowned with garlands and decked out in garments entirely made of silk and gold, jewels and all kinds of ornaments, so that no one could describe the adornment. One might behold the inhabitants, multitudinous as the waves, arrayed in all manner of various dresses." Eudoxia attributed her happy delivery to the prayers of Bishop Porphyry of Gaza. This prelate had but recently arrived in Constantinople in order to procure from Arcadius an edict to suppress the turbulent tyranny of the heathen in his diocese. St. Chrysostom suggested to him that his best course would be to interest the Empress in his favour. In return for Eudoxia's promise to lay the matter before her husband the Bishop blessed her "and moved her to a transport of gratitude" by predicting that her unborn child would be a son. Theodosius II. was the first Porphyrogenitus, or Prince born-in-the-Purple since the days of Constantine.

As the baptismal procession emerged from St. Sophia, a little scene was enacted whereby the Empress gained the Bishop's ends. St. Chrysostom who, as God-father to the infant Prince, was carrying him in his arms, stopped by pre-arrangement and Porphry placed his petition in the little hands. Arcadius took it from his child and read it, "I cannot," he said, "refuse the first commands of my son."

The Emperor strove to reconcile St. Chrysostom and Severian, and gratified at last with the coveted title of Augusta, Eudoxia herself condescended to try and smooth away the trouble she had fostered.

One Sunday, just as Mass was about to begin, the Empress was seen advancing up the nave of the great basilica with her attendants, carrying her baby son. "The complaisance of the East had given to members of the Imperial family that right to pass within the curtains of the sanctuary which St. Ambrose with courteous dignity had forbidden to Theodosius in the West." In sight however of the whole congregation Eudoxia went forward, placed the child on the Patriarch's knees and adjured him by the life of the Emperor, and by the head of the Augustus, to forgive Severian. St. John knew how to yield as well as how to stand. He perfected his severity by a holy magnanimity, but had yet to learn that his opponents could appreciate no methods and no motives but their own.

The next year, 403, saw another addition to the Imperial family, and after the birth of the Princess Marina, the strife and stress in the capital rushed rapidly to a climax.

CHAPTER II

BEFORE we go further, it may be as well to picture to ourselves the surroundings of the Imperial family. The world of luxury into which St. Pulcheria was ushered was the world denounced by St. Chrysostom. Its reign hastened to an end with every year of the Princess's growth, but in the meantime Eudoxia's court continued as brilliant as ever.

The Great Palace, called in the reverent language of the Greeks the Sacred Palace, and founded by Constantine on the acropolis of old Byzantium, had grown even by the end of the fourth century into a city by itself. Until within two centuries of the Turkish conquest it formed the residence of the Byzantine Emperors, and continually grew in size and magnificence as generation succeeded generation.

It was cut off from the city to the west by a lengthy wall pierced by five imposing gateways. The boundary line of the imperial precincts was completed on the eastern side by the sea wall, studded with substantial towers, round, square or octagon in shape, which extended for about three miles along the curve of the shore. The royal demesne stretched from a point on the south where a beacon or Pharos stood to the headland of the Golden Horn called the Point of Keras on the north. The palace was at one place substituted for the wall in about fifty feet of its length. "Fronted along its base with slabs of white marble, the edifice presented a lofty stone balcony overhanging the water, and opening on to it, a central group of three rectangular windows or doors with jambs or lintels of sculptured stone. Above, a row of seven nearly semicircular windows indicated the uppermost floor of the building called the Palace of Hormisdas."[*] On the shore of the straits themselves "was a very ornate harbour, formed on a totally different plan from any other. Curved piers of masonry enriched with marbles extending from the land, enclosed about an acre of water which was approached from the city by flights of white marble steps. On the intervening quay rested a handsome group of statuary representing a lion and a bull in the agonies of a death struggle. This was the exclusive port of the Imperial Palace, an

---

[*] Age of Justinian, Theodora," W. G. Holmes. The harbour of Bucoleon may have been constructed at a date somewhat later than that of Theodosius II. See "Constantinople," by Professor van Millingen, ch. iv., p. 94.

important segment of which adjoined the wall at this point. . . . .
Further on was a small entry leading to a chapel sacred to the
Theotokos under the title of Conductress, one of the Augusta
Pulcheria's foundations. " *

From the Palace the view lay across terraced lawns, coppices of
plane, cypress, acacia, mulberry and the majestic Trebizond palm,
to the rocky islands of the bright Propontis. Beyond the Straits
of Bosphorous lay the purple hills of Asia.

Every palace near Byzantium had its 'philopatium' or plesaunce,
a sort of enclosed park where landscape gardening attained a high
pitch of perfection, but the grounds of the Imperial Palace far
excelled all the rest. Between hedges of flowering shrubs " cut in
the forms of Greek and oriental letters, footpaths paved with
marble led to a fountain surrounded by twelve dragons in bronze.
The perfumed waters gushed forth and flowed away beneath the
branches of palms and cedars gilded to the height of a man. The
peacocks of China, pheasants and ibises strutted at liberty among
the trees, or preened themselves on ground strewn with costly
golden sand from Asia." † Under the régime of the first Eudoxia,
Pulcheria's famous mother, these gardens were continually en fête,
their arbours and parterres ever the scenes of intrigues and
trysts. There were 'sphacristiae' or tennis lawns, a splendid
'tzukanisterion' or polo ground, gymnasia and spacious paddocks.
Beautiful avenues of statues with brass plates upon their heads to
protect them from the birds, vied with colonnades of pines, like
green obelisks. High up among the sombre branches of these
graceful trees swung sweet full blossomed roses, scenting many a
long vista with their haunting perfume. There were woods of fig
and sycamore. Masses of verdure where the oleander and pome-
granate shone, alternated with walks strewn with coloured sands,
cascades and artificial cliffs, where waved the delicate mimosa of
of the Nile. Here and there were quadrangular enclosures formed
of monolithic pillars with massive architraves all garlanded with
vines. Through the gemmed thickets of the intervening bushes
came the delicious sound of plashing fountains. Terrace after
terrace led down by wide flights of marble steps to the artificial
lakes whereon floated the Imperial pleasure boats with their silken
cushions and gay bunting. Huge marble vases filled with flowers
and odorous shrubs stood here and there about the gardens, and
in the midst of all a shining column upreared a golden statue of
Theodosius the Great.

The Sacred Palace occupied the south western corner of these
grounds. It consisted of an enormous conglomeration of buildings, mostly of one storey, distributed over an area of unequal
levels. The different parts of it were connected by innumerable

* " The Age of Justinian and Theodora." W. G. Holmes, p. 37.

† " La Vie Byzantine au vime siecle." Marrast.

galleries, staircases, corridors, passages, and arcades, and were confused by a host of adjacent and independent buildings. Many private palaces had been erected within the Imperial ward. Their domes mingled with those of its many churches. Among the latter the Church of our Lady of the Pharos, and of St. Stephen in that part of the Palace called the Daphne, were the most famous. The Palace and all its dependencies were built in marble, and the roofs were covered with lead. They thus escaped the disastrous fires that so often wrought havoc in the city. Across the façades the architects designed a sort of cornice upon which it was the Byzantine custom, at least a little later, to inscribe a date or some religious maxim. "May the Lord preserve thy coming in and thy going out, now and for ever, Amen" might be read above a portico, and on the balustrade of many a balcony such an evidence of faith as this—"If the Lord be for us who can stand against us? Glory be to Him for ever." Carlo Garnier, an Italian writer, has a delightful chapter in his work "Abitazione Umana" on the Byzantine houses of the fourth and fifth centuries, but in the face of Dr. Paspates' assurance that it is impossible at this length of time to form anything like a truthful idea of the original palace, it would be misleading to build too much upon the statements of the former in this respect. The Greek archæologist himself can tell us little as to the plan and exterior look of the Imperial Palace, or as to the dates of its various parts.

From the accounts of Imperial ceremonies and usages given by the Emperor Constantine Porphyrogennetos in his work on court procedure, it is not possible to gain anything but a confused, if glowing and amazing, idea of the extent and glories of the Sacred Palace. The poetic Greek names of its various halls * and antechambers indicate the profusion and luxury of their adornment. They convey, too, an imposing impression of the magnificence, the glitter, the pomp, of court life. They bewilder far more than describe. "The Golden Hand," "the Ivory Gate," "the Thermastra," "the Halls of the Augustæus," and of "the Nineteen Couches," "the Purple Chamber," "the Bedchamber of the Daphne," "the musikos," "the Sigma," "the consistory," "the oval," "the vestiary of the Augusta," "the lights," "the Tribune," "the Octagon," "the Gallery of the Forty Saints"—all these are names among which we lose ourselves as if in the mazes of the Byzantine palace itself.

The vestibule of the Palace opened on the southern portico of the Augustæum; it was a handsome pillared hall named Chalke, or the Brazen House, from being roofed with tiles of gilded brass. An image of Christ had stood devoutly over the brazen entrance gates since the days of Constantine. The vestibule led to several spacious chambers or courts, rather of an official than of

---

* The aggregation of years of building, enlargement and adornment.

a residential character. Beyond the Chalke portion of the Palace, a colonnaded court led, on the right, to a small church dedicated to St. Stephen, the upper galleries of which overlooked the Hippodrome across the 'Place Impèriale.' On the left was an octagon chamber, the first hall in that more secluded part of the Palace called the Daphne. On the domed roof stood a figure representing the fortune of the city, erected by Constantine. The Daphne included the private reception rooms of the Emperor and Empress. Its terraces and balconies facing west overlooked the great forum outside. Beyond the Daphne again, was a further court leading to a third vestibule called the Sigma. The division of the Imperial residence to which it gave entrance was specially called the 'sacred Palace' because it contained the 'sacred cubicle' or sleeping apartment of the Emperor. The porphyry Palace was situated at some distance from the rest but was connected with it by covered galleries. It was a square building with a roof rising to a point like a pyramid. The walls and floors were covered with a rare species of speckled purple marble imported from Rome, and hence its name. It was appropriated to the use of the Empresses, and when a child was born to the Byzantine Emperor he was accordingly called a 'porphryrogennetos' one born in the purple. * Anna Comnena describes this Purple Chamber in which she herself was born, A.D. 1083, (Alexiadis Bibliotheca Teubneriana, p. 229.)

The Imperial apartments were furnished with splendour and munificence. The furniture was entirely of gold, silver, ivory and precious woods ; rich embroideries bestrewed the floors and couches, and mosaics encrusted the walls. The doors were of ivory, the ceilings lined with gold . . . . "the walls of the halls and bed chambers were of marble, and wherever commoner stone was used, the surface was veneered with gold plate. The beds were made of ivory or of solid silver, the chairs, couches, tables, stools, were of ivory or marble. The semicircular sigmas made of gold or silver were so heavy that two youths could hardly lift one." † Every article was studded with precious stones and jewels. A table is mentioned as having been carried off by way of booty in the sack of Rome, "which consisted of a single piece of solid emerald encircled with three rows of fine pearls supported by three hundred and sixty five feet of gems and massy gold." ‡ Furniture no less extravagant and costly filled the Palace at Constantinople. Its various halls and chambers were scented by fragrant sprays or fuming gums, and illuminated by beautiful polycandelae. These were huge wheels of wrought metal suspended horizontally, bearing on their margin innumerable little glass cups in which flaming wicks floated in scented oil.

---

* All these details are taken, literally in places, from Mr. W. G. Holmes "Age of Justinian and Theodora."

† Bury, "Later Roman Empire."　　　‡ Gibbon.

But "the domestic crowd of the Palace," the army of its officials and the host of its slaves and servants—to say nothing of the entire society it housed, was more than sufficient to people the ' Imperial city.' " A thousand barbers, a thousand cup-bearers, a thousand cooks were distributed in the several offices of luxury ; and the number of eunuchs [those wretched victims of oriental selfishness who under the degenerate sons of Constantine had assumed position and pride in the Palace], could be compared only with the insects of a summer's day. The monarch . . . . was oppressed by the magnificence of his dress, his table, his buildings and his train." . . . The expenses of his household surpassed that of the legions, " yet the smallest part of this costly multitude was subservient to the use or even to the splendour of the throne. The monarch was disgraced, and the people were injured, by the creation and sale of an infinite number of obscure and even titular employments, and the most worthless of mankind might purchase the privilege of being maintained, without the necessity of labour, from the public revenue. The waste of an enormous household, the increase of fees and perqusites, which were soon claimed as a lawful debt, and the bribes which they extorted from those who feared their enmity or solicited their favour, suddenly enriched these haughty menials. They abused their fortune . . . . . . and their rapine and venality could be equalled only by the extravagance of their dissipations. Their silken robes were embroidered with gold, their tables were served with delicacy and profusion ; the houses which they built for their own use would have covered the farm of an ancient consul, and the most honourable citizens were obliged to dismount from their horses and respectfully salute a eunuch whom they met on the public highway."*

The government of the Palace was as highly organised as that of the Empire, and a series of great officials whose rank or whose duties were in a scale of subordination from highest to lowest, were responsible to nobody but themselves for the administration of its myriad departments.

"The manly pride of the Romans, content with substantial power, had left to the vanity of the East the forms and ceremonies of ostentatious greatness."† Presently however "the simplicity of Roman manners was insensibly corrupted by the stately affectation of the courts of Asia." In the hierarchy of the Imperial Palace, where a multitude of abject titled dependents replaced the men of distinction and merit once grouped around an Emperor, "every rank was marked with the most scrupulous exactness, and its dignity was displayed in a variety of trifling and solemn ceremonies which it was study to learn and a sacrilege to neglect." ‡ The legal codes

---

* Gibbon, Ch. xxii. The Emperor Julian reformed these abuses, in his day, but they soon reasserted themselves, and under Arcadius and Eudoxia were as flagrant as ever.

† Ibid, Ch. xvii.   ‡ Ibid.

of the centuries onwards from Theodosius II. contain as many complicated directions as to court precedence and etiquette as to the administration of finance or justice, and in the tenth century an Emperor could devote more time and interest to the account of Imperial ceremonies and functions than to a work on military tactics. The upkeep of the Imperial Palace became practically synonymous with the government of the Empire, and in those times, its master's chief responsibility resolved itself into that of keeping the people of the capital in a good humour, well spoiled and well amused, it was of the first importance to make the Imperial pageants imposing, and the court life as brilliant as possible. The seven great officials of the Palace were not only the Emperor's domestic servants but his ministers.

The Master of Offices united the supreme administration of public affairs, to the onerous duties of his household appointment. " He was the supreme magistrate of the Palace, inspected the discipline of the civil and military 'schools,' and received appeals from all parts of the Empire in the causes which related to that numerous army of privileged persons, who as the servants of the court had obtained for themselves and their families a right to decline the authority of the ordinary judges. He also controlled the corps of Imperial messengers or spies, and enjoyed, in society, the high rank of an 'illustrious.'*

" The private apartments of the Palace were governed by a favourite eunuch . . who was styled the præpositus or Prefect of the ' sacred ' bedchamber. His duty was to attend the Emperor in his hours of state or of amusement, and to perform for him all the confidential or menial offices "* of a valet. He was in fact the Chamberlain, and had an army of deputies and servants under his command. It was this officer who so frequently, under the reigns of Arcadius and his son, abused his office and asserted a sway over the weak mind of the Emperor which was insulting to the dignity of all his other ministers. Eutropius and Chrysaphius are only two of many instances. Two important posts were held under Chamberlain, that of the Count of the Imperial wardrobe, and that of the Count of the Imperial table. The first had the care of the Emperor's gorgeous vestments and innumerable robes, jewels, mantles and ornaments, while the second exercised a vast amount of ingenuity to furnish the "winter roses " and " summer snows " all other unnatural and extravagant dainties for the Imperial meals.

The Great Logothete or Count of the Sacred Largesses was, again, minister of finance, treasurer general of the revenue, and paymaster to the Empire. But he united with this extensive office, which employed several hundred subordinates, that of controller of foreign trade, chiefly in the interests of the linen and woollen industries

---

* Gibbon, ch. xvii.

But "besides the public revenue which an absolute monarch might levy and expend according to his pleasure, the Emperors in the capacity of opulent citizens possessed a very extensive property which was administered by the Count of the Private Estate."* This 'illustrious' managed the Emperor's lands and private palaces, saw that the province of Cappadocia kept up the special breed of horses destined for his exclusive use, and was ever on the watch to confiscate and fine in his master's interest.

"The chosen bands of cavalry and infantry which guarded the person of the Emperor were under the immediate command of two Counts of the Domestics. The whole number consisted of 3500 men, divided into seven 'schools' or troops of 500 each, and in the East this honourable service was almost entirely appropriated to the Armenians. Whenever, on public ceremonies, they were drawn up in the courts and porticoes of the Palace, their lofty stature, silent order, and splendid arms of silver and gold displayed a martial pomp not unworthy of the Roman majesty."* Some of these picked men were again chosen to guard the interior apartments of the Imperial quarter, and from such posts they might aspire to the generalships of armies. These guards had their quarters in the Palace. They were divided into four companies called Scholars, Excubitors, Protectors, and Candidates, respectively. The latter body were distinguished by wearing white robes when in personal attendance on the Emperor. But the Silentiaries, a band of nobles, generally formed the chief retinue of the Byzantine sovereign.

Besides these officers and courtiers, the palace housed a host of agents, reporters, messengers, shorthand writers, secretaries, lawyers, interpreters, readers, declaimers, physicians, minstrels, and the innumerable supernumeraries of all their departments. The Empress had her own suite of Counts and ministers, her train of ladies, her bevies of waiting women and her crowds of eunuchs and servants.

When St. Pulcheria's mother was at the height of her success, the Palace was continually filled with the exotic life of the Capital. Ladies vied with each other in her boudoirs and anterooms. Their dresses were covered with pictorial embroideries, their hair was "shamelessly uncovered," and even dressed up into towers bristling with points and bars of gold, or dusted with it, and entwined with flowers. Their eyes were unnaturally dilated, their lashes and eyebrows dyed, their lips a mass of carmine, and their skin thick with enamels and preservatives. Their ears were weighted with jewellery, rings covered their fingers, and the stiff cloth of gold of their mantles was beset with pearls and precious stones. The men were scarcely less gorgeous. They wore dozens of tunics of filmy and transparent silk, their shoes were embroidered with ivy leaves, and their persons bedizened with ornaments and jewels. The successors of Diocletian followed closely in that Emperor's steps

* Gibbon, ch. xvii.

so far as the orientalisation of the Roman court was concerned. Henceforth it differed but slightly from that of a Xerxes or a Darius. The courtiers were servile, and the eunuchs all powerful.

Under the Byzantine Emperors the ' Senate' was reduced to a mere tribunal, and the consulate to a mere date. All legislative, judical and executive powers were vested in the sovereign himself. Theodosius II. was as unfettered an autocrat as ever sat upon a throne, and St. Pulcheria behind him wielded autocratic power. Yet a nominal Senate still existed, and it was formed of the higher officers of the Imperial court. When, in 451, the Emperor Marcian went to be present at a sitting of the Council of Chalcedon, he was accompanied by the Senate, namely the Pretorian Prefect, the Prefect of Constantinople, the Master of the Offices, the Count of the Domestics, the Intendant of the Privy Purse, the Master of the Imperial Stables, the Secretary of State, &c. These dignitaries aggregated to themselves an enormous number of lucrative and frivolous appointments, and revelled in the titles that the court so loved. It appears that some of these, such as ' Patricius,' were not borne in perpetuity by those who were so fortunate as to acquire them. They merely accompanied a term of office. Mr. Hodgkin tells us that the " Illustrious," conferred upon the cabinet ministers, corresponded somewhat to the modern English ' Right Hon.,' that " Spectabilio " (or Honourable), belonged to the Chiefs of State Departments, and "Clarissimus" or Worshipful, to the Governors of the smaller provinces. A law passed on March 21st, 413, addressed to Priscien, Prefect of Constantinople, defined the rank of these various nobles. The ' Counts of the first Order' ranked after the Prefects, and the Illustrious ; the Constables and Curopalates were on an equal footing with provincial Governors, &c.

The government of the Imperial city devolved on the Prefects, and on the factions of the Hippodrome. These latter existed to provide amusement for the people, and had been legalised for the purpose. The Byzantine Emperors had always encouraged their activities, influence, and animosities ; they were widespread among the cities of the Empire, and formed indeed a sort of masonic society in East and West. Each faction—there were four, the red, white, blue, and green—consisted first, of the members who subscribed annually to its funds, and to whom belonged the privilege of electing the office bearers ; secondly, of the charioteers, and thirdly of a mass of citizens who, without being subscribing members of the society, nevertheless sympathised with one or another of the factions, wore its colours and vociferously applauded its success in the Hippodrome. The fierce spirit of rivalry that animated the various parties sufficed to keep the people of Constantinople in a constant ferment, not unlike that of a modern general election. The white and red factions were more or less eclipsed by the blue and green, and swallowed up in these respectively. The city was entirely at the mercy of their quarrels and conflicting interests. The factions identified themselves with every phase of civic or political life, and even took sides in theological controversies. In the Hippodrome the blues howled down the greens, and the greens hissed the successes of their opponents. More than once the city ran with blood or withered in the frightful fires incidental to the battles of the factions. More than once the scum of the Hippodrome stables mounted to the throne of the Byzantine empire, and sat there as worthily as any Porphyrogennetos. One thing, however, stands to the credit of the Constantinopolitan circus. It never witnessed the hideous gladiatorial combats so often seen in Rome. Theodosius' noble refusal to allow its trampled sand to be wetted with human blood saved the sacrifice of a second St. Telemachus.

"To each division of the city was assigned a Curator or chief controller, a Vernaculus, or beadle, who performed the duties of a public herald, five Vicomagistri who formed a night patrol for the streets, and a considerable number of Collegiati, whose duty it was to rush to the scenes of fires with hatchets and waterbuckets." *

The Imperial Palace not only served as the home of the Emperor and Empress, the Government House of the Byzantine Empire, but as the depositary of its historic relics. The sacred Labarum of Constantine had hung idly in the perfumed air since the Emperors had ceased to lead the legions in person. The Churches of the royal ward were constantly being enriched by gifts of price and fame.

But a few years were to witness such a revolution in the Imperial household as had only been foreshadowed by the wholesale clearance effected by the apostate Emperor. Julian had reduced it to a desert forty years before, but the convent-like régime of Pulcheria was far removed from the simplicity of the man who rejoiced not only in plain living and high thinking, but in the fact that his beard was alive!

---

* W. G. Holmes, "The Age of Justinian and Theodora."

CHAPTER III

ST. CHRYSOSTOM

The epithet Chrysostom, or "golden-mouth" was only applied to St. John, Archbishop of Constantinople, when the praise it implied could no longer offend him. He died (407 A.D) before it became common, but I have used it in the story to distinguish him from the many other St. Johns.

TO return to the thread of the story. In the same year as that in which the Princess Marina was born, Eudoxia and her party found in the person of Theophilus, Patriarch of Alexandria, one who could organise and command the various forces gathering against St. John Chrysostom.

Upon this prelate had devolved the unwelcome task, six years before, of consecrating him Archbishop. Theophilus had then suffered the jealousy of a man who sees one he had tried to depreciate raised to power, and the apprehension of a traitor whose efforts to satisfy his tools had failed. He had never forgiven the unwitting Chrysostom. Moreover he was violent, dominating, and unscrupulous by nature, only too glad of any pretext for interfering in the affairs of the sister Church.

In 403 the friendly feeling shown by St. John to some monks of the Nitrian desert, who had incurred the cruel displeasure of Theophilus, was made the occasion for holding a council to deliberate upon their cause. The Egyptian prelate came to Constantinople in great state. A strong escort of Alexandrian sailors accompanied him laden with ample gifts wherewith to bribe those whom he wished to bring over to his side. He was not publicly received by St. Chrysostom and the clergy, but had a noisy welcome from the sailors of the Egyptian corn vessels in the harbour. The Empress, however, placed her palace in the Placidiana suburb at his disposal, and threw the whole weight of court favour on the side of his pretensions.

Arcadius seemed to think that St. John would hold an enquiry into the complaints brought by Theophilus against the monks, but this proud spirit took quite a different view of the case. For him, the affair of the "Tall Brethren" was a mere excuse. His idea was to convene a Synod to sit in judgment on St. Chrysostom. Even Eudoxia recognised that it would be imprudent to hold such a meeting for such a purpose in the capital. Thus Chalcedon was chosen for the scene of the affair, and Theophilus proceeded to 'pack' the council with men known to be disaffected towards the Patriarch on one count or another. The 'Synod of the Oak' foreshadowed the 'Robber Synod' of 449. St. Chrysostom refused to appear before it.

He had the humility, however, to convene a counter council of forty fairer-minded Bishops to examine the charges preferred against him. He had desired to befriend the monks, but he did not refuse to defer to this change of front on the part of the Synod. He had nothing to fear from the charges of gluttons disgusted at his frugality, of simoniacal Bishops angry at his justice, of sacreligious priests enraged at his integrity.

But the protests of his friends fell on unheeding ears. Chrysostom was condemned at Chalcedon on four of the twenty-nine charges trumped up against him, and deposed ! Theophilus had expected that Arcadius would find him guilty of high treason.

The Emperor looked on, miserably, at the doings of Eudoxia. So far he had drifted in her wake, but now he fell short of her determination. By simply confirming the decision of the council, and pronouncing on this Nathan a sentence of banishment for life, he contented nobody.

St. Chrysostom received it as became a saint. "Brethren," he said to the Bishops assembled in the Thomaites of his palace, " I see I must undergo many hardships and then quit this troublesome life . . . . remember me in your prayers. . . . You know the true cause of my fall. It is because I have not lined my house with rich tapestry. It is that I have not clothed myself in robes of silk. It is that I have not flattered the effeminacy and sensuality of certain men, nor laid silver and gold at their feet. . . . As for the doctrine of Christ, it began not with me, nor shall it die with me. . . ."

When the sentence of exile became known in the city, the common people who had grown to be devoted to the Patriarch, raised a tremendous outcry. For three days and nights a popular guard surrounded the Patriarchæon to prevent him leaving it. Meanwhile Chrysostom preached nothing but resignation and submission.

At last he escaped from the devotion of his own followers, and secretly giving himself up to the officers of the Imperial Guard, was cautiously conveyed by them after dark over the water to the port of Hieron.

No sooner was he gone than Theophilus entered Constantinopole. Eudoxia exulted in her freedom, and the people, stunned and irresolute, maintained a gloomy silence. " Soon, however, they crowded to the Church and poured forth lamentations. They were violently driven thence by the Imperial officers. Indignant and enraged . . . they loudly clamoured outside the Emperor's Palace. . . . A popular insurrection seemed imminent."

On the fourth or fifth night, however, the whole city was set shuddering and rocking in the throes of an earthquake. The Palace was shaken to its very foundations. Eudoxia awoke in horror; she rose up in the darkness and, conscience-stricken, flung herself down at Arcadius' feet crying out that it was the wrath of Heaven and protesting that Chrysostom was innocent. Would the Emperor recall him and avert the anger of the omniscient God!

The following day a clamorous crowd besieged the Palace demanding the restoration of St. John.

It was one of those dénouements only imagined by the dramatist, or realised in the lives of God's saints.

St. Chrysostom was recalled. A great procession headed by the Empress herself went out to welcome his entry to the city. He was heralded by an immense and eager concourse. Eudoxia, beside herself with reactionary excitement, flung her arms round the Patriarch's neck, and immediately, he was borne aloft amidst the flaming torches and exultant hymns of the people. That very evening his triumph was completed by the receipt of Eudoxia's impassioned letter. "My prayer is fulfilled! I have attained my purpose. It is to me a richer ornament than my diadem. I have brought back the priest. I have restored to the body its head, the pilot to the ship, the bridegroom to the bridal chamber!"

For a few months after this, St. Chrysostom was truly at the zenith of his power.

Then, suddenly, the heavens clouded over more ominously than ever. The change came quickly as the mood of a passionate woman. Eudoxia could play fast and lose even with St. Chrysostom.

Consumed by an insatiable vanity, she was now determined to claim the last honours of an Empress. The title Augusta authorised her to cause a lofty column of porphyry, bearing a silver statue of herself to be erected in the city. She chose a place of honour for it in the Augustaeum, outside the great basilica. On the occasion of its semi-pagan "dedication" the people gave themselves up to loud and licentious revelry, unchecked by the Prefect. Nothing more calculated to rouse the burning indignation of St. Chrysostom could well have been imagined. He launched a tremendous denunciation of Eudoxia's folly, and of the abandon of the people for which it gave so senseless an excuse.

Once more the Empress was filled with anger. Forgetful of all that had gone before, she determined to ruin the great preacher.

No sooner was it perceived that the tide of his popularity at court had taken its inevitable turn, than all the Patriarch's old enemies awoke to new activity. Treasonable language was again alleged against him; everything possible was brought forward to prove his rehabilitation uncanonical. A council was called to sit in judgment on the matter, and though Theophilus of Alexandria scarcely ventured to Constantinople again, his influence went powerfully to work.

The Emperor had refused to communicate at St. John's hands at Christmas—the affair of the statue had taken place in September—and now it was close upon Easter in the following year. In order to prevent a second refusal of this sort the council determined that St. Chrysostom must be deposed—by force if necessary—without further ado. Arcadius gave the order for his removal.

This time, however, the Patriarch adopted another course. He refused to yield. The Emperor, not unmindful of the awful warning of last year, hesitated to enforce the mandate.

On Easter Eve, St. Chrysostom entered his church to administer the sacrament of baptism to a large gathering of 3,000 catechumens. His enemies feared his presence there would provoke a popular tumult, and persuaded Arcadius that, since he was a deposed man he could not officiate at such a function, and that therefore the soldiers ought to be empowered to remove him. They were willing, they declared, to bear the brunt of the manœuvre.

Thus the hoarse cries of the soldiery broke rudely on the hushed air of the church where the great ceremony was going forward. The terrified catechumens scattered at the point of the sword in every direction, some with their white robes spotted with spreading crimson, while the richly vested clergy were hunted through the streets. The stricken people made, with a curious instinct, for the Baths of Constantine. There they reassembled in the darkness, panting and dishevelled, the women half undressed, and the men carrying a strange medley of sacred cloths and vessels snatched up at a moment's notice. The ceremony was just about to recommence, when a body of four hundred brutal Thracians swept down upon the constant band. Those who failed to make good their escape were haled off to the noisome prisons of the city, where they behaved like the martyrs of an earlier age. During the whole of Easter week Constantinople was in an uproar. A fierce persecution raged against the adherents of the Patriarch—Joannites as they were called. Houses were broken into and ransacked, the captives were scourged and flung into prison. Sounds of torture and blasphemy were heard even in the churches. The Bishop himself ran a constant risk of murder. He was closely guarded in his palace by a stout cordon of the people. For two hideous months Arcadius was trying to make up his mind to sign the rescript of banishment.

At last, on June 5th, 404, the golden pen went into the purple ink, and in a fit of peevish exasperation the Emperor put his name to the infamous deed.

Then St. Chrysostom gave up the struggle. His good-bye to the heartbroken Olympia and the other deaconesses, is one of the most poignant scenes in history. He said a last prayer in his church, and escaped a second time out of his own house.

Even as the breeze freshened on the Bosphorus, and the boat

plunged through the racing waves, the venerable exile looking back might have seen a flare of vengeful flame leap up against the darkening heaven and scorch its blackness. Out on the cool bosom of the night there was a vision, behind, of fire. The sky pulsated with its fitful glow. Over the sonorous waste of sea came the roar and hiss of some portentous conflagration. As the lurid scene grew brighter with the unnatural light of fire the boatmen cried out that St. Sophia was in flames.

Tragedy on Tragedy !

In the course of two tumultuous years the world and the devil had wrestled with God's champion—and thrown him. Thrown him with a fall which cost them more dearly than a victory. The rapidly shifting phases of the struggle, the violent contrasts of it, the uncertainty of Eudoxia's mood—all these things must have seemed like the vagaries of some endless nightmare. Even now the Empress might repent, reverse the decree, and stop the work of persecution.

St. Sophia stood, a blackened ruin, before her Palace gates. The gutted Senate house contained only the calcined remains of what, but yesterday, had been the fairest art treasures in the city, and the fire-scarred Augustaeum lay before the windows of the purple chamber like a withering reproach. But the Empress had gone too far to withdraw a second time.

She fell into a state of despair and apprehension from which, unlike herself, she could not rally. She followed the exile with bursts of spite which only alternated with a helpless sense of their folly. She was overwhelmed with superstitious fears, but they goaded her into an unreasoning obstinacy. It seemed as if the day of grace had passed and Eudoxia could only repent as they repent in hell. A sense of tragedy hung over her and reflected itself in the life of the court. Everything was altered. The joy of living left her, and a nameless rumour about her unborn child filled the Empress with horror. She dared not seek consolation in religion— she craved the unhallowed succours of magicians—and in her extremity, turned to her feeble husband for support. Lightly as Eudoxia had ever held it, Arcadius' love still lived.

The Emperor did his best to comfort her. If he could take no steps to repair all the evil, he had at least plenty of fears to mingle with his wife's, and could sympathise with her distress. He was constantly with her, and in the hour of her abasement forgave all the disappointment of his married life. Eudoxia was without resource in adversity and trial. She failed and sank before St Chrysostom had reached his journey's end. Her death was pitiable in its extremity of misery.

In the small hours of one autumnal morning (just a year after the erection of the famous statue), a terrific storm of hail broke over Constantinople. It lasted a long while, wrecking houses and killing people in the streets. Eudoxia could bear no more. In a paroxysm of terror she besought Arcadius to command the presence of a certain man in whose pagan charms and incantations she placed some superstitious trust. Her wretched husband yielded, and in an hour or so his wife was lying dead, her breast strewn with unavailing trinkets, and her nurses hurrying away with the corpse of a child. Such, at the age of thirty-one, was the end of St. Pulcheria's mother.

A murmur went through the city that it was the judgment of God.

It would be easy to imagine the pomp and ceremony that accompanied the interment of the Empress, since recent discoveries have shown what befitted such an occasion according to the imperial idea in the fifth century. When Maria, the first wife of Honorius, was laid to rest below the original St. Peter's at Rome "a greater treasure of gold and gems," says Professor Lauciani, "had never been found in a single tomb." Eudoxia, doubtless, was buried in the narthex of the Church of Holy Apostles, where the great Constantine himself and other members of his family already lay. The funeral procession was escorted thither through the awestruck city by the host of court officials, and the Patriarch Arsacius, an old and ineffectual man, conducted the solemn ceremony. The Empress—if we may use an almost contemporary analogy—lay in a sarcophagus of costly stone, clothed in a state robe of woven gold. Of the same material were the veil and the shroud which enwrapped her head and breast. . . . "At the right of the body was placed a casket of solid silver full of goblets and smelling bottles cut in rock crystal, agate, and other precious stones. . . ." There were also beautiful cups, a little lamp of exquisite workmanship, and four golden vases. "In a second casket of gilded silver placed on the other side," was an enormous collection of objects, gold rings with engraven stones, earrings, brooches, necklaces, buttons, hairpins set with emeralds, pearls and sapphires ; a golden nut which opened in halves, a locket and an emerald engraved with the bust of Arcadius. The letters and names on some of these trinkets proved that they had formed part of the "mundus muliebris" (or wedding gift) of the Empress. Besides the names of the four archangels engraved on a band of gold those of "Domina nostra [Eudoxia]" and of "Dominus noster [Arcadius]" were on various other articles. The little bulla or locket, was inscribed with the names of the husband, wife, and their children radiating in the form of a double cross ✳ with the exclamation Vivatis ! between each. Some of these treasures represented a portion of the state jewels which Arcadius had inherited and given to his beautiful bride on his wedding day. *

The Emperor was now left alone in the Imperial palace with

---

* These details, taken from Professor Lauciani's description of the tomb of Honorius wife, are *appropriated* to the burial of Eudoxia.

a host of sad and bitter memories, and his little children. Pulcheria was six, Theodosius, the heir, was four.

Two months later St. Chrysostom's successor died, and in February, 406, an Armenian monk, Atticus, was appointed to fill his place. The persecution of the Joannites had continued all this while with unabated cruelty. Optatus the Prefect seemed to have a genius for inflicting torture. He instituted a rigorous inquisition, and dealt out inhuman punishment. St. Chrysostom's heart in exile was torn with sorrow at the news of the sufferings his friends were undergoing. He wrote constantly to St. Olympias and—saint as he was—fretted to get so few replies. His heart grew sick with disappointment as he looked for letters : Olympias was too broken-hearted to write. He reproached her, with the easily-forgiven reproaches of love, for a neglect that at other times had no foundation in fact. He could scarcely realise that Olympias was exiled like himself, that Eutropius, his dear young "reader" had died under the torture ; that Ampructe, Nicarete, and the rest had fallen under the wheels of a veritable juggernaut ! The suspicion that the Joannites had set the Great Basilica afire was quite enough excuse with Optatus for the harshest measures. Their refusal to recognise Arsacius was a second clause against them, and the Prefect availed himself of the military to compel the Joannites to frequent the Churches. Even when Arcadius signed a tardy order for the release of those who had been languishing in prison forgotten and untried, it was accompanied by a decree of banishment against them.

Nor was the cup of St. Chrysostom's own suffering quite filled. It had turned out that Arabissus was not so far removed but that it could become the cynosure of the Christian world. You must leave no stone unturned "wrote an old enemy of St. John to Atticus, to frighten or cajole the Emperor into removing him to some still more distant and desolate spot of the Empire. . . ."

The recluse of the Patriarchaeon knew so little, save by inimical report, of its late saintly inmate, as to be prejudiced against him. Atticus, the theological student, was now burning the midnight oil less over the ecclesiastical politics of the day, than over the classics and sciences which it was his regret to have hitherto neglected. He seemed to think indeed, that the exile might be lending his weight to some sort of conspiracy of the West against the East in order to regain his see.

The names of Honorius and Stilicho could ever rouse Arcadius to jealous irritation, and he was easily persuaded to issue a decree banishing St. John to Pityus, a bleak outlandish spot on the northern shores of the Euxine.

The weary and suffering exile was hurried forward once more. His death at a wayside martyry beyond Comana, properly lay at the door of the weak-willed Emperor washing his hands of the business in langurous misery at Constantinople. He expired of grief and exhaustion on September 17th, 407, almost on the second anniversary of Eudoxia's decease.

Summer had barely come round again when Arcadius himself fell ill.   At thirty-one years of age he already felt old and hopeless. Life had lost whatever incentive it ever possessed for him and he still mourned for Eudoxia.   On the first of May he was laid to rest beside her in the Church of the Holy Apostles.

CHAPTER IV

EDUCATION IN THE FIFTH CENTURY

On the death of Arcadius, his only son, the little seven year old "Augustus," became Emperor of the East Roman world. Theodosius II. ascended the throne on the first of May, A.D. 408, and was "proclaimed" with all the customary honours at the Palace of the Hebdomon. The administration of affairs was vested in the hands of the Pretorian Prefect Anthemius and a body of co-adjutant ministers.

The Byzantine Senate was at least as capable of governing the Empire, if not of safeguarding the Emperor's minority, as Honorius might have been. Had Stilicho, the great general of the West, allowed his master to travel to Constantinople and assume the management of his nephew's dominions, disaster might as easily have befallen Byzantium as it presently befel Rome. The friendship which had existed between the late Emperor and the Persian king Isdegerd I., lent some foundation to the legend that Arcadius had rather entrusted the Empire and its infant sovereign to his chivalrous protection than to the feeble supervision of Honorius. Gregorovius remarks that since it was no extraordinary thing to witness the supremacy of Sueves and Vandals in the counsels of the West, neither would it have astonished the semi-Asiatic Byzantines to find themselves under the dominion of a Persian. Isdegerd is supposed to have despatched a courtier of his own, Antiochus, to the eastern capital as the protector of the Prince. The story is however entirely discredited. The Prefect Anthemius presided over the government of the Empire and the education of the Emperor. It is not impossible that the legend so flattering to Isdegerd arose with the Persian historians who referred in this important style to a certain chamberlain named Antiochus, whom Arcadius had appointed tutor to his son, and who kept his position in the palace until St. Pulcheria thought fit to remove him.

As a matter of history, it was to Anthemius the Prefect that the Empire looked for government and preservation during the minority of its Emperor. He was considered by his contemporaries as a statesman of rare prudence and ability, and judged by the dying Arcadius to be above self-interest and corruption. After the death of Eudoxia the Emperor seems to have exercised an amount of discretion for which events had hitherto given him no credit. He was deeply saddened by the loss of his wife, but still more filled with regret for the misfortunes and fate of the bishop whom he had consistently revered and so weakly sacrificed. He loved his little son Theodosius with that tinge of humility failure ever feels in the presence of promise, and displayed unwonted care in providing for his future. If indeed he recognised some traits of himself in the child, Arcadius could not but seek their remedy by appointing men like Anthemius to positions of responsibility around the throne.

The Prefect Anthemius proved himself worthy of the confidence of his late sovereign. During the minority of the Imperial children he administered the Empire with energy and care such as had not been brought to bear upon public affairs since the death of Theodosius the Great. "History relates nothing but good of him," sums up Mr. Oman,[*] "he made a wise commercial treaty with the King of Persia; he repelled with ease a Hunnish invasion of Moesia; he built a flotilla on the Danube . . . . .; he reorganised the corn supply at Constantinople, and did much to get back into order and cultivation the desolated lands of the Balkan peninsula from which Alaric and his Visigothic hordes had now taken their final departure." The historian of the "Decline and Fall" tells us that "the safety of the young Emperor proved the merit and integrity of Anthemius; and his prudent firmness sustained the force and reputation of an infant reign." One of the happiest results of the supremacy of this man, whose conception of duty was based on sincere religious principle, was the quiet and wholesome upbringing which he provided for the Imperial children.

On the death of Eudoxia there had been a superstitious revulsion of feeling at court, and now those noblewomen like "the most religious lady Salvina"[†] and Olympia, who throughout the recent troubles had remained firm adherents to St. John, were called upon to fill the offices of trust around the young princesses. Anthemius had two daughters, one of whom, the wife of a certain influential Procopius, may have held some position at court. Her sister Apollinaria is said to have lived among the solitaries of Sceté, under the strange guise and name of "Brother Dorotheus."

Outside the immediate entourage of the Emperor and of the nobilissimae, his sisters, the society of the populous Imperial palace remained much the same as ever. Although it lacked the brilliant leadership in which Eudoxia had delighted, the great ladies of Constantinople continued to resort thither only a trifle less frequently than they been wont to do previously. We can imagine the rivalry between the kinswomen of the late Empress and the

---

[*] "The Byzantine Empire," by C. W. C. Oman.   Story of the Nations Series. Ch. v. page 53.

[†] Epistolary phrase of the period.

wives of the ministers in power, between the older habituées of the court and a crush of less privileged women who hastened to take advantage of the exceptional circumstances to obtain an entry there. The Imperial princesses might be disregarded while the dead Empress's friends were striving to queen it over one another in her stead. While the Emperor, though a mere child, could already command the obsequious homage of his ministers and guardians, Pulcheria and her sisters were not as yet facts in the case. Society scarcely realised that they might presently become a power in the Palace.

Anthemius, however, was a man of observation.

He confided the Imperial sisters to the care of those ladies of the court who inclined to the Joannite faction. In the absence of any word about their upbringing, inference at least, would lead us to believe that the early years of Pulcheria, Marina, and Arcadia were scrupulously preserved from worldly and indifferent influences. All their after life reflected the pious, sober and dutiful characteristics of their training. Only good and religious ladies were admitted to the entourage of Anthemius' Imperial wards. Had it not been so, we can hardly suppose that the character Pulcheria inherited from her grandfather, would have persisted though the weakness of her father, the vanity of her mother, and the deterioration due to circumstances of pomp, luxury and flattery. It must have been largely owing to the judicious provision of Anthemius that Pulcheria received an education, without which she might never have become the right hand of the Emperor, or a saint in the eyes of the Church.

The persecution instituted by the opponents of St. John Chrysostom against his adherents, after his exile in 404, had not spared some of the noblest and wealthiest women in Constantinople. The lady Olympia, widow of a Prefect, and deaconess of St. Sophia, was banished to Cyzicus ; the illustrious Pentadia, widow of one of Theodosius' master generals, was compelled to withdraw into even greater seclusion than the voluntary privacy in which she had hitherto lived.

Nicareta, one of the Patriarch's most zealous helpers among the poor and sick, was mulcted of the bulk of her property and reduced to poverty. The lady Salvina herself, princess of Mauretania and niece by marriage of a Roman Empress, was only saved from similar consequences by the supremacy of her rank.

At this time she was living in austerity and retirement, " the model of widows," at Constantinople, as she had also been in Rome.

On the death of the Great Theodosius in 395, half the eastern court had accompanied Honorius to Italy. Those who, as children, had all been brought up together in the Imperial nurseries of this child-loving sovereign, became widely dispersed. Time was to identify many of them with events and interests disintegrating to the empire, while, on the other hand, the fortunes of others were to be the only links remaining between East and West. To Rome went

Serena, Theodosius' adopted niece, there to play a brilliant part as the wife of Stilicho, the mother of Maria and Termantia, and victim at last of the Senate's cowardice. To Rome went Placidia, Honorius' step-sister, destined for thrilling adventures—first as Gothic Queen, then as Roman Empress. To Rome went Olympia, once the betrothed of the Emperor Constans, to Rome went half the society of Constantinople, and to Rome went the Princess Salvina.

After the death of Hebridius, her husband, Salvina associated herself with the famous group of St. Jerome's women friends on the Aventine. If she had shared the intellectual pursuits as well as the intimacy of Marcella, Albina, Furia, Blesilla, Paula, Eustochium and the rest, she would have been exceptionally qualified to preside over the education of Pulcheria and her sisters. She had returned to Constantinople, probably after the fall of Rome in 410, when so many of the noblest Roman families fled *en masse* to Africa and the East. She had very possibly known Demetrias and her mother; Melania and her husband; that Volusien whom St. Augustine tried to convert; Eltheria who travelled to the holy land and sent home to Spain an account of the ceremonies at Jerusalem in Holy Week A.D. 385, together with a host of other noble and historic people. She may, indeed, have read St. Jerome's work dedicated to Loeta, the first treatise on the education of women conceived in the Christian spirit, and as an ardent admirer of St. Chrysostom, have imbibed also his views on that subject.

The great Patriarch laid it down that women, especially mothers, are the natural educators of children. While the Prefect Anthemius, himself an adherent of St. John, reserved the case of Theodosius for still further consideration, he may well have invited the Princess Salvina to take up her residence in the Imperial Palace at the head of Pulcheria's suite.

There is something always a little pathetic about the education of royal children. For them it is not merely the weariness it is to most others, but a responsibility, the mere contemplation of which is entirely unfitted for their years. Whether or not the lessons of a Byzantine princess in the fifth century were as important as the sums of a Victoria in the nineteenth, the education of her brother was of the greatest moment. Theodosius was a delicate child, and cared more for drawing letters than for reading them. Pulcheria watched him already with the eyes of love, and made haste to fit herself to superintend his work so that it should be neither friutless for his mind nor harmful to his body. Ahead of him at the outset in capacity and purpose, she was ready, at the age of fifteen, to select the professors and direct the studies of a boy only two years younger than herself.

It would be misleading to estimate the standard of woman's education at this date, when culture was very generally neglected, by such figures as those of Hypatia of Alexandria, Athenais, Mariana, and Asclepigenia of Athens. These were the daughters of savants and philosophers whose delight it had been to find in the bosom of their own family their most appreciative pupil. But they belonged to a world which had little in common with the spirit of the times. They were not Christian, nor did they mix in any but the most exclusive circles of intellectual sociey.

Alexandria in the fifth century was the home of the widest and most varied culture. Pagan philosophy lived there side by side with Christian theology, and whatever poetry of distinction the age produced was written in that city. In Athens, on the other hand, the traditions of Hellenism were preserved with greater purity. Hypatia and Athenais were the recipients of a many sided education. They were deeply versed not only in those sciences of which their fathers happened respectively to be the masters, but also in the special subjects of such academic friends as found it agreeable and profitable to pay intellectual court to professors' daughters. They studied literature, philosophy, mathematics, rhetoric, and such sciences as the times could distinguish from charlatanry.

On the other hand, the epistles of St. Jerome reveal an equally high order of intelligence in the women of his following at Rome. The Scriptural studies of the ladies in the Aventine Palace are in every way worthy of comparison with the interests of Hypatia and Mariana. They were, however, no less exceptional. They no more form the criterion of Christian female education in the fourth and fifth centuries, than the attainments of Athenais form that of a still more widespread culture.

It seems, nevertheless, that no wealthy establishment in Byzantium was complete without its tutor. Gregorovius puts in some special pleading for the ladies of the capital. They, at least, availed themselves to some extent of such an advantage. Even Eudoxia had profited more by the instructions of the Christian philosopher Pansophius, than ever Arcadius and Honorius had done by the tutorship of Arsenius and Themistius. The Emperor of the West was incredably ignorant. Indeed we are told that the education of a Constantinopolitan lady at this date might put the modern woman to the blush, just as the culture of the ladies of the renaissance is not yet discountenanced by that of the Girtonian or Newnhamite. The scholarly German even instances Pulcheria herself, in the same category as Hypatia, to illustrate his point.

The Augusta indeed was well equipped for the duties of her station. She knew both Greek and Latin, and could transact the business of state departments in either language. She had that appreciation of art, literature and history which only cultivation can give, and had moreover imbibed such a respect for learning that those who possessed it were ever personae gratae with her. No stronger proof of the solidity and liberality of her education can be brought forwaid than the fact that during her brother's reign a

magnificent university was founded at Constantinople.   It was
a truly Imperial undertaking, and should be a lasting glory to the
name of Theodius II.

Amid all the charitable enterprises and institutions which had
hitherto exercised the ingenuity and occupied the attention of
the Christian clergy, schools had hitherto found no place.
There were seminaries for the priesthood in various cities—
or rather the Bishop's household comprised a certain number
of students who aspired to the service of the Church.   The
monasteries possibly sheltered a little love of learning, but even
St. Chrysostom seemed to consider the pulpit all that was
necessary for the instruction of the masses.   The holy Patriarch,
who knew by experience what the moral atmosphere of the
state schools was like, and who was certainly the last man to
undervalue a knowledge of letters, when weighing the arguments
for and against a public education, decided that the risk was too
great to be compensated by the intellectual advantage.

Moreover, the edict of Julian the Apostate, which forbade
Christians to teach grammar and rhetoric in the schools was
largely responsible for the low ebb of Christian education for
some time.   Ammianus Marcellinus tells us that in the early part
of the fifth century, "the acquisition of knowledge had no charm
for the nobles"; the state-supported rhetors and grammarians of
the provincial schools had but little occupation.   The curtained
alcoves and porticoes of the streets and public places where their
classes were held, sheltered few scholars, and the poor "Calculo"
who depended upon teaching the three r's to the urchins of the
city, might very likely starve.   The "grammaticus" who succeeded
him in the educational course of things was more popular when he
lectured on music than on the classics.

"Mental culture, even in the mansions of wealthy Byzantines,
occupied a very subordinate place.   Everywhere might be seen
dice and draughts, but books were usually conspicuous by their
absence.   Bibliophiles there were   . . .   but who rather valued
the fine parchments, dyed in various tints and handsomely
inscribed with letters of gold or silver, bound in jewelled covers
or in plates of carved ivory, than the literary contents."*

A young patrician's education began and ended with rhetoric, for
only in this art could he hope to attain any distinction at the bar,
in the pulpit, or the Senate.   Roman despotism had crushed
political life, and the range of human thought became restricted in
these centuries of decline to theological subjects.   Within that
range it reaped, truly, a plentiful crop of endless controversies and
metaphysical subtleties.   Popular interest fastened upon the
debates of an ecclesiastical Synod with the fervour it had shown
in earlier times for the discussions of the Senate.   The very

* W. G. Holmes, "Age of Justinian and Theodora."

tradespeople could neglect the counting of their change to discuss the nature of the Godhead with a passing customer.

A visit to the city of Athens was looked upon as the final touch to a man's education. To have studied there gave it a distinct cachet. The beautiful Greek city had an irresistible attraction for students. Their enthusiasm blinded them to the fact that its classic glory was now a thing of the past, and that its repute was declining. The fathers of the Christian Church tolerated the study of the classics there more freely than anywhere else. In the East the feeling towards the old Pagan literature, where its faiths clung less obstinately to life than they did in the West, was more indulgent. St. Chrysostom could admire Libanius, St. Basil and St. Gregory could sigh for the love of Athens, while St. Augustine was reproaching himself for his devotion to Virgil. It was notorious that the Emperor Anthemius, supposed to be the best educated man of his day, numbered the works of Sallust, Livy, Tacitus, Plautus and Virgil among the treasures he carried West with him in 465.

But for all this, the only books commonly read at the time when Pulcheria sat at the feet of the Princess Salvina, were "the Satires of Juvenal and the fabulous histories of Marius Maximus."* During the whole period from Diocletian to Theodosius, literature was in a wretched condition, and Ausonius, the only poet of the time is stigmatised as "incredibly bad."* History itself was only written by epitomisers. With the Spanish Emperor however, a new spirit had been infused into letters, and the last half of the fourth, together with the whole of the fifth century is looked upon as the classical age of some branches of Christian literature St. Pulcheria had the works of St. Augustine, St. Athanasius, St. Ambrose, St. Jerome and St. Chrysostom to read, the biographies, letters and homilies they wrote; she had the hymns of St. Ephrem, the poems St. Gregory of Nazianzen dedicated to St. Olympia, and may, too, have known this holy Bishop's passion play. The writings of the Christian poet Prudentius would not have been banned from her library. "They blended Horatian love-poetry with Christianity, as it were warm wine with cool water, and the mixture suited the taste of the day. The asclepiads of Severus Endelechius, 'on the deaths of cattle,'"† told a pastoral tale, with the charm of contemporary romance, but with the Christian sweetness of taste. "Two swains are introduced complaining of the loss of their herds through plague, and as they talk Tityrus, a Christian, enters, driving along animals which the pestilence had not injured." They had escaped, so he explains, because the sign of the cross—"Signum quod perhibent esse crucis Dei"—was branded on their foreheads.

Pulcheria would scarcely have appreciated the tone of the

---

* Niebuhr Lectures.   † Bury, "Later R. Empire."

fiction of her own day. Its amorous gallants, barbarous brigands, cruel pirates, "disparted" lovers, its children lost in infancy, reared by shepherds, and recognised by tokens long years afterwards, its faithful servants—all these would have had no charm for her. While the celebrated "Daphnis and Chloe" of Longus, the "Leucippe and Cleitophon" of Tatius, were charming the literary circles of society, Homer and Euripides were being studied by the serious, and Nonnus' paraphrase of St. John by the devout.

The German historian Gregorovius comes to a sad estimate of the Imperial children's lot. They grew up—this little brother and his sisters—"among loveless strangers, cold and polished flatterers, state and court officials, the great ladies of society, priests and eunuchs, ... their ascetic habits prove that they experienced a joyless childhood under the pressure of court ceremonial and of ecclesiastical discipline."* He draws an unattractive picture of their lives in the gorgeous wilderness of the "sacred" Palace. But it does not necessarily follow that because their upbringing was sedate and serious, the children were unhappy. When, later on, Pulcheria is contrasted with Athenais, the bright and sunny Greek, the comparative sombreness of her character but reflects the tone of these early and impressionable years: and if the influence of good and gentle guardians could make for happiness in the childrens' lives, Theodosius and his sisters had some meed of it.

The Patriarch Arsacius died within a very short time of his succession to St. Chrysostom. He had been brother to Nectarius, and was old and feeble in the year 405. He was followed on the archiepiscopal throne of Constantinople by a man well fitted to watch over the spiritual interests of the Imperial orphans.

Atticus was an Armenian monk of sterling if unpolished character. As a young man he had devoted himself so exclusively to the study of theology, that his education in other directions was somewhat neglected. He was quick to perceive this drawback on his appointment to the Patriarchate of Constantinople, and immediately set to work with the resolution of manhood, if not the enthusiasm of youth, to mend his rough accent, to acquire a knowledge of literature, and to fit himself in every way for the discharge of his varied and important duties. He studied by night with immense perseverance, and was able in a short while to silence those who had twitted him with his ignorance. His success was as assured as it was modest. He was satisfied when he had attained so much of worldly grace and wisdom as his conception of his office made a matter of duty, and remained the man of God he had been before his elevation. If his sermons were in no way remarkable, his charity was. The historian Socrates draws a picture of St. Atticus which impresses us all the more for its brevity and homeliness; for its unlikeness to a mere panegyric.

---

* "Athenais," F. Gregorovius.

He quotes a letter which reveals the man, and shows the spiritual influence under which Pulcheria grew up, better than any other words could do.

"Atticus to Calliopius [a Priest of a church at Nicaea] salutations in the Lord.

"I have been informed that there are in your city a great number of necessitous persons whose condition demands the compassion of the pious. As therefore, I have received a sum of money from Him who with a bountiful hand is wont to supply faithful stewards, and since it happens that some are pressed by want that those who have may be proved who yet do not minister to the needy—take, my friend, these three hundred pieces of gold and dispose of them as you may think fit. It will be your care I doubt not to distribute to such as are ashamed to beg, to the exclusion of those who through life have sought to feed themselves at other's expense. In bestowing these alms I would have no distinction made on religious grounds, but feed the hungry whether they agree with us in sentiment or not." *

Atticus was extremely gentle in his judgments, and had no difficulty in admiring a man's character while condemning his opinions. He was friendly with the Novatian bishop Asclepiades, and used to say that he would have agreed with Novatus himself in refusing to eat those things which had been sacrificed to idols, although the censoriousness and harshness of the sect disgusted him.

He was, at the beginning of his Patriarchate, thoroughly hostile to the exiled St. John, and an opponent of the Joannites. In this he resembled St. Cyril of Alexandria. In the year 418, however, he could set an example to the latter and insert his glorious predecessor's name in the dyptichs of St. Sophia. During the whole period that elapsed between St. John's banishment and the honourable translation of his relics from Comana to the Imperial city, in 438, the Joannites had refused to communicate with his successors, and were fast drifting into schism. Not for a moment had Anthemius allowed the princesses to become really identified with the party who carried their loyalty to the holy bishop beyond a point he himself would sanction. But throughout her life Pulcheria displayed a perfectly sure instinct as to the faith, where even grave ecclesiastics hesitated. She revered the memory of St. Chrysostom as of a Saint, and yet submitted to the guidance of St. Atticus. Complete harmony now existed between the Palace and the Patriarchaeon. The Augusta was only eight when St. Atticus took up his residence in the latter, but eleven years later he dedicated to her that little Treatise on Faith and Virginity which so profoundly influenced her life.

The ecclesiastical ferment of the last few years died down presently, under the tactful administration of Anthemius.

---

* Socrate's History, Bohn's Translation.

In 410 the news of the fall of Rome before Alaric shocked the Empire from end to end, but the Eastern government felt no obligation to come to the rescue of the West so long as Honorius maintained himself safely—if ignominiously—in Ravenna. Two years previously General Varanes had been sent to aid that Emperor against the upstart Attalus, but Anthemius possibly realised that the masterly *dolce far niente* of his late master's brother, would keep him in Ravenna more safely than a military cordon.

In 409 Theodosius II. had assumed the honours of the consulate for the first time, and in 413 an attempt is said to have been made against his life. The story originally given by Damascus, and retailed, like an oasis in his desert of facts, by Tillemont, has a legendary value of its own. It is handed on by Photius who considered that truth alone constrained the non-Christian writer to preserve it. Lucius, a pagan, and the Byzantine consul for that year, in a fit of mistaken zeal went to the Imperial palace to assassinate the twelve-year-old Emperor.

Three times he was on the point of drawing his sword, when his arm was paralysed by fear. A beautiful vision of a woman appeared behind the child, shielding him, and fixing a proud and terrible look upon the treacherous consul.

The only event of much importance which marked the end of this phase of affairs was the commencement, in 413, of a new wall on the West side of the city. The public spirited Perfect conceived the project of so enormously extending the fortifications of Constantinople as to embrace the area over which its suburbs had been spreading since the time of Constantine. These walls, or portions of them, are still in existence, and constitute practically all that remains to-day of St. Pulcheria's city. They were planned on a magnificent scale, and consisted of embankments, parallel lines of towers, terraces, scarp and counter scarp, moat and formidable breastworks. They were garrisoned by sentinels in every tower, and pierced by ten "gates." Some of these were connected with the highroads of the Empire by massive drawbridges and guarded by twin towers. The others, military ports, were also strongly fortified. But none of them, such as the "Circus Gate," the "Gate of Charisius," the "Pempton Gate," the "Gate of St. Romanus," the "Gate of the Holy Spring" or the "Reghion Gate" could compare with the great entrance to the Via Egnatia.   "The Golden Gate," flanked by two marble towers, had been built to commemorate the victory of Theodosius I. over Maximus, and was now included in Anthemius' plans. To the original inscription

"Haec loca Theodosius decorat post fata tyranni" was now added in his grandson's name

"Aurea saecla gerit qui portam construit auro." *   It was built,

---

* Translation. "Theodosius adorns this place after the doom of the usurper," and " He who constructed the Golden Gate, brings in the golden age."

like the triumphal arches in Rome, in three divisions, and one of these was probably used as a chapel. It saw the processions of the Emperors as they passed beneath it on their way to be proclaimed at the Palace of the Hebdomon, and it witnessed the receptions accorded to the envoys of the Bishops of Rome. The Prefect Anthemius, however, was destined to see little more than the beginning of this enormous undertaking. He died the following year, 414, and was succeeded in the Prefecture by Aurelian.

Pulcheria was now fifteen, and, in the judgment of her brother and the Senate, capable of assuming the Imperial authority. The entire burden of the State thus devolved upon her, and the day that saw her declared " AUGUSTA " closed the short era of her girlhood.

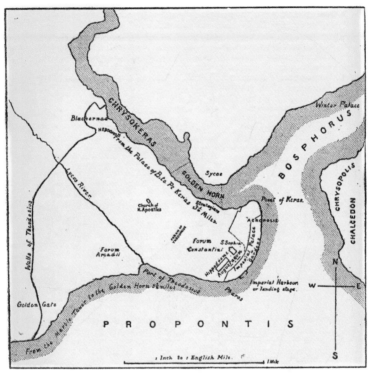

SKETCH MAP OF CONSTANTINOPLE SHOWING THE EXTENT OF THE CITY.
[*An Historical Atlas of Ancient Geography. Dr. Wm. Smith and Mr. Grove, Pt. v. adapted from.*]

CHAPTER V

In his " Age of Justinian and Theodora," a history of the Sixth century A.D. Mr. W. G. Holmes devotes a few pages of his initial chapter to the pre-Roman history of Byzantium. Later on he gives a circumstantial and very picturesque description of Constantinople prior to the reign of Justinian. But the topography of the city, despite all the researches of archaeologists, is an obscure question. For the purposes of this sketch the writer has followed the little plan of the heart of Constantinople, given by Professor C. W. Oman in his " Byzantine Empire " (Story of the Nations Series), rather than the more elaborate one in Messrs. Lethaby and Swainson's " St. Sophia." The great authority on Christian Constantinople is of course Du Cange, but the present writer, designing to draw a *picture* rather than a plan of the city as St. Pulcheria knew it, has availed herself of the picturesque details given by a host of other writers, such as Gregorovius, Gibbon and the Abbé Marin.

The description of the new wall of Anthemius brings us naturally to the subject of this chapter. It can hardly be a digression at this point to try and picture Constantinople as it was in the time of St. Pulcheria.

But in order to do so we must dismiss from our minds all that we associate with that distinctive Byzantine art and spirit which had not yet begun to characterise the great eastern city. We have to realise that the first Constantinople was a purely Roman creation, planned and built by men who brought only western traditions to bear upon their work. Constantinopolitan archaeology is a vexed subject in itself with a literature of its own, but even this takes us little further back than the age of Justinian. The transforming enthusiasm of that versatile genius (to whom posterity owes St. Sophia as a Byzantine masterpiece, A.D. 532) has indentified itself to such an extent with our whole historical conception of the city, that we scarcely realise the original Constantinople to have been purely Roman.

When the Emperor Arcadius died, the capital of the eastern Empire was not yet a hundred years old. New Rome, or Constantinople as it was popularly called in honour of its founder, remained, down to the time of Theodosius II., much as it was on the festival of its dedication (May 11th, A.D., 330.

The old Greek city of Byzantium had occupied the extremity of a tongue of land on the European side of the Straits of Bosphorus. The site determined by the first Christian Emperor for his new capital included this, but embraced a much larger area, and was roughly triangular in form like the land it covered. The

4

apex pointed across the sea to Asia; the two sides were washed, on the south by the waters of the Propontis, on the north by the Golden Horn, and a wall built from shore to shore on the western side formed the artificial base. Viewed from the sea, the land lay low. The "seven hills," five of which were included by the spear line drawn by Constantine to define the limits of his city, could only be detected by the mild outlines and contours of the town. "Bays, gulfs, creeks and seas were stretched in endless vistas on every side. . . . Out of the waters from point to point there rose terraces, gardens, towers, palaces, and churches, radiant in marble and gold, thickly strewn with groves of beech, acacia, arbutus and cypress; dotted about with fruit trees. . . . The Golden Horn ran far up into the land," * its banks were steep and rocky on the Pera side, and from their heights the inlet looked like the broad estuary of a river. The Bosphorus itself gave the impression of a yet nobler flood flowing past the city at right angles to the Horn and the headland of Keras. The blue hills of Asia stretching right across the view from north to south seemed more like the opposite side of this gigantic stream than the coast of a separate continent. The harbours of the city were crowded with the "dromons or warships of State, with their brazen beaks and banks of long oars . . . with the bright-sailed merchant vessels from east and west: from Amalphi, Durrachium, Barium, Naupactus, Cherson, the Ægean, the Propontis, Smyrna and Rhodes. . . . Behind those miles and miles of wall, battlement, tower and gate, the Seven Hills of New Rome rose into the sky, one after another in picturesque confusion of terrace, dome, cloister and palace, all bowered in groves of flowering shrubs. . . . And all round this vast and variegated pile . . . there mounted up into the blue welkin ranges of wooded hills, crags, headlands and far off mountain outlines, softly folded in pencilled lines and mists of white haze." † To the south the Burgala with its double peak rose behind the Asian suburb of Chalcedon. The Giant's Hill, and the Arganthonius covered with oak forest, kept guard over the Straits of Bosphorus, while Olympus could be seen far away in the distance covered with its pall of perpetual snow.

The main part of the city of Constantinople lay westward of the sites chosen by the Emperor around the old Acropolis, for the Imperial, or 'Sacred' Palace, the principal forum, and the most important buildings. From the fact that the neighbourhood could furnish no good building stone, nor even any material suitable for bricks, Constantine's architects were obliged to adapt timber, largely, to the purposes of their designs. Although the capital was planned out with all the spatial magnificence due to unity of purpose, this drawback in material, and the fact that the whole undertaking was less the creation of original genius, than an architectural revival,

* F. Harrison, "Theophano."   † Ibid.

must have denied unblemished splendour to the original city. At this date the art of building had fallen into complete decay. Niebuhr expressly tell us that everything belonging to the age of Constantine was, from an artistic point of view "contemptible." During the erection of Constantinople the Emperor found himself obliged to cause schools of design and construction to be opened everywhere throughout the Empire, that men might be trained for the work. Vitruvius had to be studied afresh, and his chapters on the building properties of woods were doubtless much consulted. Although the Romans had mastered the difficulties of domic construction and stone roofing long before the transference of the capital, they would have little opportunity of using their knowledge at Byzantium. Everything was roofed with wood: the Churches and the Palaces were also tiled with brass. Constantine was wholly dependent upon marble for the beautification of his city. The essential features of such places planned as a whole, like Palmyra, were long avenues of columns forming the main thoroughfares, issuing under triumphal arches into piazzas and fora. Much attention was bestowed upon the façades behind these columns. No booths or nondescript markets were allowed to be held beneath their shadow, hiding the beauties of the street. The whole Empire was put under contribution to supply the wherewithal to make the new Rome beautiful. Doubtless richer quarries than even those of Egypt and Thessaly whence came monoliths of imperial purple and green, were found in the old temples of many a declining city. Their noble shafts of porphyry and cippolino would be invaluable prey, and the harbours of the Golden Horn were filled with the enormous barges specially constructed to bear them to the rising capital. Only a few miles away, in the island of Proconnesus, an easily wrought marble of dazzling purity was found in abundance, and every day gangs of workmen might be seen rolling shafts and columns along wooden stocks to the sites they were destined to adorn.

"Parian marble, the most beautiful of all white marbles, from the island of Paros; Pentelic marble from Pentelicus; Hymettan marble from the mountains of Attica; rich yellow giallo antico from Numida; cippolino with its beautiful green waves from Carystos; purple pavonazzo from Phrygia; black marble from Cape Matapan; green and red porphyries from Egypt; alabaster from Thebes; serpentine from Sparta; jasper and fluor-spar from Asia Minor; lapis lazuli . . . from Persia; countless varieties of the so-called Lumachella marbles; rare and beautiful breccias;"* Luna marble (the modern Carrara,) from Italy; all these were borne overland and oversea to the busy shores of Bosphorus.

Building went forward with incredible swiftness. Constantinople with its streets and piazzas, its basilicas, offices, palaces, villas,

---

* "Rome," M. A. R. Tuker and Hope Malleson.

quays, barracks, granaries, baths, fountains, aqueducts, cisterns, circuses, theatres, gymnasia, its promenades and cincture of fortifications rose about the site of the old Byzantium.

But, as at Rome " the solidity of the public buildings seems to have been in marked contrast to the flimsy nature of the common dwellings. . . ." These latter "were roofed with timber or thatch." In the more crowded or poorer regions of the city, "they were often of several stories and perilously high ; many of them were built of unbaked bricks, with projecting upper floors, and they were constructed with wooden framing filled in with rush and plaster so that when fires broke out in the city whole streets and quarters were laid waste in a few hours." * New Rome was, unfortunately in no position to profit by the experience of the mother city. Hasty as much of the work soon proved, and retarded by these constant conflagrations, the result of this stupendous activity was yet not unworthy of the Imperial design to transplant a capital and build it within one generation. For once the colonnades were reared, the pediments set, the arches and porticoes constructed, the fora paved, the shores embanked, the gardens laid out, the harbour planned and its cable carried across the Horn, the ways connected, and the Churches and Palaces in readiness, Constantine had the art treasures of the world, and the wealth of the Empire, to lavish on their decoration.

The city was so peopled with statuary that thirty years later a special magistrate was appointed to take note of them and provide generally for the care of public ornaments.

The Augustæum, or " Place Impériale," as Professor Bury calls it, was adorned with the finest masterpieces of art collected throughout the provinces of Greece and Asia. In the great forum on the second hill, traversed by the main thoroughfare of the city, a pedestal of white marble twenty feet high upheld a colossal statue, renamed to represent the Emperor. It had a sceptre in its right hand, a golden globe in its left, and a crown of rays glittering on its head. As time went on this statue was constantly replaced ; under Arcadius the column bore a figure of his illustrious father Theodosius the Great. The "spina" of the Hippodrome was crowded between the "metæ," or goals, with statues, columns, and obelisks ; while everything that was costly, rare or remarkable in art or history found a setting on the shores of Bosphorus. The palaces were furnished with a luxury and lavishness of display which was soon, however, enormously to increase. The beautiful desmenes belonging to them were designed to meet all the requirements of taste, indolence, and pleasure. The courtyard, or atrium, of every basilica was more beautiful in Constantinople than it could have been in Rome. Filled with statues, and with gloomy bushes exhaling the warm and honied odours of

* Ibid.

the East, its gleaming pavement strewn with blossoms, it must indeed have merited its poetic name, and have truly been a "paradise."

The Imperial palace has already been described, so no more need be said about it here, save that the Imperial precincts communicated with the city through the Gate of Meletus and the Passage of Achilles. Immediately beyond lay the Augustaeum, the great forum of Constantinople, where civic life flowed at its fullest and richest. It was a magnificent oblong paved with marble, crowded with statuary, and issuing at either end under triumphal arches in the highways of its "Region."

Along one side stood three stately buildings connected by a colonnade, the Baths of Zeuxippus, the Senate House, and the Patriarchaeon, or palace of the Archbishop. Facing these was the Hippodrome, the great racecourse of Constantinople, beyond which, northwards, stood the Church of the Holy Wisdom (St. Sophia) the Hospital of St. Sampson, and the Church of St. Irene. Between the Hippodrome and the Patriarchaeon stood the famous Milion from which all the roads of the east were measured. It was a small domed building surrounded by an arcade of seven pillars embellished with statues, among which were those of Constantine and his mother, St. Helena. The Sacred Palace was connected with St. Sophia by a private gallery, the "Skepaste Scala," whose wooden arches spanned the Chalkoprateia and led into the catechumens' gallery. It had also a private staircase, called the "cochlea," leading to the "kathisma," or Imperial Grand Stand at the northern end of the Hippodrome. Opposite the Senate House (in Theodosius II's time this building dated from Julian's reign) stood the Nymphaeum, a place in which those who had no house of their own could celebrate their weddings. At the date of which we write there was also to be seen the Basilike, the library recently founded by the apostate Emperor. When it met with its destruction in the reign of Zeno it numbered 120,000 books.

"A particular description of the city, composed about a century after its foundation enumerates a capitol or school of learning, a circus, two theatres, eight public and one hundred and fifty-three private baths, fifty-two porticoes, five granaries, eight aqueducts or reservoirs of water, four spacious halls for the meeting of the Senate or courts of justice, fourteen churches, fourteen palaces, and four thousand three hundred and eighty-eight houses, which for their size or beauty deserve to be distinguished from the multitude of plebeian habitations. In less than a century," Gibbon continues, "Constantinople disputed with Rome itself the pre-eminence of riches and numbers. New piles of buildings crowded together with too little regard to health or convenience, scarcely allowed the intervals of narrow streets for the perpetual throng of men, of horses, and of carriages. The allotted space of ground was insufficient to contain the increasing people; and the additional foundations which, on either side, were advanced into the sea, might alone have composed a very considerable city."* In the first Region alone there were four private and fifteen public cornmills.

Such, in a bird's eye view, was Constantinople at the time of St. Pulcheria.

In point of size, Rome and its eastern namesake were originally much alike. The first wall of the former measured thirteen miles in length, and Constantine gave to the new Byzantium a circumference of ten or eleven, which increased to fourteen if it included the suburbs of Sycae and Pera on the opposite shore of the Golden Horn. Under Aurelian, Rome had so grown in size as to necessiate the erection of new walls twenty-one miles long. Constantinople had so spread by the time of Theodosius II., that Anthemius' new fortifications included "the narrow ridge of the sixth, and the broad summit of the seventh hill." Houses built on piles of wood had run out into the water about the harbour, and extended all along the shores of the Propontis and the Golden Horn. An organised ferry plied between Pera and the opposite side, and the "chelandia" or Imperial galleys were often to be seen mingling with the crowded craft on those waters. Some writers speak of Chalcedon as a suburb as it was easily attained from the European shore. About the Chalcedonian Stairs, one of the chief landing places at Byzantium, there must have been a constant coming and going of vessels plying backwards and forwards on business or pleasure between the two cities.

Under the régime of St. Pulcheria, security of life and property tended greatly to increase the prosperity of the metropolis. An orator of the time† observed that no longer was the vacant ground in it more extensive than that already occupied. " The beauty of the city is not as heretofore scattered over it in patches, but covers the whole area like a robe woven to the very fringe. The city gleams with porphyry and gold . . . its former extremity is now its centre. Were Constantine to see the capital he founded, he would behold a glorious and splendid scene." During the reign of Theodosius II. the appearance altered more than at any time since its building. A new harbour was built on the Propontine shore, there rose the most impregnable line of fortifications history has ever known, and owing to Pulcheria's zeal for religion and philanthropy, innumerable new churches and hostelries were founded.

In the Appendix to his article on St. Pulcheria (Mem. Ecc. v. xv.) Tillemont gives a list of these. And the Abbé Marin, in his invaluable work on the Monks of Constantinople, supplements it by a beautiful picture.

"Whilst monasteries and churches were in course of building in the new capital, in their shadow were gradually being raised many charitable houses to aid the unfortunate of every description.

---

* Gibbon, ch. xvii. † Themistius.

Christian charity was to be found in as many forms as there were forms of human misery to call it forth. Du Cange mentions nearly forty of these institutions founded by emperors, empresses, princes, high functionaries or wealthy individuals; very many were established prior to the tenth century. There were "xendochia," closely resembling our hospitals of to-day, "gerontocomio" or "gerocomia" for the aged; "orphanotrophia" for orphans; a "lobotrophion," or home for the infirm; a "brephotrophion," which would now be called a crèche for little children; a large number of "ptochotrophia," where food was distributed to the poor, and a "pandochion," or general refuge, where food and shelter could be found for a hundred men and a hundred horses." There were also a 'lobotrophion' for cripples, and St. Helena's asylum for the aged in the Psamathia quarter. Under Arcadius, the Patrician Florentius founded another of these, and under Theodosius II. Dexiocratus, Anthemius, Narses and other noblemen, kept up the philanthropic spirit of Constantinopolitan society.

Over the entrances to these institutions—vast religious settlements—there was generally some invitation of this description : "Come, friend, whoever you may be, take place without shame among us for this is the house of God. When you knock at the door say why you ask admission, and wait patiently until it shall be opened. Enter then with joy mingled with respect, and offer your prayers to the Lord. Speak nothing of the vanities of the world, for you discourse with men who have renounced them all, but rather may your bearing be edifying and agreeable that your return home may be blessed and happy." *

"One remarkable feature" in the philanthropic life "of the city, and to be encountered at every turn, was an elevated shed which could be approached on all sides by ranges of steps. These "Steps," as they were briefly called, were stations for the gratuitous daily distribution of provisions to the poorer citizens. Every morning a concourse of the populace repaired to the Step attached to their district, and each person on presenting a wooden tessera or ticket, inscribed with certain amounts, received a supply of bread, and also a dole of oil, wine and flesh." † More than fifteen public bakeries, chiefly situated in the bakers' quarter, the Artopolia, furnished the daily supply of bread.

A medical officer, entitled an arch-physician, with a public stipend, was attached to each parish to attend gratuitously to the poor; and the monks of the many convents in and about Constantinople, busied themselves with the visitation of the sick, and stimulated by their own example the zeal of the "copiati" or guild of the buriers of the poor.

From the outset the young city on the Bosphorus was as

---

* *Cf.* Theodore of Studium, Carmen xxix.
† Mr. W. G. Holmes, " Age of Justinian and Theodora."

populous as some of the modern capitals of Europe. When Constantine transferred Rome from Italy to Greece he used every possible means to people the new seat of government. Inducements were held out to the nobility to remove their princely establishments and accompany the court. Privileges unworthy of the foresight of a statesman were bestowed upon the common people. The Imperial founder would have emptied Old Rome to fill the New, but notwithstanding this exodus, only eighty or so years afterwards—when the Goths invested the Capital on the Tiber—her walls sheltered a population estimated at twelve hundred thousand souls.

That of Constantinople must at least have equalled it, for by the time of Theodosius II. we are told that the city far surpassed Rome both in wealth and population. People of every race and tongue poured into the great mart for commerce and pleasure. When in A D. 378 the Goths desired to besiege it, its enormous extent defeated their design. The cosmopolitan character of its inhabitants was naturally reflected in the aspect of the city. The influence of Persians, Slavs, Arabs, Goths, and of all the other nationalities attracted to the capital of the Empire was traceable in various quarters, and although, as we have seen, the original Constantinople was a Roman city, the frequent restorations and entire reconstructions constantly necessitated by fires and earthquake shocks, soon began to modify taste in accordance with a growing Greek tradition. The growth of Byzantium between the ages of Constantine and Theodosius gave place to a revival of more purely Greek styles, so that in the fifth century the appearance of the capital recalled substantially the age of Pericles.

Increase of wealth and luxury went hand in hand with the orientalisation of life. Women drew apart from men and lived in their own apartments, in comparative seclusion, attended by bevies of slaves and eunuchs. The consequent tendency to confine all signs of domestic life to the interiors of the houses took away something from the animation of the streets. Women were missed amid the busy " via-via " of the Theodosian city almost as markedly as they are to-day in the thoroughfares of Stamboul.

The life of Constantinople differed little from that of other contemporary Roman cities, except in so far as it was the life of a capital in which the Emperor was resident. It was even more bright and brilliant than in Alexandria, more strenuous and bustling about the quays and harbours than in the port of Rome, more vivid even than in witty Antioch, more businesslike than in Carthage, more varied than in the miserable, amphibious Ravenna, and quite as full of polemical interest as ever the presence of St. Jerome contrived to make Jerusalem.

The " illustres," " spectabiles," and " clarissimi," of high society inhabited palaces of their own in vast self-sufficing establishments, while the poor lived in tenement blocks, or " insulae," much on the

W. 80.   1865-97.

ALLEGORICAL FIGURE OF CONSTANTINOPLE.
DYPTICH, SIXTH CENTURY.
ENDURING TYPE.

Continental system of the present day. All classes shared in common the luxurious lounging places of the city. On payment of an insignificant sum the beggar could avail himself of the comforts of the public baths equally with the haughtiest senator. Different streets and quarters were signalised by different occupations and markets—such as the Chalkoprateia or street of the Jewish brass workers, one of the principal thoroughfares. But in each of the fourteen Regions, private palaces of the Empresses, or the opulent mansions of municipal or military officers—such as the Strategion of the Praetorian Prefect—formed neighbourhoods of grandeur and importance. The Empress Eudoxia had a private residence at Pera and another in the Mariana district. St. Pulcheria had a house in the third region, and her sisters also had palaces elsewhere. The Palace of Blachernae in the fourteenth ward was situated outside the walls and formed a township in itself.

* * * * * * * *

In order to understand the greatness of Constantinople it is not enough merely to reconstruct a picture. It is not enough to enable us to appreciate Anthemius or Pulcheria, to see nothing but the life and stress and colour in the streets of the capital. For we have to realise that Constantinople was more even than the metropolis of a great empire.

Constantinople was the Empire!

"The history of the Empire," says a modern writer,* "is the mere history of the capital." Again, such a history "is that of a government, not of a nation."

In the fortunes of Constantinople lay the fate of the eastern half of the Roman world. By the strength or weakness of the city's grasp upon the provinces which belonged to her, the confines of the Empire were determined. By the impregnability of her mere walls its existence was prolonged years after all administrative, military or financial order had ceased to be, and the Roman power, long extinguished in the West, had, like the substance of the Dead Sea apple, crumbled away within the brave exterior of the city. After the division of the Empire in A.D. 395, the history of Constantinople is first, that of its rapid rise and aggrandisement. Its golden age began with Pulcheria's grandfather and endured until the beginning of the Crusades. During all this time the city was without a rival even within the Empire. It was the centre of all the art, learning, commerce and civilisation of the "dark ages." It was the heart and brain of that State which "cherished the flame of culture and literature when it was well-nigh extinct throughout western Europe . . . . until such time as the nations of the occident were once more prepared to receive the gift and to despise the giver." St. Pulcheria was Empress then, at a glorious period in the career of the great Eastern Rome. The old fashioned school of historians is accustomed to hold this history up to contempt as the most corrupt and decadent the world has known. True, we hear of little save palace intrigues during the seven centuries that elapsed between Theodosius' time and the Crusades, yet these years were the true glory of Byzantine history. The Byzantines were the precursors of the Holy Cross Knights in defending Christian civilisation. "Had pagans, fire-worshippers, or Mussulmans, and devastating hordes [of Isaurian brigands,] succeeded in piercing their walls before the fifteenth century, the course of civilization would have been seriously changed." Only at brief intervals, and under exceptional rulers, however, did the city rise to a sense of its high vocation, just as it is only the exceptional historian * who can rise above his disgust at her internal corruption to take this high view of her destiny. The eastern Emperors for the most part certainly led the lives of murderers, liars, and debauchees, while the Empresses were often female monsters. The administration accordingly suffered. But modern writers have done much to place the subject in a less prejudiced light than these facts alone would throw upon it. Constantinople is entitled to the gratitude of Europe as being the fortress and bulwark of mediæval Christendom. Before her walls invading hosts of Saracens were constantly repulsed, and the tide of Islamism was restrained, until all the land it threatened to overwhelm behind her had settled into national and religious order.

The later history of the city is that of an isolated state convulsed by internal factions, its borders rent by incursions of barbarian peoples, and its frontiers forever shifting according to the fortunes of decades of wars.

Certainly one of the most important aspects of this history is that obtained from the Christian point of view. The foundation of Constantinople "removed the seat of government from the presence of those awful temples to which ages of legend and glory had attached an inalienable sanctity. . . . It broke the last link which combined the pontifical and imperial character. . . . The Senate, and even the people, might be transferred to the new city, but the deities of Rome clung to their native home and would have refused to abandon their ancient seats of honour and worship. Constantinople arose, if not a Christian city, certainly not a pagan one." * It was defaced here and there by buildings designed to meet the basest requirements of a wicked age, buildings the existence of which only the realist would care to record, but if the new capital of the world were peopled by the heirs of the vices of the older state of things, it at least "had no ancient deities whose worship was inseparably connected with its more majestic edifices and solemn customs." † In the midst of Constantine's magnificent museum of art stood a statue which preached the Gospel. It was that of the Good Shepherd.

* Bury, Harrison, Freeman, &c.   † W. H. Wheeler Bush, " St. Chrysostom."

CHAPTER VI

SOME historians tell us that the child-Emperor's eldest sister was declared Augusta as soon as Anthemius was dead; others affirm that it was only when she had proved herself capable of ruling, after the lapse of a twelvemonth, that Theodosius conferred this title on her.

To be an Augusta was the highest honour to which the wife, mother or sister of an Emperor, could aspire. It carried with it special prerogatives and privileges. Eudoxia had been the first Empress who had borne it in the East, and the conservative government at Ravenna had been deeply offended at its bestowal upon the Frankish beauty. The traditions of the title were wholly noble. It was an old sacred word, used [previously to its application to Augustus Ceasar] only in the language of the priests, and never applied to any human being. It was appropriated in B.C. 27 to the man who had been the saviour of Rome, whom the popular belief had already begun to regard as a human incarnation of the divinity. "This sacred name marked out the man to whom it was applied as one apart from the world, standing on a higher level, possessor of superhuman power in virtue of the name, and transmitting that power through the name to his descendants." To be called Augustus, was then, originally, as if the Church should call a man 'Saint' during his life.

In the course of time the supremacy of the title came to be of greater significance in its aspirant's eyes than its religious character. Although an Augustus still wrote, and was still addressed, far on in the Christian era, in such terms as seem almost blasphemous to us now, the words 'sacred,' 'eternal' and 'sublime' as applied to him became no more than the unctuous phraseology of official language, and by the fifth century the significance of the title had become wholly worldly. It lost its exclusive character and could be bestowed on lesser members of imperial families for reasons of state,* or courtesy, and even upon cities. Eudoxia, the 'barbarian' Empress had received it; Pulcheria honoured it; the wife of Theodosius II. came to bear it; and the luckless sister of Valentinian III. had it thrust upon her. The Romans encamped at Richborough spoke of the city on the river to the north [London] as 'Augusta.'

* It would seem that the title Augusta carried with it punctilious restrictions with regard to marriage, and that a Princess so distinguished could only hope to select a partner from the very highest sphere.

One of the ' privileges of an Augusta' was that of being ' adored ' equally with the Emperor throughout the Roman world.   This homage was also a survival from the days when the title Augustus made the sovereign a sort of incarnation of the Roman genius and, as such, a partaker of the worship addressed to it.   The concession of this tremendous distinction to Eudoxia had involved that erection of statues in her honour which caused St. Chrysostom to utter in the capital of the East, the indignation felt by the western court. When, however, the title Augusta was conferred upon Pulcheria, it was not seemly that any of the usual ceremonies or rejoicings should be omitted.   These honours were customary in Constantinople and the East, and so long as there was no repetition of the " orgiastic dances, loose mimes and noisy buffooneries" which in 404 had disturbed the services of St. Sophia, the Church had no serious objection to raise.

It was the custom at the beginning of a new reign to erect portrait busts of the Emperor and the Empress in the most honourable buildings and thoroughfares of their capitals, and to send copies to the sister court at Rome or Constantinople.   The unveiling and ' consecration' of these effigies, or ' labrata' as they were called, in the case of Theodosius and Pulcheria, took place with dignity and decorum in the Senate House of Byzantium, A.D. 414.   Civil ceremony as it was, it seems to have borne the stamp of a religious function.   The Perfect Aurelian shared the honours of the occasion with the Archbishop Atticus.   We should be reading S. Pulcheria in a light other than that of her own century were we to suppose that she herself saw any impropriety in her title.   It had lost the significance paganism had attached to it, but no such excuse might palliate the offence, to a Christian way of thinking, of its various accompaniments.   That the Augusta herself perceived this fact, and presently endeavoured to disembarrass imperial state of its blasphemous attributes, was sufficiently manifested in a law by which Theodosius sought to restrain excess in showing honour to the imperial statues.

It was a matter of great difficulty to uproot habits of flattery which custom had sanctioned for ages.   Pagans, however, had not failed to justify their own idolatrous practices against the reproaches of Christians on this very ground, and the distinctions made in reply were not altogether convincing.   St. Chrysostom's horror of the titles courtiers would so willingly have bestowed upon him, and righteous indignation of their employment even in connection with the Emperor only voiced the feeling entertained by the more sincere and thoughtful.   Thus in the year 425 Theodosius ordered that when a statue was to be erected to the Emperor, the Governor of the city should assist at the ceremony in order to honour the majesty of his sovereign, but also to see that the people indulged in no superstitious ' adoration' of it. Moreover, when such an image or statue was carried in public procession, no more respect was to be paid to it than a earthly king might receive, all further honour being reserved for the Divine Majesty alone.

True the preamble to the Theodosian Code, published in 439, would seem highly inconsistent with these reforms. But the Emperor himself, so far from encouraging its preposterous phraseology was necessarily to some extent the victim of tenacious custom. He who composed the speech from the Throne in the fifth century hardly dared break away from imperial traditions, and set a precedent derogatory to the Emperor, even were he sure of his master's private approbation.

The great day which placed the reins of government in the hands of St. Pulcheria was the fourth of July 414. It had a dual significance in the eyes of this girl of fifteen. She made her assumption of the imperial power the occasion of a ceremony in the Great Basilica which was at once a religious profession and a coronation, before either of those rites, strictly speaking, had come into existence.

The Patriarchal Church had been restored since the disasters of 404. Shortly after the funeral of the late Prefect, all signs of mourning were removed from the city. All the palaces and porticoes were freshly crowned with garlands ; beribboned festoons of flowers swung from column to column along the avenues of the great thoroughfares, while gaily painted 'Venetian' masts upheld the lines of bunting which every where bedaubed the brilliant streets with colour. The great arena of the Hippodrome was carpeted with flowers, and from an early hour on that radiant summer morning the Augustaeum was filled with an expectant throng. The Basilica witnessed a concourse vast as ever the passion of St. John's eloquence had attracted thither. The day wore on while the great ones of the State were getting through the civil ceremonies in the Palace.

Pulcheria, beautifully robed in the Imperial 'sticharion,' a long veil, or 'maphorion,' upon her head, and above it a golden fillet sparkling with gems, long lappets of pearls striking the colour up upon her cheek—Pulcheria bore herself with the grace and pride of a Roman princess. This was the single great court function of her life. * It was, virtually, her accession to the throne : the rulership of the East Roman world had devolved upon her, and the ceremony of her vows was to follow, and confirm, this Imperial consecration.

"One of the most wonderful things in all this wonderful history," says Professor Freeman speaking of Rome, "is that for ages this mighty fabric of despotic administration, as it went on without being supported by any national life, went on without any definite rule by which the powers of that despotism should pass from one hand to another. This is true," he continues, "of the

---

* Her marriage in August, 450, could scarcely compare with the ceremony of her vows.

Roman Empire at every stage from Augustus to the last Constantine. A monarchy went on for five hundred years without any definite law of succession. The Empire was neither elective nor hereditary." Even in the dawn of Roman history, the kings, although they had no right to transmit their power to their sons, seem to have sometimes exercised an influence over the succession. This anomalous condition of things was responsible for some of the first crimes recorded in that long and varied tale. "Down to the very time of Justinian, the legal theory was that the Roman people by a special act in each case transferred to each succeeding Emperor the powers which were inherent in the people themselves." But as Professor Bury adds, the sovereign himself soon discovered the expedient of securing the recognition of his son as heir during his lifetime, whereby a dynasty might virtually be founded without ostensibly violating the elective theory.

Theodosius had been declared Cæsar at his birth, and from that moment was looked upon as the successor of Arcadius his father. He became Emperor in 408. But his sister Pulcheria succeeded, at Anthemius' death, to the responsibilities of the supreme position, and by the unanimous consent of her brother, the Senate, the army and the people, became virtually Empress.

No sooner were the civil ceremonies of her investiture concluded, than the whole court proceeded to the Basilica of St. Sophia for the great religious function by which the Augusta designed to dedicate herself to Almighty God and to the trust of the Empire.

For Pulcheria had resolved to make a vow of perpetual virginity. It behoved her to safeguard her brother's throne from the pretensions of possible rivals. She would be the Augusta—her sisters too were daughters of the Imperial house—her husband, and even theirs, could easily sweep Theodosius aside should they be so minded. A court intrigue, an émeute among the factions, a rising in the city, disaffection in the garrison—any of these things would suffice to overthrow the child-Emperor and crown a rival's ambition.

The sacrifice Pulcheria was thus called upon to face, probably cost her less than the renunciation of her desire for religious life. Were she to become a nun, or even a deaconess of St. Sophia, Theodosius might be still less likely to retain the purple. And yet the Princess suffered a holy envy of Demetrias, Euphemia, Paula, Melania and Olympias. Her only course lay in an heroic compromise. She resolved to make a double sacrifice, that of the cloister as well as that of the world. She determined to lead a nun's life in the Palace of Byzantium, to be hidden, simple, prayerful and chaste in the midst of the very court.

That her vow was dictated by a true spiritual impulse, far above any mere political consideration, the story of her life and reign should sufficiently prove. Had it been founded on love for her brother alone, would she have persevered to her life's end despite every disillusionment and ingratitude which might sap her resolution? This were surely not basis enough for a sacrifice so supernaturally borne, for a life so consistently lived. If in later years the Augusta dared look back upon the brave-heartedness with which she had made her initial renunciation, in which she had taken the burden of the state upon herself, it was in order to nerve her love and resolution to fresh endurance, not to seek a plea for dispensation. At the outset of her life she had no reason to mistrust her brother or herself, and with the confidence of unlimited devotion she felt that no sacrifice would be too great to make for him and for his interests. But had she not been actuated by motives unassailable by shock and disappointment she would scarcely have persevered, when she was forced, time after time, to face the truth, that all her hopes of Theodosius were doomed to fail. She fought against misgiving as the Emperor grew up, and only arrived at the truth that after all his character was a weak one, at the latest moment her devoted faith in him might survive. It is a grave time for a man, although he may not know it, when she who has most to lose in losing trust and esteem for him, admits the light of truth into the empty recesses of her heart. And so it proved for Theodosius. But St. Pulcheria kept her vow to the end. Her temptations and her opportunities for breaking it were numberless. She might have married many times and have braved public opinion with the gorgeous aplomb of an Irene or Theophano. Or she might have abandoned the thankless post of duty and sought her soul's true satisfaction in some sequestered cloister. She was, however, proof against herself in either guise, and true throughout her life to one of the most peculiar 'vocations' which the Church has recognised.

The sacrifice of marriage was scarcely so imperative in the cases of her sisters, Marina and Arcadia, yet they made it, sweetly, purely, quietly, looking to Pulcheria's example, as she looked for their support. The Imperial sisters were nuns by choice and not perforce of circumstance. Their sacrifice was rather of the cloister than of the world.

In the Great Basilica then, on that glorious summer day nearly fifteen hundred years ago, the three Princesses, in the presence of all the people, vowed their hearts to God, and their faith to their father's house. Theirs was an exceptional case, and the conditions of the 'velatio,' or religious profession of the time, were waived for Theodosius' young sisters. In the hush that always attends a solemn moment, St. Atticus pronounced the beautiful exordium. His voice was lost to the greater part of that enormous concourse, and midst the ordeal of imperial publicity, St. Pulcheria felt the sacred charge made a solitude for her soul with God.

" Accipe puella pallium quod preferas sinc macula ante tribunal Domini nostri Jesu Christi, cui flectit omne genu caelestium et terrestrium et infernorum.

"Benedicat te Conditor caeli et terrae, Deus Pater omnipotens, qui te eligere dignatus est ad instar sanctae Mariae matris Domini nostri Jesu Christi ad integram et immaculatam virginitatem, quam professa es coram Deo et angelis sanctis. Idcirco serva propositum, serva castitatem, per patientiam ut coronam virginitatis tuae accipere merearis. Nunc exoro Domini nostri Jesu Christi divinam misericordiam ut hanc virginam consecrare ac sanctificare dignetur usque in finem.

"Benedicat te Deus Pater et Filius et Spiritus Sanctus omne benedictione spirituali, ut maneas sinc macula sub vestimento sanctae Mariae matris Domini nostri Jesu Christi." (v. Mgr. Duchesne.)

"Accept, my Daughter, the vesture which thou must bring spotless before the throne of our Lord Jesus Christ, before whom bends every knee in Heaven, on earth and in hell.

"May the Creator of Heaven and earth bless thee, God the Almighty Father, who has deigned, at the prayer of holy Mary, Mother of our Lord Jesus Chist, to elect thee to that life of whole and immaculate virginity which is now professed in the sight of God and of His holy Angels.

Therefore observe chastity, that by patience thou mayest merit to receive the crown of thy virginity. Now I pray and beseech the divine mercy of our Lord Jesus Christ, that He will deign to consecrate and sanctify this virgin to the last.

"May God the Father, Son and Holy Ghost bless thee with every spiritual blessing, that thou mayest remain unspotted in the vesture of holy Mary, Mother of the Lord Jesus Christ."

Lastly came the unveiling of the Augusta's 'apophoretum.' She had, like a bride, bestowed a wedding gift upon the Church. It consisted of a magnificent golden altar, inlaid with masses of precious stone and studded with pearls. Upon it were inscribed the vows of Pulcheria, Arcadia and Marina. Thus, says the pious Tillemont, the Augusta took not only the Archbishop, the clergy, the Senate, the court, the soldiers, and the people, to witness her solemn engagement, but also Almighty God and the hierarchy of Heaven.

What then had the Augusta done? Cut herself off from the world and yet not become a nun? How did the Church regard such a course of action? Pulcheria was neither contemplative nor deaconness; she had done more than was required of the 'consecrated virgin.' What examples had she found among the women of that age for such a life as she professed to lead?

CHAPTER VII

FOR some centuries after the legal establishment of Christianity, the woman who took a vow of virginity need not necessarily leave her home. Even in the writings of St. Ambrose there is no sugges- tion that the widow, or the maiden who vows chastity shall seek seclusion or solitude. Neither in the letter of St. Hilarius of Poitiers to his daughter Abra is there any suggestion that the woman who embraces religion should dwell apart from her family. There came, in this way, to be a recognised class of 'consecrated virgins,' distinguished only from other women by the modesty in their dress, the use of a veil, and their precedence of married women at the communion rails. They made their vow, at any age, into the hands of a priest, and were regarded with respect.

The deaconnesses approached more nearly to the religious ideal. These were ladies of age, experience, and leisure. The Church prescribed certain gentle rules, by the observance of which their pious and charitable undertakings could gain the merit of obedience. To them many duties were allotted which would otherwise have fallen on the clergy. They visited the sick, prepared female catechumens for baptism, had the charge of the 'gynaikitis' or womens' gallery in the church, relieved the poor, and cared for the linen of the altar. A deaconness was required to be of advanced age. She assumed a distinctive dress, made her vows into the hands of a Bishop, and was solemnly blessed by him. Her life was required to be modest, unassuming and exemplary. There were forty deaconnesses attached to the Church of St. Sophia : St. Olympia had been one of these.

The tendency of Christianity had been from the first to emancipate and elevate womenkind. In proportion as the spirit of independence, equality, philanthropy, gained ground among them, they were looked upon as advanced. Old fashioned people regarded St. Chrysostom's deaconnesses, and St. Jerome's disciples much in the same light as our grandmothers would regard the modern athletic girl, lady doctor or woman barrister. Their life implied a complete revolution in the female sphere. Select Byzantine society would refuse to know a woman who sought publicity—unless under the ægis of religion. A contemporary Bishop exaggeratedly asserted the great virtue of a woman to be

5

that neither her name nor her person should ever cross her threshold! Greatly as St. Chrysostom loved and esteemed the order of deaconnesses, graced by women like Olympia, Nicarete, and Ampructé, he was extremely severe upon those women who made of their religious dress and profession an occasion for coquetry and scandal. This sort of thing was one of the crying evils of his time. The 'agapetae' or 'spiritual sisters' of the clergy added much to the disedification of the Church. Even actresses and women of the lowest character found it profitable to adopt the religious dress as a fit disguise for masquerade.

St. Pulcheria might, indeed, have become a deaconess of St. Sophia had she been free to consult her inclinations, for in no wise would such a step have been deemed derogatory to the dignity of the Emperor's sister. But from the fact that many years afterwards, when the opportunity of embracing such a life not only occurred but pressed itself upon her, she refused to do so, we might suppose that she would rather have imitated Euphemia and Demetrias and retired to a convent. The order of deaconesses had already passed the period of its lustre. It failed to receive ecclesiastical approbation any longer about the sixth century, in the West, but in the schismatically inclined East it lingered on into the middle ages. Had St. Pulcheria been as free as the ladies of her own court, had no responsibility to her brother and the Empire weighed upon her, she would most probably have sought the "sanctuary of the world," and hidden herself in one of St. Melania's or St. Paula's convents at Jerusalem or Bethlehem.

Religious life in the eastern capital had an extremely chequered career. A learned Augustinian, Père Pargoire* tells us that the materials for its authentic history, between the years 330 and 450, are not only scarce but contradictory. But the Abbé Marin in his exhaustive work on the "Monks of Constantinople" has collected an enormous number of interesting and picturesque details illustrating that history from its beginnings to the age of Photius. Helyot, again, describes the various orders of oriental monks which traced their origin to St. Anthony, St. Pachomius and St. Basil, but none of these historians supply much information on the subject of the nuns.

Women, however, were no less emulative of men in the fifth century than they have been at any other time. Wherever men could so live as to be independent of women, the latter would outstrip their sacrifice. It would be strange if the story of the Byzantine monks had no complement of this description. But convents were not at this date numerous in the city, for when the daughter of Antigonus set Emperor, mother, father, lover, at defiance in favour of the cloister, she took the veil in Egypt; and the sister of Arcadius' minister Rufinus, became an errant nun, or pilgrim.

* "Les Débuts du monarchism à Constantinople." Revue des Questions Historiques, Jan. 1899.

Constantine the Great, may or may not have founded monasteries in his city. But the Arian Emperors who succeeded him certainly did so, and to some extent their efforts were crowned with a fleeting success. In proportion as sovereign or bishop persecuted Catholicism, so any orthodox communities of monks existing in Byzantium were suppressed (and even martyred) in favour of the heretical bodies. Thus, remarks Père Pargoire, heretics are the first religious known to history in that city.

"Founded to uphold error, only existing on account of error, these houses were almost of necessity bound to disappear when civil and religious power ceased to favour them; all the more so when they actually pronounced against them." Under the Apostate, all these religious congregations died out, and at the date of the accession of St. Pulcheria's grandfather only one monastery is known to have existed in the city.

Twenty years later there was "une floraison des maisons re-ligieuses dans la capital." Some of these contained large communities numbering a hundred and fifty subjects. With Theodosius the Great the era of historic monasticism opened for Constantinople, and the beginning of many great Byzantine convents coincided with his reign. There were, under Arcadius, three religious houses of special note in the capital, that of Dalmatius, that of Rufinus, and that of the Acoemeti. In her study of St. Theodore of Studium, a celebrated monk of the eighth century, Miss Alice Gardner has drawn a picture of the monastic life which began three hundred years earlier, under Theodosius II. The Studium, or foundation of the devout Patrician Studius, dated back to the reign of that prince, and the order to which its monks belonged "was founded early in the fifth century by a certain Alexander, a man of noble birth who had fled to the desert, first to escape the world, and later to avoid the office of bishop. . . ." The rule observed by these Constanti-nopolitan communities was that of St. Basil, extracted from his dialogues and compiled from his maxims. In a note Miss Gardner says that Helyot "represents the latter Studites as wearing green cloth with a double cross of red on the chest. But his information is not very exact."

During the reign of Theodosius II. the monastery of St. Dalmatius took precedence of all the other religious establishments in the capital. Its Superior, the 'Archimandrite,' * was a power in the state, and despite his vow of 'clausura,' (enclosure) exercised great influence at court. The monastery at Chalcedon, founded by Rufinus, suffered at the outset from that minister's disgrace. But it was peopled subsequently under St. Hypatius, and flourished. At the death of St. Dalmatius, his dignity officially passed to his successor Faustus, but it was to Hypatius at the Apostolaeum that

---

* An 'Archimandrite' was the head of a number of religious houses, but an 'hegou-menus' was simply the abbot of one.

all eyes turned as to a father. He was held in the greatest esteem by the Emperor and the Augusta. The Princesses one day had recourse to the threat that they would force the door of the monastery, unless he would consent to grant them an interview in the neighbouring mansion.

Theodosius himself often visited the monk, and kept up a filial correspondence with him. In 426 when the Constantinopolitans raided the monastery of Alexander on account of the strange proceedings of the Superior, the monks found refuge with St. Hypatius, and remained there unmolested under the protection of Pulcheria. The Augusta seems to have had considerable authority over the religious establishments around her for, after the deposition of Abbot Eutyches in 451, the Pope wrote requesting her to see that his successor was orthodox and fitted for the post.

Amidst all this history Père Pargoire tells us nothing of Byzantine nuns. But since the innumerable hostelries and infirmaries with which St. Pulcheria enriched the capital * were served by women as well as men, perhaps the Abbé Marin's description of these establishments and large religious settlements as they existed at that date, may illustrate either side of the subject. And Helyot, in his first volume on the "History of Monastic Orders," gives a number of pictures illustrating the dresses of the ancient oriental nuns. St. Chrysostom speaking of the religious women of his day says that they wore a black gown and girdle, pointed white shoes, and a white veil half hidden under a black mantle, which covering the head, enveloped the entire figure.

It is quite possible that the young Augusta had to look to Milan, Hippo, or Bethlehem, for the model upon which to mould her life, that of her sisters, and of the numerous retinue of like-minded ladies who were to form a sort of religious community in the Imperial palace. The "religious sisters" of St. Olympia had all been dispersed during the Joannite persecution. Severe as their observation had been, it may well instance what St. Pulcheria found elsewhere. These women had clothed themselves in sackcloth, been satisfied with mats thrown down on the floor for beds ; they had kept long vigils in the night; they walked barefoot, never broke their fast before evening, and never tasted ought but pulse and herbs. They had occupied themselves with prayer, manual labour, and the care of the sick of their own sex.

The Augusta turned the private apartments of the Imperial palace into a convent of this sort. The "purple chamber" of the Byzantine empresses no longer beheld the gay scenes nor witnessed

---

* One of her sisters, the Princess Arcadia, founded the monastery of St. Andrew ; Paulinus that of SS. Cosmas and Damien, often called the convent of Anargyres ; the Patrician Dexiocratus built one under his own name ; the Consul for the year 412 founded the monastery of St. Theodore Tiron. The Emperor Marcian, successor to Theodosius II., founded the Convents of St. Zoé and St. Irene, "but as for those which the city owed to the liberality of St. Pulcheria, Sozomenus cannot ennumerate them."

the wordy altercations between favourite and minister which Eudoxia's presence there used to occasion. All state business was transacted elsewhere. No man's foot ever crossed the threshold. Only the child Emperor came every morning to join his sisters at their prayers.

Pulcheria, Arcadia and Marina with a chosen band of noble-women devoted themselves to the mortifications, the recollection, the monotony, the exercises, of religious life. Daily Mass was already a liturgical function in the Church, and to the several hours of the day and night which the sisters already spent in psalmody and prayer, the private chaplains of the palace would add the office of 'vespertina.' The nuns in St. Melania's convents in the East seem to have communicated somewhat rarely. We have no means of knowing what might have been St. Pulcheria's practice in this respect. In the fifth century the Church allowed the faithful to communicate more than once on the same day provided the fast were not broken. Women received the Blessed Sacrament in their hands covered by a clean white cloth called a 'dominical.' During Lent Mass was celebrated at three o'clock in the afternoon. St. Pulcheria loved the liturgical offices. She is said to have instituted new offices appropriate to certain days, and to have encouraged the practice of processions.

The Augusta abolished all luxury and waste at her table; its pomp vanished with its ceremonies, and the Emperor's sisters "interrupted by frequent fasts their simple and frugal diet." The custom of 'lecture' during meal times was already common in the East before St. Angustine adopted it in his community at Hippo.

The Imperial sisters dressed very simply. They wore, probably, the white of the gynecaeum, and were scrupulous according to the fashion among modest women at that time, to keep every ripple of hair concealed beneath a veil. If their robes exhibited the gorgeous embroideries common at that date, the subjects of their pictorial panels, borders and widths would be taken from the gospels. Around their necks hung beautiful little lockets of gold beset with gems, enclosing relics or an extract from the Scriptures.

The Augusta herself, however, probably wore the purple. This colour was forbidden to all without the Imperial family circle, and even within it, only those of the rank of Cæsar might enjoy this privilege. In the year 424 Theodosius addressed a law to Maximin, Count of the Sacred Largesses, ordering him to require all those possessing purple robes and materials to relinquish them without compensation. It had been illegal ever to possess them, and constituted the crime of lese-majesté.

The Imperial sisters lived in great retirement. Their days passed quietly in prayer and study, and it may be doubted whether they ever appeared in the pageants so dear to the Byzantine people, or took any part in the official life of the court. " They all pursue the same mode of living," says Sozomen, in the present tense, "they are sedulous in their attendance in the house of prayer, and evince great charity towards strangers and the poor. These sisters generally take their meals and walks together, and pass their days and their nights singing the praises of God. Like other exemplary women they employ themselves in weaving and in similar occupations. Although of royal birth and educated in palaces, they avoid idleness as unworthy of the life of virginity to which they have devoted themselves. The favour of God has been, for their sakes manifested towards their family and the state; and the Emperor in proportion as he has grown in years has increased in power, while all seditions and wars [this must have referred to the Persian and Italian campaigns] undertaken against him have spontaneously come to naught."

It is curious that the only examples of Byzantine needlework, and of the textile fabrics of the fourth and fifth centuries that have come down to us are those from some Coptic tombs found in Upper Egypt. The dry, still air preserved them as it preserved the infinitely older cloths which swathed the mummies. These torn and faded fragments link together the fabrics of India and Byzantium. Their evidence covers a period of four hundred years, from the third to the seventh century, a period which, without them, would form a hiatus in the story of the needle and the loom. These bold designs in wool upon a linen ground, in the Egypto-Roman style, are the earliest examples of Christian textile ornament, and probably illustrate the industry of the Imperial princesses at Byzantium. They are not embroideries but the product of small looms. They were woven in the form of medallions or squares, strips or borders, and applied to a linen vestment, made the "tables" so strikingly characteristic of the Byzantine cassock. They were filled in with figures more or less bold in design, and the gradual increase in brightness and variety of colour indicates the advance of time. There is at the British Museum "a large and handsome linen bier cloth . . . . embroidered in coloured wools with a frieze of cherubs holding collars or necklaces, and baskets of flowers and fruit. In the centre two cherubs are supporting a crown within which is worked the cross . . . . and the rest of the cloth is ornamented with birds, vases of fruit, and flowers, rosettes, diamond shaped ornaments," and other small decorative forms. "This rare piece of work, which is probably the only complete example in Europe," dates from the third or fourth century. There are other, and beautiful examples of the same sort at South Kensington.

It was also one of the fashions at that time to border dresses with elaborate scenes wrought in silk and golden thread. Not unfrequently the Sacred Scriptures furnished the subjects for these pictures, and a Byzantine lady would totter to her litter on the arms of her slaves, bowed down by the weight and number of her ornaments, with such a figure as that of Lazarus pendant on a scarf or sleeve. The gold work in these embroideries was heavy and substantial. Indeed whole robes were covered with it, and the dress in which an Empress might be buried, if melted down might weigh an incredible number of pounds. Roman writers ennumerate five or six sorts of needlework, each of which included a large variety of stitches (the 'opus pulvinarium,' the 'acu pingere,' etc.) styles and materials. Some of these possibly necessitated the use of frames and drums. The rich and florid embroideries of Persia undoubtedly served as patterns for the Roman needle-woman. They were bright with gold, resplendent with flowers and 'semé's' with precious stones. The textile silks of the period exhibit gay designs of horsemen and hunters, birds, flowers, and conventional subjects, and the colours, dark and mellowed by time, were originally red, yellow, blue, white and black.

The robes of Theodosius were magnificent; the purple "mandye," which he wore as Emperor, was emblazoned with gold, and embroidered with the imperial dragons. The diadem itself was a band of nicely worked silk woven with pearls and the choicest rubies and emeralds. The Count of the Sacred Largesses who supervised the manufacture and dyeing of all fabrics intended for use in the Palace, and who directed the numerous establishments of women where such work was carried on, often ordered the consignment of costly silks and broideries to the Superintendent of the Augusta's household. And the "Nobilissimae" Arcadia and Marina, worked in their secluded palace, while their ladies read aloud, or played hymn chants on the organ.

But these occupations which formed the business of her sisters' lives, were St. Pulcheria's recreations. She had the education of the Emperor to supervise, and the business of an Empire to transact. Moreover she was no sooner mistress in the Imperial court than she had reforms to undertake.

Constantinopolitan society was no longer without a head. The anti-Joannite remnant found it easy to forget its prejudices now that people generally took their tone from the alterations at court, and if the Marsas and Castricias of the old days of luxury and passion were still alive, they probably now took to piety with the ease of fashion's slaves. For the most part however Pulcheria's régime would be voted dull by those who remembered Eudoxia, and the gayer portion of society would console itself for an interval of quietude by the reflection that Theodosius would marry.

CHAPTER VIII

IT was upon Pulcheria alone, of all his descendants, that any portion of the mantle of the Great Theodosius fell. She, only, seemed to have inherited anything of his character and capacity.

The founder of the dynasty was undoubtedly a man of sterling qualities and forceful personality. He was a fine type of " Roman," tempered by sincere religion. His faults were manly, unlike the effeminate vices of the pagan Emperors, and his virtues were those of a Christian. The moderateness of his ambition, so well resigned after the disgrace of his father to find its satisfaction in the prosperity of his private estate in Spain, was in no way inconsistent with his latter conception of imperial greatness. "The whole period of the history of the world," says Gibbon, "will not perhaps afford a similar example of an elevation to the purple so pure and at the same time so honourable," as that of this Spanish soldier. Even as sole Emperor of the Roman world Theodosius knew how to be not only a devout son of the Church but one of her most submissive penitents. She has honoured him less for the benefits his reign conferred upon her, than for the example of his magnificent humility after the massacre of Thessalonica. Throughout his life the justice and temperateness of Theodosius' natural disposition never betrayed his dignity, nor belittled his majesty as Emperor. His private life was full of harmony. If he could love his living wife more constantly than her memory, who shall say that consideration for his children, who were everything to him, had not much to do in bringing about the happiness of his second marriage? The princess Pulcheria had escaped the feebleness of her father and the frivolity of her mother. It seemed as if she had been rather the daughter than the grandchild of this man. Yet how did it come about that the responsibility of the administration devolved upon Pulcheria in 414 rather than upon a ministry similar to the last? Did seniority alone entitle Pulcheria among the Imperial sisters to the rank of Augusta? Would a child, a girl, herself little older than the Emperor, have assumed the reins of government had any other member of the Theodosian family in the East been better qualified to do so than she? Would Anthemius' cabinet have recognised the young Princess as regent unless it already saw in her a capacity beyond her years? The Perfect Aurelian might

"Perpetuae semper Augustae."
Fourth or Fifth Century.

have been appointed to carry on his predecessor's work: just at that moment there was more than one man in the Byzantine ship of state to whom the conduct of affairs might have been confidently entrusted. But it was felt that Pulcheria possessed not only the right of kinship to the Emperor, but the qualifications of a well-trained mind and a balanced judgment to claim for her an office whose demand for loyalty she could best meet. The young Augusta would succeed to absolute power; she had already known how to submit to discipline. She would have the wealth of the Empire at her command; she had already determined that self-denial was nobler than luxury. She would be the final arbitress of the destinies of every one of her subjects; she was filled with the true spirit of religion. The regent would have to allow the star of his supremacy to pale before the rising light of the Emperor—who could do this more gracefully, personally and politically, than a devoted sister? The annals of Byzantine history furnish few instances of deliberations like these. Whether Pulcheria took up the administration as a result of them. or simply because no man forced himself to the front at that critical moment, it is difficult to say. But that she proved herself worthy of the best estimates formed about her, is incontestible.

The Princess probably retained the cabinet of the late Prefect. Her first care was to banish Antiochus—her brother's tutor, from the court, and to surround the young Emperor with men in whom she could repose more trust. She lost no time in providing Theodosius with the best masters it was possible to procure. A law of the 30th of November hastened to confirm all privileges granted to Professors of the liberal arts, and to bestow further immunities on Doctors of medicine and their families. Constantinople was not wanting in savants, and indeed, men of letters and culture flocked to the capital from all parts of the Empire in the hope of obtaining some position at court about the boy Emperor. St. Pulcheria was sincerely anxious that her brother should profit by his education to the fullest extent, and in this particular he certainly repaid her zeal. She was too clearly convinced of its importance to restrict herself in the choice of his professors. Scrupulously Catholic as she was, Pulcheria had too great a reverence for learning, too broad minded an example in her grandfather, too little fear of the classics, not to entrust the direction of many of her brother's studies to distinguished pagans.

Theodosius himself loved books and every sedentary occupation. He devised a little lamp which should replenish itself with oil so that his night long studies need not keep his servants waking. Down to the thirteenth century codices of the Gospels from his pen were still in existence, and displayed the text arranged leaf by leaf in careful crosswise form.

The Augusta's next care was to purify the Palace of the favourites and parasites who infested it, and who clogged the working of every department with their exactions, and their tortuous conduct of the smallest affairs. "As a tender girl," says Gregorovius, "she changed the corruptest court of Christendom into a convent." The evil was of long standing and her ministers, to the very end, were hardly blameless in respect to peculation, nepotism and venality. Eunapius says that these scandals flourished in the administration. Amedée Thierry makes no attempt to dispute the point even when he speaks of "l'esprit du sévère equité qui fait le cachet du gouvernment de Pulcherie." His remark is abundantly substantiated by one of the Augusta's early reforms. The law, as it stood, authorised the viva voce testaments of dying persons, provided there were witnesses, even to the prejudice of written documents. This was abused by people who expected a handsome douceur when they swore that the deceased had left his property to the Prince. St. Pulcheria ruled that this law ceased to carry any weight when the sovereign or any powerful legatee should be involved. In such a case the bequest must be in writing.

This was the same spirit which, later, prompted the Imperial moderation and justice of the edicts against popular "adoration" of the Emperor's statue.

Such reforms, however, are always the work of time. The young Augusta could but inaugurate a better state of things. Her attempt to check the wastefulness and dishonesty of the administration ought at least to clear her, personally, of the blame of a long standing state of corruption.

It has been said that the manner in which Pulcheria contrived to make a young Byzantine prince into a God-fearing man, to solve the problem of morality for her brother in the midst of the vice of the Palace and the capital, would alone entitle her to admiration. It might be added, that for the Byzantine court to incur no further odium than that arising from its venality during these years, would be another tribute to Pulcheria.

"It appears to me," says Sozomen, who began his History about the year 443, "that it was the design of God to show by the events of this period, that piety alone suffices for the safety and prosperity of princes ; and that without piety armies, a powerful empire, and political resources, are of no avail. He who alone regulates the affairs of the universe, foresaw that the young Emperor would be distinguished by his piety, and therefore caused his education to be conducted by his sister Pulcheria. This Princess was but fifteen years of age, but was endowed with astonishing wisdom and prudence. To avoid all cause of scandal, and opportunity for intrigue she permitted no man to enter her palace. . . She superintended with extraordinary wisdom the transactions of the Roman government ; concerted her measures well, and allowed no delay to take place in their execution. . . She caused all affairs to be transacted in the name of her brother, and devoted great attention to furnishing him with such information as was suitable to his years. She employed masters to instruct him in horsemanship and the use of arms, and in literature and science. He was also taught how to maintain a deportment befitting an Emperor by his sister ; she showed him how to gather up his robes, and how to take a seat ; and taught him to refrain from ill-timed laughter, to assume a mild or a formidable aspect as the occasion might require, and to inquire with urbanity into the cases of those who came before him with petitions. But she chiefly strove to imbue his mind with piety and with the love of prayer ; she taught him to frequent the Church regularly, and to be zealous in contributing to the embellishment of houses of prayer ; and she inspired him with reverence for priests and other good men, and for those who, in accordance with the law of Christianity, had devoted themselves to philosophical asceticism. Many troubles which would have been excited in the Church at this period," continues St. Pulcheria's contemporary, " by the influence of erroneous opinions, were averted by her zeal and vigilance. It is mainly owing to her prudence, as we shall have occasion to show in the after part of this history, that we are at the present time preserved from new heresies. It would take a long time to describe the magnificent houses of prayer which she erected, the hospitals for the relief of the poor and of strangers, which she founded, and the monastical establishments which she endowed. . . Almighty God heard and answered her prayers, and on many occasions bestowed on her a knowledge of future events. Such indications of Divine love are not conferred upon men unless they have merited them by their good works. But I must pass over in silence the manifestations of Divine favour which were granted to the sister of the Emperor, lest I should be condemned as a mere panegyrist."*

M. Amedée Thierry, among modern writers, contributed an article † on St. Pulcheria to the Revue des Deux Mondes for October, 1871. Incomplete as a biography, it yet forms a charming chapter in her life. It draws a picture of these early responsible years full of scholarly detail, and yet instinct with grace and freshness. It cannot be enough regretted that so delightful a writer and capable an historian, did not devote a volume instead of an article to this unique Princess.

He tells us that history has perpetuated the memory of her beauty. Pulcheria's mother had been a notoriously lovely woman, with the fair complexion and blue eyes of her Frankish race. The descriptions of Arcadius were not so pleasing. He was of short stature, thin person and sallow skin. His hair was dark and his eyelids drooped listlessly and lazily over his eyes. His aspect was that of a man always half asleep or in indifferent health. We

* The Ecclesiastical History of Sozomen. . . Bohn's Series.

" † Pulcherie et Athenais."

can scarcely think of Pulcheria 'the beautiful' as inappropriately named. The coinage of her reign preserves her effigy, but from the stereotyped female head which served equally well for Placidia, Eudocia or Pulcheria, little can be gathered from the point of view of the painter. The Roman Empresses were often represented on the coinage, (this indeed seems to have been one of the privileges of an Augusta), and at a period when the currency was at a high artistic level, these portraits were really fine. But in the fourth and fifth centuries the numismatic art was at a very low ebb. The coinage was debased and the design poor and stereotyped. The bust of the Augusta Pulcheria bears no comparison with the head of a Faustina. It seems as though the die sinkers of the imperial mint at Byzantium made little attempt at portraiture. A certain effigy, derived perhaps from an ancient model, had become the accepted emblem, rather than the likeness of the reigning Empress. The same profile served equally well for three contemporary Empresses. The head was adorned—not as we should expect, with the Byzantine veil hiding the hair,—but with a sort of encircling cap of jewels ; the ears were pierced by pendants, and the neck was ornamented and draped like that of a Greek icon. In every case a small hand held over the head a tiny wreath or diadem, an emblem probably of the almighty power of the Father, since it also appeared in contemporary mosaic pictures of the Saviour. Such a coin can do little more than suggest the queenly poise of the Augusta's head, her royal gravity and presence, and the calm intelligence of her regard.

The art of the period was mainly confined to ivory carving, but Mr. Holmes tells us that the portraiture on the annual consular diptychs was not more ambitious than that on the coins. Thus, if the head on the quaint little plaque " Perpetuæ semper Augustae " might possibly be that of St. Pulcheria, it does not assist the enquiry as to her likeness, to any appreciable extent. It has however a unique interest enhanced by the element of this likelihood.

M. Thierry's article on " Pulcherie et Athenais " mainly concerns itself with those years during which the Augusta's influence was unchallenged in the court. It deals with her young womanhood, with the uneventful term of Theodosius' preparation for public life, and fills up the meagre outline of history from the year 414 to the date of the Emperor's marriage. It invests the least striking portion of his reign, but the most responsible period of St Pulcheria's life, with a charm only a French writer could give. While M. Thierry ceases not for a moment to be the exact historian, while he nowhere yields to the temptation of psychology or romance, he yet writes of the girlish Augusta with a sympathy, an appreciation, a lightness of touch which illumines these years and relieves Gregorovius' estimate of their sombreness. The asceticism of the Princesses was neither the outcome of unnaturally religious environment, nor the cause of a mirthless youth, but the spontaneous expression of their piety. And so M. Thierry makes us believe. The sweetness of such a life could well be interpreted by a writer of the same nationality as the creator of "Eugénie Grandet." Frenchmen write most pleasingly of simplicity, of abnegation ; perhaps they alone can make pathos so spiritual that is not sad. M. Thierry lifts St. Pulcheria's young life into so sweet and fair a light, the pity is he loses the transfiguring gleam of her spiritual life. For the girl Empress was upheld by something more than the strength of her own character, and whatever may have been the struggles waged within her woman's heart and soul, it were derogatory to the ideals by which she conquered, to suppose her filled with smothered jealousies and vain regrets.

The education of the young Emperor was the Augusta's chief care. She chose the companions of his sports and studies, and associated him with herself and her sisters in all his religious exercises. Theodosius joined the imperial nuns at their offices and prayers, and observed the canonical hours together with his sisters. While, however, " Plucheria sought in her devotional reading a certain rule whereby to guide her faith through the labyrinth of controversy and opinion, her young brother showed a different temper. In this respect he was least amenable to his sister's influence." He reposed an exaggerated confidence in himself, and displayed a desire to judge and regulate matters beyond the capacity of his mind—a trait which was one day to contradict that high estimate of his orthodoxy which his contemporaries formed from the uprightness of his life. How often a weak nature deems itself strong at the point where an admittedly finer character is content with lowliness and submission !

Theodosius received liberal instruction in all the arts and sciences. At about twelve years of age he began to apply himself to the study of grammar, dialectic, rhetoric, geometry, arithmetic, astronomy and music. His subjects were taken in two courses of two and six years duration respectively. His ' phonascus ' taught him not only how to speak, and punctuate his oratory with imperial gestures, but how to sing, declaim and recite. He probably learnt how to accompany these performances upon the lyre, or upon the simple form of organ known to musicians of that age. Under the heading of philosophy the pale boy studied his relationship to the state he was called upon to govern, and Theodosius II. afterwards became the first Christian Emperor who systematically fostered that science "by creating a faculty at Constantinople and extending clearly to philosophers the immunities granted to other professors." * But besides these

* Mr. G. W. Holmes. " The Age of Justinian and Theodora." This writer tells us that a treatise on education written by an African, Martianus Capella, " seems to contain all the book work a student was expected to do, while under oral teaching by the professors."

important subjects, which St. Pulcheria had mastered before him, Theodosius studied a variety of curious things, such as the medicinal properties of herbs, the rarity, significance, and value of gems, and the art of penmanship.

He led a secluded and sedentary life. The unstable state of his health seemed to Pulcheria sufficient reason for leaving his chaste and gentle temperament to its own leisurely maturing. Theodosius' days passed as quietly and as studiously as those of his younger sisters. At eighteen his thoughts were wholly centered on his clerkly manuscripts, his illuminations, and his dainty paintings in molten wax. He was in no haste to assume the burdens of his rank, and hardly cared to realise that he had the right to dispense with his sister as soon as he reached man's estate. Every now and again it behoved him to show himself in public, in the Hippodrome, in the Great Basilica, at the Campus Martius, or in the midst of one of those gorgeous Imperial pagents on the feast of the dedication of the city, which were always so dear to the Byzantine populace. Then the pale youth would play his splendid part, as Gregorovius says, "like an Imperial doll," glad when it was over. On the other hand, he loved horsemanship, and willingly spent hours in the polo ground belonging to the Palace. He became an excellent rider, archer and huntsman, and was inseparable from a companion whose bright and manly bearing was at once a contrast and an incentive to his own. This was Paulinus, the son of a Count of the Imperial Bodyguard, and a special favourite of St. Pulcheria.

Mr. W. G. Holmes enables us to get a very good idea of the routine of the Imperial day. "Every morning at seven o'clock," he tells us, "the Grand Janitor of the Palace taking his bunch of keys, proceeded with a company of Guards and Silentiaries, to open all the doors which led from the Augustaeum to the Consistory or Throne room." After the lapse of an hour "the Emperor [and the Augusta were] summoned to open the business of the day.' The antechamber had already become crowded with dignitaries of state, senators, prefects and the hundred and one persons desirous of an audience with the sovereign. "Among the throng at these receptions were always a number of officers of a certain rank who, on vacating their posts had the privilege of 'adoring' or kissing the purple" . . . . . "In the absence of urgent business the audience closed at ten o'clock; at a sign from the Emperor the Janitor passed into the antechamber with his keys which he jangled noisily as a signal of dismissal. The Palace was then shut up, but at two o'clock it was reopened with the same formalities as before, for the further transaction of affairs. At five it was again closed, and the routine of Imperial administration ended for the day." On the Dominica or Sunday, the assemblies were most numerous "and took part in the domestic Mass at the Palace."

Bishop Theodoret tells us that the Emperor was "adorned with many excellent qualities, among which may be mentioned his philanthropy and mildness, and his placidity of mind," which nothing could stir to anger. On one occasion some rather masterful monk presumed to excommunicate the Emperor for refusing to comply with his request. Theodosius would not begin his meal unless the excommunication were reversed. He was assured by the Patriarch and other priests above the monk in authority, that he need not have the least scruple on the point, that the ban was already removed had it ever for a moment held good. But nothing would satisfy the Prince until he who had uttered the sentence, returned, and personally removed it.

On another occasion Theodosius showed a truly Imperial firmness in adhering to his sense of right. One day whilst he was witnessing a combat of beasts in the amphitheatre, the people sent up an excited cry of demand to the Kathisma. They begged the Emperor that a gladiator might rush in and give the *coup-de-grâce* to a particularly formidable brute. Theodosius rose with dignity— a small figure in that vast expanse, but with a noble face and peerless glance, and returned the severe reply, " You forget! Human blood flows not in my presence! "

One of the Emperor's friends once asked him why he never condemned a man to death. " Because," Theodosius replied, " I should immediately wish it were in my power to restore him to life."

CHAPTER IX

FOR six or seven years the Augusta Pulcheria continued to act with full Imperial authority in the east Roman Empire. They were years of tranquility, unbroken at least in the capital, by events of serious import.

In 415, the date at which the history of Sozomen suddenly breaks off, the tumults in Alexandria which culminated in the savage butchery of the renowned Hypatia, attracted the attention of the Imperial court. The Augusta sought to bring about a better understanding between St. Cyril and the Prefect Orestes, but external influence could do little with the factions of that proud Egyptian city. Some few years later this Patriarch yielded to the exhortations of St. Isidore of Pelusium and inserted the name of S. John Chrysostom among those venerated in the Serapaeum. Some of the credit for this tardy reparation of an outworn prejudice may be attributed to St. Cyril's friendship with the Byzantine princess.

In the summer of 416 Theodosius, and possibiy Pulcheria, left the capital, to spend a few months at Eudoxiopolis, erstwhile called Salambria, a town on the sea coast between Constantinople and Heraclia, where they probably had a palace. The Emperors of the fifth century travelled very little. In the whole course of his reign Theodosius never left the capital for more than a month or two at a time, and the longest journey he ever took was to Cyzicus, or possibly to that spot near Antioch where the column of St. Simeon Stylites upreared itself like a pulpit, that its marvellous solitary might preach to the congregations of the world. The Emperor Arcadius had owned a summer palace at Ancyra, but Theodosius II. seems to have preferred Eudoxiopolis and Nicomedia when he had occasion to take an Imperial holiday.

The life of the capital went on without much superficial change. The Augusta could scarcely modify a system of goverment which was the outcome of centuries of Roman law and custom. The masses of the poor in the city were kept from starvation by official alms, and, as Kingsley * says, " were drugged into good humour by a vast scheme of public spectacles, in which the realms of nature and art

* Hypatia.

were ransacked to glut the wonder, lust, and ferocity of a degraded populace." In true Byzantine times the Empresses never appeared in the Hippodrome, but so early as the first half of the fifth century the traditions of old Rome still obtained in society to a large extent, and the Augusta Pulcheria may sometimes have appeared beside her pale and listless brother in the Imperial Grand Stand.

Below the very seats of the Emperor and his suite were the vaulted porches closed with massive iron grilles, whence the chariots dashed forth for the race. One of these was set apart as a Chapel. From end to end of the immense course stretched the massive divisional wall called the 'spina.' The people clustered thickly on it, about the bases of its monuments and obelisks, and were stung and choked by the fierce spattering sand and dust as the racing chariots tore thundering past. Often they had the spectacle of a furious collision as the maddened teams, striving to out-manœuvre each other at the turning point, crushed together, and the skidding wheels of the lumbrous cars became inextricably locked. Then the reek of the roaring horses mingled with the hot smell of blood, and a frightful wreck of men and beasts was hidden in the dust of its own agony and confusion.

"A picture of life in the fifth century," wrote the author of "Hypatia," "must needs contain much that is painful . . . . . it has to represent a very hideous though a very great age; one of those critical and cardinal eras in the history of the human race in which virtues and vices manifest themselves side by side—even at times in the same person—with the most startling openness and power. One who writes of such an era labours under a troublesome disadvantage. He dare not tell how evil people were ; he will not be believed if he tells how good they were." It is a curious spectacle —that of the austere and pious Augusta presiding over the shows in the Byzantine Hippodrome !

Theodosius' visits to the churches were regulated by the festivals of the calendar. "On the eve of these processions the devout intention of the monarch was proclaimed by the heralds. The streets were cleared and purified : the pavement was strewn with flowers ; the most precious furniture, the gold and silver plate, and silken hangings were displayed from the windows and balconies, and a severe discipline restrained and silenced the tumult of the populace. The march was opened by the military officers at the head of their troops ; they were followed in long order by the magistrates and ministers of the civil government ; the person of the Emperor was guarded by his eunuchs and domestics, and at the church door he was solemnly received by the patriarch and his clergy. . . . . The most convenient stations en route were occupied by the bands of the blue and green factions of the Circus . . . . . from either side they echoed in responsive melody the praises of the Emperor."

* Gibbon.

In the year 418 an indiction or revision of the taxes of the Empire took place. This was a great administrative undertaking whose recurrence every fifteen years served to mark the financial condition of the people. A system of fixed and regular spoliation obtained throughout the Empire, and of peculation and bribery at court. Eunapius points this out clearly enough, but does not ascribe the fact to the personal character of the Augusta. St. Pulcheria did everything in her power to relieve poverty and distress. She incurred much jealous blame for the lavish way in which she dispensed her private fortune among the hospitals of the city, and she ever lent a ready ear to the intercessions of bishops, like the great Theodoret, on behalf of plague-stricken districts and unfortunate provinces. The reign of Theodosius II. was marked by two royal acts of charity. All arrears of taxation were twice remitted, in 414 for forty years, ending in 408, and again in 443 for twenty years, ending in 428. The comparative simplicity of the Augusta's court exonerated the Emperor from the blame of luxury and wastefulness, though Pulcheria took particular care that her economy should by no means give the people cause for dissatisfaction. The Byzantines loved pomp, ceremony, and show. The reforming and financially cautious Emperors always forfeited their popularity, and Pulcheria endeared her brother to the populace by fêtes as distasteful to herself as to him. Thus while the poor provincials groaned under heavy burdens, and the wealthy classes shrank from filling offices which implied large demands on their private incomes, the life of the capital went on as gaily and sumptuously as ever.

Theodosius was now nearing his majority. The question of a marriage for him was not mooted so early as that of Arcadius had been, but as he often remarked in the hearing of others, that neither birth nor wealth would weigh with him in the choice of a wife so much as his taste and affection, the Augusta began to fear some court intrigue like that which had introduced her mother to her father. Had Theodosius not worn the diadem, had the dynasty he represented any hope but in himself, the nun in his sister might yet awhile have silenced the politician. She may indeed have felt reluctant to bring about so radical a change in his life, and her own, as a marriage would involve, but at all risks St. Pulcheria determined that so far as it lay with her, Theodosius should not be entrapped or hurried into a life-long mistake. She had foreseen the dangers of such a time, and with the solicitude of a sister, the prudence of a Queen, and the self-effacement of a Saint, had already given the matter thoughtful attention. She had need to secure the religious tenor of life in the Imperial palace by a very careful choice of the woman who would henceforth lead society. She had to choose a bride who would know how to be an Empress and yet not a ruler ; a wife, not necessarily a stateswoman ; a sister, not a rival. For, as time went on, it became clear to St. Pulcheria that the burden of sovereignty would largely remain upon her own shoulders. Theodosius showed less eagerness than she would have welcomed to relieve her of responsibility and to undertake the conduct of affairs with manly resolution.   As a daughter of the house of Theodosius she had no intention of resigning her rights in favour of the Empress, and if her brother still required a co-adjutor on the throne, it should still be his sister.   Experience and success had confirmed the rights with which she had been invested in 414, and could transfer them to none other.   This beautiful young girl could crown another with a diadem more lustrous than her own, and give place in her brother's love, and in the eyes of the world, to the Empress ; but she could not resign the duties which were so integral a part of her peculiar vocation.

The laws of birth and rank which were supposed to limit the sphere in which a Roman Emperor might seek a consort, were sometimes disregarded. Although from the time of Constantine I. ambassadors from the noblest families of barbarian (and particularly of heretical) blood, were discouraged as suitors for the hand of a Byzantine prince or princess, the observance of such restrictions was not very scrupulous.   St. Pulcheria was not at all hampered by them.   She made a most impartial survey of the ladies of Constantinople, barbarian or Roman.   The case of her own father only escaped illegality since Constantine, in his definitive legislation on the subject, had made special exemption for the Franks.   He admirec the fidelity and valour of that people, and thus paved the way for the exaltation of Eudoxia.

St. Pulcheria was deeply immersed in these cares, when an extra-ordinary chain of circumstances led her to the very bride whom she feared it would be so hard to find.   She was ready, in 420, with an alliance to suggest to Theodosius, which brought all the unworthy schemes of self-interested and ambitious courtiers to nought.

CHAPTER X

THE great Greek philosophers who, in the classic age of human speculation founded whole schools of thought, burned in the vacancy of men's heavens like suns. They were the centres of systems, they were the source of all other intellectual life. Around each, minds grouped themselves in constellations, and the smallest satellite that proved a point of brightness, even at the distance of time's most revolutionary cycle, traced its radiance back to Plato.

During the latter decades of the fourth century there flourished in Athens, Leontius the sophist, one of those philophasters who called themselves the Neo-Platonists.

Athens was still a wholly pagan city. Many of the monuments of its ancient glories were yet standing; age scarcely seemed to touch its architectural grandeur; the everlasting youth and untroubled spirit infused into the masterpieces of Phidias and Praxiteles still informed them with unrivalled beauty. The commercial or political ferment of the empire was stilled in this old world spot of dignity and peace. Classic studies flourished there unrebuked even by the most zealous of the Christian fathers. In no other Greek town did the new religion have greater difficulty in gaining a foothold and arresting the attention of society. The dogmatic struggles of the Byzantine Church passed unheeded there, even by the sparse community of Christians. Yet change was at hand.

The theosophy expounded by the latter-day philosophers, of whom Leontius was an example, took the form of a pantheistic development of Platonic ideas, in opposition to the Christianity which seemed to be so gaining on the world. "The beautifully bespangled card-castle of Neo-Platonism had, at this date, all its work cut out to maintain itself against the knots of . . . . sophists, the wrecks of the old Cynic, Stoic, and Academic schools, who, with venom increasing after the wont of parties with their decrepitude, assailed it as an empty medley of all Greek philosophies with all Christian superstitions." * In the gradual elevation of the Soul from materialism, her purification from sensualism, and her mystic union with the Absolute, paganism had attained the level of a spiritual religion for the highly cultivated few who could thus apologise for it. According to his admirers the Emperor

* Kingsley " Hypatia."

Julian was a product of this exotic Hellenism; Hypatia was its last high priestess; and Athenais, the subject of this chapter, its fair apostate.

Athens was, however, no more than a museum of antiquity. The edicts of Theodosius I. against pagan forms of worship, had closed the doors of the temples, though their further condemnation was not carried out. Nowhere in Greece, least of all in Athens, had the imperial imposition of Christianity succeeded. And yet Synesius of Cyrene wrote disappointedly of his visit there, to Hypatia at Alexandria. Greek enthusiast far more than Christian bishop, Synesius had perhaps too sincere a love for ancient culture and its beautiful Alma Mater to view Athens with the petty jealousy of an Alexandrian. The enthusiasm of the youthful student, intoxicated with delight in finding himself upon the Acropolis, could blind him to the observation Synesius shrewdly made. The glory which still rested on the city and drew men's longing gaze, was not the noontide splendour but that of the after-glow.

The name of Leontius the sophist is only rescued from oblivion by the fame of his lovely daughter. Little is known of him, but the shrewd conjectures of Gregorovius give us a hint or two. He cannot say whether Leontius was a native Athenian or not, but he adds that, whoever his masters in philosophy may nave been, the great minds of Athens had already passed away before the young man could have begun to frequent the schools. As a boy, Leontiuus may have witnessed the Emperor Julian's attempts to revive paganism, and as a man he saw them reversed by the enactments of Theodosius. In the autumn of 395 Athens was threatened by Alaric, and the sophist may have been among those impoverished by the terms upon which the inhabitants were allowed to capitulate. "The Gothic prince with a small and select train was admitted within the walls; he indulged himself with the refreshment of the bath and accepted a splendid banquet provided by the magistrate. . . . . But the whole territory of Attica . . . . was blasted by his baleful presence, and if we may use the comparison of a contemporary philosopher, Athens itself resembled the bleeding and empty skin of a slaughtered victim."* Leontius was a man of influence, popularity and wealth. Olympiodorus was enabled through his good offices to found a chair of philosophy at Athens, and Synesius of Cyrene may have known him, though the jealousy twixt philosopher and sophist may have condemned friendship to unripe acquaintance in the latter case.

Leontius had two sons, Valerius and Genesius, and a daughter was born to him at some date after Alaric's visitation. Historians differ considerably as to Athenais' age at the time of her marriage. It is an important point in the light of after events. Seven years

* Gibbon.

or so count more with a woman in middle life than in youth, and could this year be determined, the fact of Athenais' exact age in 440 might do something to exonerate or condemn her memory.

The sophist dedicated his little daughter to Pallas Athene, and Athenais grew up a worthy child of Hypatia's sovereign goddess. She received her education at the hands of her devoted father, and at those of his many distinguished friends. She became an excellent writer,'an enthusiastic student of Homer and Demosthenes; she spoke with ease and fluency in public and held disputes in the schools on literary and philosophic subjects We may picture Athenais escorted to her lecture hall, as Kingsley has drawn Hypatia, surrounded by a crowd of dilettanti, not one of whom would have had manliness enough to defend her in an hour of need. Often may she, too, have needed to dash the tears away when the thought occurred to her that beauty and not learning drew her audience !

" Seated beneath the fig tree that grew before her father's house, when the sun had disappeared in the Gulf of Salamis, and a gentle evening breeze wafted the perfumes of Hymethes down to her, Athenais sang to her lyre's accompaniment the rhapsodies of ancient Greece. Her song was of Leda carried by the swan ; of Hecate who ruled the mysteries of the night, and whom the Athenians regarded as the goddess of their hearths ; of Endymion sleeping beside his heifers whilst Diana descended from Olympus to contemplate the pastures of Ionia. Then her voice rose as she chanted the exploits of the Homeric heroes, the woes of Priam's children, the triumphs of Platæa and Marathon."*

She was brought up a pagan, and had Leontius voluntarily closed his eyes to the grandeur of Christianity, it would have been an easy matter for him to withhold all knowledge of it from his daughter. A girl is not led to question the faith that satisfies an honoured father. She accepts it as trustingly as she confides her love, and no revolution at her very door affects her *unless* she hears its echoes in the house. Even to the present day, so long as there are educated people, the old mythologies of Greece must continue to exist artistically. Leontius could perceive no qualification ; for him the philosophy of this mythology was the religion of the educated—Christianity might suffice for the ignorant, or for the preoccupied majority.

Often as Athenais may have come into contact with Athenian Christians at the house of a Christian aunt, her father had little fear of their influence upon a mind that reflected such credit on his training. His daughter, however, would never have witnessed the gladsome processions of old in honour of her tutelary goddess, nor could she have offered prayers and flowers in the Temple of the Muses, had not the custodian of the Acropolis sometimes

* Poujoulat Hist. Con.

allowed her to behold the friezes of the Parthenon. Only in her own home could she have assisted at the rites of her religion, and even for this infringement of the edicts Leontius was liable to a penalty. But on one occasion when Athenais fell dangerously ill, her father risked a visit to the Temple of Pallas Athene to pray for her recovery.

Leontius lived a quiet and studious life. He had less professional ambition than Socratic virtue. He loved his daughter, but with the infatuated complacency of one whose outlook on life was wholly impractical and self-sufficing. On the strength of the revelations of her horoscope Leontius could calmly abandon Athenais to the providence of an unknown future. When he died, about the year 416, he left the bulk of his property to his two sons. His daughter was dowerless save for her beauty and the reputation of her learning ! We think of her as the fallen idol of a pedant whose pride must have equalled his philosophical superiority to the common cares of life. Leontius' wits seem to have deprived him of the foresight of less lofty-minded fathers. His was the fatuous action of a man who chose to ignore the facts that Athenais was a woman as well as a scholar, that brothers can mask impatience and nurse jealousy, that men care little for penniless beauty, and that the world is rough and rude despite all the explanations of philosophers.

The fair Athenian found herself, indeed, in a sorry plight. Valerius and Genesius practically chased her from the home, and were glad to throw away the miserable sum of a hundred aureis to see the last of her. So much, at least, Leontius had left her, " I desire that a hundred pieces of gold be given to my beloved daughter whose happiness is above that of any other woman." Weeping, Athenais besought her brothers to allow her a third part of their joint inheritance. Truly " happiness " seemed far enough from her, as she fled to her father's sister for shelter and condolence.

From her aunt's house Athenais instituted legal proceedings against her brothers. It seems that they were unsuccessful, for her next step was to go to Constantinople to throw herself upon the protection of the Augusta Pulcheria. However legal matters fared with her—and the world was no kinder to the weak and dispossessed in the fifth century than it is inclined to be to-day— Athenais' name, and the news of her misfortunes acted as an open sesame with the Emperor's compassionate sister.

St. Pulcheria befriended the daughter of Leontius, and Athenais was welcomed by the cultured society of the capital and the court. She may indeed, have been admitted to the palace as one of the Augusta's suite, and have taken up her residence under the wing of her Athenian relative, within the precincts of the Imperial ward.

She was in all probability about twenty years of age. In default of that picture of her with its gay blue background, which, later, won the Emperor's heart, we had best recall the image of a gracious Grecian lady, tall and radiant. Athenais was famed for the beauty which could be regal in the modest draperies of a Thorwaldsen nymph. Though the rippling fillet-bound hair of a Hebe was now confined by the bejewelled mitella of a Roman lady, or concealed by the Byzantine veil; though the sweet firm feet of a muse were now shod with embroidered shoes, no accidents of dress could disguise the serene brows, and the finely turned lips of a clear-eyed Grecian goddess.

As a pagan the fair suppliant won St. Pulcheria's affection, but until she became a Christian it is hardly likely that the brilliant dénouement of her career suggested itself to the Augusta's private thoughts. Her conversion came about between the years 416 and 421. It may have been due, in some degree, to the influence and friendship of the Imperial sisters, and to the exhortations of the Patriarch Atticus, but even more sincerely, to the schooling of adversity. Neo-Platonism had not dried her tears, nor salved her wounded heart. Athenais' conversion must have greatly rejoiced Leontius' sister and have richly repaid the sacrifice she had made of home in order to accompany her niece to Constantinople. The beautiful orphan became a willing convert to Christianity. She seems to have retained a gentle feeling towards the old faiths and ideals of her girlhood, more out of love for the memory of her father and for associations' sake, than in any spirit of comparison or of poetic regret. There was no rancour, either, in Athenais' soul, against Leontius or her brothers. Her mind was wholly sweet and forgiving and ready to be impressed by a faith her heart could well assimilate.

If indeed, as Gregorovius suggests, the confession of Cyprianus, (which, as part of the legend of SS. Cyprian and Justina, Athenais afterwards rendered into verse) had a peculiar interest for her, it may have been because it described a similar process to her own conversion. In this light the passage may almost be regarded as autobiographical, and is of the greatest interest in a story which has so little else to guide it.

"Followers of Christ," it exclaims, "you who truly cherish in your hearts the well-praised Saviour, see my streaming tears and learn whence flows my grief. And you who are still snared in the dark illusions of idolatry, mark what I relate of its lies and deceptions. For never has one lived more wholly devoted to false gods than I. To none but me have the demoniac arts been so deeply taught. Yes, I am Cyprian, whom my parents dedicated to Apollo as a child. The orgiastic tumults of the festival of the grey dragon were my lullaby. At seven I was presented to the sun-god Mithras. I lived in the glorious city of Athens, and, as it pleased my parents, became its citizen. When I had attained the age of ten, I kindled the torch of Demeter and immersed myself in Cora's dirge. I bore Palla's serpent to the citadel as temple-lad.

"Then to the summit of wooded mount Olympus I climbed like the fools who seek there the radiant habitation of the holy gods. I saw the hours and found there the multitudinous winds, day's clamorous chorus, and all those winged fantasies in whose illusions life slips away. . . . . . . Then for the first time the demons' weakness was revealed to me."*

In the meantime love sprang up between St. Pulcheria and her charming protégée. Athenais underwent a course of religious instruction imparted to her, in all probability, by St. Atticus himself, and presently the wonderful future forseen by Leontius in his daughter's horoscope, revealed itself to the astonished world.

From the date of Leontius' death to that of Athenais' wedding, the facts of the story are so few and far between that only imagination may fill up the intervals. It is impossible to say how long a time elapsed while the fair philosopher was disputing her father's will in Athens, or before she relinquished all hopes of prevailing upon her brothers to provide for her. She may have spent some years in the capital, or even in the palace, without coming directly into contact with the Emperor. Theodosius had never seen her, if anything may be based upon the story of the Paschal chronicle, before the Augusta introduced her to him as a likely bride. The young princess had a thousand court intrigues to forestall, and society machinations to circumvent, in this delicate business of her brother's betrothal, and it would have augured ill for the success of her plans to expose them to criticism by drawing attention to Athenais as the possible bride. The beautiful Greek suffered nothing in Pulcheria's eyes by comparison with the eligible maidens of Constantinople, nor, we presume, in those of the Archbishop. None of the daughters of the senators could rival her, and the Augusta saw in her position the very guarantee of that graceful docility for which it might have been vain to hope elsewhere.

Such a marriage might sorely disappoint a large section of the ambitious court, and despite the theory that the Emperor ennobled the woman he married, be looked upon as a mésalliance. Justinian could impose the infamous daughter of a charioteer upon society as its Empress, yet the Roman princess Placidia *demeaned* herherself by marrying a barbarian king. By that law of Constantine which Justinian had such notorious occasion to set aside, the Senators of Byzantium (and how much more its Emperor!) were forbidden to marry women unfitted to rank as their wives. The definitions of this law were called so frequently in question, that in 454 Theodosius' successor, made an effort to limit them strictly to their incontestable meanings. "God forbid," said the charitable

* From Gregorovius' German version of the original Greek.

edict, "that poverty should ever be synonymous with infamy, since we well know how many who have been among the poorest, have for that very reason acquired much glory, the proof of their goodness and integrity."

Athenais' dowry of beauty, culture and faith, entirely satisfied Pulcheria, but she doubtless bestowed some portion on the maiden, out of her privy purse, as a shield against the criticism of the world.

The story of the seventh century chroniclers has it that the Augusta sprang her choice upon Theodosius like a lovely vision. Delighted with a picture of Athenais, and curious to behold one of whom his bosom friend Paulinus also spoke in terms of the highest praise, the young Emperor besought his sister to present the Athenian to him. The moment in which a curtain was drawn aside, and the lovely Greek advanced with the three obeisances of court etiquette, is one of the most picturesque records in the romance of Byzantine history. Fable or not, we can ill afford to discard so delightful a picture, though M. Thierry thinks it frivolous, and Gregorovius draws his pen across it.

The rapid course of an Imperial betrothal was soon run. But in the meantime Athenais had been received into the Church.

The catechumens of the fifth century were generally baptised on the vigil of the feast of Easter, the preceding forty days of Lent having been spent in preparation. So soon as Athenais became a "competent" her name was given in on the day before Quadragesima, and an examination was held by St. Atticus as to her fitness to receive the sacrament. St. Pulcheria supplied her mother's place and answered the bishop's interrogatories, "Does this woman lead a good life, is she obedient, not given to wine nor deceitful?"

For the next few weeks the fair Greek had to be as assiduous in her attendance at instructions and exorcisms as the humblest convert. "Beginning from Genesis, the bishop went all through the Scriptures during that time, explaining them first literally and then unfolding them spiritually." Athenais next learned to recite the Christian creed, with the greatest care and reverence. After the 'redditio' or profession of faith made before the bishop, St. Atticus thus addressed her.

"During these seven weeks you have been taught all the law of the Scriptures, you have also heard concerning the faith and concerning the resurrection of the flesh . . . . but the teaching of the deeper mystery, that is of Baptism itself, you cannot hear, being as yet a catechumen. But lest you should think anything is done without good reason this, when you have been baptised in the Name of God you shall hear . . . . during the eight Paschal days. . . .*

---

* V. Mgr. Duchesne "Christian Worship" and the Appendix.

When at last the beautiful convert stood in the baptistery of St. Sophia,* surrounded by the deaconesses, and accompanied by the Augusta, the Imperial sisters and their ladies, she began by turning to the West, the land of darkness, and holding a wax taper in one hand and extending the other with a queenly gesture, pronounced the formulary of rejection.

"I renounce thee, Satan, thy pomps, thy works and all thy worship!"

Then turning to the East, the realm of light, she again repeated the creed of Nicaea.

There was a little stir as the deaconesses now came forward to divest the neophyte of her garments and robe her afresh in white. She was then anointed from head to foot with the chrism and plunged thrice into the consecrated waters of the font. St. Pulcheria stood by as god-mother, and Athenais emerged as Ælia Eudocia. Once again she was anointed on the forehead, ears, nose and breast with the holy oil, and turning to the East, repeated the Lord's Prayer.

After Athenais had assisted at the holy sacrifice for the first time and had received communion, she was given a draught of mingled milk and honey, according to the Alexandrian custom of the time.

St. Pulcheria now looked upon her protégée with as much more than her former interest that the further tie of sisterhood could draw them no closer together. The spiritual relationship contracted between them was regarded in the fifth century as a very real bond, and was taken in all earnestness on either side.

The baptism of Athenais was more than a theme of congratulation and rejoicing, it was a triumph of Christian friendship, and the Augusta, with all her liberal appreciation of learning and culture, gloried in having overthrown the Greek divinities in Eudocia's eyes. She was now free to enjoy without reproach or reservation an intellectual companionship which had charmed her from the first.

Theodosius himself found in Athenais' mind and disposition an even greater attraction than her exquisite physical beauty. The temperament of this young Byzantine prince was not unlike that of St. Edward of England. He was gentle, religious and studious, more monk than bridegroom, more clerk than king. At this date he was twenty years of age, and not without good looks. He was of middle height, had dark eyes and an open glance, a fine clear-cut profile, clean-shaven lips, and the unusual contrast of fair hair. His manner with men was amiable and princely, and with women, dignified and courteous.

* We are quite justified in supposing that Athenais was baptised in the baptistery of St. Sophia rather than in one of the domestic churches of the Imperial precincts, since in the early centuries each diocese had only one baptistery, and that one was attached to the Cathedral. Rome alone had more than one baptistery. In the fourth century the bishops were the ordinary ministers of the sacrament of baptism.

During the few days that elapsed between the ceremony of the betrothal, (the 'subharratio' or ring-giving), and the wedding, Athenais was strictly sequestered. But her union with the Emperor was no mere state convenience hedged round with the formalities of rank and custom. It was a true romance, a lovely union of Christian and Grecian ideality. The daughter of Leontius—Athenais as we may continue to call her since she never discarded that name—might, truly, recall her father's augury with a smile merited rather by its happy event than by its parental folly.

CHAPTER XI

Marriage, according to Roman law in the fourth century A D. was essentially a civil function, and could be entered into without any religious solemnization whatever. But the Church had already elaborated those beautiful ceremonies, some of which survive in the Greek rite to-day, by which devoutly minded people might be reminded of the sacramental character of this great step in life. The scenic details of the present chapter are woven together from a variety of sources, chiefly from Dr. Paspates "Imperial Palace of Constantinople," and although each one by itself is sufficiently authentic, the writer would beg every indulgence for the manner in which she has arranged the pictures. They do not aspire to be antiquarian reconstructions of the vanished scenes, but just that approximate setting which serves the simpler purpose of this book.

IF the wedding ceremonies of the fifth century already approached the elaborateness of those described by the Emperor Constantine Porphyrogennetos, the Imperial Palace now witnessed such scenes as had not been enacted there since the death of Eudoxia.

The only contemporary picture we might hope to obtain of them would be from the pen of the western poet, Claudian. Laureate at the court of Ravenna, he composed an epithalamium to celebrate the nuptials of Honorious and Maria in 398. It is however difficult to imagine that Theodosius, Pulcheria, and Athenais would care for the "fescenninae" of the day. These were verses, more or less pagan in cast, recited at the wedding feast to provoke the laughter of the company by their satirical humour and obscenity. They had been prescribed as far back as the time of Augustus as of immoral tendency. Claudian's epithalamium is merely a compliment conceived in the vein of the old mythology, to Honorius Maria and Stilicho. Cupid boasts to his mother Venus of the Emperor's capitulation and begs her to "Prospera, regalibus adnue votis," or in modern parlance, abundantly to bless the newly-wedded pair. Venus proceeds to fulfil the request of the officious little god of love, but first reminds Maria that she has travelled all the way from Cyprus. All this is alien to the spirit of Pulcheria's court, although it probably found some excuse for its presence at the Emperor's wedding, in the social conventions of the day.

It was in the height of summer. The entire city of Constantinople was once again en fête and thronged with the holiday making populace. The Prefect Florentius and all the public officials had taxed their ingenuity to devise a brilliant programme for the week-long celebrations, while the numerous private palaces at the disposal of the Emperor and his sisters were filled with ambassadors, provincial bishops and governors, and the great guests of the occasion.

At an early hour on the day itself—June 7th, 421—all the senators presented themselves at the Great Palace and proceeded to robe in the Consistory. Three porphyry steps at the end of this apartment led to the throne "an elaborately carved chair adorned with ivory, jewels, and precious metals." It stood beneath a silver dome raised on four pillars just sufficiently high to permit of the Emperor standing upright. "A pair of silver eagles spread their wings on the top of this canopy, and rich curtains which might be drawn so as to close the interior, hung between the columns." *
Here Theodosius formally received the senators, seated, and robed so richly that his appearance almost defies description. His ample purple robe of state, the mandye, fell to his feet and was fastened on the shoulder by an enormous clasp or fibula of gold and precious stones. Its simplicity was enriched by two squares of embroidered cloth of gold which approached from the back and front to the division on the right side, but which were partially hidden by the "scaramangion," a mantle of ermine and rare furs, which depended from the shoulders. Purple hose, bejewelled scarlet buskins consisting of heel and toe caps laced across the instep and fastened with the golden eagles peculiar to the Emperor, and a white tunic sleeved to the wrists, and girt with a crimson scarf completed the princely costume. Upon the Emperor's head glittered the Imperial crown, with its silken cap, its golden intersecting arches surmounted by a cross, and its lappets of pearls pendants on either side of the pale and youthful face. In his left hand Theodosius held a globe again surmounted by a cross. He was surrounded on the "accubiton" or dais of state by an order of Patricians, styled the Fathers of the Emperor, garbed in white, with purple "tables" (embroidered squares) on their mantles, red girdles and black shoes. The surrounding guards made a blaze of generous colour with their green tunics faced with red, their white hosen, thick rings of gold round their necks, their long spears and their oval shields bordered with blue and widely starred from the centre in black on a red ground. Their Count or Captain was distinguished by his red and purple breasted tunic, and by the Christian monogram of his shield in yellow on a green ground.

Close to Theodosius stood the young Paulinus, the bravest and the handsomest of his guards and personal friends.

After the Senators had robed, at the command of the Emperor, who seems to have personally directed the more stately portions of the ceremonies, they proceeded to the Golden Hand, which

---

* Mr. G. W. Holmes "The Age of Justinian and Theodora."

apartment led into the great Hall of the Augustæus. Here they advanced, prostating themselves thrice and kissing the feet of the Emperor—a mode of approach only dispensed with on Sundays—and after some interval allowed for the throng of noble guests to rank itself in befitting order around the Hall, the Master of Ceremonies entered attended by five of the silentiaries.

The Emperor now motioned for the Patriarch to be conducted from the Church of St. Stephen in the Daphne, where he had been waiting, to the presence; on his arrival Theodosius rose to greet him. Behind the venerable Atticus came an imposing procession of ecclesiastics. Presently all the guests drew aside and formed an obsequious avenue through which the Emperor passed on his way to the " Apse " where the wedding ceremony properly began.

During the whole of this time the bride-elect was waiting elsewhere in the palace. The " Præpositus " was now dispatched to fetch her and to conduct her to the Emperor's side. Clad in the sticharion,* and modestly veiled, the beautiful Athenian now took precedence of the Augusta. St. Pulcheria, the most noble ladies Marina and Arcadia, and a train of titled women accompanied her to the Apse, and immediately the Patriarch began the wedding rites.

Eudocia took candles, and lighting them one by one, like twinkling stars, handed them to the various officials who supported her. When the Emperor drew aside the bridal veil it was so held by the cubicularii as to screen her from the public gaze, whilst the bridegroom received her mantle from the Patriarch and cast it round her.

At the time when the Emperor Constantine Porphryrogennetos wrote his descriptions of court functions the ceremony of coronation had become an imperial as well as a bridal rite. But at the date of Athenais' marriage to Theodosius it had not yet been instituted in the royal sense. Athenais was crowned as a Greek bride is crowned to-day, but neither she nor her husband were ever crowned by the State. Thus if St. Atticus next blessed a diadem among the other hereditary ornaments of the Byzantine imperial brides, it was as a part of the marriage service and in no way as a civil act. These jewels were each and severally handed from the Bishop to the Emperor and bestowed by him upon the lovely person of his bride.

After this came a pause and the confusion of a mass movement of high dignitaries. The Patriarch and his clergy withdrew to another apartment, whither the Emperor and Empress presently repaired to hold a congratulatory reception. All the jealousies of the court were momentarily allayed by the contagious enthusiasm which the beauty of the bride aroused. Only those whose egotism had stifled the last generous impulse of which the heart is capable, could nurse resentment against the radiant young

---

* A mantle falling from the shoulders.

Athenian in this moment of her pride and joy. Her progress to the audience chamber was acclaimed by a delighted throng. All those ministers, officials, officers, dignitaries and noblemen who had been invided to the wedding were now introduced by the Master of Ceremonies, when they made a series of profound obeisances before the Imperial pair. These presentations occupied a long time, and must have become, after awhile, as wearisome to the sovereigns as to all those who, their brief moment of importance over, relapsed into the rôle of onlookers. But the interminable succession of these great ones came to an end at last.

Thereupon the silentiaries of the Palace Guard received the order to proclaim the Emperor and Empress throughout the vast establishment. The retirement of the clergy was a signal for the entrance of the Augusta and her court, who in their turn, repeated the homage just performed by the Senators and the male aristocracy of the capital. The great ladies of Constantinopolitan society were ushered in by the "ostiarius," and, guided by the signals of his wand made the court courtesies of the fifth century.

When all was over, the Imperial bride and bridegroom repaired to the other audience chamber, called the Golden Hand, the Empress being attended by the entire concourse of ladies recently assembled. On reaching the "Onopodium" she was greeted by general acclamation. "For many faithful years!" Disguising her fatigue under the gracious demeanour de rigeur in a queen, Eudocia next made a sort of bridal tour through the principal quarters of the Palace, everywhere acclaimed by the delighted guests and ministers. She passed along, bowing on either hand, her bosom full of suppressed emotion. At this overwhelming moment of her incredible fortune Athenais' greatest longing was to recall herself to her brothers' love. She went through the succeeding ceremony of the adoration of the Cross in one of the Imperial churches, with the fervour of a recent convert, and afterwards rejoined the larger part of her retinue in that Hall of the Augustaeus whence the great day had begun, as it seemed, an eternity ago.

The remainder of the wedding service had yet to be concluded. In the Church of St. Stephen in the Daphne Theodosius II. and Athenais, daughter of the Athenian sophist, were finally made man and wife. The Patriarch then said Mass. At the end, the bridal pair received their nuptial crowns of flowers, or of gold and silver leaves, and their return to the palace was once more the cause of an outbreak of loyalty and hymeneal song. They laid down their crowns in the nuptial chamber, and only now were permitted to rest in the Hall of the Nineteen Couches.

A magnificent banquet followed. "The floor of the banqueting hall was paved with precious marbles now covered with rare carpets and rugs," and the Emperor and Empress, the Augusta, the Patriarch and a small selection of the highest ministers of state dined at the crescent-shaped golden table.

Even when twilight crept over the sea, and despite all illuminations, darkness gradually filled the odorous gardens around with
the restfulness of night, a murmur went up from the festive city.
For days the courtly entertainments were continued, and many an
Imperial pageant made high holiday for the rejoicing citizens.

One of the ceremonies that found a place among these fêtes
was the filling of a new reservoir, which bore the name of Pulcheria,
since the Augusta had ordered its construction the previous year.
One Saturday the Emperor unveiled a new statue of his father,
which had been erected on a magnificent column in the midst of
the Arcadius piazza on the Xerolophe hill. After the bridal wreaths
had been returned to the altar of the Church, the term of Byzantine
honeymoon drew to its close. Portrait busts of Theodosius and
Eudocia were duly despatched to Honorius at Rome or Ravenna,
and all the obligations of the great occasion were fittingly fulfilled.

The young Augusta, upon the grave current of whose life this
brilliant event must have broken somewhat strangely, had the
satisfaction of finding her days revert to their wonted monotony of
prayer and duty.

It is curious to reflect that she who had assisted Eudocia to the
enviable forefront of Imperial life, and who, personally now withdrew behind the scenes more than ever, was herself as youthful, and
almost as beautiful, as the bride. The Empress took her place in
society at once, with exquisite grace and breeding. She became
immediately the attraction and the ornament of the court, and
doubtless relieved the Augusta of many of its social and festive
obligations. St. Pulcheria was little over twenty. But she had
played so grave, so responsible, so sober a part in the counsels of
her brother and in the elevation of Eudocia that we think of her as
considerably older.

Her choice of Athenais seemed fully justified. The married
life of Theodosius opened under happy auspices, and the young
Empress brought the most winning graces to bear upon her new
position. It was one requiring all a woman's tact and ingenuity to
fill, although from an Imperial point of view it carried few
responsibilities. Her term of office as maid of honour to the
Augusta had accustomed the philosopher's daughter to the
ceremonial of palace life. However much it was inevitable that her
Greek spirit should sometimes faint a little under the burden of
Imperial etiquette, and long for the silence and freedom of the
groves of Athens, Eudocia had the power to quickly adapt herself
to the brilliant circumstances of her lot. Nevertheless her path was
difficult. As wife of the Emperor her demeanour necessarily lost
something of its naturalness and spontaneity. She had to move,
act and speak, with the greatest circumspection in order to disarm
the envy her success had occasioned amidst the defeated intriguers
of the Imperial court. She had to receive the homage of great
ladies, whose breasts harboured nothing but criticism and spite

7

against her, with the graciousness of one whom these things can neither frighten nor surprise. She had to wield her influence judiciously not to infringe upon her sister's Imperial prerogative, and to wear all the semblance of an Empress, without possessing the substance.

With her husband and with Pulcheria alone could Athenais remain herself. She became the bright centre of a circle of intellectuals, and held many a lively discussion with the poets and philosophers of her husband's court, while Theodosius himself reverted to his dreamy studies. His marriage had scarcely bestirred him or awakened him to the facts of life. He loved his beautiful bride with the same peaceful love he bestowed upon his books, and although she certainly filled all the space his nature could make for a wife, he remained the gentle, unimpassioned prince he had been from the beginning.

One day St. Pulcheria read him a lesson on his absent-mindedness, and pointed it as forcibly as she knew how. He had affixed his signature to a certain document, as often happened, with no knowledge of its contents. It had sufficed him to note the green ink of the Augusta's annotating. A short while afterwards, he chanced to ask for his wife, when Pulcheria replied that she was no longer at his beck and call. He had just signed her away into slavery—bound his wife in fact to his sister! Gregorovius thinks that this little anecdote belongs to the later time when unhappiness had begun to creep in between the Augusta and the Empress. He sees in it some desire on Pulcheria's part to teach Athenais herself a lesson. If this be so, it must be admitted, regretfully enough, that the beautiful Greek in time deserved the reminder.

When Athenais' two brothers heard of the marvellous fortune that had befallen their sister, they fled from home in fear lest her resentment might now overtake them. They seem to have misunderstood her nature as only blood relations can. Athenais was not only incapable of harbouring her wrong, but unable to forget her love. Surrounded now with new ties, new faces, new friends, and new environments, her heart yearned wistfully for those who were her own. As Empress of Byzantium, she yet felt strange, and longed for some link with the past in Athens. The news of her brothers' flight and consternation filled her with the eagerness of a kind design. She immediately sent for them to come to Constantinople. The story runs that they were accompanied thither by seven Grecian sages in the superfluous character of intercessors. No sooner were Valerius and Genesius ushered into the presence of their radiant sister than she sprang towards them with a happy torrent of forestalling pardons. "If you had not treated me badly," she protested, "I should not have been compelled to visit Constantinople, and I should never have become an Empress. The diadem to which by birth I had no claim you have bestowed upon me! It was really my good fortune that was the cause of your not yielding to my wishes, and not your disposition towards me."

A woman dares not analyse the happiness she is willing to rear upon foundations of forgiveness. It is a mercy that she dares forget. Love perforce is blind.

Valerius is said to have become Prefect of Illyricum—possibly he was the Consul with Ætius in 432, and Genesius took up his abode in the capital as a minister of state.

The seven sages, whose names are all solemnly recorded, met with no scanter courtesy from the populace of Constantinople than they bestowed upon it. Their contempt for all they saw and heard in the young city, smacked of the invincible self-sufficiency of pedants. The foolish old "sages" little supposed that they cut the figures of buffoons. The quaint legend of their adventuring invests the story of Athenais' reconciliation to her brothers with a touch of humour not unworthy of treatment by a Shakespeare.

Scarce a year elapsed before a daughter was born to the Imperial pair. Once more a golden cradle stood in the Purple Chamber of the Empress, and the people of Byzantium kept another holiday. The Patriarch baptised the royal child and named her Licinia Eudocia. Athenais had proved herself all that Pulcheria hoped, and with the birth of the infant the last hesitation as to her worthiness of the highest dignity disappeared. She was forthwith invested with the full regalia of Imperial rank, and proclaimed Augusta, Jan. 2nd, 423.

The Western Emperors from Gratian

TO

Valentinian III., A.D. 423-455.

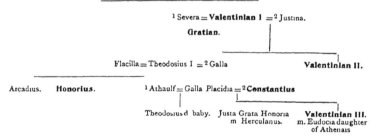

THE story of the court-life at Byzantium must be interrupted at this point in order to pick up the thread of Western history. The two halves of the Roman world had been drifting steadily apart since the accession of Theodosius' sons to their respective thrones in 395, Arcadius at Constantinople and Honorius at Rome. The one half was becoming Greek and the other was breaking up. But now for a moment the strange adventures of the Princess Placidia were to renew the alliance between East and West. This woman, whose romantic and chequered career is a history in itself, was to learn from her niece in Constantinople those lessons of prudence and wisdom necessary to fit her to occupy the sister throne of Ravenna. Just as the novelists of fifty years ago loved to develop the separate plots of their tale until the moment when their union could invest the whole narrative with fuller interest, so the story of Placidia is something apart from that of Pulcheria, and yet necessary to it, after the date at which we have arrived. The personal history of these two queens epitomises the history of the Empire they ruled. The events of their individual lives determined a temporary respite in the process of its decay, and knit the ties of friendship which alone enabled Rome to breast the tide of adversity for yet a few more years.

The Princess Placidia was the daughter of Theodosius the Great, and his second wife Galla. She was born in A.D. 388, shortly after her father had securely seated the young Valentinian II. on the throne of Milan, under the paternal care of St. Ambrose. For three years Theodosius remained in the West, but scarcely had he returned to Constantinople than the news overtook him that all the work of his recent campaign had been undone. Valentinian was dead, and a usurper Eugenius, presumed to send his ambassadors to the Eastern court. The Empress incited her husband by her tears to avenge her brothers' fate, and a second war began. Before the victory of 394, however, Galla died in childbirth, and Theodosius followed her very shortly to the grave.

The Princess Placidia was but a baby when she made her first appearance in the Imperial Palace at Constantinople. She was the step-sister of Arcadius and Honorius. As soon as the war was brought to a conclusion the Emperor sent for Honorius to join him in Italy in order to receive the sceptre of the West. "The arrival of Honorius"—then a boy of eleven—"at Milan, was welcomed by a splendid exhibition of games in the circus, and the Emperor, though he was oppressed by the weight of his disorder, contributed by his presence to the public joy. But the remains of his strength were exhausted by the painful effort which he made to assist at the spectacles of the morning. Honorius supplied during the rest of the day the place of his father, and the great Theodosius expired during the ensuing night." * Had the little Princess Placidia accompanied her brother with half the Byzantine court to Italy, both the wives whom the Emperor had loved so tenderly would have been represented by their children at his bedside. Placidia was then seven years of age. The historian of the "Decline and Fall" tells us that she received a royal education in the Palace at Constantinople, so that some doubt must attend the date of her journey west. It seems, however, that when she did arrive in Italy, she was entrusted to the protection of the great Vandal Stilicho, and, like Honorius himself, found in Serena his wife, a foster-mother. This lady was a niece of the late Emperor, and consequently cousin to her Imperial wards. She had a palace at Milan and another in Rome, and was altogether the greatest noblewoman in the West.

The first years of the child-Emperor's "reign" were troubled by the revolt of the usurper Gildo in Africa, but Stilicho undertook a war against him and brought it to a successful conclusion in 398. The joy of the African triumph was happily connected with the nuptials celebrated between Honorius and the General's elder daughter Maria. The ceremony took place at Milan, but owing to

* Gibbon.

the extreme youth of the bridegroom (Honorius was only fourteen) Serena arranged that the marriage should be no more than formal.

In the meantime it devolved upon the minister to superintend the education of the Augustus. "The experience of history," says Gibbon, "will countenance the suspicion that a prince who was born in the purple received a worse education than the meanest peasant in his dominions ; and that the ambitious Stilicho allowed him to attain the age of manhood without attempting to excite his courage, or enlighten his understanding." Honorius was certainly less cultured than even the lazy Arcadius.

If Placidia herself, in after years proved more able a ruler than either, it must have been rather in virtue of her woman's wit than in that of any education. She passed through the school of experience and adversity, and owed more to her emulation of St. Pulcheria than to the foresight of Serena.

Stilicho and his wife cherished secret hopes of a second alliance with the Imperial family ; Placidia was for them the destined bride of Eucherius their son, and consequently needed only that amount of education which would enable her to appreciate his fitness to share, if not indeed to occupy, the throne of the western Empire. Such were their ambitious plans, destined as nobler ones have been, to the ruin that dogs the faith placed in princes.

In the year 402 Italy was first invaded by Alaric with the Gothic nation at his back. Stilicho immediately took the field against this formidable foe, nerved with the consciousness that in himself alone lay any hope for Honorius. Daily messengers hurried to and fro between the Palace of Serena and the shifting seat of war ; the whole city of Rome hung upon the news they brought. It went half mad with relief and joy when it heard of the victories of Pollentia and Verona.

Placidia probably went to Rome in her brother's train when " Honorius was directed to accept the dutiful invitation of the Senate and to celebrate in the Imperial city the auspicious era of the Gothic victory and of his own sixth consulship." The suburbs and the streets from the Milvian Bridge to the Palatine Mount were filled with the Roman people, "who in the space of a hundred years had only thrice been honoured with the presence of their sovereigns. While their eyes were fixed on the chariot where Stilicho was deservedly seated by the side of his royal pupil they applauded the pomp * of his triumph." Honorius resided for many months in the city, and guided by the minister, did his best to make himself popular among all classes of its inhabitants. He may indeed have visited the Lady Marcella in her palace on the Aventine, and Placidia would probably have known Melania, Paula, Eustochium, Fabiola, Principia, and the other members of that distinguished society which formed the 'ecclesia domestica' of St.

* Gibbon.

Jerome. The games given in the circus to celebrate Honorius' presence in the city, are ever memorable as the last at which gladiatorial combats were permitted to take place. The heroic indignation of St. Telemachus was not lost upon the young prince, whose piety, if feeble in comparison with the zeal of his father, was at least susceptible and true.

Placidia seems to have remained in Rome notwithstanding the Emperor's frequent withdrawal to Ravenna. The Goths retreated from Italy for a space, in 403, but two years later another invader, Rhadagasius, led a terrible horde of savages and pagans to defeat at the siege of Florence. Before this event Honorius, "anxious only for his personal safety, had retired to the perpetual confinement of the walls and morasses of Ravenna." It seems that Placidia remained behind in Rome until its fall in 410.

In 408 Maria died, whereupon the Emperor married her sister Thermantia. Virgin wives or not, neither bore any child, and the great General's ambition to see the purple on the shoulders of his son might have been realised had Placidia, now twenty years of age, hurried into the marriage. Stilicho, however, was tottering to his fall. His authority over Honorius was being undermined and flouted by advisers at Ravenna, and the people in general had begun to distrust the policy of the only strong man in the government. When Arcadius died in 408, Stilicho's opposition to Honorius' intention of going East "to regulate with the authority of a guardian the provinces of his infant nephew Theodosius"* was the immediate cause of his own undoing. Honorius looked upon him as a tyrant and longed for release. There was trouble at Pavia, and the soldiers, instigated by Stilicho's enemies at court, massacred a large number of his friends and supporters. The General himself, unwilling to plunge the country into civil war on his behalf, fled to Ravenna and took sanctuary within a church. He was roughly seized and promptly executed. The flight of Eucherius was intercepted, and the death of that innocent youth was soon followed by the divorce of poor Thermantia. "The adherents of the late minister were subjected to a fierce persecution, but Serena his widow was spared for the moment." A year later she was strangled by order of the cowardly and suspicious Senate during the siege of Rome. Placidia was in the city through all the horrors of that awful time, but it is difficult to understand what fear or pressure was brought to bear upon her, that she gave a ready consent to the execution of her cousin, involving herself with the ingratitude shown by Emperor and people alike, to the family of the great Vandal.

The Princess must have suffered the extremity of famine like the rest of the citizens high and low in the beleagured city. As the terrible weeks wore on and the selfish hoards of the rich became

* Gibbon.

no less exhausted than the resources of the charitable, Tisamene and Læta, imperial ladies themselves, were reduced like Placidia and numberless others, to the revolting fare left over from the soldiers' mess.

Long after the sentinels upon the walls had ceased to look for the first portions of the nameless brew of cats and dogs prepared in the public cauldrons,—long after plague-stricken corpses had become familiar horrors about the streets and squares,—long after the fear of Alaric's coup-de-grace had given place to a desperate desire for it—the pride of the Senate held out.

Long after the congregations of the various Basilicas could no more drag themselves together, or heed the comforter whose voice would be stilled to-morrow,—long after the hope of relief from Ravenna had given place to despair,—long after all these interminable phases of misery, the resolve of Alaric to reduce the city remained determined as ever.

When at last Rome capitulated (408), the immense ransom demanded still further beggared those who, for want of food to buy, had money or treasure left. The Goth stripped off the rags of Roman pride and inflicted a worse defeat on the city than that of arms.

Placidia's captivity spared her the further horrors of the sack of Rome in 410. She may not indeed have been carried off by the Gothic host until that time, but as the city was virtually at Alaric's feet during the weary interval, the conqueror would have provided for the safety of so illustrious and valuable a prisoner. The failure of all his amicable or diplomatic overtures to the government of Honorius, exasperated Alaric and drove him to the quaint expedient of creating a compliant Emperor of his own. When he appeared a second time and threatened the city through the port of Ostia, Rome had little hesitation about opening her gates and submitting to the dictates of her master. Placidia would have seen the elevation of the Prefect Attalus and possibly have shared the indignation of St. Proba at that turn of fortune. The inhabitants generally were in high spirits; only the rich house of the Anicii was dismayed at the new order of things. Honorius himself was terrified, and at once thought of flight to Constantinople. The hostile advance of Alaric and Attalus upon Ravenna was only checked by news of reinforcements sent thither by Anthemius from the East. Rome was again reduced to a sad plight by the loyal action of the Count of Africa in stopping the supply of corn. Were Placidia with the Gothic forces she would have seen the degradation of Attalus in the plains of Rimini; were she in Rome she would have known her fate was once more trembling in the balance of fresh negotiations between her brother and Alaric. The accession of an enemy to Honorius' side once more frustrated Alaric's pacific intentions, and turning back he marched a third time upon Rome. It was in August, 410. "The Senate without any hope of relief, prepared by a desperate resistance to delay the ruin of their country. But they were unable to guard against secret conspiracy . . . . . . at the hour of midnight the Salarian gate was silently opened and the inhabitants were awakened by the tremendous sound of the Gothic trumpet." * Rome was surrendered to a six days' pillage. If Placidia or Marcella or any of the great ladies of the city "dared look forth from the marble terraces where so often they must have gazed over Rome † shining white in the sunshine in all her measured lines and great proportions, her columns and her domes, what a dread scene must have met their eyes," what a nightmare of terror must have smitten their hearts! "Clouds of smoke and wild gleams of flame—the roar and outcry and slaughter mounting up into the air and soiling the very sky." What a terrible flight of women through the darkness in the lost battle borne down by the flying, all bent upon safety within some church. The gloom was lit by the savage gleams of fires; the air was full of shrieks and the terrible sobbings too deep to be articulate; the Tiber rushed onward, swift and strong, swallowing in a second, those flung into it by the press and jostle of the throng.

Placidia was saved from all this as a captive in Alaric's hands. Moreover Athaulf his kinsman, who had been Count of the Domestics in Attalus' fleeting day, took especial care to ensure her safety.

When the host rose up and marched away southward, as a flock of vultures might leave a skeleton to whiten on the Campagna, Placidia was carried with it. Alaric died in Brutii before the year was over. The soldiers buried him in the bed of a stream, and then raised Athaulf on their shields to be their king. Wild shouts of "Thiudans!" rang through the Gothic camp, and stirred the heart of the captive princess in strange unison with the rest.

Athaulf, or Adolphus as Gibbon calls him, was brother to Alaric's wife. He had married a Sarmatian and was the father of a family when he fell in love with Placidia. The royal lady accepted her captivity with marvellous resignation, and seems to have had no difficulty in reconciling herself to its courteous conditions. The rapid succession of Honorius' ministers had, at this juncture, placed at his right hand a man who had long loved his sister, but whom Placidia disliked. She probably foresaw the pressure Honorius would be persuaded to bring upon her in order to force her into a marriage with Constantius. For this reason too, she may have been all the more content to forget she was a Roman. The Goths were however Arians. It must have been a blow to Honorius and a scandal to the Church that the sister of the Emperor should unite herself to one whose faith was held in abhorrence, for at that time the line of demarcation between

---

* Gibbon. † Mrs. Oliphant "Makers of Rome."

Catholic and Arian was rigidly drawn. But the circumstances of the marriage are, generally, so obscure that it is impossible, at this distance, to judge them. Unless Athaulf were a widower he must have divorced his Sarmatian wife—if wife indeed she were, to marry the Roman Princess, and hence another blot on Placidia's fair fame.

She must have greatly loved the king thus to have braved the opinion of the world, or at least thus to have endured, four years of fruitless bargaining. The Gothic army remained some time in Italy "spoiling the land," though some historians think that the King and the Emperor came to an understanding and Athaulf engaged to suppress the tyrants who had risen up in Gaul. However this may have been Placidia was still held captive—if not against her own will, greatly against that of Honorius and Constantius. Athaulf was far more disposed to side with Jovinus and his party than with the Emperor. But owing to quarrels, jealousies and complications arising among the Gothic leaders, things so fell out that "Athaulf finally decided to war against him whom he had come to assist, and defend the rights of the Emperor whom he had intended to oppose." * Surely the moment of his embassy to Ravenna would have been a favourable one for Placidia to stipulate for her restoration had she so desired. The great aim of Honorius was to recover his sister, but the goverment was unable to carry out its part in the engagement whereby Athaulf was to be supplied with corn—as the king probably foresaw—and everything was cancelled by a renewal of hostilities. In the attempt to take Massilia, Athaulf was desperately wounded by the hand of a man destined in after years to be Placidia's viceroy in Africa. This crisis had its own weight with the lovers. Hitherto Athaulf had felt it due to his own dignity as Gothic King that Honorius should countenance his marriage with Placidia, while the Princess had been well content with the homage of the camp. During the whole time of her warlike and nomadic captivity, the daughter of Theodosius had been treated with the utmost respect. Indeed the deference of Athaulf was all the more acceptable to her in that it sprang from a deeper source than mere consideration for her pride. Brave and manly as Alaric had been, his successor "excelled in the more attractive qualities of grace and beauty," and she could not remain insensible to him.

Placidia and the King could only rejoice that death had come no nearer than to break down the barriers of their last hesitation.

At the end of that same year, 413, the pair were married at Forli or at Imola. The January following, there was a grand celebration in the house of one, Igenius, a leading citizen of Narbonne. The occasion must have been supplementary to a quiet wedding.

* Gibbon.

" The bride attired and adorned like a Roman Empress, was placed on a throne of state, and the King of the Goths who assumed . . . the Roman habit, contented himself with a less honourable seat by her side. The nuptial gift which according to the custom of his nation was offered to Placidia, consisted of the rare and magnificent spoils of her country. Fifty beautiful youths in silken robes carried a basin in each hand, and one of these basins was filled with pieces of gold, the other with precious stones of inestimable value. Attalus, so long the sport of fortune, ... was appointed to lead the chorus of the hymeneal song. The barbarians enjoyed the insolence of their triumph ; and the pro-vincials rejoiced in this alliance which tempered . . . . . the fierce spirit of their Gothic lord." *

The Gothic king's admiration for everything Roman was greatly augmented by his marriage. His sentiments were rendered still more enthusiastic by the birth of a son to Placidia, although the exclusiveness and lasting resentment of Honorius did little to encourage them. The Emperor deplored his sister's marriage and remained implacable towards her husband, while Constantius was consumed with jealousy and disappointment, and ill disposed to countenance his successful rival.

The Queen's little son Theodosius, died in infancy at Barcelona. He was buried in a silver coffin in one of the churches of that city, Athaulf having been " gently pressed " into Spain by the Imperial generals.

Placidia's happiness was short lived. Athaulf had received into his service a certain Dubius erstwhile a follower of his enemy Sarus. One evening the king had gone to the stable to look after his horses as was his custom, when this man, who had long awaited the opportunity, stabbed him to death. The deed was instigated, possibly, by Singeric, Sarus' brother, who immediately siezed Placidia and put to death Athaulf's children. All six had fled to the arms of the Bishop Sigesar for shelter. The bloody tragedy was followed by the bitterest humiliation for Placidia. She was compelled by Singeric to walk before his horse in the company of captives, for twelve interminable miles.

Within seven days this barbarity was itself avenged. Singeric in turn was slain, and Wallia became King. The death of Athaulf rejoiced the heart of Honorius and was equally acceptable to his minister. When the news of it arrived at Constantinople on Sept. 24th, 415, there were illuminations and Circensian games. So deeply had the Roman people taken to heart the mésalliance of a princess of their Imperial house ! The young Queen was alone in her unfeigned grief.

The policy of the new Gothic leader reversed that of his pre-decessor, and so the restoration of Placidia to her brother at Ravenna

* Gibbon.

was the principal condition of the peace concluded with the Imperial government early in the year 416. This restoration could now be accomplished without detriment to Gothic honour, and in a few months Placidia found herself worried into the marriage from which she had thought to escape by uniting herself to the Goth. Honorius brought his authority to bear upon her in support of Constantius' prayers. On the first day of the January following, the General's hopes were realised, and the ex-Queen became his wife. Placidia seems to have escaped any taint of heresy she might have contracted from the Goths, for she became in after years a creditable daughter to the Church. St. Barbatian, her confessor, kept the secrets of her early life locked within his priestly heart, and history itself has guarded them no less securely.

The description of Constantius contrasts him unfavourably with Athaulf. " When he walked in public his eyes were downcast and he looked askance ; he had large eyes, a large neck and a flat head ; when he rode his whole body inclined over the neck of his steed, and he used to cast his eyes obliquely hither and thither ; all deemed his appearance that of one who might aim at Empire. At feasts and carouses he was amenable and sociable, descending even to vie with the mountebanks who performed for the guests.*" He was a thorough Roman. He was as able as any of the men who aspired to rule the Emperor, and had in fact elaborated a scheme for conferring local autonomy on the inhabitants of the provinces. He loved Placidia with the devotion of a dog. The beautiful woman exercised an absolute dominion over the mind of her grateful husband, and came gradually to feel that life with him was not so dark as she had feared.

In 418 a daughter, Justa Grata Honoria, was born in the palace at Ravenna. Her father's character afterwards came out strongly in her. On July 3rd of the following year Placidia gave birth to a son, and named him after her uncle Valentinian.

With the commencement, in 420, of Constantius' third consulate, Honorius conferred the titles of Augusta and Augustus upon his sister and her husband, while the infant became a Nobilissimus. Strongly as the Emperor of the West had objected to the assumption of the former dignity by Eudoxia at Byzantium, he saw nothing to deter him from bestowing it upon one whom the Gothic soldiers in Ravenna still claimed as their queen. Constantius was still more closely associated with Honorius in the government, and became, in fact, coadjutant-emperor. Constantinople utterly refused to recognise him or his title, and erected no statues in his honour, even as a consul. The rough soldier found the restraints of Imperial rank extremely irksome. " Rarely has the world had so frank a confession of the unjoyousness of a kingly life," says Mr. Hodgkin, " as it received from this clumsy, roystering and yet not

---

* Olympiodorus quoted by Professor Bury.

altogether odious husband of Placidia."* He died very shortly, in the seventh month of his reign, and the Augusta became for the second time a widow.

After Constantius' death the relations between Honorious and his sister became very close and affectionate. There was no reason why it should not have been so; the Emperor had always loved Placidia, and she had seen enough of sorrow to be grateful for his tenderness. Slanderous tongues, however, were not wanting to put a vile construction on their love even as the fraternal affection of Theodosius and Pulcheria was to suffer from them in the East.

A cabal was formed in which Leontius, Placidia's steward and two of her women, Spadusa and Elpidia, played a prominent part in fostering suspicion and bad feeling. There were frays in the streets of Ravenna, and the barbarians who had accompanied their ex-queen from Barcelona struck blows for her fair fame.

The breach widened, and at length the Augusta and her two young children were banished from the city. She sought an asylum in the old home at Constantinople, even as her mother had once fled there before her. She had nowhere else to go.

Now that Athaulf and Constantius were dead, the government of the eastern empire was prepared to show every kindness to the unhappy lady. Placidia could ill afford to harbour resentment against her niece and nephew for the festivities of five years back. Had Honorius long survived the obscure quarrel, complications might have arisen between East and West in consequence of Theodosius' pity for Placidia.

She arrived in the Imperial city on the Bosphorus in the midst of the rejoicings at the conclusion of a Persian war.

---

* " Italy and her Invaders."

CHAPTER XIII

THE campaign against the Persians, of the year 421-422, insignificant enough in itself, connects the history of the reign of Theodosius
II. with that of the great Neo-Persian Empire. The mighty duel
between Rome and Persia lasted for seven centuries, from the
death of Crassus to the time of Heraclius. The ambition of Rome
was to grasp the whole vast realm of the Sassanian kings and to
seat her emperor upon their very throne, while that of Sapor and
his successors was to dispute the sovereignty of the world. Only
at intervals it seemed that the mighty game were drawn, and that
a settlement between the adversaries might bestow peace upon
their respective empires.

The Romans had been virtually at peace with the Persians
since the long campaigns of Sapor the Great (308-380 A.D.)
had revived the ancient military prestige of that people. The
commencement of the Sassanian dynasty a century still earlier, had
been synonymous with the re-establishment in all its pristine
fervour of the Zoroastrian faith. The memory of Artaxerxes, the
founder of the Neo-Persian Empire, continued to be venerated as
long as his descendents occupied the throne, both as that of the
saviour of his nation, and as that of a legislator whose enactments
and maxims of government were considered the fundamental
institutions of the country. When Christianity became the
established religion of the Roman Empire, the Persians, instigated
by the Magian priesthood, took alarm at the close alliance between
a faith which has begun to gain ground among themselves and
their hereditary enemies. Henceforward the policy of the Persian
government from being one of toleration and good-will towards the
Church, changed, and became identified with its political hostility
to the Roman Empire. The friendship of Yezdegerd I. for the
Greek Emperor Arcadius led to a toleration of the Christians
within Persian dominions, to which the Zoroastrian priesthood took
violent religious and patriotic exception. The reign of Yezdegerd
was disturbed by trouble and dissention ; the monarch himself was
surnamed "Alathim," the sinner, on account of his Christian
sympathies.

At the time at which we have now arrived in the story of

Constantinople, St. Maruthas was the Bishop of Vagrit in Mesopotamia, a province on the borders of Persia, but subject to the Oriental Roman Empire. This prelate occupied himself in zealously protecting the Christian population from the oppression of their neighbours, and in compiling the acts of the martyrs who suffered in the old persecutions under Sapor. St. Maruthas' hymns were as popular as those of St. Ephrem, and possibly resounded in the church of the Holy Wisdom in Constantinople itself. The Emperor Arcadius appointed this Mesopotamian bishop as Ambassador to Yezdegard I. Two years after the accession of this Persian King, St. Maruthas made a journey to Byzantium to induce Arcadius to use his interest in favour of the Persian Christians. The court, however, was too much taken up in 403, with hostility to St. Chrysostom to spare attention for Maruthas. The following year he undertook the enterprise again, and at the Patriarch's instance, sought to interest "the most religious lady Olympias" in his cause. St. John directed her to assist him, and to promote what he himself had begun in favour of a Church for which he had already expressed an extraordinary zeal. This was in the year of the Synod of the Oak. St. Maruthas attended its sittings, and stumbling one day, in his heavy way, across the foot of Bishop Cyrinus, occasioned that succession of hideous gangrenes in which men saw the punishment of God.

Nothing seems to have come of these journeys. A few years later on, the Government at Constantinople honoured Bishop Maruthas with the commission of two successive embassies to Persia. Their object was the conclusion of a lasting peace, since Arcadius sought to avert as many dangers as possible from the opening years of his son's reign. Yezdegerd conceived the highest esteem for Maruthas, calling him "the friend of God." The Magians fearing that the Prince might be converted to the Christian faith had recourse to a base trick. They hid a man under the ground in the Temple, who, when the King came to adore the perpetual fire, exclaimed, "Drive forth from this holy place the king who impiously believes a priest of the Christians!" Yezdegerd thereupon would have dismissed Maruthas, but the latter persuaded him to repeat his visit to the Pyraeum, that the floor of the holy enclosure might be opened and the imposture revealed. A signal punishment befel the Magians, and the Bishop was immediately authorised to erect churches wherever he pleased. A considerable number were rebuilt in various parts of the country, and Maruthas made a long stay during his second embassy. He held two Synods at Ctesiphon—the latter in 414, and rejoiced at the flourishing state of the Church under his care.

But the Persian Christians, who had long ago received their baptism of blood, were now to be confirmed through trial. In A.D. 414, the zeal of Abdas, Bishop of the royal city of Susa, precipitated another era of persecution. This enthusiast led an attack on one of those sacred enclosures wherein the hallowed flame symbolising the Soul of the Universe was kept perpetually burning. His uncompromising refusal to rebuild it at the expense of the Christians forced Yezdegerd to retaliate. Thereupon a violent persecution broke out in which Abdas was among the first to lose his life. This terrible storm lasted for thirty years. It was raging in the year 422, and causing multitudes to seek refuge within the borders of the Roman Empire.

Thus the campaign against the Persians serves to illustrate the history of the Church in Persia, and also—which is more to the purpose of this book—to introduce two or three of the leading men at Theodosius' court.

The Alan family of the General Ardaburius was one of the most powerful in Constantinople, and played a conspicuous part in the nomination of succeeding emperors. The patrician Maximin conducted many successful embassies in the service of his imperial master, and finally attained the highest offices of responsibility that his merit could deserve. An obscure soldier, Marcian, whose private adventures form a romance by themselves, rose by degrees in the confidence of his officers and the esteem of the Senate, until finally the Augusta Pulcheria, called him to her side and seated him upon her brother's vacant throne. A certain Saracen prince (the Saracens were in submission to the Persians) was ordered to the frontier to turn back Christian refugees, but, touched by compassion for their sufferings, he not only abstained from molesting them in their flight but assisted them to the utmost of his power. As soon as this came to the knowledge of Yezdegerd, Aspebet as the Prince was called, retreated to Constantinople. He was received by Anatolius, the Master of the Armies of the East, and given a command among the Saracen allies of the Empire.

King Yezdegerd died before the outbreak of hostilites. The Magi had so incensed his subjects against "the Sinner," that the crown had been next offered to Chrosroes, a man in no way related to the deceased monarch. The elder of Yezdegerd's two sons failed in an expedition against the intruder, whereupon Baharam— or Vaharanes, (the name is spelt in a variety of ways) the second son, who had been absent from court at the time of his father's death, undertook the enterprise. The story of his success is too picturesque to omit. He suggested to Chrosroes that the crown of Persia should be placed between two famished lions as its temporary guardians, and that he who succeeded in recovering it from them, should, by general consent, be permitted to wear it. The king agreed. But at the moment of the ordeal he failed to step forward, so Baharam boldly advanced. After a life and death struggle with the ferocious brutes, both of whom he succeeded in slaying, he siezed the ball of Persia's sovereignty, and amid the deafening plaudits of both delighted armies, proudly placed the diadem upon his head.

This Baharam was a fanatical hater of Christianity. No sooner had he attained the throne than he sent an embassy to the Emperor Theodosius demanding the extradition of the Christian refugees. For some time previously there had been friction between the Byzantines and the Persians, the latter having plundered some travelling merchants, and refused to send home some labourers hired to work their gold mines. But these causes of complaint were not brought forward by the Romans, who contented themselves with refusing this demand about the Christians, and refrained from making any counter claims. "Christians have succoured Christians," replied the Emperor, "the Empire has given its protection to those who sought it. If war were the only alternative to surrendering them I should say, 'Let it, then, be war!'" If we compare the firmness of this message with the feebleness of the negotiations carried on with the Huns at a later date, when St. Pulcheria's influence over her brother had waned, we can but see her spirit in this noble defiance. The Augusta could scarcely have been ignorant of the fate awaiting these poor Persians, should her brother abandon their cause. The writings of Bishop Maruthas would have acquainted her with the martyrdom of St. James, who was butchered to death, joint by joint, and limb by limb, under Sapor I. Nor would the poignant tales of Maharsapor, Parses, and Sabutaca, martyrs all, have failed to˜ rouse her pity, and bespeak her championship for the defenceless refugees.

The moderation of the Roman attitude was not appreciated at Persepolis. Baharam "declared the peace to be at an end and immediately made preparations for war." *

The command of the Roman army was entrusted to General Ardaburius, who hurried his troops through Armenia into the fertile province of Aryanene. There he encountered Narses, the Persian Surenas † whom Baharam had sent against him. He obtained a victory yet not a decisive one; and plundering the country as he went, hastened forward into Mesopotamia to protect it from a threatened inroad of the Persians. Narses then threw himself into the fortress of Nisibis, a famous frontier city, and there stood on the defensive. He sent an envoy to the Roman leader to arrange some mutual plan of campaign, and to ask for the appointment of some suitable place for a second engagement. Ardaburius returned the haughty reply that his Emperor did not fight at the dictates of the enemy. But for some time he did not feel himself strong enough to invest the city. Presently, receiving reinforcements, however, he marched forward into Persian Mesopotamia, and commenced the siege of what had once been a Roman stronghold. "Hitherto Baharam, confident in his troops or in his good fortune, had left the entire conduct of the military operations to his

---

* "The Seventh Great Oriental Monarchy." Professor Rawlinson.
† Or General.

general, but the danger of Nisibis—that dearly won and highly prized possession—seriously alarmed him, and made him resolve to take the field in person with all his forces. Enlisting on his side the services of his friends, the Arabs, under their great Sheikh Al-Amundarus, and collecting a strong body of elephants, he advanced to the relief of the beleaguered town." *

The Arabs had no sooner pitched their tents in the neighbourhood of the relieving army, than, for some unaccountable reason, believing themselves surrounded by the Romans a panic spread and the whole host took to flight. Baharam lost a large number of his allies, but the remnant having rallied, they again took the field, and the Persian king at the head of a large force encamped near Nisibis. This time the Imperial army took alarm. The immense number and size of the elephants with which the Romans saw themselves confronted, terrified and demoralised them to such an extent that Ardaburius, judging it imprudent to risk a battle, drew off from the siege, burned his artillery, and retired.

The Persian elephant crops was at this date of supreme importance to their army. It was recruited from India and placed under the direction of the ' Zendkapet,' or Commander of the Indians. Centuries before the time of this campaign, the Punic elephants of the Carthaginian armies had sufficed to rout the Romans. The Persian cavalry was entirely of the heavy kind ; the horses were effectively armoured, their riders wore coats of mail, strong vizor'd helmets, and carried shields, spears, swords, bows and arrows. But the archers formed the élite of the Persian army. It was not until their cloud of arrows had been discharged from behind the wattled breastwork of their shields, that Ardaburius' men felt themselves upon even terms with the enemy. The common footmen stationed behind the archers, and armed with swords, spears, and darts, were a fair match for the Roman legionaries.

Instead of pressing on the retreating Roman forces, the Persian king led his army against Resaena † a fortified town lying some distance south of Nisibis. The place was without a garrison, but the citizens led by Eunomius, their Bishop, were prepared to defend it. For an entire month Baharam remained before it, making every effort known in warfare at that time to reduce the gallant town. The Persians were noted for failing to follow up their successes, and for ill conducting their sieges. Baharam opened trenches under cover of which his men might reach the ditch below the city walls and fill it up, he directed innumerable attempts at escalade, and tried to rear towers and rams against the

* Professor Rawlinson.

† Or Theodosiopolis a city built by the reigning Emperor in the Roman portion of Armenia near the sources of the Euphrates. It was defended by strong walls, lofty towers and a deep ditch or moat.

battlements, but all without effect. The citizens continued to hold out. At last a parley was held, but the blasphemies of the Persian envoy so outraged the religious sense of the stalwart Christians of Resaena, that a projectile was hurled at him from the great balista called " St. Thomas " and his brains were dashed to the ground. The superstitious Baharam immediately raised the siege and withdrew.

" While the fortified towns on either side thus maintained themselves against the attacks made upon them, Theodosius gave an independent command to the Patrician Procopius and sent him at the head of a body of troops to oppose Baharam. The armies met, and were on the point of engaging, when the Persian monarch made a proposition to decide the war not by a general battle but by a single combat." * Areobindus, the Roman champion, slew Ardazanes, a Persian Goliath by entangling him like a gladiator in the meshes of a net, and the victory was accredited to Procopius.

In the meantime Ardaburius who probably still commanded in Mesopotamia, had drawn the Persian force opposed to him into an ambuscade and had defeated it. The war had gone everywhere against the Persians. The incidents of the campaign are not related by the authorities in chronological sequence, but as it seems clear that the war only lasted two years, and that the incidents already related would have been sufficient for its first and most important phase, the stories and legends with which the historian Socrates fills out his account probably belong to the closing months. A vision of angels is said to have appeared to some travellers in Bythnia, charging them with a message of reassurance and encouragement to the Roman forces. The Byzantine Generals Ardaburius, Procopius and Vitian showed themselves thoroughly good tactitians. Acacius, Bishop of Amida, distinguished himself by an act of charity like that of Bishop Deogratius in Africa after the sack of Rome by the Vandals in 455. Having heard that 7000 Persian captives were in his neighbourhood he gathered his clergy around him, and reminding them that Almighty God had no need of ecclesiastical treasures, being All Sufficing in Himself, proposed to sell the gold and silver vessels belonging to his Church. With the price he ransomed the captives, and after having nursed them until they had recovered from the effects of their privations, sent them to the Persian king as evidences of the true spirit of Christianity.

At length Baharam determined to sue for peace. The truce necessitated by the opening of negotiations was, however, rudely broken by an act of perfidy on the part of his followers. The corps d'élite of the Persian cavalry, the Immortals, persuaded the king to allow them to make a surprise attack on the Roman camp. The treacherous design was discovered in time for Ardaburius to

* P. Rawlinson.

prepare. His men received the onslaught so well that the Immortals, one and all, were slain.

Baharam could only affect total ignorance of the affair lest the sacred standard of Persia, the famous 'durufskawni' or leathern apron of the blacksmith, should be more deeply disgraced than by defeat. The negotiations were accordingly reopened. The patrician Maximin as Assessor to the Roman General, and Helion another diplomat, were appointed to discuss the terms of peace with the Persian representatives.

The war was wholly successful in its object, for Baharam not only ceded the point about the Christian refugees, but granted religious toleration in Persia. Theodosius also obtained relief from persecution for the Armenians, who were, at this time, oppressed by their Zoroastrian King, and whose religious interests were identical with those of the Persian Christians. A Christian feudatory King was placed once more over Persian Armenia, and Baharam was induced to forego his attempts to suppress the Christianity of his Armenian subjects. " A truce of one hundred years," Gibbon tells us, " was solemnly ratified " between the Romans and the Persians, "and although the revolutions of Armenia might threaten the public tranquility, the essential conditions of this treaty were respected near fourscore years by the successors of Constantine and Artaxerxes."

The mountainous country of Armenia had formed a bone of contention between the Roman and the Persian Empires for the past two hundred years. The great struggle betwixt the two was, in all its phases, influenced and complicated by the Armenian question. A little state inhabited by a race of sturdy and spirited mountaineers, Armenia was ever of the greatest diplomatic and strategic importance to both the mighty belligerents between whom it was perpetually interposed. The Armenians had early embraced the Christian faith, and throughout centuries of change and struggle, distinguished themselves by their profound attachment to it. Seldom as circumstances allowed them to cherish the dream of national independence, this aspiration was always subordinated to the interests of religion. Armenia was continually falling under the sway either of Rome or of Persia, but she was so far from losing her national spirit, or from sacrificing her religious freedom to the exigencies of these alternations as to ever present an independent problem. While she looked to Persia to preserve her from annexation to Rome, and to Rome to save her from the imposition of Zoroastrianism, she dreamed of a national freedom which had perhaps been realised on more than one occasion but for internal dissentions. The peace concluded in A.D. 422 between Theodosius and Baharam was as beneficial in Armenia as in Persia, to the Church but a few years later the interposition of the Greek Emperor was again requisite and resulted in uniting the interests of the Armenians still more closely with those of the Roman Empire.

During the whole period of the war Constantinople was kept in touch with the armies in the field by Palladius, a second Pheidippides, who hastened backwards and forwards with incredible speed. Ardaburius' proud boast to Baharam that his master's domains were of such vast extent that the news of this war in Persia had not even reached the Emperor's ears, was belied by the fame of Palladius. It was said that the messenger could traverse the distance between Constantinople and the Persian frontier within three days!

> "So, when Persia was dust, all cried ' To Akropolis'!
> Run, Pheidippides, one race more! the meed is thy due.
>
> .   .   .   .
>
> He flung down his shield
> Ran like fire once more : and the space 'twixt
>   the Fennel-field
> And Athens, was stubble again, a field which
>   a fire runs through,
> Till he broke : ' Rejoice, we conquer'!
> Like wine through clay
> Joy in his blood bursting his heart, he died—
>   the bliss ! "
>
> BROWNING, " Pheidippides."

So might the Empress have written. For Athenais vied with the poets of the day in celebrating the campaign. The return of Ardaburius and the magnificent ovations he received in Constantinople, the popular enthusiasm for the soldiers, and the religious pæans of thanksgiving together with the stories of the war would have furnished her muse with subjects for a hundred songs. The Empress might well " feel proud to think that the daughter of Leontius was able to twine a spray of laurel around the diadem which the wife of Theodosius wore." Her poem has not survived, but it was received with great applause ; and by literary courtesy was acknowledged to have carried off the palm. This spirited performance earned for her the epithet ' Carminum Studiosa.' In an age when the Romans nicknamed everyone, from the ' sausage-eater' and the ' cabbage feeder' of the common crowd, to the Emperor ' calligraphos' (beautiful writer), so original an Empress could scarcely hope to escape some sobriquet.

During the war the trade of Constantinople suffered some depression, and the Augusta's charities increased. The silk weavers stood to lose the most. The raw material from China was at that time conveyed either by land through Central Asia, or by sea via Ceylon and the Persian Gulf, to the Imperial city. The enemy had control over both routes, and until peace was concluded the Master of Offices may frequently have had occasion to represent the distress of the poorer weavers to the bountiful Princess.

The worst result to the Empire of this campaign was that it laid all the country north of Constantinople open to the ravages of the Huns. Ammianus Marcellinus records the quaint discovery of an old squared stone, hidden in the very centre of the walls of Chalcedon, which, when the latter were thrown down "in order to build a bath at Constantinople" (in A.D. 375 apparently), revealed, in Greek verse, a terrible prophecy.

> " When young wives and damsels blithe, in dances that
>   delight
> Shall glide along the city streets, wi h garlands gaily
>   bright
>
> Then shall the Huns in multitude break forth
>   with might and wrath
>
> And nou ht but loss of life and breath their course
>   shall ever stay."*

This prophecy was verified in 423, and the last line of it might sadly enough, serve as a text for the latter history of Theodosius' reign.   The brief empire of the Huns now stretched over all the lands north of the Euxine and the Danube.   Under chieftains whose appearance alone was a nightmare to the Greeks, the Hunnish hordes overran the land as far as Adrianople and Phillipopolis.   The Senate had no resources whereby to stem the tide of this invasion.   The army was engaged upon the frontiers of a distant kingdom, and the home forces might only suffice to protect the capital.   The entire province lay at the mercy of the Huns.   In a weak moment the Government adopted a dangerous but not an unprecedented expedient.   It bought off the barbarian horde by the ignoble promise of an annual tribute equal to £31,000 in modern money.   Thus the seed was sown of that terrible harvest of trouble which Theodosius began to reap in 441.

Meanwhile the ex-Queen of the Goths, the pitiful widow of Constantius arrived in the eastern capital, and the children of Placidia and Athenais met.

---

* Ammianus Marcellinus. Bk. xxxi. ch. 1.   Bohn's translation.

GALLA PLACIDIA AND VALENTINIAN III,
FIFTH CENTURY.

[*Face p.* 119.

CHAPTER XIV

VALENTINIAN (III)

The Emperors were not, so early as the fifth century, numerically titled, but distinguished one from another by some epithet or adjective, as 'the Great' or the 'Younger.'

THE Empress Placidia had been received in Constantinople with every mark of courtesy and kindness.

But she came back after a lifetime—a long one it must have seemed to her—to find the old Palace peopled with relations who were utter strangers. The Athenian Empress, for her part, was now brought into contact with other of her husband's relatives, and we can imagine that while St. Pulcheria and her aunt had something in common, Athenais might intuitively divine the differences between them.

Placidia's disposition needed the education of adversity, and even then it might fail here or there, while Pulcheria's deep piety had established her whole nature on a firm foundation.

It was a curious group that circumstances brought together in the year 423. Only a master hand could draw it—the youthful brother and sister, sovereigns of the East, sombre with a Spanish gravity, the mature beauty of the world-worn Placidia, and the alien yet harmonious grace of Athenais. In the foreground three children—mere names in history—complete the picture, as their lives wind up the story of their house. Eudocia still lies, a baby, upon her mother's knees, Valentinian aged five, pushes himself before the cross-grained child Honoria.

The ex-Empress Placidia had been declared Augusta, and her son Nobilissimus (one step below the 'Caesar,') in Ravenna, but the East had not recognised their right to these titles. Now however this courtesy was extended to the illustrious refugees, and Constantius, in his grave, was forgiven.

A few months elapsed when the inaction of the situation was suddenly broken by the news of the death of Honorius. This occurred on August 13th, 423. It was kept from the public for awhile, Theodosius' first care being to send off a force to Salonae, the capital of Dalmatia, in order to suppress any excitement on the frontier. When at last it was announced, the gates and shops of Constantinople were closed for seven days, and an official mourning reigned with somewhat more indifference or hypocrisy than usual.

The people of the eastern Empire cared nothing for Honorius. Nor, we imagine, could his death have much afflicted the Imperial family itself, unless Placidia's conscience were assailed by the tenderness of disproportionate regret. Her tears however were quickly brushed aside in astonishment at what happened next.

An embassy arrived at Byzantium from the 'primercerius' John! It seemed that this court secretary had usurped the vacant throne, and now took this lordly way of intimating that fact to Theodosius. "History," says Gibbon, "has attributed to his character more virtues than can easily be reconciled with the violation of the most sacred duty." That duty had assuredly been to lay the western crown at the surviving Emperor's feet.

John's ambassadors were summarily imprisoned, and on their release were chased out of Constantinople with the utmost ignominy. Then the usurper's designs of contracting an alliance with the Huns were interrupted by the necessary preparations for immediate war, which were likewise busily pushed forward at Constantinople.

The son of Arcadius might at this moment by right of consanguinity alone, have reigned sole and legitimate Emperor over the entire Roman world. His generals were soon to add the title of conqueror to that of heir, and the grandson of the man who had divided East and West, might have welded the Empire into a whole again. Instead, however, of "listening to the voice of ambition," instead possibly, of burdening the East with the failing West, "Theodosius resolved to imitate the moderation of his grandfather and to seat his cousin Valentinian on the western throne." Not only the justice, but the sage foresight of this decision seem to show it as emanating, in the first instance, from the counsels of St. Pulcheria.

The East Roman Empire was as unwieldly, unless under the rule of a king of men, as the West, and the Augusta must have felt that her brother had few of the imperial qualifications which might justify his assumption of double his present responsibilities and cares. The recent alarm of war with the Huns, while as yet the armies had not returned from Persia, demonstrated clearly enough the impolicy and futility of burdening the Government at Constantinople with the "laborious task of waging a distant and doubtful war against the barbarians beyond the Alps; or of securing the obedience of the Italians and Africans whose minds were alienated by the irreconcilable difference of language and interest." If the Augusta had discussed with Placidia those novel ideas of Constantius, * by the exercise of which Honorius' co-adjutor had hoped to have somewhat disburdened the central government at Rome or Ravenna, she must have felt confirmed in her opinion that it were unwise to extend the already gigantic borders of Theodosius' own dominions. The ex-Empress would have been only too glad to agree with Pulcheria's point of view, since it promised to secure the succession for her son. It were a simple act of justice, should Theodosius relinquish his claim to the West, to cast the purple mantle of Honorius upon the infant Valentinian. The poor defrauded Empress and defenceless widow, regained her courage and her spirit in this bright change of her fortunes.

She sped to the altar of St. Stephen (or of St. Sophia) and made a fervent vow that she would build a glorious Church in her beloved Ravenna should it please Heaven to send her safely back!

A chill struck the heart of Athenais as she saw the un-accustomed blood mantle in her husband's cheek, his manuscripts pushed aside, and his military accoutrements brought forth. And St. Pulcheria, in the midst of her councils and audiences with the ministers and generals, sent for the court physician. She was not only a stateswoman, but a solicitous sister.

The army was again entrusted to Ardaburius, and to his son Aspar. The former engaged to embark at Salonae with the infantry and go by sea to Italy, across the head of the Hadriatic, while the latter with the cavalry was to conduct Placidia and her children along the coast to Aquileia. Theodosius with a brilliant retinue, accompanied his aunt and his young cousin Valentinian. He had not proceeded further than Thessalonica, about a third of the distance, when his health, at all times feeble, broke down and demonstrated the impossibility of his engaging personally in the war. He turned back, leaving Placidia in the charge of Count Candidian, and the army went forward via Sirmium, and over the Julian Alps to the first great city of the Venetian March held by the adherents of the usurper John. Aquileia was assaulted and taken, but this success was marred by the intelligence of a terrible disaster that had befallen the fleet.

A storm had arisen and scattered it far and wide; two galleys only could be accounted for, and these were prisoners in the port of Ravenna. The leader Ardaburius was on board. The news of his capture filled the Byzantines with consternation, and Con-stantinople felt the infection of fear. Ardaburius however enjoyed a certain degree of liberty which he used, or abused, to revive the loyalty of the garrison. The usurper's general, Castinus, hesitated to take any decisive step until the arrival of some Hunnish reinforcements, to the number of sixty thousand men, under the ex-consul Ætius. In the meantime the secret machinations of his illustrious prisoner derived all the force they could from Ardaburius' strong personality. The conspiracy so far prospered as to encourage the plotter to despatch secret instructions for Aspar to advance. A shepherd—the devout historians say an Angel, engaged to conduct the cavalry across the fordless morasses north of Ravenna. After a short struggle the fears of the Byzantines were dispelled, the gates of the city were thrown open and the usurper was handed over to the victors.

Placidia condemned him to death. The right hand of the quondam secretary was cut off, and the wretched man, driven through the circus of Aquileia on an ass, was exposed to the ridicule of the populace and the scorn of the soldiers. He was then executed.

The news of the 'conquest of Italy' arrived at Constantinople at a dramatic moment. The people were all assembled in the Hippodrome; the Protectors or guards massed in the Stama (a stage below the Imperial stand) had just raised the standards bearing the two-headed Byzantine eagle, to greet the entry of the Emperor. No sooner had Theodosius made the sign of the cross in the air, and the answering cries of adulation had subsided, than the chariots wheeled out from the Manganon beneath the Kathisma and formed up abreast by the rope. But the Demarch of the Greens had scarcely dropped the 'mappa' for the start when a horseman galloped in to Constantinople and held a headlong course for the Palace. His news was soon out, and Theodosius, rising to his feet quelled the uproar in the circus and called upon the people to give thanks. The charioteers were left struggling with their horses unheeded on the track, while the people poured out of the Hippodrome and streamed off behind the Emperor to the Church of St. Sophia. The Augustaeum was filled with the vociferating throng, and the echoes of hymns and shouting penetrated to the quiet apartments in the Palace where the nieces of Placidia awaited the news of her happy restoration.

The Patrician Helion—the same probably who had acted with Maximin in the conclusion of peace with Persia—was Theodosius' plenipotentiary at Placidia's side. By Imperial authority he solemnly invested Valentinian, on October 23rd, 425, with the diadem, the purple and the title of Augustus. The child had already been made Cæsar, and by this final ceremony, which took place either at Rome or at Ravenna, he became Emperor of the Western world. The Augusta Placidia was appointed guardian to her son, and when the Byzantine troops withdrew, she remained Regent in Ravenna as Pulcheria had been in Constantinople. Her power was equally unfettered; the care of Valentinian's education and training, and the supervision of affairs of state devolved in this instance upon a mother, and a woman of the world, who showed herself less equal to this onerous vocation than her remarkable niece, at fifteen.

"Placidia envied, but she could not equal, the reputation and virtues of the wife and sister of Theodosius; the elegant genius of Eudocia, the wise and successful policy of Pulcheria." (Gibbon)

Her first care, however, was to pardon Ætius, instead of banishing him like Castinus, for his share in the recent rebellion. She showed a confidence in the man, (so recently her enemy), who was to become the main support not only of her own administration but of her son's entire reign. Ætius had arrived on the scene of action, with sixty thousand Huns at his back, too late to be of any assistance to the usurper John. But such was his influence over these troops that he was able without much difficulty to dispatch them peaceably whence they had come. Placidia may not have realised how dangerous a man she had admitted to her confidence, but the verdict of history exonerates him from suspicions of treachery once he had distanced all rivals. Valentinian is supposed to have asked the opinion of a courtier as to whether he had done well or ill, at the close of his miserable reign, in killing Ætius. " I know not Sublimity," was the dry reply, " I only know that you have cut off your right hand with your left."

The Eastern Empire received some recompense for the heavy expenses it had incurred on behalf of Valentinian. The rich maritime province of Dalmatia was a substantial indemnity, but to acquire the sovereignity of Pannonia and Noricum (all three belonged to Western Illyricum) was a questionable gain. These provinces had been harried and ravaged for twenty years by various tribes of the northern barbarians and might well be a thorn in the side of any government. While, however, the treasury at Constantinople may have immediately proceeded to reimburse itself to some extent out of this concession, the territory was not finally made over to the East until the year 436, when the marriage took place of the second-cousins Valentinian and Licinia Eudocia. Its acquisition was one of the political stipulations agreed upon at the time of the betrothal, but in an age and an Empire when autocracy flourished without question, the Imperial son-in-law could make a personal present of his frontier lands to his august co-adjutor.

While the Empire thus preserved the dual character it had borne since 395, more friendly relations were established between its two courts than had existed during the last few years. The betrothal of the young Emperor Valentinian to the infant daughter of Theodosius and Athenais, drew close the bonds of personal friendship. In one particular, however, the two halves of the Roman world were more sharply divided than they had been before. From this time onward it was decreed thar all future laws and edicts should hold good only within the dominions of their respective authors, unless they happened to be expressly adopted in East and West alike.

Thus the second of the two brief wars which marked the first half of Theodosius' reign, was brought to a scccessful conclusion. They bear of course, no comparison with the terrible struggle waged against the Huns, towards its close. But if a comparison be drawn between the conduct of these campaigns, the policy they furthered, and those of 441 (and onwards), some explanation will be needed of the deplorable contrast. It may be considered that undue emphasis has been laid upon St. Pulcheria's influence in her brother's counsels. When, however, the result of her absence is displayed, it will be granted that, all unobtrusive as she was, the Augusta wielded Theodosius' power until it was beguiled from out his hand and turned against her.

The salon of which the young Empress had become the centre in the imperial palace, had a decided charm even for the austere Augusta. St. Pulcheria had no less esteem for the gifted Paulinus, and no less an appreciation of the arts and sciences than Athenais herself. She took part in these literary réunions, and it must have been, one day, a substantial cause for congratulation, that they were honoured by her interest.

For it is impossible to attribute the revival of the Constantinopolitan University entirely to the zeal of the sophist's daughter had this not been supported by Pulcheria's interest and approval.

This institution * had been the only imperial foundation of a distinctly Christian character, designed in the interests of education. It had fallen into such a state as to necessitate entire remodelling, and Athenais, who deplored the scarcity of Greek professorships, was delighted to collaborate with her husband in an undertaking equally congenial to his tastes. "The inauguration of the University," says Mr. Bury, † "was an important measure for Byzantine life and indicates the enlightenment of Theodosius' reign. It was intended to supersede the University of Athens, the headquarters of paganism . . . . . . and thereby to further the cause of Christianity." It was also intended to provide more liberally for those Greek studies which were gradually beginning, in the eastern Empire at least, to outnumber the Latin. All through the fourth and fifth centuries the Byzantines (that curious mingling of Greeks, Barbarians and Asiatics which called itself Roman), were struggling back to a national consciousness distinct from the imperial idea, and a university in which there were more Greek professorships than Latin, did much to further that tendency. On more than one occasion a Prefect ventured to issue a decree in Greek, an experiment which pleased the people generally, even if it drew down the censure of conservative officialdom.

The University as Theodosius re-established it, was governed by a President called the "Oecumenicus" because he was supposed to be a sort of walking encyclopaedia. It consisted of some blocks of newly-purchased buildings situated some distance from the sea. It numbered seven librarians, and its professors were maintained at the public expense. They each had their public class rooms, and were not prohibited from teaching privately outside the University,

---

* The University buildings were situated in the Forum of Theodothius, on an eminence called the Capitol.

† "Later Roman Empire."

but laws were passed to prevent them seeking any field for their activities beyond the capital. The candidate who aspired to a chair in the University was obliged to undergo an examination before the Senate, and it was necessary for him to possess an irreproachable moral character, as well as to prove that his learning was profound. The term of twenty years' service secured for the professors the title of Count and placed them among the nobility of the Empire." * The Latin language was represented by ten grammarians or philologists, and three rhetors; the Greek, by ten grammarians and five rhetors or sophists. One chair of philosophy and two chairs of jurisprudence received liberal endowments. Although Athens must have lost considerably by this transfer of the centre of intellectual gravity, the world as a whole, and Constantinople in particular, gained to an enormous extent. The Church attached to this Academy was served by sixteen monks, and prelates were often chosen from the ranks of the professors to fill the first sees of the Empire. These brethren, like those of the celebrated Studium, may have rendered literary services not only to their own generation but to later ages, both by their studious products and still more by their "invaluable work as careful copyists of ancient [and patristic] writings." The Studite rule, which in its infancy was contemporaneous with the revival of the University, "was copied in many details by those who, from the tenth century onward, created a system of monastic rule on Mount Athos. And our debt to the monks of Mount Athos is one that scholars are coming more and more to appreciate." † The professors of the Theodosian University, emulating the culture of Studium, set, together with its celebrbated monks, the model for those careful and laborious workers for whom the modern world has shown too little respect. Who can tell what literary treasures still remain hidden in the obscure Greek monasteries of the East?

In 426 St. Pulcheria lost one whom she loved as a father. On the occasion of his last visit to Nicaea, the aged Bishop Atticus had remarked to his friend Calliopius "If you desire to see me again you must come at once to Constantinople." It seems he had a premonition of his death, which took place on the 10th of October. He was buried with all fitting honour, but the Emperor could not attend the obsequies in person, being absent—at Thessalonica some say—at the time. Tillemont, however, notes that Theodosius spent the June to November of 426, at Nicomedia.

Shortly after this event the metropolitan Bishops met in the 'catumencia' of the Great Basilica, to vote for St. Atticus' successor. Mgr. Duchesne ‡ describes the ceremony of a fifth century consecration when the candidate was presented to the congregation,.

---

* Finlay, "History of Greece."
† Miss Gardner, "Theodore of Studium."
‡ "Christian Worship."

surrounded by the local clergy and those higher ecclesiastics whose ranks he was about to enter.

The President of the assembly interrogated the people as to the identity of the candidate, and as to his qualifications for the office of bishop.   The questions were put solemnly three times, and met with the response " He is worthy."   Whereupon three of the Bishops present approached the altar, the elected priest knelt down, and the President recited the consecration prayers over him whilst two deacons held the Book of the Gospels open upon his head.   The newly consecrated Bishop was then conducted to his seat, and saluted with the kiss of peace.   Finally he celebrated Mass.

But in the case of a Patriarch of Constantinople (or Archbishop as he should as yet be more properly called) the fiat of the Emperor played an important part, and could confirm or veto the choice of the Bishops and people.   Having arrived at a selection of three candidates, the conclave then conducted their nominees in religious procession to the Hall of the Candidati in the imperial palace, there to await the sovereign's final choice.   In the instance of St. Atticus' successor this decision was given in favour of a certain venerable old man, Sisinius.   Immediately the whole body of clergy present, together with the Senators, and possibly, the Empress and Augusta, proceeded to the "Manaura" where, according to Porphyrogennetos, Theodosius thus addressed them :—

" The grace of God, and our Empire which proceedeth therefrom, hath promoted this most holy man to be Patriarch of Constantinople. The holy Trinity through the Empire which It hath granted us, promoteth thee to be Archbishop of Constantinople, the new Rome."

After this Sinisius, accompanied by a large following of the clergy and nobility, was inducted into the Patriarchaeon, while the Emperor returned to his own apartments.

About the time of Theodosius the Great the eastern half of the Empire had been divided for the purposes of Church government into the five enormous dioceses of Egypt, the Orient, Pontus, Asia and Thrace, and the metropolitan sees were respectively those of Alexandria, Antioch, Caesarea, Ephesus, and Constantinople.

It was not until some years after the Council of Chalcedon (451) that the 28th canon, which tried to raise the capital of the eastern empire to pre-eminence among the sees, obtained any sort of recognition.   But the Bishops of Constantinople strove so long and so consistently after the Patriarchal dignity, and the precedence of Alexandria and Antioch, that at last the loud protest of Rome became silent.   Since the first attempt to aggrandise Constantinople was made at the second General Council in 381, and this is, consequently, regarded as the beginning of its patriarchal dignity, the convenience of referring to its Archbishop as the Patriarch is not altogether an anachronism.   St. Chrysostom indeed was consecrated at the hands of Theophilus of Alexandria, and Sisinius at those of the Bishop of Heraclia in Thrace, but from the year 381 the Bishops of Constantinople exercised almost Patriarchal authority over Thrace, Asia Minor and Pontus (three enormous provinces consisting of twenty-eight 'districts,') and they seemed with few exceptions unable to resist the lust of power. When their ambition was seconded or spurred by that of the Emperor it could defy Rome, but it belongs to the history of St. Pulcheria to relate how, for a while, despite heresy and pride, she kept the Church in the East true to the see of St. Peter.

CHAPTER XV

PROLIFIC in heresies as the East had been from the first Christian century onwards, two more sprang into prominence under Theodosius the younger.

It had been the calculating policy of Constantius, who inherited the great Constantine's political ideal of unity, to enlist every likely force to that end. That Arianism, a creed which favoured principles of secular authority, should flourish temporarily throughout the empire was the natural result of this worldly-minded imperialism. The persecution of St. John Chrysostom, savouring as it did of the Cæsar-papism of a later time, had been but one of the evils resulting to the Church in the East from the Arianism of the first Christian emperor's successors. Inasmuch as the homogeneity of these vast realms necessitated the stern repression of distinctive national feelings and aspirations in its various parts, it was the aim of the Imperial government to break any intimate connection between the people and the Church, to reconstitute the latter on the lines of the civil administration, and subject her to its authority. This was peculiarly the case in Greece. The characteristic political genius of the Greeks had been obliterated under the Roman yoke, but as soon as Christianity began to make headway among them, their national traits and their exhausted spirits began to revive. The local government of the bishops replaced the system under which every Greek city had been a capital, and the people once more perceived in the Church a communal ideal. With preaching, oratory revived, and by oratory alone the Greek nation could be reinvigorated. The political influence of Christianity thus revealed itself almost immediately in the East : the new religion spread with almost incredible rapidity, and " the Greek Church had grown to be almost equal in power to the Roman state [even] before Constantine determined to unite the two in strict alliance."* " When Christianity became the religion of the emperor, the political organisation and influence of the Christian communities could not fail to arrest the attention of the authorities." Constantine was largely influenced in his choice of Byzantium for the new capital of the empire by the presence in the East of so large a body of Christians. " The Senate and Roman nobility remained firmly

---

* Finlay, " History of Greece."

attached to paganism, which was converted into the bond of union of the conservative party in the western portion of the empire, and thus the Greeks were enabled to secure a predominancy in the Christian Church."* When, however, Arianism was in the ascendant, a church identified with the national interests of a people whom the imperial government desired to deprive of their individuality, was a Church at variance with the emperor. When her bishops opposed him they were deposed and exiled.

The superb Catholicism of Theodosius the Great had done much to repair this blight of heresy, and to lay the ghosts of that paganism more recently revived by Julian ; but two evil effects remained, which were checked for half a century under Theodosius II. and his saintly sister. The government at Constantinople had so far arrogated all things to itself that the Church of the East already stood in danger of a fatal schism, or of that subjugation to which it afterwards succumbed. But Pulcheria's devotion to the See of Rome no less than her jealousy for the welfare of her own peoples checked any development of this threatening aspect of affairs, while the asceticism of her life discountenanced the incredible worldliness of a court which had long enjoyed every precedent for the luxury and extravagance against which the Patriarchs themselves scarce dared to raise a voice.

The Greek nation, apart from the Byzantine court, remained consistently orthodox all through the fourth and fifth centuries, for the favour shown to the Arian (imperialistic) clergy, only had the effect of inclining the popular ear more attentively to the Catholic (nationalistic) priests. Moreover this resistance of the faithful, which endured some centuries of persecution, gave assurance that the triumph of orthodoxy would be finally secured otherwise than by the civil patronage inflicted on the Church. Under the Great Theodosius, who owed so much that was finest in his character to the direction of St. Ambrose, a reconciliation took place between the government and the Church. The division of the Roman world between Honorius and Arcadius tended to bind either sovereign more exclusively to his own subjects, and to restore the individuality of the respective nations. Thus under Arcadius and his son an orthodox and yet national Greek Church existed, a church which had still to recognise that subservience to the Emperor could only be safe so long as the Emperor was subservient to Catholic unity.

It was an extremely precarious position. Perhaps it is not too much to say that only the profound Catholicity of St. Pulcheria, only her extraordinary instinct in religious controversy, preserved the Church in the east through the storms of Nestorianism and Eutychianism. St. Cyril of Alexandria was the recognised Catholic champion of the first campaign, as St. Flavian was the

* Ibid.

9

martyr of the second, but the Augusta, by her firm fidelity in a wavering court, succeeded in preventing its official secession to the side of heresy. The warp, however, so early given to the relationship between Church and State in the east, was past her power to permanently set right. It issued in the subjection of the Greek Church to the Russian Czars.

For the final schism of 1054 took its rise among the heresies continually forming and being dispelled around the great controversies of the fourth and fifth centuries. A hundred strange sects, with names only interesting to a student of theology, gradually found themselves without the pale of the Church. It is strange that though the intellectual stress and subtlety of the Hellenist orientals gave rise to this body of dissent, the Church into which they all subsequently crystallised should have thenceforth remained stationary, with an infant theology, an inelastic discipline, and an uninspired monasticism. All signs of life from that time onward were mainly manifested in the West. An eminent French writer* throws some light upon this subject which also illustrates the character of St. Pulcheria's subjects. The Greeks, he says, as masters of the world, " always inclined to put themselves in opposition to the dominant influence that lay nearest to them." Surrounded by the unprogressive nations of the East, they exhibited the greatest intellectual, philosophical, commercial and æsthetic activity, and in the presence of oriental supineness, were occidental in character. When once, however, the nation fell under the sway of Rome, and so far from having to fear the contagion of torpor, found itself enveloped by an energy even greater than her own, the tendency of the Greeks was to become jealous and conservative, to reverse the tables. Greece became, then, oriental in her immobility, in her desire to preserve the heritage of civilization against the shock of western barbarism. That the Greek Church remained behind the Latin from the moment when she began to refuse subscription to the decress of the General Councils was therefore the result of this " singular contention between the instinct and the intellect of this people." Under Theodosius the Great, as we have seen, the eastern half of the Empire began to lose its Roman character, as the army itself began to care less for its traditions than for its sources. As soon as this tendency was sufficiently pronounced the old " contention " reappeared, and made the Greek Church what it is to-day.

In the fourth and fifth centuries Christianity was by no means so wide spread or so generally accepted throughout the Empire as the prevalence of continually recurring heresies would seem to indicate. It was not until the time of St. Pulcheria's grandfather that any zealous stand was officially made against paganism.

---

* M. Viollet le Duc. " Lectures on Architecture."

During the times of peace that intervened between the various persecutions, Christians were exposed to temptations which must have corrupted all but those of the finest calibre, and thrown them back into the pagan world. " It could not be otherwise ; the net of the Church gathered together fish of every sort," from dissolute Corinth, from the learned schools of Athens and Marseilles, the waggons of wandering Tartars, the huts of wild Numidians, the museums of Alexandria, and the temples of Persia. " Christian and pagan were thrown together in the utmost confusion . . . the same complicated questions which trouble Catholics, and especially converts, now, might perplex Christians then . . . when one at a dinner party might be offered meats sacrificed to idols, or be called upon to wear crowns of flowers in honour of Bacchus or Venus."*

The schisms that continually troubled the infant communities of Christians, wherever such existed, must also have done much to hinder the growth of the faith. These heresies and quarrels can only be accounted for when the heterogeneous character is remembered of the soil on which the Seed was flung. No sooner had the Church emerged from the first age of persecution, than she found herself confronted anew with the gigantic task of teaching a hundred different nations, according to the injunction originally given by her Divine Founder. And no sooner had she put her hand to the plough of this enormous undertaking than the nearest field of her labours, the Roman Empire, began to be overrun by all the unsettled and uncivilised elements which were to form the nations of the subsequent mediæval world. In the face of this overwhelming mission the wonder should be, not that perplexities arose, but that the Church's teaching was not rather torn to shreds, her truths far more misapprehended than was actually the case, and her very identity extinguished. The heresies called to the front great controversialists as well as zealous missioners, and the labours of the fathers from St. Athanasius to St. Augustine and St. Cyril, helped the Spouse of Christ to that great buckler of her faith, the Creed, without which she never could have borne the fray !

With the exception of Arianism, the heresies of the fourth and fifth centuries—to treat them with scant courtesy—seem to have generally arisen out of the intellectual cantankerousness, or the mere rivalries, of some bishop or abbot, and to have died out with the last of his partisans after the inevitable condemnation. Perhaps this clashing of opinions, this pride of speculation, this warfare of conceptions was an inevitable phenomenon, when in those decadent times, the beauty of the Christian ideal of holy living was neglected in the effort to frame formulas for the universal belief of races who could not possibly have anything else

---

* Father Dalgairns, " History of Holy Communion."

in common. The Church directed the eyes of all men to the figure of the Saviour, but the Gothic understanding of that sublime spectacle was other than the Roman, the Roman than the Syrian, the Syrian than the Greek, the Greek than the Frankish, the Frankish than the Teutonic. The Church had her ideal of unity, a spiritual unity, the unity of truth. She found herself called upon to understand the capacities of all these nations; to see with their eyes and hear with their ears; to enter most intimately into their several civilisations, and cope with their individual superstitions, beliefs, traditions and tendencies; to allow for the extent of their education in her stupendous charge. She was divinely aided in the work, of course, by the galaxy of saints of every age and country, raised up to preach unity and truth, refute error, correct mistakes, and support the orthodox. Before the missionaries the Druids fled, and idols went down, while the Gregories, Basils, Cyrils, Augustines, Jeromes, and Chrysostoms stamped out the virulent plagues of heresy as they arose. Pelagianism, Nestorianism, Donatism, Eutychianism and the rest, were strangled; but not indeed before they had severally lived long enough, and spread wide enough to do much temporary harm.

Truly, in spite of all the present age can say against the Creed, the Councils and the Doctors, Christianity itself without them (humanly speaking) could scarce have survived the fall of the Roman Empire.

No heresy can properly be of note merely to the " ecclesiastical specialist." But from an historical, as distinct from a theological point of view, perhaps it is not rash to speak of greater and lesser controversies. Thus none of the hundreds of 'minor' heresies combatted by the Bishop of Hippo were to compare in danger to Arianism. Under Theodosius I. Catholicism had so revived in Constantinople as to make it possible for a Catholic to carve out a distinguished career. The heretical sects were discouraged, paganism declined, and St. Chrysostom's struggle was rather with worldliness and immorality, than with speculative error.

It seemed nevertheless, as if one danger were no sooner averted than another broke out. St. Pulcheria had completed the work of St. Chrysostom in a way he would not have dared to hope, but heresy reappeared.

Sisinius had only occupied the Patriarchal throne of St. Sophia a year or so, when his death occasioned a fresh appointment to the Imperial See. The most popular candidate was Proclus, Archbishop of Cyzicus. This holy man was a native of Constantinople, and had been a 'reader' at St. Sophia in the days of St. Chrysostom. St. Atticus had ordained him a priest. Even after his promotion to Cyzicus, the well-known preacher remained in the capital as the inhabitants of the former city were unwilling to acknowledge the jurisdiction of the Constantinopolitan Patriarch. But the canons forbade the 'translation' of a prelate from one see to another, and Proclus' nominal authority at Cyzicus was an impediment to his promotion at Constantinople.

The man upon whom the Emperor's choice then fell, was a priest from Antioch, Nestorius by name, so full of zeal, repute and monastic piety, and endowed with such eloquence that the people believed they were called upon to welcome a second John. Nestorius was the recipient of cordial congratulations and good wishes from Rome, Alexandria and the other great sees. The Pope, St. Celestine, wrote * to him that he had been anxious as to the bishops successively appointed at Constantinople "because good is apt not to be lasting; and what joy we had in the successor of the blessed John, Atticus of blessed memory, the teacher of the Catholic faith; then in the holy Sisinius who was so soon to leave us, for his simple piety and pious simplicity; and when he was removed the relation of the messenger who came rejoiced our soul; and this was straightway confirmed by the relation of our colleagues who were present at thy consecration. . ."

"He was chosen," wrote St. Cyril to the Emperor later, "as one practised in the doctrines of the Gospels and the Apostles, trained in godliness, and holding the right faith altogether blamelessly. Your Pious Majesty longed to have such a man, and all who were set over the Holy Churches, and I myself also. And, indeed, when the letters of the most pious Bishops about his consecration were sent round by those who advanced him thereto, I wrote back without delay, rejoicing, praising, praying that by the decree from above all choicest good should come to our brother and fellow minister." †

The Augusta Pulcheria, however, felt a nameless misgiving about the new Patriarch.

It seemed to her that impetuosity and an impeachable judgment, joined to a certain self-sufficiency were grave warnings in the temperament of a man called to support weighty responsibilities. She seemed to divine the existence of these defects in Nestorius side by side with that very zeal for orthodoxy with which he was so widely credited. Perhaps he had, nevertheless, the strong personal attraction of a man who is at once ascetic and enthusiastic, and the individual force of a leader. The Augusta could only trust it was a prejudice, and not a piece of insight that Theodosius' decision obliged her to smother.

She was not however wholly alone in her mistrust. Dalmatius, a hermit of great influence and sanctity, contrary to all precedent refused to allow the newly-consecrated Nestorius to enter his cell in order to obtain his benediction.

In his inaugural sermon Nestorius personally addressed the Emperor. "Oh Emperor! drive heretics from thy Empire, and I will grant to thee the kingdom of Heaven; strengthen my hands

* Ep. St. C. ad Nest. Conc. Eph. P. 1. c. 18.
† Apol. ad. Theodos. Conc. Eph. P. 3. c. 13.

in putting down the enemies of the Church, and I will aid thee in conquering the Persians!" *

Some of his very first activities were directed towards obtaining from Theodosius new edicts against the remnants of the Arian party, and other heretical sects of more recent growth. But in 429 Nestorius belied the purity of his zeal and made it evident to the world that the championship of his own opinion was dearer to him than that of the Catholic faith. After the Council of Carthage in 418, when the teachings of Coelestius and Pelagius had been condemned, the Pope censured those Bishops who should receive and " communicate " with the exiled heretics belonging to their sect. In spite of this Nestorius extended official hospitality to some Pelagians visiting Constantinople in 429. This was the first overt indication of his intractability, the first justification of Pulcheria's misgivings. Theodosius himself perceived the danger, and presently ordered the refugees to leave the city, but no sooner was trouble from their influence thus averted than the Patriarch plunged the Church into new difficulties.

---

* Manual of Universal Church History.   Alzog. t. 1 pg. 415.

CHAPTER XVI

Neither history nor archaeology seems to have preserved or reconstructed any description of the original St. Sophia. The magnificent Byzantine masterpiece with which Justinian replaced it (A.D. 532) has obliterated interest in the previous church. In the description of that basilica in which St. Pulcheria made her vow, the writer has used considerable license, asserting the details of a picture that is only probable by analogy, and ascribing to St. Sophia features of other, but contemporary, buildings. All sorts of errant notes have been pressed into the service, such as those derived from the history of mosaic work, and of these no one can deny, at least, the chronological appositeness.

The St. Sophia of St. Pulcheria's day bore that general resemblance to its original which any building may do, whose frequent restorations only stop short of being reconstructions. It had been founded, if not completed, by the Emperor Constantine on the site of a temple on the akropolis of the ancient Greek city. Its architect is said to have been one Euphrates. It probably reproduced the style of two sister churches, since Constantine designed to honour, by three ecclesiastical foundations, the Peace, the Strength, and the Wisdom of Almighty God. The new city on the Bosphorus was sufficiently supplied with churches. From the age of Constantine to that of Justinian, three typical forms were in vogue, the rotunda, or sepulchral church, the 'dromikon,' like old St. Peters' at Rome, and the detached chapels and oratories which served as adjuncts to most important, civil, or eccclesiastical establishments. There were about fourteen churches within the city proper of Constantinople about the beginning of the fifth century, and among so many these three typical forms may each have been exemplified. Size and costliness of material were the signs of a degenerate architectural taste, and the basilicas of Constantine may have compared with the building of his predecessors, as his triumphal arch in Rome compares with that of Titus. But if the original edifices of Constantine were only decorated by marbles and by paintings in tempera, and encaustic, a decade or so later, the Alexandrine art of mosaic was copied at Byzantium with a success destined rather to decline than to improve. In Constantinople itself, in Rome, but chiefly in Ravenna, churches are still standing whose form and appearance must substantially reproduce the buildings of the fifth century. Bearing in mind the architectural details which are specially characteristic of the age of Theodosius II. (e.g. the impost capital) it is probably not too much to say that the description in the text of the pre-Justinian St. Sophia (gathered as it is, from existing monuments), may be taken as an approximate picture.

ONE beautiful summer morning in the year 429 a group of wondering strangers found themselves in the Augustaeum of Constantinople. They were exiles from Italy and Africa, the companions in distress of some of those western bishops who had fallen into the Pelagian heresy, and been driven from their sees.

They stood looking about them with unfeigned astonishment; even those from Rome and Carthage felt provincial here.

From the beautiful pavement of the spacious forum their view was bounded on all sides by the noblest buildings of Constantinople. A canopy of heavenly blue shed floods of sunlight over the peerless prospect of glancing marbles, shining façades, cool purple-shadowed colonnades and cavernous archways. Only the tall cypresses that topped the walls of the Archbishop's Palace gardens touched a natural note in the magnificent artificiality of the scene. At the northern end of the Augustaeum, beyond the hospitable Patriarchaeon (the only building that the strangers recognised) the sun struck a peculiar green sheen out of the gilded brazen tiles on the roof of St. Sophia, and threw the lateral walls into a shade that well became their plain and unassuming length. But it played, like a bright expression, over that part of the façade which rose above the walls of the atrium, or courtyard in front, bringing out the figures in its blue mosaic, and filling the enclosure below with a warmth the fresh zephrys from the sea could scarce dispel.

The Italians moved in the direction of the church, but before they reached the wide flight of steps * leading up to the porticoes from the piazza, they were beset by a crowd of Byzantine beggars, and importuned by the ‘ paternostrari ’ † of St. Sophia's precincts, to buy the thousand and one little objects of piety which, to-day, are still hawked on the steps of many a cathedral in Europe. But they had, apparently, attracted the interest of one of those black cowled Greek kaloyers ‡ who seemed ubiquitous, and to his authoritative interference they owed their extrication from the crowd. He led them into the comparative quiet of the ‘ paradise,’ that beautiful space fronting the church, where statuary gleamed amid massed flower banks, and odorous shrubs ; where the water from a fountain in the centre, welled out of the mouths of dolphins, and, betwixt the leaves of flowers and cones in bronze, flowed round the porphyry columns that upheld a canopy, into the surrounding marble basin.§ A shady cloister ran round the court, and here stood or knelt the occasional figure of a ‘ Penitent,’ one of those whose sin, not yet absolved, forbade his venturing into the sacred building. The Great Emperor Theodosius himself had not dared thrust his presence further, until St. Ambrose had shriven him for the sin of Thessalonica. The garth of St. Sophia was spacious and courtly as a palace garden, unlike the sun-smitten tangle of orange trees and roses in some old-world Spanish cloister, but at least as warm and perfumed. The Greek monk now revealed the secret of his interest in the strangers.

* There were thirty-five at old St. Peter's in Rome.

† Term used by mediæval pilgrims to designate the vendors of beads, etc.

‡ Monks.

§ Taken from the description of the fountain at old St. Peter's.

His keen wits had told him at a glance who they were, and he was unable to resist this golden opportunity of thrashing out a heresy. Pelagianism was much discussed in the cloisters of the east since the dispersion of its confessors had roused more interest in their ideas than had the condemnations pronounced by western Councils. The subtle Byzantine was charmed to argue on those original problems which had suggested themselves to the brain of a British monk, with some of his adherents. The Italians, on their parts were no less delighted to match the intellectual nimbleness of their defence against the trained dialectics of the Greek. It was a unique chance, thought the kaloyer, thus to meet with the Patriarch's guests! Had he too, like Nestorius, been one of those susceptible thinkers upon whose ears arguments fall with new force when put by the men who originate them, he might have run some risk. The decisions of St. Augustine were discussed, under the blue shadows of the ambulatory of St. Sophia, before either the Greek or his companions could have forseen the convocation of such a Council as that of Ephesus.

But as time went on, and the increasing stream of worshippers passing through the paradise and up the steps of the narthex into the basilica, indicated that the hour was approaching for one of those sermons from the Patriarch which had already begun to attract attention by the unfamiliarity of their ideas, the monk hastened to conclude the discussion into which the exiles had plunged no less enthusiastically than he.

Still talking eagerly, however, the whole party traversed the narthex—a sort of corridor running the entire length of the façade —and entered a second spacious hall where those converts preparing for the catechumenate were mustered. The Pelagians* were determined to take advantage of the friendly reception accorded them by the Patriarch of Constantinople, to hear Mass in St. Sophia, and the kaloyer offered to conduct them to a spot whence they might obtain a view of the sanctuary, and of the Emperor and Empress when the latter should arrive. The 'audientes' (or 'hearers'), followed the Italians with their eyes, as the latter drew each others attention to the inscription on the font into which they dipped their hands. It read, curiously enough, either backwards or forwards, "Wash away your sins and not your countenance only." ΝΙΨΟΝ ΑΝΟΜΗΜΑΤΑ ΜΗ ΜΟΝΑΝ ΟΨΙΝ. The 'beautiful gates' which led from the hearers' station into the body of the church were hung with curtains of the richest crimson material. They swung aside and fell again ponderously as the kaloyer ushered his companions forward.

This silent blotting out of the exterior world enhanced the

---

* Pelagianism never formed an ecclesiastical sect, but merely a theological school. It died out about the middle of the fifth century, but not before Pope Leo the Great had instructed the bishops not to receive any Pelagian to communion without an express recantation.

grandeur and solemnity of the scene before them. Only in Rome itself had the Pelagians seen anything to compare with it.*

An imposing vista receded before them. Avenues of majestic columns, forming low double aisles on either hand of the high rectangular nave, conducted the severe line of the horizontal architrave to the glowing apotheosis of the central northern apse with its semi-dome roof of mosaic and gold. On either side smaller apses closed the aisles, and their half-spheres gleamed no less resplendently above the screens that hid them from the Church. The floor was paved with lustrous marbles; mellow hues as of some cool fresh cavern of the deep suffused the air. Beautiful monolithic columns of Numidian giallo antico, of warm honey colour, of sombre porphyry, marble and cippolino, were enhanced in serried mystery by the clouded light, like gold dust, that streamed from the brilliant heavens through windows of talc, sliced alabaster and veined marbles. Rich embroidered curtains hung in the spaces between the columns, stilling the soft air and hushing every echo. The roof was hidden by a carved and gilded ceiling of cedar wood, placed just above the clerestory, whose windows admitted a stained diffused brightness admirably calculated to heighten the harmonious effect of all this wonderful blending of colour.

The nave ended in a magnificent round-headed arch upon the face of which shone great pictures in mosaic. The beautiful 'concha' it framed, was filled by a colossal figure of the Saviour, above whose head a hand appeared "extended from the clouds, and holding a crown, an emblem of the almighty power of the Father whose representation in human form was not then tolerated." † The background was dark blue with lovely purple clouds edged in gold ; sparkling palm trees and brilliant rivers filled in the noble composition. The two smaller domes were equally radiant. One of them was "filled with the most exquisite green-gold tendrils upon a dark blue ground, above which the Lamb of God appeared with four doves." ‡ In the other were "golden stags advancing between green-gold arabesques upon a blue ground towards a fountain, an emblem of the conversion of the heathen." § A broad ribbon of pictures in mosaic ran along the walls of the nave. "The arrangement of the figures and the delicate feeling for colour pervading the whole . . . showed . . . a genuine splendour and beauty which have been lost to the world in the destruction of the later decorated buildings of Imperial Rome."

* See note at head of the chapter.

† Layard "Italian Schools of Painting." It is curious to observe this same device of the crowning hand—with the same interpretation?—on the Imperial coins of the period. The mosaic described is found in Layard, p. 14.

‡ Baptistery of the Lateran in Rome, A.D. 432-440?

§ Mansoleum of Galla Placidia.

Conscious silence and immense isolation reigned in the vast spaces of the basilica. The assembling multitude had no power to disturb its majesty and peace. Even the porphyry, silver and ivory statues seemed to partake of the pervading serenity, and to have no part with the human throng.*

The ambo, or pulpit, a huge erection just within the 'beautiful gates;' the choir; the spaces reserved on either side of it for the Emperor, senators, and nobles, for the Empress and her train of ladies; the 'iconostasis,' a marble screen dividing the chancel from the rails of the sanctuary, all conspired to obstruct the nave. The ambo was a marble platform reached by flights of steps, around which ran light columns of precious stone supporting a canopy of alabaster and mosaic. The choir was a space reserved within a low marble balustrade for the readers, chanters, acolytes, deacons and inferior clergy. To the right the Emperor's throne, or 'solium,' stood within the 'senatorium,' and on the left, that of the Empress paired with it in the 'matroneum.' The high marble screen immediately in front was hung with little lamps whose wicks floated in perfumed oil before a resplendent array of ikons. All the available spaces about these divisional screens and balustrades were filled with bowls of lovely flowers whose scent distilled itself in the circumambient air.

A flight of seven porphyry steps led from the chancel to the 'bema,' or raised floor of the sanctuary within the apse. Around the walls ran tiers of seats for the clergy, in the midst of which, at the back stood the curule chair, the 'cathedra,' of the Patriarch. Innumerable lamps in the shapes of bowls, and crowns of gold and silver, hung down above the altar. The latter raised in the midst of the sanctuary, along the chord of the apse, was hidden from view by marble railings, supporting a canopy (ciborium) on columns and arches of silver, from which veils, or embroidered silken curtains were suspended, closely drawn. All the appurtenances of the sanctuary, from its 'holy gates' of vine wood cased in silver, to the gong of gilded iron which recalled the attention of the worshippers, were of the rarest and richest materials. The altar had an antependium of gold and precious stones; the Blessed Sacrament was reserved in a beautiful silver dove that hung above it called the 'peristerion.'

The apse on the right hand served as a 'lakonikon' or sacristy in whose 'amaria' and 'scrinia' (cupboards and book cases) the sacred books and vessels of the Church were kept. It led into the baptistery. On the other side of the sanctuary the 'prothesis' was

---

* The Emperor Constantine had filled St. Sophia with statuary, to much of which a new Christian signification must speedily have attached. Among the new figures were a complete series of the Roman Emperors, and three statues of St. Helena. The celebrated figure of St. Peter (which Professor Lanciani believes to have been all that Catholics claim for it) was, possibly, reproduced in St. Sophia, or in the Holy Apostles, although, like more classical works of art, this copy may have been destroyed in some fire which ruined the whole quarter.

used for preparing the bread and wine for consecration at the Holy Sacrifice.

The congregation was accommodated in the nave and aisles, the men and the women on different sides, the latter overflowing into back of the nave on crowded occasions.   But here, more properly, stood a third class of 'penitents' (beside those in the hearers' station and the paradise), called the 'substrati,' and beyond those again, around the ambo, stood the 'consistentes.'

Mgr. Duchesne's description* of such a Mass as that celebrated by the Patriarch of St. Sophia in the fifth century transports us in imagination into the midst of an imposing and magnificent ceremony.   The modern Catholic while recognising the Holy Sacrifice feels as if in a dream, so much is familiar and so much is most strange.   The mere historical account of the liturgy reads impressively, and we come to the end of the few pages dealing with "the Mass in the East" feeling as though we were issuing from the great basilica itself.   Mgr. Duchesne gathers his material from the Catechism of St. Cyril, an exposition of the ceremonies of the Mass drawn up for the use of the newly baptised.   It began at the point when the catechumens were dismissed, and the Bishop, having washed his hands prepared to celebrate the sacred mysteries.

The reading of the 'lections' and of the 'dyptichs' was over; the homily delivered from the ambo had occasioned its accustomed stir in the congregation, and then a solemn hush succeeded the retirement of the catechumens.   Two deacons stood beside the altar gently waving the 'flabella' to keep insects away from the holy oblation, and presently, at the appointed signal, came a long procession of communicants.   First the Patriarch himself received, then the priests, deacons, sub-deacons, lectors, psalmists and 'ascetae.'   Next came the deaconesses, virgins, widows and children, and finally the general congregation.   Towards the end of Mass the kiss of peace was exchanged between women and women, men and men, from the altar to the doors.   Finally the people were all dismissed as at the present day, and after the Emperor and Empress had retired by the Skepaste Scala, the Byzantine crowd poured out into the blazing Augustaeum, and like the wind carried word of the Patriarch's latest utterances to every quarter of the city.

When Nestorius first ascended the throne of St. Sophia, he found the religious world of Constantinople divided into two parties according to the view that the Blessed Virgin Mary was the Mother of God or merely the mother of Man.   The love and honour of 'Panaghia,' sanctioned by the truths of the Nicene Creed, had already led some of the Fathers† to speak of her as the

* " History of Christian Worship."

† S.S. Alexander, Athanasius, Cyril of Jerusalem, Gregory, Chrysostom, Ambrose ; Cassian, Origen, Eusebius, S. Vincent of Lerins, &c., &c.

Mother of God. As it was, indeed, by the death of God Incarnate, that mankind was redeemed, so Mary was truly the Mother of God. Had she been but the mother of Man the death of her son could not have availed to save the human race. Thus to deny her the former title was to deny the central, divine Fact of Christianity. "The heresy" it has been beautifully said, "stumbled at man's wonted stumbling block, the Love of God in the Incarnation, 'when Thou tookest upon Thee to deliver man, Thou didst not abhor the Virgin's womb.'" At the beginning of the fifth century there was a certain school of theologians at Antioch, who, basing their ideas upon those of a certain Gaulish monk, named Leporius, denied this divine motherhood of the Blessed Virgin. They took exception to the "Theotokos," as the Arians had taken exception to the "homoosia." The question turned, like the other so-called 'Christological' controversies of the age, on the relation between the divine and human natures in the Person of Jesus Christ.

Nestorius promised to give the faithful of his new flock "a clearer and more satisfactory explanation than they had yet received on the nature of the Son of God."* He himself did not exactly agree with the Antiochene controversialists, but modelling his thought upon that of his friend, Bishop Theodore of Mopsuestia, arrived at a compromise which he now tried to teach at Constantinople. Both he and his companion Anastasius, preached against the baldest form of the new heresy, but they merely added confusion to error. They explained, in a course of sermons, that the Blessed Virgin might indeed be less than the Mother of God, yet more than the mother of Man. She was the Mother of Christ; she "gave birth to a man in whom the union of the Logos had begun, but was still so incomplete that he could not until after baptism, be rightly called the Son of God." The Archbishop filled in his argument with new and fatal explanations. He held that there were two distinct Persons in Our Blessed Lord, joined by any sort of union but the hypostatic,† the Godhead dwelling in His Humanity merely as in a temple. This was a denial of the Incarnation, and one of the most dangerous heresies that had ever menaced the internal peace of the Church.

The attitude of the Patriarch with regard to the whole controversy filled all the east with alarm, and confirmed the Augusta Pulcheria's worst forebodings. The monks of Constantinople took their stand with entire accord on the side of the Theotokos, and the heresy "met everywhere," says Dr. Alzog, "with the most determined opposition." St. Pulcheria, whose devotion to Panagia, the All-Blessed, had been shown by the erection of many a church in her honour, strongly opposed herself

* Alzog. tI. pg. 415.

† The Hypostatic Union. The union of Christ's body and soul with the Person (or hypostasis) of God the Son. Simple Dic. for Catholics C.T.S.

to Nestorius, and exerted all her influence to counteract Theodosius' leaning towards him. For the Emperor truly loved the Bishop, and waited, hoping that the faith he felt in him might justify itself in spite of every appearance to the contrary. When once he had impulsively committed himself to the admiration of this man, the weak-natured Emperor clung to it with pitiful perseverance. It was an obstinacy that defied argument or common sense, for although Theodosius' faith escaped perversion, he allowed it to run every risk. His heart remained the truer for the misgiving of his mind.

The Empress Athenais was too true a Greek not to take an extreme interest in the intellectual subtleties of the controversy. In herself she exemplified that " belief in the power of argument [which] was a legacy of the pagan Greeks to the Eastern Church*." This theological problem supplied for her the place of the old profitless disputations she had followed so eagerly between her father and his sophist friends. As Leontius had delighted to crack his brains over the hard points in philosophy, so his daughter now rushed with somewhat unbecoming intrepidity into the battles of her new faith. She leant so patient an ear to the waverings of Theodosius, that it seems she herself inclined to the Nestorian party. Pulcheria, at least, was unsupported at court, in the opposition she offered to Nestorius. The Empress prepared strangely for the part she was to play later on as a leader of Eutychian schismatics, by taking up so tentative an attitude in the Nestorian controversy.

Popular feeling ran extremely high. Nestorius was often loudly contradicted in the very pulpit ; placards hoisting him on the petard of his own utterances were everywhere displayed about the streets ; he resorted to cruelty and force to check the monks who constantly challenged him to discussions in the very highways of the city.

One day two priests named Basil and Thalassius went to the Patriarchaeon to ask for a definite statement of Nestorius' views. The Patriarch himself had invited them. In the letter they afterwards addressed to Theodosius, they gave an account of the infamous interview. The moment they broached the subject of his heterodoxy Nestorius had them seized, stripped, beaten, flung down and kicked, loaded with chains, struck in the face and finally imprisoned. Their letter went to the Emperor " not to demand vengeance for our wrongs but to implore assistance for the Church."† Indeed, it became a popular cry at Constantinople. " A King we have ; a Bishop we have not ! " The people refused, after a while, to frequent the churches, where their faith was liable to be so travestied, and scarcely any would communicate.

---

* " History of the E. Church," Stanley.

†This incident is taken not from a Roman, but from a Anglican authority. See the Introduction to the volume on St. Cyril in Pusey's Library of the Fathers.

St. Proclus, the Bishop of Cyzicus placed himself at the head of the faithful, and for a time his exhortations swayed the unstable sympathies of the court in the right direction. He was an intrepid champion of Our Blessed Lady, and preached with the eloquence of spiritual and virile love in defence of her glorious prerogatives, calling her to Nestorius' very face, "the Light Cloud which bore Him which sat between the Cherubim."

For three years the Constantinoplitan Church was afflicted and rent by Nestorius. He hurled anathemas against those who refused to communicate with him ; his writings and utterances were widely disseminated and hotly debated ; and the confusion of the city was reflected in the court.

CHAPTER XVII

AN ANTI-NESTORIAN HYMN

In Bethlehem is He born,
Maker of all things, everlasting God !
He opens Eden's gate,
Monarch of Ages !   Thence the fiery sword
Gives glorious passsge ; thence
That severing mid-wall overthrown, the Powers
Of earth and Heav'n are one :
Angels and men renew their ancient league,
The pure rejoin the pure
In happy union !   Now the Virgin-womb,
Like some Cherubic throne,
Containeth Him, the Uncontainable :
Bears Him, Whom while they bear
The Seraphs tremble : bears Him as He comes
To shower upon the world
The fulness of His everlasting love."

" Hymns of the Holy Eastern Church."

WRITTEN (C. 430) BY S. ANATOLIUS : TRANS. BY REV. J. M. NEALE.

St. Pulcheria herself took a queen's, and not a theologian's interest in the Nestorian controversy.   As a faithful daughter of the Church, it was of the first importance to her, that whatever influence she could wield should be exerted in concert with Bishop Proclus and the monks.   We need not study Nestorianism to understand her attitude.   But we must indeed follow the events that brought about the overthrow of the Patriarch, and study the men and women who acted in the drama, in pursuit of the Augusta, for around this crisis formed one of the greatest trials of her life.

It so happened that the Archbishops of Alexandria were brought into yearly contact with the Churches throughout the East by the annual letter which they wrote to announce the day upon which Easter would fall.   The circulation of Nestorius' tracts in Egypt first occasioned St. Cyril to write against his heresy.   " There can be little doubt," we are told, " that the powerful mind of St. Leo, who, later, became the soul of the Council of Chalcedon, was taught through these writings as St. Cyril himself had been taught through those of St. Athanasius." *   For some time Nestorius took little

---

* Introduction to St. Cyril.   " Pusey's Library of the Fathers."

notice of the new champion who had appeared against him. But the Alexandrian prelate was deeply concerned at the progress of a heresy, which fastened upon that subject of the Incarnation, which had been a favourite theme of his during all his priestly life. His Paschal Letters had been full of it, long before Nestorius ever raised the standard of revolt; so much so that even the Letter of the year 429, was scarcely regarded as exceptional. "Since this is a question of faith," he wrote, "and all the Churches in the whole Roman Empire are offended, what shall we do who are entrusted by God with the Divine Mysteries?" He next felt it his duty to write a letter to the monks of Egypt, exposing the dangers and the fallacies of the new doctrines that were serving them for so much meditation and discussion. This it was which at last attracted Nestorius' angry attention. From this moment St. Cyril stood forward as his first opponent, and the eyes of Christendom fastened upon the two.

For the past three years, St. Cyril had watched the trend of events at Constantinople, not without fear, and a deep sense of his own responsibility. But he had only broken silence thrice. The fiery nephew of Theophilus had learnt a lesson from his early prejudice against St. Chrysostom, and was resolved, with the self-command of a saint, not to allow his indignation against Nestorius to overrule his sense of justice for the second time. He wrote, indeed, to the Emperor and to the Imperial family, but omitted all mention of the Patriarch, and abstained from quoting any of his catchwords. It was his endeavour to retain their loyalty to the Church; not so much to discredit the *man*, as his teaching and opinions.

He does not seem at first to have understood that the Augusta required less exhortation than her sisters and the Empress, but he came to perceive later on that it might be largely through her support that the ear of Theodosius could be won. St. Pulcheria witnessed her brother's vacillation, and the questionable attitude of the court with keen anxiety, and had fallen there into the opprobrium that attends those who sink themselves in an unpopular cause. A cabal had already begun to form against her in the interests of the Empress, and Theodosius could accuse St. Cyril of seeking to split the court in two, by taking advantage of the differences existing in it. "He had no business," wrote the Emperor, "to address the Imperial sisters in a different tone to that he used towards himself, and to court notoriety by 'meddling' with the 'private affairs' of the Augustae." As though catechetical instructions turned on "private affairs!" The Patriarch had written a long treatise setting forth the simpler aspects of the controversy to the Princesses Arcadia and Marina, and a more difficult exposition to Eudocia and Pulcheria. But a vile report had been spread that the Augusta's enmity to Nestorius arose because he had accused her to the Emperor of improper relations with the Patrician Paulinus. There were no grounds whatever for the slander, (which, as the wind of malice veered round was later on fastened upon Athenais), but even as such, it hints to us across the silence of so many centuries, the intrigues of the court factions. It shows the strengthening cause of an unworthy jealousy in Athenais, and throws a gleam through the mists that shroud the action of that far off scene, on changes in the plot of the story. For the purposes of such a book as this, the intimation, the guiding thread, the link in the chain that this slander affords, is of greater value than the history in which it lies embedded.

The same charge, probably legendary, which subsequently attempted to account for the disgrace of Athenais, and the death of Paulinus in 440, did as much injustice to the Empress, as her apologists would do to Pulcheria. It suggested that the love of the Court Marshal really accounted for the rivalry which had been growing up between the two ladies for an indefinite time, and modern historians fly to so obvious an explanation of the matter. It had, however, no foundation in fact, either with regard to Pulcheria, in 429, or to Athenais eleven years afterwards; and, as the former's biographer remarks, " it is very profoundly unjust to credit a baseless and imaginary surmise of this sort, against the honour of so good and amiable a Princess." * The rancour of religious controversy had robbed men's minds of common chivalry and reason. Pulcheria, who had fostered Theodosius' friendship for Paulinus from the time when both were lads, and who rejoiced that his culture had so materially assisted the beautiful Athenian in 420, to assimilate the conditions of her new life, was not the woman to descend to anything unworthy of herself, of Athenais, and of their mutual friend. She would not, as a woman of thirty, suddenly involve herself in disgrace and infamy with a man she had trusted for a score of years, and to whose friendship she had confided Theodosius as a boy. But the Nestorians were not content with this. They went farther, and accused the Augusta of a crime which only the depraved imagination of the day could suggest. Historians have pitied Theodosius for his position twixt wife and sister, and have praised the management by which he is supposed to have preserved the peace for years yet to come. They would do better to pity St. Pulcheria, and to admire the heroic fortitude she must have displayed in enduring her part. She was resolved to sustain St. Cyril and St. Proclus, and content to leave her own cause to the vindication of time.

St. Cyril's anxiety augmented. In the independent and dangerous attitude of the Constantinopolitan Patriarch and in the support he seemed to be deriving from the countenance of the Emperor, the Alexandrian doubtless foresaw the ' Caesarpapism '

---

* Tillemont Mem. Ecc. Ste. Pulquerie.

† Caesarpapism. The imperial domination of the Church—the anomaly exhibited in the later Byzantine Empire, and in all ages where the head of the State is in absolute authority over the head of the Church.

of a later age. He wrote, accordingly, to Pope Celestine I., and to the other bishops of the west, in order to submit the whole controversy to their arbitration. He did not however take this step before his correspondence with Nestorius had enabled him both to grasp the points of his argument and the character of its champion.

"Never was there a case in which the contending parties approximated so closely; both appealed to the Nicene Creed." St. Cyril declared it not enough to subscribe this creed without also accepting the sense of it according to the interpretation of the Church.

Nothing tended more to the elevation of the Pope than his magnificent attitude as arbitrator in these successive eastern controversies. The weakness of the empire in the west increased his power, assured his independence, and saved the Church from the imperial patronage under which she laboured in the east. The ecclesiastical history of those ages which intervened between classical and mediaeval times demonstrates the rise of the first see in Christendom from a standing scarcely recognisable, in the eyes of the world at least, from equality or rivalry with Constantinople, Alexandria or Antioch, to a position of unquestioned supremacy. The eastern Emperors longed to establish the superiority of an imperial over an apostolical see, their principle being that the ecclesiastical rank of a bishopric should be regulated in accordance with the civil standing of the city. This very point came uppermost in a council held during the reign of St. Pulcheria, but owing to her fidelity to Rome the very bishops who advocated Constantinople's claim were temporarily silenced. The unstability of faith in the east helped to subject its storm-tossed Churches to the Pope, and to direct all eyes to him for authoritative guidance.

Thus Celestin responded to the appeal of St. Cyril and took an active part in the Nestorian controversy. He held a council in Rome, the result of whose unimpassioned deliberations was the condemnation of Nestorius' propositions, and his deposition from office.

St. Cyril, at the desire of the Pope, also held a Council in Alexandria. Nestorius replied to the anathemas it pronounced against him by an equal number of charges, insultingly and contemptuously worded, against the orthodoxy of St. Cyril and his adherents. The whole matter might well have ended with St. Celestius' ultimatum, but that the Emperor Theodosius now yielded to Nestorius' demand for the decision of the universal Church.

In the name of the two Emperors, Valentinian and Theodosius, the Third Œcumenical Council was convened to meet at Ephesus during the season of Pentecost, 431. Not knowing of his recent death, the Emperor sent a peculiarly respectful invitation to St. Augustine to attend; but his letter to the Archbishop of Alexandria was, clearly, dictated by Nestorius.

"It is plain to everyone," wrote Theodosius, "that religion has its firmness not from anyone's bidding but from intelligence. Now then, let thy Piety instruct us, why, overlooking us (whom thou knowest to have such care of godliness) and all the priests everywhere, who could better have solved this dispute thou hast so far as in thee lies, cast confusion and severance into the Church. As if a rash impetuosity became questions as to godliness rather than accuracy; or as if carefulness had not more weight with Ourselves than rashness; or as if intricacy in these things were more pleasing to Us than simplicity. And yet We did not think that Our high estimation would be so received by thy Piety, or that everything would be thrown into confusion, inasmuch as We, too, know how to be displeased. But now We shall take heed to the sacred calm . . . . We will that all shall be laid open at the holy Synod, and that what shall seem good shall prevail, whether the defeated obtain forgiveness from the Fathers or no . . . . So then thy Reverence must come at the time appointed in the other letters sent to all the Metropolitans, and must not expect to recover the relation to Ourselves in any other way than that, ceasing from all grievousness and turbulence, thou come willingly to the investigation of these questions . . . . If thou willest to do otherwise We will not endure it . . . . " *

The Emperor was unable to attend the Council in person, so he was represented by Count Candidian, the Captain of his bodyguard. He extended special protection to Nestorius, who was the first to arrive at Ephesus, accompanied by sixteen Bishops and an armed escort. But his party was far outnumbered by that of St. Cyril who came attended by fifty Egyptian Bishops, besides a host of monks, a deputation from the celebrated congregation of the Alexandrian 'parabolani,' and a large retinue of sailors and servants all massed under the banners of St. Mark and the Holy Mother of God. St. Cyril "was not gracious of aspect" we are told, "and looked more likely to refuse a favour than to grant it. His eyebrows were dense and bushy, large and arched; his face was broad but half hidden by a thick and flowing beard whose rippling lengths of grizzled hair added to the venerable appearance of his bald forehead and straight Greek brow. Truly a man to wield authority, strongly to build up and to pull down, with little respect to the persons of men; . . . . but not to descend to the littleness of personal pride or mean ambition, nor to shed unnecessarily one drop of the blood of his fellow man." *

Such was Nestorius' redoubtable opponent. He came charged to uphold the Pope's decision. His cause was seconded by Memnon, Archbishop of Ephesus, with forty suffragan Bishops from Asia and twelve from Pamphylia, and by the general voice of the monks and people. Pope Celestine was represented by two Bishops, Arcadius

---

* Conc. Eph. p. 1. c. 31.

† St. Cyril and the Tumults of Alexandria.—"Dublin Review."

and Projectus, and a priest Phillip. These envoys however did not arrive from distant Rome until after the first sittings of the Council, and Nestorius' chief supporter, Bishop John of Antioch, was also late. He sent excuses for his delay "alleging that some of his party had been taken sick on the way, that his horses had been disabled, and that the inconvenience of travel was very great," * although so thorough was the provision made by the state for journeys of this sort, that "a Vicar could dispose of a train of ten horses and thirteen asses on a dozen occasions in the year," on the public roads, merely "to make tours of inspection throughout his diocese."† " A fortnight was consumed in this way, when John sent word to Cyril 'that if his arrival should be delayed, the Council need not be deferred on that account, but should proceed with the necessary business.' "‡

St. Cyril's first intention of awaiting the Antiochenes was presently changed. The heat at Ephesus was terrible; many of the Bishops had suffered a good deal on the journey thither, and were now stricken down with illness. The poverty of others made it imperative that their absence from home should not be too long protracted. On June 22nd, therefore, the President opened the Council without further ado. The Imperial Commissioner protested against it, and Nestorius himself refused to appear until the gathering was full, but in spite of this, the business was opened. Nestorius' heretical sermons were read, and carried their own condemnation. The sitting closed late that night by a sentence of deposition against the Patriarch. The entire populace of Ephesus went wild with delight. The people broke out into joyous clamour, the members of the Conclave were escorted to their several lodgings with torches and flares, women ran before them burning incense, and the city was en fête from end to end.

The finding of the Council was communicated to Nestorius next day, but he immediately sent an indignant protest to the Emperor, whose representative then declared the decree invalid. Under the imperial protection, John of Antioch, who arrived a few days later with forty-two bishops, proceeded at once to hold a separate Council (the Conciliabulum) in the palace assigned to him. It pronounced a sentence of deposition against St. Cyril and Archbishop Memnon, and excommunicated the other bishops of their party! When at last Bishops Arcadius and Projectus with Philip the priest, arrived from Rome, St. Cryil opened a second session (July 10th) followed by five more, in the course of which the Council issued several circular letters, and drew up six canons against the Nestorian and Pelagian heresies.

The imperial commissioner, Count Candidianus, took care that

* Alzoz Universal Church Hist. Sec. 119.

† W. G. Holmes. "The Age of Justinian and Theodora."

‡ Alzog.

no representations from St. Cyril and his side should reach the Emperor from Ephesus. A monk, however, disguised as a beggar, finally brought the news of the deposition of Nestorius to the capital. He carried a letter in the hollow of his stick. From the very first the Archimandrite Dalmatius—Superior of the Constantinopolitan monks—had, like the Augusta, mistrusted Nestorius. On receipt of St. Cyril's letter giving an account of the doings at Ephesus this holy old man was much preplexed as to what course of action to pursue. The monks throughout the city were in a state of ferment. For forty-eight years Dalmatius had never been seen in the streets. Often had he refused the Emperor's prayers to come forth and head processions in times of storm and earthquake, but now was this the occasion to break his vow of clausura, lead a mighty throng to the gates of the imperial Palace and speak out strongly for the Mother of God? The hermit prayed and considered; hours passed by, and the responsibility weighed heavily upon his conscience. Suddenly in the night time, there came a reply to all his questioning, " Dalmatius, go out from this place."

When the venerable hermit suddenly appeared in the Augustaeum, in the vanguard of an immense concourse of people, Theodosius hastened with all deference to accord him an audience. The Emperor was surprised beyond measure at the relation of Dalmatius, and demanded, with no slight degree of confusion, why the Patriarch of Alexandria had not kept him informed of these things himself? Dalmatius replied that no messengers had been allowed to reach him from any member of the Council, and that Count Candidian had hindered the transmission of all reports except those of the Nestorians. Theodosius had recourse to an expedient. He could not bring himself to desert his favourite, but neither could he disregard the representations of the Archimandrite, the exhortations of Bishop Proclus, or the sorrowful pleadings of Pulcheria.

Dalmatius withdrew, and mounting the ambo of a neighbouring church, gave the people an account of his interview with the Emperor.

The feeble compromise, however, by which Theodosius summarily confirmed all three conflicting depositions (those of St. Cyril, Memnon, and Nestorius), was further made ridiculous by the reconciliatory mission of one of the high officers of the Court.

Theodosius was sorely troubled by the ferment in the Church, the Capital, the Palace, and in his own mind.

One day as he rode out to the Palace of the Hebdomon attended by his guards and courtiers, he drew rein at the door of a hermit's cell, and forbidding any to follow him, asked permission to enter. First he removed his diadem that the solitary might not know it was the Emperor who knocked. No sooner had the monk received him than both fell to prayer, and afterwards sitting down simply by his side Theodosius asked his host what manner of life the Fathers of the Desert led. "They occupy themselves with intercession for your Majesty and all your ministers," the monk replied.*

Theodosius glanced round the cell, and preceiving a little dry bread in a crock besought the father's benediction, and permission to eat with him. The solitary rose, filled a little vessel with water into which he spilt some salt, and moistening the bread shared this meal with the Emperor. If ever peace sat at board with that weary man it was then. He revealed himself—unnecessarily it would seem, to his humble host, whereupon the monk prostrated at his feet. "Oh!" said Theodosius speaking aloud his thoughts, "how blessed are you solitaries, who, free and unharassed by worldly concerns, lead sweet and tranquil lives, with no care but the salvation of your souls, and no thought but how best to merit eternal life! as for me—I was born in the purple, I occupy a throne, and I can truly swear I have never sat down to meat without a spirit full of care!"

He withdrew refreshed, and that night the hermit fled still further from the haunts of men, and went away into the solitudes of Egypt.

At the suggestion of the envoys from Rome, the Council petitioned Theodosius to release St. Cyril and Memnon from the imprisonment and quarantine to which they had been condemned by the unauthoritative Conciliabulum. Nestorius' supporters attempted to vindicate their orthodoxy by transmitting to the Emperor a creed in which they admitted the term 'Theotokos,' and interpreted it with reservations of their own.

The Emperor received both deputations, and sent them back to Ephesus to summon eight representatives from either side to retire to the comparative seclusion of Chalcedon, and there debate the question in his presence.

Historians hesitate when this smaller gathering is assembled, to account adequately for Theodosius' change of front. "After fruitless efforts to come to a settlement, the Emperor ordered that the Council should be dissolved, permitted the Bishops to return to their respective sees, granted liberty to Cyril and Memnon," and from having favoured the schismatic throughout, now rent his imperial robes at hearing Nestorius' familiar blasphemies, and "ratified his deposition."† He banished him to his Asian monastery, although allowing him the honour of a voluntary abdication, in October, 431. This was nothing less than a tardy acception of Pope Celestine's original fiat.

Nothing marked the power of the sovereign over the eastern Church more strongly than Candidian's conduct of affairs at Ephesus; nothing marked the counter-significance of St. Pulcheria's influence more signally than the way in which the controversy ended.

---

* Tillemont, Hist. des Emps. T. II., a. v.

† Alzog.

Nestorius' discomfiture must be attributed, in the Council to St. Cyril, and in the court of St. Pulcheria, although in both instances history is so abrupt that the dénouement is difficult to trace. The gratitude of the Alexandrian Patriarch to the Augusta was geniune and unbounded. He certainly considered that his victory was largely due to her support. He has been accused of bribing the Augusta and important members of her suite to further his cause with Theodosius, but St. Pulcheria was already in alliance with Dalmatius, the monks, and Bishop Proclus, before St. Cyril came to to their rescue. That St. Cyril made presents to the Princess cannot be denied, but the fact should be judged from the standpoint of the Byzantines and the fifth century. At that time no one could approach a superior, no matter how just his cause might be, without the recommendation of a gift. It was a mere point of etiquette. In sending offerings to the Court, St. Cyril showed himself a man of address and breeding. St. Theodore of Studium, one of the most upright and inflexible figures of monastic history had no conscientious scruples against such a custom. In a letter he wrote during a period of captivity, much like the quarantine of St. Cyril at Ephesus, he expressly thanked a lady for having bought consideration for him by her gifts to his goalers. It was, apparently, a recognised means of effecting one's purpose according to the adulatory ideas of the day. The charge of corrupt practices which modern historians are so glad to bring against St. Cyril originated in a sufficiently unworthy quarter. The powerful eunuch Scholasticus was a traitor. He had been in sympathy with Nestorius, and when afterwards, ostensibly allied with the Cyrillian party at court, he desired a means of discrediting the Patriarch of Alexandria in the Emperor's eyes, he threw a false light on these overtures of St. Cyril, and accused him of bribery.

A new Patriarch, Maximinian, ascended the throne of St. Sophia, but the heretical party of Nestorius persisted for two years before it attempted to become reconciled to the Church. " A reconciliation was finally secured through the combined mediation of the Pope and the Emperor; the prudent negotiation of Acacius, Bishop of Beroea, a man universally respected, and who had attained the vererable age of a hundred and ten years; the kind offices of Paul of Emesa, Symeon the Stylite . . . . Isidore of Pelusium, all of whom laboured earnestly to quiet the troubled minds of the citizens of Autioch."† The Emperor Theodosius himself went on a journey to consult the marvellous ascetic on his mountain column, but whether the connection with the Nestorian ferment or with another, does not seem to be quite clear. When, at last, the Antiochenes recognised the authority of Maximinian, they fully concurred in the condemnation of his predecessor, and at the instance of Bishop John himself, Nestorius was taken from the

† Alzog. Universal Church History, Sec. 119.

cloisters of St. Euprepius and sent into exile. From Oasis he went to Panopolis, thence to Elephantine, only to be recalled. He bore meekly the punishment he had once arrogantly inflicted on others, and consoled himself by writing an autobiography, called a "Tragedy." He died some time after the year 439, but the exact date and place are unknown. Tradition assigns him a grave in Upper Egypt.

The Nestorians who had been banished found a protector in Barsumas, Bishop of Nisibis (A.D. 435-489), and under his successor they perfected their ecclesiastical organisation. It is curious to reflect that in far-away tracts of Kurdistan, in remote places in India, in the deserts of Tartary there remain to this day the descendants of those Nestorians, who in the fifth century wandered from Constantinople, Edessa, and the cities of the east Roman Empire, carrying their marvellous civilisation with their dogmatic errors into the interior of Asia.

While shut up in his own room at Ephesus, St. Cyril elaborated his theological letters to the imperial ladies into a "Treatise on the Right Faith." As soon as he returned to Alexandria he expunged from his writings such expressions as had given offence in various quarters, and sent his ten books written in refutation of the Emperor Julian, to Bishop John of Antioch.

In the year 423 St. Sixtus succeeded St. Celestine at Rome, and in 425 Maximinian died at Constantinople.

At length the objections of those who had consistently opposed the promotion of St. Proclus were overcome, and this estimable man, who had never taken possession of the see of Cyzicus, was appointed to that of the Imperial city. All through the recent troubles he had strenuously fought Nestorius. Now, however, he treated the most inveterate among the schismatics with remarkable mildness, and displayed nothing but kindness, and the paternal solicitude of his office. He kept up a correspondence, and lived in close union with the Pope, St. Cyril and Bishop John. We can only suppose that he exerted all his influence to heal the domestic sorrows in the Palace, and to encourage St. Pulcheria. It seemed indeed, as though his Patriarchate had come about just at the moment when its peaceful and beneficent character could do most to allay the recent storms, and obliterate their traces.

Theodosius had alienated himself from the affections of the populace. His endurance of a Bishop they so feared and hated, lowered him in their estimation, and when in 435 there came a famine in the city, the crowds actually stoned him as he was on his way to the public granaries to expedite the distribution of corn.

The Augusta Pulcheria, however, was the more popular for her loyalty to St. Cyril and to the Holy Mother of God.

CHAPTER XVIII

THE Augusta Pulcheria had now passed the meridian of her life. She had outlived not only the éclat of her early years, but the love and gratitude of the woman she had raised to a throne above her own. Never had the sacrifice of her vow seemed more thankless than at this moment. Theodosius had belied her most tenacious faith, and it seemed as though her influence at court were no longer productive of anything but contradiction. But a saint's capacity for suffering may only be compared with a woman's fidelity to love. St. Pulcheria still consoled herself for her brother's manifest defects by her trust in his good qualities, and held herself in readiness to waive all but essentials in favour of his views. A woman who would prefer her own opinion to a man's, in affairs like those of a great Empire, and bravely face all consequences of her contradiction, must be either peculiarly justified by her capacity, or animated by one or another of the master passions of history. The Augusta had no personal ambitions. It were a great act of humility for her to defer to Theodosius and his small-souled counsellors, unless she still clung to that faith in him which her heart cherished, after it had been abandoned by her intellect. She had won the battle at court which St. Cyril had won in the Council, and had now but the domestic disfavour to encounter of Athenais and the discomfited Nestorians.

Strangely enough, at such a moment, Pulcheria found herself brought face to face with the revelation of a career, which might have been her own, but for the grace of God. If anything were wanting to prove the spirituality of her resolve and vow, it were surely supplied by the contrast of her niece's lot. The Empress Placidia made in her daughter's regard the very mistake that historians make about Pulcheria, and imagined that motives of political expediency were sufficient to prompt heroic virtue. An Imperial mandate, however, could not do the work of the pure grace of God, and the story of the unhappy Princess Honoria is a dramatic foil to that of St. Pulcheria.

It forms one of the most passionate and unredeemed of forgotten of human tragedies. The irresistible craving of her womanhood, thwarted and pent by the very mother who bore her ; the fruitless appeals to the pity or chivalry of men ; the effort to accept religous consolation and the final imprisonment and pining to an obscure death, make up a theme which the world's masters in art have been blind to neglect.

The ex-Queen Placidia had not been married to Constantius above a year, when a daughter was born to the strangely assorted couple. Shamefully repugnant as this second wedding had been to Athaulf's grief-stricken widow, the devotion of her husband presently availed to reconcile her to her new life at Ravenna. The difficulties of Constantius' undisciplined nature came out strongly in his daughter, but before Valentinian was born in the succeeding year, Placidia had become comparatively happy once again. The boy's character was totally different to his sister's. It may have resembled his mother's, but he was spoiled and corrupted from the first, and it were unfair to Placidia to trace his faults to her.

The Empress, however, loved her son to the exclusion of her daughter. Honoria's life was sacrificed to Valentinian, and after Constantius' death in 420, their mother gave full play to her favouritism.

Justa Grata Honoria grew up in the Palace of Laurelwood, at Ravenna, an unhappy and unheeded child. It occurred to the Empress to have her created Augusta, in order to place her in rank, when she should arrive at marriageable age, above the aspirations of possible suitors. Coins struck in her honour when she was only three, exhibit this title, and around the sacred monogram on the other side, runs the "improper legend" Salus Reipublicæ. The voluntary sacrifice Pulcheria had made for Theodosius, was imposed on Honoria for Valentinian.

Placidia has been suspected of trying to render her son unfit for his inheritance by neglecting his education, in order to remain in power herself. Were this the result of design, the blow aimed at Honoria may have also been dictated by wholly selfish motives. But it is difficult to form so harsh a judgment of the Empress. She had taken up the reins of government in the West, filled with the desire to emulate her niece at Constantinople, and was sufficiently religious minded to appreciate Pulcheria's uncommon fame, and to aim at a similar reputation. She had, however, been spoiled, as many good women are, by love and flattery, and by the golden linings to her clouds of sorrow. She was young enough, sanguine enough, and ignorant enough in 423, to be imperious and arbitrary. She may well have supposed that so much education as had sufficed for her would also suffice for her son, but in causing the dignity of Augusta to be conferred on Honoria, she may not have aimed so much at a regency for herself, as at gaining another Pulcheria in the person of her own daughter. There are people who can so ill appreciate another's standpoint, especially when they scarcely wish to do so, as to be surprised when the laws their own convenience lays down meet with little favour. This is all the more so, when such convenience dictates a course of action which might be supposed beneficial to the one who has to follow it. Placidia, sympathising little with her daughter, perhaps knowing her not at all, raised her to the inaccessible height of an Augusta.

The Princess could not bear this official stifling of her passionate young nature. Restive like the burly Constantius had been under the restraints of court life, and as determined as he not to be fettered by them, Honoria "detested the importunate greatness which raised her above the hopes of the most presumptuous subject, and which forever excluded her from the comforts of honourable love. . . She yielded to the impulse of nature, and threw herself into the arms of her Chamberlain Eugenius." She presently met her mother with the proud reproaches of a neglected daughter. Wretched as such a fall must ever be, there was something fine in Honoria's defiance. Moral judgments must always be " checked and enlightened by perpetual reference to the special circumstances that mark the individual lot," and only those whose sympathy with human nature is truly catholic should judge Honoria. She needs no plea but this ; the age and her Imperial circumstances constitute no ground for her defence. Honoria allowed herself to be morally defeated by a passion which was rather that of liberty than of love, since, for her, no high religious motive might transfigure the sacrifice Pulcheria had made. She scarcely felt her responsibility to the Empire, and she certainly had no love for its youthful Emperor.

Placidia was furious. And worse still, the young brother at whose door Honoria's misery also lay, was filled with hypocritical and selfish indignation. He and his mother promptly decided to purge their Palace of this scandal. Doubtless Eugenius was executed, and "after a strict and shameful confinement," Honoria was banished to the remote Constantinople.

She travelled in disgrace with a retinue of eunuchs and goalers. "On all the main roads an elaborate system of public posts was studiously maintained," * and the Imperial couriers hastening backwards and forwards en route, would keep both Ravenna and Constantinople informed as to her obscure progress. Poor Princess ! she probably completed each day's journey at the public " mansion " or wayside establishment, where a "sufficient number of light and heavy vehicles, of draught horses and oxen, of pack horses, sumpter mules and asses were kept" for the accommodation of those travelling on the public service.

At last she arrived at the Imperial palace and was received by the aunt whose very name she hated. The sight of the beautiful child Eudocia, destined to be her brother's bride, filled her with a passionate sense of her own wrong. Whether Honoria retired to the seclusion of St. Pulcheria's own cloistered apartments, or to some convent in the city, it is impossible to say. Did the disappointment of the Imperial nun's own life lead her to deal

---

* Mr. G. W. Holmes, "The Age of Justinian and Theodora," ch. II.

sympathetically with her intractable niece? Could Pulcheria make allowances for a nature so different to her own, or did she share Placidia's indignation at the disgrace the Princess had brought upon the Imperial house? The sister of Theodosius was a true daughter of the founder of their dynasty, and shared his conception of the dignity of the purple. Her character was lofty, severe and steadfast, rather than mild, and yet it would be contradictory to suppose that one whose heart was softened by suffering, and always full of compassion and forbearance, had no gentleness for the black sheep of her own kin.

Honoria possibly stayed in the palace and "reluctantly imitated the monastic assiduity in prayer, fasting, and vigils of the imperial sisters and their chosen band," or some mandate of Theodosius may have compelled her to take the religious veil. For the weapon of tyranny was already forged by which many a succeeding Byzantine Emperor ridded himself of mother, wife, or sister. It was, indeed, to be presently turned against St. Pulcheria herself. All this happened in A.D. 434. For twelve or fourteen years the miserable Honoria languished in an atmosphere which, despite all St. Pulcheria could do, was uncongenial to her. She was sixteen when she arrived in Constantinople, and had attained the age of twenty-eight when a second act of desperation brought another imperial storm about her head.

During the whole interval nothing was heard of her. She was forgotten in her home and in the world. Even the wedding of Valentinian and Eudocia on October 20th, 436, brought no release or solace to the captive.

In 435 the Empress lost her younger daughter Flacilla,* and in this common grief much of the estrangement that had lately crept in between brother, wife, and sister was forgotten. An unforeseen domestic crisis will often solve a situation before it reaches a critical point. St. Pulcheria had much to bury in the grave of the little princess, and the Empress may have learnt more of Christianity in her hour of woe than ever the Nestorian controversy taught her.

In 436 the young Emperor of the West attained his seventeenth year, and the government at Ravenna intimated to that at Constantinople his readiness to claim the hand of the Princess Eudocia. Fourteen years ago the two children had been affianced; never in the interval had they set eyes upon each other. Eudocia, now fifteen, was to receive a bridegroom of whom she had not the faintest and most childlike remembrance. Valentinian could better recall the lovely little girl, but scarcely troubled his head now to decide, whether the latest accounts of her beauty rendered him in love with love, rather than with his bride-elect. Volusianus,

---

* Instead of being a younger child of Theodosius, the Facilla who died in 435 may possibly have been his eldest sister.

the Prefect of Rome, and one of the greatest nobles of the West, came to Constantinople as Placidia's ambassador, to make the diplomatic* arrangements necessitated by the approaching marriage.

During the whole interval the two courts had maintained cordial and close relations. To review them as briefly as possible we must revert to the year 422 when, by the aid of Theodosius' troops, Valentinian III. was seated on the throne of the West.

It is a curious fact that, of the two commanding men who supported the Regent's power, one should have been her enemy allied with the Huns in the interests of the usurper John, and the other should have lost Africa to the Empire. "In the melancholy season of Placidia's exile and distress, Boniface alone had maintained her cause with unshaken fidelity, and the treasures and troops of Africa had essentially contributed to extinguish the rebellion.† When in turn, the count, as victim of his rival's intrigues and of his own credulity, was besieged in Hippo by the Vandals, Placidia again besought the assistance of the East, and "the Italian fleet and army were reinforced by Aspar who sailed from Constantinople with a powerful armament in A.D. 430." The defeat sustained by the united Roman forces decided the fate of the province, and all the cities of the East and West were filled with those unfortunate refugees who fled before the victorious barbarians. The letters of Bishop Theodoret recount the adventures and sufferings of some of these. Many sought refuge in Constantinople, conducted thither by the returning fleet, and the government made all the provision it could for them, out of sympathy for the bereaved Empire of Valentinian.

The Empress Placidia had penetration enough to receive her discomfited viceroy at Ravenna with magnanimity and confidence, his losses and blunders notwithstanding. The influence of Count Boniface, who was a loyal subject and sincere Catholic, might have made for good with the young Augustus, had the minister not met with an untimely end as the result of a duel with his exasperated rival Ætius. The Empress immediately deprived the latter of his military command, proclaimed him a rebel and obliged him to retire beyond the confines of the empire. "The republic was deprived," says the historian, "by their mutual discord, of the service of the two men," who might fittingly be called "the last of the Romans." Notwithstanding the support of Ætius and Boniface, from the year 423, Placidia had ruled by the light of no wisdom or valour superior to her own, when the empire might have had the benefit, and Valentinian the example, of really great administration. Ætius was indebted to his constant friendship with the Huns for the influence which presently enabled him to reinstate himself with

---

* Such as the final surrender to the Eastern Empire of Western Illyricum bargained for in 422, see. c xiv.

† Gibbon.

Placidia's government. From 433 to 454 Ætius ruled in the West, as Stilicho had done before him, as commander-in-chief of the army, as patrician and frequently as consul. "His prudence rather than his virtue, engaged him to leave the grandson of Theodosius in the possession of the purple, and Valentinian was permitted to enjoy the peace and luxury of Italy, while the patrician appeared in the glorious light of a hero and a patriot, who supported near twenty years the ruins of the Western empire."

Thus in 436 the irresponsible young Augustus was enabled to take a leisurely journey to the East and to prolong the festivities of his marriage. The ceremony was to have taken place at Thessalonica, midway between the two empires, but Valentinian pressed on to Constantinople, there to meet not only his bride and her parents, but the Augusta Pulcheria, and possibly his sister Honoria.

The Empress Athenais had now reached the zenith of her career. It was fitting that she who had been raised to imperial rank should, in turn, see her daughter married to an emperor. Eudocia had been betrothed so long that the ceremony of the 'subarrhatio,' or ring-giving might have been repeated, but until the day of the wedding, the bride and bridegroom were not permitted to meet. Life for a Byzantine maiden was secluded enough in the fifth century. Before reaching the marriageable age of fourteen or fifteen, she was persistently immured in the women's apartments of her father's house, and high or low in station, was never allowed to meet the man whom her parents, or a professional match-maker, should secure for her husband, until the wedding evening. The installation of a wife generally took place amid such scenes of riot and debauchery that St. Chrysostom exhausted even his invective in denouncing them. But in a devout court like that of Theodosius and Pulcheria, we may suppose the bridal of Valentinian and Eudocia to have been most decorously conducted and accompanied by a holy function in St. Sophia or in the Imperial Chapel of St. Stephen in the Daphne.

In the meantime the ministers of the Court settled the details of the dowry, and the Prefect of Constantinople put the city in readiness for a week of fête and holiday.

There is a human interest about such an event as a wedding which is the same in all ages. Difficult as it may be now to recall with any vividness the atmosphere and life of the Byzantine court of the fifth century, it only requires an effort of sympathy to divine the most intimate thoughts and feelings of that far-away bride and her parents. It needs only the heart at this moment, to tell of Theodosius, Athenais, and their daughter; of Placidia and Valentinian, or even of Pulcheria and Honoria. The play which is always played so brightly against the impenetrable curtain of the future which only rises on its sequel, was enacted in 436 at Constantinople, amid the tears and smiles, the hopes and prayers, which have been its accompaniment from the beginning, and will be to the end. If the happiness of Eudocia only served to throw Honoria's misery into still more violent contrast, it showed the inequality there ever is in human lives. Honoria's heart may well have broken with self-pity, all the more pathetic for its loneliness: the proud and happy Athenais little thought she would never see her only child again. St. Pulcheria prayed lest the vows made to man should disappoint a trusting soul as those to God have never done.

The Imperial Palace was filled with the retinue of the Western emperor, and all the nobility of Constantinople mingled with that of Rome and of Ravenna. The two halves of the empire were once more closely knit together in the happiness of a bride, and every augury, down to the blessing of the venerable Patriarch, St. Proclus, spoke well for the coming years. The newly wedded pair left Constantinople shortly afterwards, and wintered at Thessalonica en route for Italy. Before Eudocia reached Milan, her mother had set sail for the Holy Land on a pilgrimage of gratitude.

Eudocia's love for Valentinian was deep and lasting, only he who can account for a woman's heart may say why. It seems that the Byzantine bride had pledged her constancy to the husband imperial fate bestowed upon her with a gladness as fortunate as convenient! She loved him at first sight, with the unreasoning love which only time may justify—or sap. And in her case, as in many another woman's, her love was without the pride which might mitigate the woe of disillusionment. The griefs in store for her could inflict only a sense of outraged long-suffering which no anger against him might anæsthetise. For Valentinian proved a vicious as well as a feeble descendant of Theodosius the Great. His upbringing had entirely spoiled what original worth his nascent character possessed; but for this the times were more to be blamed than his mother. The age was only comparable in luxury to the last century of the Republic and the first of the Empire. Valentinian had neither courage nor the instinct of his rank, only its license and pride. Nothing but imperial tradition, and the semblance of sovereignty, could be honoured in so unworthy a scion of a great house. His effeminate education had rendered him incapable of the conduct of war and government, and had engrafted upon him a taste for the lowest pursuits and vices. His ordinary associates were soothsayers, charlatans, fortune-tellers. Although he had in Eudocia a wife whose devotion, birth and beauty, left him nothing to desire, his life was chequered by irregular passions and entanglements. He sacrificed his wife, as nobler men may do for nobler ends, to the circumstances of his lot, and to the limitations of his own nature. Within a short while Eudocia bereft herself of every argument love could suggest whereby to induce his loyalty, and when she saw them failing constantly, her hope failed too. For her greatest bitterness was only prompted by her love, and when a man takes a loving woman at her angry word he unwittingly reveals the narrowness of his own soul.   So she lived through nineteen wretched years, getting so little used to her griefs, that when at last an avenger's sword struck Valentinian down, his widowed Empress wept over this latest of them as though it overshadowed all the rest.

If Placidia had forseen this life in store for her daughter-in-law, Theodosius and Athenais had not.   The marriage with Valentinian was a brilliant match for their daughter and a useful tie between the halves of the Empire.

Honoria, the supernumerary in all that crowded pageant, remained in exile.   Her brother came—and went, and his sister's heart kindled with such a hatred of the fortunate, and such a bitterness to Rome, that presently she did not hesitate to stoop to any degradation to revenge herself upon the empire and its rulers.

CHAPTER XIX

DURING the embassy of the Illustrious Volusien at Constantinople there came a lady to that city, at his distinguished invitation, whose humble guise as a nun from Palestine, and whose modest retinue detracted nothing from that fame of her which had long ago been noised throughout the Roman world.

St. Melania enjoyed the hospitality of the Patrician Lausus, a noble Byzantine who had been, if indeed he was not for the second time in 437, Grand Chamberlain at court. Through her host no less than through the western Ambassador, Melania could have compassed a personal, beyond a formal, introduction to every member of the imperial family, but especially to the Augusta Pulcheria. For it was owing to special representations from St. Cyril that the latter had again advanced the Patrician Lausus to an influential position in which his staunch orthodoxy might tell against Nestorianism in high places.

The Palace of Lausus was situated in the most aristocratic region of Constantinople, near the western flank of the Hippodrome, on the beautiful highway of the 'Mese,' which led from the Augustaeum to the Golden Gate. It was cut off from neighbour-ing buildings by the narrow streets which in Constantinople as in Pompeii, must have obstructed every view and vista, and filled the city with shadow. High walls on either side of these lanes hid the houses and courtyards behind them, whose balconies or sun-stages ('solaria') supported on light columns overhung the street, and were furnished with flights of steps leading to the pavement below.

All the sunshine and cheerfulness of the neighbourhood were concentrated in the avenue of the Mese. Every now and again as the litter of some clarissimus stopped at the monumental portico of one or another of the palaces, the gate opened giving a glimpse of a classic garden within, radiant with greenery and snow-white statuary. The thoroughfare was crowded with sumptuous carriages and richly caparisoned horses; with the trains of persons of consequence who never stirred abroad without attendants carrying chairs, fans, etc.; with the favourites of the factions, the charioteers or 'heniochi' accompanied by crowds of patrons and admirers; with monks, and ecclesiastics; with philosophers in long grey cloaks, rhetoricians in bright crimson, and physicians in their distinguishing blue. It was a scene full of vivacity and colour, only to be described by a Lombard* or a Sienkiewicz.†

Slaves lounged about the steps of the porticoes, whiling away their idle hours with the incidents and the gossip of the street; occasionally a slight diversion was caused when a beggar or an unkempt rustic monk stopped to apply at the porter's lodge. Sometimes quite a little assembly gathered in the itinerant guest chamber of one of the larger palaces, when the servants gave themselves airs in virtue of their lord's liberality. Here the slave who scoured out the hypocaust in the baths, lounged with the grace of an Athenian athlete; there the eunuch custodian of the servants' quarters discussed theology with the bearers of my lady's litter ; and yonder a pretty page or two, more like girls than boys, played mora in the sun with their companions.

Within the courtyard of the Palace of Lausus all was sunshine, charm and freshness. Much wealth had been expended in order to give the garden-like enclosure the appearance of a landscape in miniature according to the fashion of the day. Trees waved and fountains played, and artificial cascades poured over counterfeited cliffs into pools stocked with fish. The air was musical with the plash of water, and sweet with the scent of the flowers which everywhere clustered round the marble basins of the fountains, and reflected themselves in the shining pavements. Here a gardener dictated operations to a group of underlings, soberly garbed in short sleeved tunics of undyed wool, with a belt round the waist and a hood against the sun; there a workman ruminated on the latest sermon in St. Sophia, as, squatting on his heels in his multicoloured cassock, he arranged the tesseræ on some new piece of the mosaic path. The quadrangle was so filled with palms and shrubs and statuary that much of the façade of the palace was hidden from sight.

The main building—that portion which faced the portico and contained all the principal apartments inhabited by the Patrician and his family—had a sunny aspect. Its two-storied elevation was accordingly graced by a sort of double portico, above and below, or rather by two covered galleries, which not only formed a convenient means of communication between all parts of the house, but which gave the building character and features. The massive square, pillars in front of the lower storey supported a plain or carved entablature, upon which rose the more ornamental columns, with a balustrade between them, of the upper floor. This gallery was framed in marble, and under its yawning shadow, white statues and the white dresses of women made blue patches in the brilliant picture. In the vestibules and galleries of the palace were collected many of the most famous gems of Grecian art, the celebrated Venus of Cindos ; a nude work of Praxiteles ; the

Lindian Athene in smaragdite ; the Samian Hera of Lysippus ; a chryselephantine, or ivory and gold statue of Zeus by Phidias which Pericles had placed in the temple at Olympia ;* and innumerable other treasures. A stairway open to the air led from the court-yard and the lower portion of the house, to the upper corridor. It issued under a graceful portico of its own, whose projecting cornice and airy columns added much to the beauty of the façade. Mosquito nets flapped lazily across the doorways and the perforated windows ; festoons of graceful creepers made wreaths around the marble shafts, and streamed over balustrade and balcony in bouquets of oriental colour. All was beautiful as a classic, and luxurious as an eastern, dream.

On either side of the courtyard ran the annexes of the palace, suites of apartments in which guests like Melania, and possibly like the Empress Placidia's envoy himself, were courteously lodged. Here also were accommodated all the more important officers of the Patrician's household. Everywhere the men were separated from the women, but on both floors the distribution and destination of the various rooms and cubicles were alike. The 'gynæcaeum' or women's portion exactly corresponded to the men's. The architec-tural ingenuity of the Byzantine builder had been, however, much exercised to devise the means of communication between the various parts of the palace, as, according to the dictates of its importance, its diversity had grown. The simple plan of the original house had been in the course of time confused by the addition of baths, oratories, pavilions, courts, granaries, vaults, storehouses, stables, greenhouses and new gardens.

The transition from her grave and quiet convent in the remote Holy Land to this luxurious establishment at Constantinople must have turned St. Melania's thoughts to her own old home in Rome, and, leading them back in retrospect over the years of a lifetime nearly spent, have confirmed her in the faith that renunciation had been the better part.

The resources of the Palace of Lausus were far more taxed by the reception of the Illustrious Volusien and his Roman train, than by the housing of his niece and her attendants. Within the high blind walls of that great establishment all was life and animation. Down in the cool underground kitchens an army of cooks and scullions prepared the banquets, and painted more crosses and sacred monograms than ever upon their pots and pans and walls and tables, to ensure a blessing on their work.† Never were the

---

* The description of the Palace of Lausus is, roughly, adapted from the account of a Byzantine mansion in a work " Abitatione Umana " translated from the French, but the enumeration of its art treasures comes from Mr. W. G. Holmes' " The Age of Justinian and Theodora."

† During this reign there was some legislation to restrain the too familiar use of these sacred signs. They were forbidden, for instance, to be painted or engraved upon the pavements or on the commoner objects in daily use.

'apothecae' more richly stored with flasks of oil and wine, with chests of grapes and olives; never were the wardrobe closets so filled with precious stuffs and flowing silken robes; never had the wine presses poured such an incessant stream of purple juice, nor the slaves of the whole establishment been kept so constantly busy. Even the students in the library had to close the amaria and leave dust to accumulate on their patrons' scrolls and manuscripts, in order to place their time and pens at the service of his noble guests. In the womens' quarters needles flew and shuttles darted quite as fast as tongues, and nothing was talked of from morning till night but the approaching marriage of the Princess Eudocia and the consequent festivities.

In the comparative seclusion of her own apartments, however, the Lady Melania was occupied with other cares than these. She had come to Constantinople with an object far beside them all. Her uncle, Volusien, had sent for her to meet him there, but neither he nor she could have forseen how timely their interview was to be. The Roman Ambassador was now an old man. He had been, all his life a pagan, and even St. Augustine had failed to persuade him as to the truth of that religion which dictated the ascetic life his niece had led. The distinguished member of a noble Roman family, Volusien, like so many others, had taken refuge in Africa after the fall of Rome in 410. His mother had pressed the Bishop of Hippo to open a correspondence with her son with a view to his conversion. St. Augustine readily complied, urging Volusien to read the Christian scriptures and to submit to him the difficulties he found in them. The young man replied with great courtesy and respect. He was then living and thinking with a circle of friends at Carthage whose comments on the conduct of the virgin Demetrias in 414, and of the view taken of it by Christian thinkers like Augustine and Jerome, doubtless ill-prepared him to appreciate the religious ideal as it was then enthusiastically exemplified by the educated women of his own rank and wealth. He wrote, certainly, to St. Augustine about his difficulties, and the letter was covered by way of explanation, by one from Count Marcellinus, the Bishop's friend, who had presided at the celebrated Conference against the Donatists in 411. Nothing came, however, of this correspondence, and St. Augustine must have spoken regretfully of the incident to Melania. St. Augustine died in 430, and every word of his was now treasured in the memory of his friends. When the aged nun set foot in the great city whither Volusien had come, the admonitions of their mutual friend were present to her mind. When the Ambassador from the Court of Ravenna fell ill and lay near to death in this strange capital, the great Bishop's recommendation of him to her solicitude and prayers seemed to have borne fruit at last. St. Melania was now looking for one of those unlikely conversions which never astonish faith.

This lady came of that galaxy of 'valiant' women whose

unparalleled renunciations, half a century ago, had filled all Rome with consternation and astonishment. Her grandmother, the elder Melania, had been the intimate friend and associate of St. Jerome's converts on the Aventine, and like Paula and Eustochium, herself left Italy for the East and spent the rest of her life at Jerusalem. Only once did she return to Rome, and that happened in 408, on receipt of the news that her son's daughter, Melania the younger, having lost both her children, had gained the consent of her husband "that they should bind themselves by mutual vows to serve God in perpetual chastity."

The elder Melania "advised Pinian and his wife to give what they possessed to the poor and to choose some remote retirement. This counsel they readily embraced," in concert with a number of relations. After an interval of four years, during which Publicola, the father of Melania the younger, died, his mother again set out for Palestine, accompanied part of the way by Albina, her widowed daughter-in-law; Melania her granddaughter, and Pinian; a niece Avita and her husband; and their son and daughter—all having vowed themselves to a life of chastity and prayer.

"Albina, Melania the younger and Pinian," continues Alban Butler, "first made over their estates in Spain and Gaul, reserving those which they possessed in Italy, Sicily and Africa. They made free eight thousand of their slaves, and those who would not accept their freedom they gave to the brother of Melania. Their most precious furniture they bestowed on churches and altars. Their first retreat was in retired country places in Campania and Sicily, and their time they spent in prayer, reading, and visiting the poor and sick in order to comfort and relieve them. For this end they also sold their estates in Italy, and passed into Africa, where they made some stay, first at Carthage, and afterwards at Tagaste, under the direction of St. Alypius, who was at that time bishop of this city. In a journey they made to Hippo to see St. Augustine, the people there seized Pinian demanding that their bishop should ordain him priest. But he escaped out of their hands by promising that if he ever took holy orders it should be to serve their Church. The poverty and austerity in which they lived seven years at Tagaste appeared extreme. Melania by degrees arrived at such a habit of long fasting as often to eat only once a week, and to take nothing but bread and water, except that on feast days she added oil to her bread. Their occupation was to read and copy books. In 417 they left Africa for Jerusalem where Melania the elder had died some years before. They continued to lead the same manner of life, and the years passed on most peacefully, marked by the deaths of first one and then another of the unworldly company. First St. Eustochium died, and then St. Jerome. In 433 Melania laid her mother Albina to rest, and barely a year before the date when we find her with Volusien in Constantinople, the saintly wife had closed her husband's eyes, and looked for the last time on the face of the dearest companion of her life and sacrifice.

At the moment when her uncle's missive reached her, St. Melania had just retired to a convent she herself had built and was now about to rule.   She was called upon to exchange her cell, the coarse rug upon the floor that formed her bed, and her penitential fare for the luxuries of a long forgotten life in the world's great eastern capital.   Aged and worn, she had no hesitation in undertaking the arduous journey, buoyed up, as she was, by the hope of succeeding at last where St. Augustine had failed !

It seems as though Volusien fell ill after the marriage of his imperial master with the Byzantine Princess, for the negotiations that preceded it were neither interrupted nor delayed.   Thus Melania had some opportunity of acceding to the wishes of the Augusta Pulcheria, who longed to receive her at court, and to hear from her lips the account of such a life as had inspired the ruling of her own.

Emperor, Empress, and Augusta were at one in their esteem for the holy and renowned Melania ; she was received at court with the utmost cordiality and deference.   Theodosius treated the saintly visitor with filial rather than imperial respect, and Athenais conceived for her immediately a strong and beautiful affection.

She came indeed into the imperial circle like that earthly angel, who winning all, serves all, and makes a common confidence the imperceptible basis of reconciliations and new peace.   The Emperor listened to her counsels with a silence prompted as much by their intrinsic wisdom as by the dictates of courtesy.   But woman's logic and woman's theology never count for much, nor can age sustain argument without discomfiture at the hands of an ungenerous opponent. We need not imagine that the worn and fragile Melania held any wordy disputes with Theodosius or the Nestorians.   In her distant home among the nuns and monks of the Holy Land she had indeed followed the recent controversy with an interest like St. Pulcheria's, but what she said about it now had the profundity of the soul rather than of the intellect.   It seems to have sufficed.   It bore good fruit.   The city was still agitated by the subsiding tumult, and Nestorius' tracts and pamphlets served to keep alive the controversial spirit so inimical to religious peace. Melania persuaded the Emperor to suppress these, and something of the assurance of her own transparent faith entered into his vacillating soul and stilled its restlessness.   He never seems to have looked back again upon the doubts and regrets it was his duty to forget.

The Empress, too, benefited by the conversation of Melania. The beautiful Greek bore a sad heart under her magnificent robes, and despite a brave front lifted to the world, she wept for the loss of her children.   With the departure of Eudocia, Theodosius and Athenais were left childless, and there seemed to be no likelihood that the Theodsian dynasty would continue, at least in the eastern Empire. St. Cyril seems to indicate by a phrase in one of his letters that in 430 the Empress had given birth to a son, and other slight inferences point to his name as Arcadius, but this child must have died in his earliest infancy to account for the historians' total silence on the point. An air of sadness seems to have settled down upon the court. Athenais was too intellectual a woman to have been spoilt by the show of things ; even Imperial greatness had not dazzled her outlook on life, and now that something of its promise had failed she was ready for the lessons Melania might have to teach her. In the course of a few years such sorrows as are peculiar to mothers, be they high or low, had softened her sympathies, and the force of Christian holiness came home to her, in the presence of this nun, as it had never done before.

Only a truly holy woman can efface herself for the encouragement of another's influence where her own has failed ; only a Saint can rejoice when a stranger succeeds by means which, in her own hands, have been too familiar to carry weight. St. Pulcheria's heart must have been strengthened in the silence with which it leaned on Melania's. The anxious and state-worn Augusta welcomed this graceful intervention, and noted the effects of it as gratefully as did the Patriarch.

There was something in Melania's aged face that reflected the sunsets of the Holy land. There was an air of peace about her like that which rested on the hills of Bethlehem, and a serenity caught from the spacious silence of nature and the inward life. Her presence in the Imperial court was a beautiful anomaly. Her conversation was the gentle easily-satisfied talk of an old lady too familiar with her subject to present it with any art to her listeners. She had little to relate, only something to describe. And to her fifth century audience, the Imperial sisters, the Empress, and their ladies, the interest would lie in her account of the buildings, the ceremonies, the relics and the ecclesiastical personel of the Holy City, rather than in its eternal hills and mystic atmosphere. They would talk of St. Helena and the Holy Sepulchre, of Bishop Juvenalis, of the monks and convents, of St. Melania's own oratory now building, of the pilgrims and the hospitals, of the stream of Romans from the west, rather than of the holiest memories connected with Jerusalem. Thus the Byzantine imagination enshrined the earthly traces of Our Blessed Lord as in an ornate frame. The simplicity of His life, copied in Melania's poor dress and simple mien, was honoured at Jerusalem in this manner, as the nun herself was honoured by the deference of a Byzantine court. The Emperor and the Augusta gloried in legend and tradition, and loved to hear how the great ones of the earth heaped their treasures on the holy sites. And the idea of pilgrimage took vivid hold on Eudocia's lively mind, diverting it from its sorrows, and kindling new enthusiasms.

During the dying illness of the Patrician Volusien, St. Melania remained in Constantinople, constantly at his side with her gentle ministrations and her words of Christian consolation.   She had little difficulty now in persuading him of the "sweet reasonableness" of a faith in which, if it is difficult to live, it is extremely comforting to die.   To some minds, perhaps, the solution that faith affords of all the perplexed problems of existence, is never welcome until the sands of vigorous life run out so far, that hope must be given up of arriving at a human understanding of them. The humility of our mortality is to such men a greater blessing than the power of intellect.   And so Volusien,* at last, perceived. He was baptised, and died shortly afterwards in St. Melania's arms.

Thereupon her task was done.   Anxious to return home for Easter in the following year, 438, Melania left Constantinople as soon as might be.   The Empress had already announced her intention of making a pilgrimage to the Holy Land in obedience to Theodosius' wish that she should return thanks at the Holy Sepulchre for the happy wedding of their daughter.   But Melania went as she had come, humbly and noiselessly, not waiting for the escort of the Imperial retinue.   She may have seen the departure of Eudocia and Valentinian for the West, or indeed, she may have left the capital before the bridal pair.

It was very possibly her presence and her conversation that suggested to the Emperor this votive journey of his wife. Theodosius felt an earnest wish to thank Heaven for all the blessings of his life and reign, and as neither he nor the Augusta could absent themselves for any length of time from the conduct of affairs, the glorious duty of making a pilgrimage to Jerusalem fell to Eudocia's happy lot.   In the fourth century the Holy City was not only the sanctuary of the Roman world, but the cynosure of all thoughts and devotion.   The journey thither was become so popular that its dangers and fatigues counted for less than they do to-day.   There was an Itinerary drawn up giving all the routes and hospices on the way from Bordeaux to Jerusalem, the Baedecker of the day as it has been called.   Pilgrims high and low from all the corners of the Empire travelled slowly eastwards, and made of their journey and their sojourn in the Holy Land an epoch in their religious life.   In an article entitled "Un pèlerinage en Palestine et en Egypte de 386-387." (Revue des Deux Mondes t. 57).   M. Amedée Thierry takes us this very pilgrimage with St. Jerome and St. Paula, and in the "Peregrinatio Etheriae," we have the original account of a Holy Week spent in Jerusalem by a lady who had come all the way from Galicia in Spain.

The Empress Eudocia set out upon her journey late in the

---

* There is some question as to the identification of Placidia's envoy with the Volusien of St. Augustine's correspondence, but Catholic writers consider them to have been one and the same.

year 437, or early in 438, historians differ slightly. There is no reason to suppose that unhappiness between herself and the Augusta served to recommend the project to either of them, as modern writers, glad of some commonplace motives, would suggest. Pulcheria and Eudocia were not yet estranged to that extent, nor had anything so far occurred which had not speedily yielded to some reconciliatory influence. Tillemont scouts the idea that before this journey either the Augusta or the Empress had found it difficult to live in charity with one another. Eudocia was entrusted by her husband with large sums of money for Bishop Juvenalis to distribute among the poor of Jerusalem, and, among other royal gifts and presents, with a golden cross beset with gems, to be erected in the Martyrium. Her 'pilgrimage' seems to have been a very brilliant affair. It served as an occasion of fête for all the fortunate cities en route, and moreover, for an outburst of classicism on the part of Athenais, who rejoiced once more at Antioch, to look round on an audience of eager faces. The Empress, despite her sincerely religious intention, meant to make of her journey a progress in Imperial state. She was equally pleased to receive the flattered hospitality of the Asian cities, as the religious welcome of their Bishops, equally ready to bestow her smiles upon the people as her alms upon their Churches.

One January day, then, the Empress took leave of her husband and his sister, and amid a large gathering of senators and nobles stepped into the gorgeous barge waiting to convey her and the principal members of her suite to the vessel in which they were to sail. It seemed as though an entire fleet weighed anchor, so enormous was the train and escort of the wife of an Emperor of the East. The people densely lined the quays along the shore, cheering enthusiastically as the purple sails bellied in the wind, and the silken bunting streamed out before it, brilliant flecks of colour against the sunny blue. "Long life to the Empress Eudocia! Long life to our Augusta Eudocia!" roared the people, and across the water came the responsive shouts.

Nothing is more impressive than the departure of a majestic vessel. So proud and beautiful, so strong and dauntless, and yet such a mote in the immensities of sea or sky! Away she moves with her frail human freight, into infinitude and silence. What above, below or around but the Providence of God, and the loneliness of unbroken light!

CHAPTER XX

ONE day in the year 437 the Patriarch ascended the ambo of St. Sophia and began to preach upon his predecessor John.   He was interrupted by applause, and presently the attentive multitude broke out into the demand "Restore to us our exiled Patriarch. Restore to us the body of our father John!"

St. Proclus hastened to the Emperor and the Augusta, and both assented with alacrity to his proposal.   For thirty years the embalmed body of the exile had been lying in its humble tomb in the Chapel of St. Basiliscus on the road to Pityus.   It was now decided to translate these relics to the capital.

"In every city through which the coffin was carried it was received by the rejoicing homage of multitudes of ecclesiastics as well as of the people.   At Chalcedon Theodosius had sent an Imperial tribune to receive it; and he himself awaited its arrival in the midst of his senators and high officials and soldiers."   The Augusta Pulcheria and her ladies formed the second most important group to do the cortége honour.   This may have been one of the rare occasions when the disgraced Honoria could fittingly appear in public.   "It was now January 27th, 438.   So vast was the concourse of vessels of all sizes that in the rhetorical figure of the contemporary historian 'the Propontis was transformed into a Continent.'   It was night, and the surface of the sea reflected the blaze of innumerable torches as the citizens poured out in their myriads to welcome home the mortal remains of 'the teacher of the universe, and the mouth of gold,' as Pulcheria and Theodosius called him.   No sooner was the coffin transferred from the Imperial dromon to the shore than a stately procession formed to conduct it to the Church of the Holy Apostles.   The entire route was densely lined with crowds among whom no two opinions any longer existed as to the merits of the quarrel which, so many years ago, had convulsed the city.   Women who had been among the most inveterate of the saint's enemies, now saw the court itself doing reverence to one who had never made a truce with its vanities and vices, while the Patriarch shed tears of joy over the restoration of his master.

To St. Pulcheria and to Theodosius, above all, the event was deeply moving.   They desired that this translation should not only be a triumph but an act of penitential reparation. They accompanied the holy remains to the church where their father and mother lay—where Flacilla had been recently interred, where they themselves would one day lie among the bones of their Flavian predecessors. No sooner was the coffin set down than Theodosius knelt before it side by side with Pulcheria. Then he stripped off his purple mantle and laid it over the saintly relics. Leaning his forehead against the coffin he prayed aloud for the forgiveness of Arcadius and Eudoxia, while his sister prayed inwardly that this silent reconciliation on earth might have its counterpart in the other world whither her mother's shrinking soul had been so dreadly summoned. St. Chrysostom had come back, brought by willing hands along the dreary track of his relentless journey. The pitiless suffering of soul and body was over now and counting to his eternal glory ; the weary pressing onward, at every step farther and farther away from those to whom his heart yearned back, was all reversed. Olympias herself had rejoined him in that sweet Country to which he had turned all her thoughts. But on earth, the little infant princess who had lain in his arms at baptism, now grown a woman after his own ideal, was making reparation before the whole wide world. Before the corpse was finally enclosed in the golden shell prepared for it, St. Proclus seated it upon the Patriarchal chair to which it had done such honour in life, and a great shout of salutation arose " Receive thy throne once more, Oh Father ! " Then, not far from the tombs of Arcadius and Eudoxia, the body of St. Chrysostom * was reinterred, and he who had been the Bishop's devoted secretary read the solemn prayers in the liturgy for a translation of holy relics.

This event seems to have taken place during the absence of the Empress, or at least just before her departure. The Constantinopolitans already congratulated themselves upon the wealth of holy relics which had gradually accumulated in the churches of their city, but Eudocia hoped to bring something back with her from Jerusalem which should enhance still further the reputation of their sanctity. The historian Tillemont enumerates these treasures, and leaves the truth of his list and of their authenticity an open question. In the year 440 St. Pulcheria discovered a treasure trove of this description in Constantinople itself, and added the bones of the celebrated forty martyrs to the altars of St. Thyrsus. We should be despising one whole aspect of that age if it were of no interest to us to know that the Byzantines prided themselves on the possession of the head of St. John the Baptist, in the Church belonging to the Palace at Hebdomon ; that the Church of the Holy Apostles possessed the relics of SS. Andrew, Luke, and Timothy, and of the Prophet Samuel !

---

* His relics are now at St. Peter's in Rome.

The Christians at Jerusalem are said to have sent the Augusta Pulcheria—possibly by the Empress—some garments supposed to have belonged to the Blessed Virgin Mary, among them, her girdle, which was entrusted to the Church of the Palace at Blachernae. The famous portrait of the Holy Mother attributed to St. Luke, also found its way thither. It continued to be venerated through the centuries until "when the Turks broke in," Mr. Hutton tells us, "the Janissaries seized the picture and cut it into fragments for charms."

To follow, then, the Byzantine Empress on her pilgrimage to the Holy Land:—

The fleet which carried her through the Hellespont sailed on past the Grecian archipelago, by Lesbos and Chios, the island home of Homer, by Samos, Rhodes and Cyprus, to the shores of Syria. The Imperial lady landed at Seleucia and proceeded in great state to Antioch, where she received an enthusiastic welcome, where she pronounced an oration in the Senate, and where she conceived the idea of writing an epic on the local martyrs Cyprian and Justina. At the date of Eudocia's visit, Antioch stood in its last Græco-oriental magnificence, and many of its most venerable monuments were falling into ruins. The palace of the 'Tetrapylon,' and the wide avenue of columns that cut right through the city were still the great features of the place, although age and the ravages of earthquakes had destroyed their pristine glory. In the myrtle and laurel woods of the Orontes Christian basilicas had taken the place of temples to the gods, and the oracles of the groves of Daphne had long been silenced. The most recent associations of the place were not even those of the caustic Emperor Julian, but of St. Chrysostom and Theodosius the Great, and lastly, of Nestorius.

The Empress was welcomed to the city, as became her highness, by the Patriarch and his clergy, and the Count of the East who had his residence there. She made a tremendous impression on the Antiochenes, and herself caught the infection of their high spirits. She pronounced her oration in the Senate house, from a throne of gold and gems, and declared her intention of enlarging the walls of the illustrious city whose guest she was. Seized with the proud remembrance of her Greek origin and Athenian education Eudocia concluded her address with the Homeric line.

"Of your race and blood to be I also glory!"

The people were transported with enthusiasm, and immediately voted her two statues, one of bronze to be erected in the Academy of Sciences and one of gold to be set up in the Senate House. Eudocia, indeed left many traces of her visit to Antioch. At her request the Emperor allowed the walls to be extended to the Daphne gate whose brazen doors were then gilded after the style of the Porta Aurea in Constantinople itself. A new and imposing

Basilica was built, statues of Theodosius and Valentinian were erected, the baths of Arcadius were restored, and large alms bestowed upon the poor.

The Itinerary compiled in 333 A.D. for the use of pilgrims to the Holy Land describes the route which Eudocia now took. It led from the Palace of the Daphne at Antioch to the Mediterranean viâ Laodicea and Tripolis, then to Berytus and by the old Phoenician towns of Tyre and Sidon, still celebrated for their costly textures and purple dyes. The Empress then sailed down the coast to Ptolemais, and passed the venerable Mount Carmel before she reached the busy Caesarea on the confines of the Province. Here she was received by the Byzantine Governor Palestinas, and by the Bishop of the city. She was conducted thence still farther through the country, by Maximinopolis, Stradela, Scythopolis to Aser and Nicapolis and to Aelia Capitolina itself. The Roman names throw a strange light over Bethesda, Sychem and Jerusalem, like that with which the incongruous history of this Imperial progress invests their memory. St. Melania came out to meet her "daughter," and escorted by a company of religious women Eudocia entered the Holy City. The unbroken chain of destiny, Gregorovius remarks, had led her from the olive groves of Athens to the palms of the distant city of David and Solomon. "Both wonderful centres marked for her the outset and the close of life: both were the opposite poles of human culture. Hellas was the objective of the intellect, as Jerusalem that of the soul. What Greece had been for the men of old, Palestine was for the new humanity. The Gospel had supplanted Homer. In the old capital of the Jews there had arisen religious ideas in the souls of poor high-minded men potent enough to overcome the long established dominion of the Olympian gods, the brilliant insight of philosophers, and the sum of antique knowledge. All the genius of the Hellenic past, all its science and art went for nothing in sight of the barren hills where Jesus had wandered speaking to His disciples of the grass and the little red lilies of the field." The key to the mystery of Jerusalem could only be found in those emotions of faith, devotion and renunciation which had sanctified Melania. Could the daughter of Leontius, the gorgeous Empress of Byzantium, hope to understand "the strange deep flowing poetry of Old Testament Judæism, the divine melancholy of the Psalms, the Sybilline sublimity of the Prophets, the titanic sorrow of Job, or the spirituality of the ancient world of the pastoral patriarchs?" These questions arise as the German writer dwells on his theme, but if a Greek or a Frenchman had written of Eudocia's journey might he not have asked something different? We cannot, at this distance of time, and through so different a perspective, undertake to say what might have been the thoughts prompted in Eudocia's mind by all she saw at Jerusalem. There is always the modernness of the present to overcome in appreciating the past ; the present at Jerusalem in the fifth century was a thing of force and obviousness.   Moreover the Empress was more sincere a Christian than they can ever be who regret Greek idealism.   If comparisons arose in her mind between the 'religion' she had abandoned and the faith of Christ, they would scarcely have been tinged with that sentimental tenderness which moderns are too ready to excuse.   She probably thought and felt, in the presence of the holy places, much as Pulcheria would have done, touched to the heart by their tender and sacred associations.

The Roman legions of Vespasian had long ago changed the blooming gardens of Herod into an arid wilderness around the city. Jerusalem herself, as Our Blessed Lord had known it, had been levelled to the dust, and the Ælia Capitolina to which Jerome and Paula's steps had turned, was but the city built by Hadrian from the ruins left by Titus.   By Eudocia's day, however, the pagan temples which had everywhere sprung up and desecrated the most holy sites, were replaced by Christian churches.   The Temple of Jupiter which had replaced that of Solomon on Mount Moriah had been torn down.   St. Helena restored the holy Sepulchre to the devotion of Christians in 326, when a temple to Venus being thrown down, this most sacred spot was believed to have been discovered in the foundations.   At the time of Eudocia's visit to the Holy City, the three principal churches were Anastasis, or Sanctuary of the Resurrection, containing the Holy Sepulchre, the Sanctuary of the Cross, and the great Basilica of Constantine, called the Martyrium. It was in the Anastasis that the daily offices, described by the Spanish pilgrim Etheria, took place, but the Eucharist on Sunday was celebrated in the Martyrium.

St. Gregory of Nyssa, who died in 394, has left us a terrible account of the moral corruption of the "lay" inhabitants of Jerusalem at that time.   He warned the pilgrims flocking thither that all the cities of the East were infected with pestiferous vices, but that Jerusalem was worse than any.   He branded it as filled with thieves, adulterers, murderers, poison-mixers and idolaters.   It was populated, on the banishment of the Jews, by a low class of Syrians, whose religion was nothing but a mixture of Christianity with the cults of Astarte and Mithras.   If the Crusaders of later times were unable to live up to the standard of religion they professed, and disgraced the Holy Land with their revelries and crimes and feuds, little wonder that the streams of pilgrim-adventurers in earlier centuries came out of the ordeal no better.   The domestic vices of Jerusalem increased with the popularity of the pilgrimage, but were not sufficient to strip this of its ideality, or to destroy the inexpressible joy with which it was undertaken by the devout.   Nothing has ever been able to extinguish the halo which surrounds Golgotha and the Mount of Olives, or the light which lies on Bethlehem and the holy river Jordan.

But the city of Jerusalem was also peopled by monks and nuns ;

with the exception of Egypt, no other province of the Roman Empire numbered so many ascetics, religious and hermits as Palestine. There were cells in the Holy City, upon the surrounding hills, in the ravines and waste places. The Empress Eudocia stayed, so historians suppose, at the Convent of St. Melania, and the venerable foundress introduced her to the holy places, and to the nuns of St. Paula, and others. She studied the 'Onomasticon' of Eusebius, a sort of religious guide to Palestine and Jerusalem, which St. Jerome had translated, enlarged, and revised.

One day, on the occasion of the dedication of Melania's Oratory on Golgotha, the Empress received some hurt to her foot, but upon her return home to the convent it was found to be as well as ever. The fact is noted by those who would like to cry " A miracle!" in the story of her pilgrimage.

Bishop Juvenal, who had been one of St. Cyril's ardent supporters at the Council of Ephesus, was probably known to the Empress, and now played an important part as her ecclesiastical host at Jerusalem. She must have had many interviews with him relative to the disposal of the large sums of money she was entrusted to place in his hands. So well and so charitably were they spent that the Athenian lady became Jerusalem's greatest benefactress after St. Helena. Every facility was accorded her to attend the various religious ceremonies in the great basilicas, and to behold their treasures. If Eudocia were in the city during Easter week, either in 438, or in the following year, her letters to Byzantium (full and enthusiastic as those of so literary a lady were likely to be), may have substantially resembled those of the Spanish pilgrim Etheria. Perhaps it would be no dishonesty to quote these by way of illustration.*

"When the morning of the Sabbath begins to dawn," she says in one of them, "the Bishop offers the Oblation. And at the Dismissal, the Archdeacon lifts his voice and says, "Let us all be ready to-day at the seventh hour in the Lazarium." And so all go to the Lazarium, that is, Bethany, situated at about the second milestone from the city. And as they go from Jerusalem to the Lazarium, there is, about five hundred paces from the latter place, a church in the street on that spot where Mary the sister of Lazarus met with the Lord. Here, when the Bishop arrives, all the monks meet him, and the people enter the church, and one hymn and one antiphon are said, and that passage is read in the Gospel where the sister of Lazarus meets the Lord. [Now forasmuch as in that province some of the people know both Greek and Syriac, while some know Greek alone and others only Syriac; and because the Bishop, although he knows Syriac, yet always speaks Greek and never Syriac, there is always a priest standing by who, when the Bishop speaks Greek, interprets into Syriac, that

---

V. the 'Peregrinatio Etheriae' appended to Mgr. Duchesne's "Christian Worship."

all may understand what is being taught. And because all the lessons that are read in the church must be read in Greek, someone always stands by who interprets them into Syriac for the people's sake, that they may always be edified. Moreover, the Latins here, who understand neither Syriac nor Greek, in order that they be not disappointed have (all things) explained to them, for there are other brothers and sisters knowing both Greek and Latin who translate into Latin for them]. Then, after prayer has been said, and when all have been blessed, they go thence with hymns to the Lazarium. And on arriving at the Lazarium so great a multitude assembles that not only the place itself, but also the fields around are full of people. Hymns and antiphons suitable to the day and place are said, and likewise all the lessons are read. Then, before the Dismissal, notice is given of Easter, that is, the priest ascends to a higher place and reads the passage that is written in the Gospel, "then Jesus six days before the Passover came to Bethany," and the rest. . . . . . . Then all return to the city direct to the Anastasis, and lucernare [which they call here licinicon] takes place according to custom."

Eudocia would have written to Pulcheria of "Eleona, the very beautiful church which stands on the Mount of Olives," of Syon, of "the Imbomon, the place whence the Lord ascended into Heaven," and of the ceremony of the 'adoration' of the Cross on Good Friday.

"Before the sun rises they [the pilgrims] all go at once with fervour to Syon to pray at the column at which the Lord was scourged. And returning thence they sit for awhile in their houses and presently all are ready.

Then a chair is placed for the Bishop in Golgotha ; . . . . the Bishop duly takes his seat in the chair and a table covered with a linen cloth is placed before him ; the deacons stand round the table and a silver gilt casket is brought in. . . . . The casket is opened and (the wood of the Holy Cross) is taken out, and both it and the Title are placed upon the table. Now . . . . the Bishop, as he sits, holds the extremities of the sacred wood firmly in his hands, while the deacons who stand round, guard it. It is guarded thus because the custom is that the people, both faithful and catechumens, come one by one, and bowing down at the table, kiss the sacred wood and pass on. And because, I know not when, some one is said to have bitten off and stolen a portion of the sacred wood, it is thus guarded . . . . lest anyone should venture to do so again. And as all the people pass, one by one, all bowing themselves, they touch the Cross and the Title, first with their foreheads and then with their eyes, then they kiss the Cross and pass through, but none lays his hand upon it to touch it. When they have kissed the Cross . . . . a deacon stands holding the ring of Solomon, and the horn from which the kings were anointed ; they kiss the horn also and gaze at the ring . . . . . . all the people are passing through up to the sixth hour, entering by one door and going out by another. . . . ."

"On that day no announcement is made of a vigil at the Anastasis because it is known that the people are tired: nevertheless it is the custom to watch there. So all of the people who are willing, or rather, who are able, keep watch . . . . those of the clergy who are young and strong keep vigil there, and hymns and antiphons are said throughout the whole night until morning; a very great crowd also keep night-long watch, some from a late hour and some from midnight as they are able.

"Now from Easter to the fiftieth day, that is, to Pentecost, no one fasts here, not even those who are Aputactitae (taking only one meal a day). . . . On the fortieth day all go after the sixth hour to Bethlehem to celebrate the vigils . . . . in the church wherein is the cave where the Lord was born."

It would interest the Augusta at Constantinople to know how beautiful the churches were in Jerusalem. "It would be superfluous," says the letter, "to describe the adornment of the church in Golgotha, or of the Anastasis, or of the Cross, or of Bethlehem [on the feast of the Epiphany]; you see there nothing but gems and gold and silk. For if you look at the veils they are made wholly of silk striped with gold. The church vessels too of every kind, gold and jewelled, are brought out on that day, and indeed who could either reckon or describe the number and weight of the cereofala (candles on tall candlesticks) or of the cricindelae (tapers?) or of the lucernae (lamps), or of the various vessels? And what shall I say of the decoration of the fabric itself which Constantine, under his mother's influence, decorated with gold mosaic and costly marbles, as far as the resources of his kingdom allowed him?"

Surely such would have been the burden of Eudocia's circumstantial letters to her husband and sister, while she reserved the deeper thoughts and reflections for those poems of which so few, unfortunately, have survived until the present day.

The Empress returned to Constantinople shortly before the death of St. Melania, which occurred on December 31st, 439. She was entrusted by Bishop Juvenal with the arm of St. Stephen the Protomartyr, among other presents to the Imperial city, and a priest was told off specially to accompany this treasure on its journey.

The Augusta Pulcheria is supposed to have had some premonition of the approach of the Empress, thus preciously laden, and she probably accompanied Theodosius to Chalcedon to meet his wife. Eudocia came back amid rejoicings as hearty as her Godspeed had been, and it only wanted the discovery of 440 to make Constantinople itself a goal of pilgrimage for the devout.

About the year A.D. 320, forty Christian soldiers had suffered martyrdom under Constantine's pagan colleague Licinius, at Sebaste in Armenia. Their remains, transported at some subsequent time to Constantinople, were kept for many years in a garden outside the walls by a deaconess named Eusebia. When this lady found herself on the point of death she bequeathed the property to a community of monks from whom in turn she exacted the promise that they would bury her with the martyrs' remains placed over her head, and also that they would keep the whole transaction a profound secret. The monks faithfully fulfilled their engagement. At the same time they built a small oratory below Eusebia's tomb and above it was erected a small building with its flooring so contrived that access could easily be obtained by those who knew the secret to the relics which lay beneath.

In course of time an imperial officer of high rank, named Caesar, lost his wife, who happened to have been a dear friend of Eusebia. He had her interred close to the dead deaconess. Moreover he subsequently bought the whole plot of ground from the monks with the intention of building on it a sepulchre for himself near to that of his wife. In parting with the property the monks still preserved the secret of the relics of the forty martyrs. No sooner had Caesar obtained possession of the land than he caused it to be cleared of the little oratory already standing in order to build there a splendid church in honour of St. Thyrsus. It is related that after this building had been completed some years, the Augusta Pulcheria had a series of extraordinary visions. The martyr Thyrsus appeared to her three times and revealed to her that the remains of forty Christian martyrs were concealed in the foundations of the church! He enjoined upon her to take steps to have them placed beside his own tomb in order that they might share the honours accorded to himself. A similar communication was made to the Augusta by the forty martyrs themselves, who appeared to her in shining robes.

Inquiries were at once set afoot with a view to discovering the whereabouts of the relics. All the monks who knew anything about the circumstances of Eusebia's burial were already dead, with the exception of one called Polychonius. This aged recluse naturally refused to divulge a secret with regard to which he, like the rest of his community, had pledged himself to perpetual silence. Still, by dint of cross questioning, so much information was deduced from his replies as ultimately led to the discovery.

When the Augusta was at length informed of the probable locality in which the martyrs' remains would be found, she gave orders for the work of excavation to be begun. Near the pulpit of the church erected by Caesar, the coffin of his wife was found and at a short distance also that of Eusebia. Within the latter, when opened, was found a box bound round with bars of iron and lead, containing the sought-for treasures!

Into the aperture which appeared on the top of this box one of the courtiers who stood by thrust his cane, and thereupon such a delightful fragrance was exhaled on the air, that no doubt existed as to the nature of the casket's contents. As soon as the discovery was reported to St. Pulcheria, she hastened to the spot accompanied by the zealous Patriarch Proclus. They caused the coffer to be carefully opened. Two silver cases were exposed to view, embedded in all manner of pleasant perfumes and containing the precious relics. The princess, says an eye-witness, could scarcely find words to express her deep gratitude to Almighty God for having accounted her worthy to be their discoverer. She had them placed within a costly vase, and transferred with becoming ceremony to their more honourable destination.

It is a beautiful tale and full of the religious spirit of the times. The Church has always loved her dead, and seen in ashes of the the martyrs not only the material of their glorious resurrection but her ground of hope in the intercession of the Saints. " In spite of its flightiness and changeability," says the Abbé Marin, " the spirit of the Byzantines was profoundly religious. Their devotion, albeit somewhat naïve and credulous, was nevertheless always stirred by theological discussion and by the subtlest of Christian metaphysics. But, beyond everything, they loved exterior show, sacred hymns, pompous ceremonies and solemn processions : this population so volatile, so frivolous, so corrupt even, had yet, by some singular contradiction, a limitless admiration, a reverence pushed to the verge of superstition, for the austere-faced monk," the martyr, and the saint.

THEODOSIUS THE YOUNGER.

From a contemporary Coin, enlarged.

[*Face p.* 181.

CHAPTER XXI

THE great accomplishment of the reign of Theodosius the Younger was undoubtedly the codification of the Roman laws.

The year 438 witnessed the publication of the celebrated legal code known to history and to students of law, as the Codex Theodosianus. The labour of its compilation had extended over a period of nine years, and so great an undertaking entitles that mild and insignificant successor of the Caesars, who then occupied the eastern throne, to the gratitude and the remembrance of the whole civilised world. For this standard of justice not only out-lasted the fall of Rome and gave stability to the Byzantine Empire, but inspired barbarian peoples with that spirit of equity and temperance upon which modern legislation has been built. The Theodosian Code, moreover, prepared the way for that still more scientific effort at revision known as the Justinian; and incidentally, it forms the most copious and authentic source of information on the state of the Roman Empire from the time of Constantine to that age when the Byzantine spirit had so far declared itself as to extinguish exclusively Roman traditions on the Bosphorus.

The whole reign of Theodosius II. was characterised by the efforts made to elucidate, simplify, and reduce, the bulk of legal compilations which had been accumulating through centuries, to a manageable compass, and to extract therefrom rules adapted to the conditions of the time. Historians ascribe the inception of this clerkly effort to the genius of Theodosius himself as much as to the influence of Antiochus, the Emperor's early tutor, whom St. Pulcheria had, at one time, banished from court. This man had been reinstated in imperial favour, and now exercised so much influence in state affairs that he might be called the master rather than the minister of the royal authority. St. Isidore of Pelusium wrote to warn him that the assiduous reading of the Scriptures was no guarantee for the right administration of justice, but the Patrician seems to have acquitted himself admirably as President of the Law Commissions. The design of reducing the legislation of the Empire to some sort of order must have originated in a brain clear and perspicacious, one that could organise and reform, that would labour obscurely with perseverance. M. Amédée Thierry attributes the conception, in the first place, to Pulcheria; to her from whom the Emperor drew all the inspiration of his acts. In legal matters Theodosius, unlike the student and artist that he was, loved abbreviation and retrenchment.   He aimed at curtailing all superfluous procedure; in 428, for instance, he passed a law doing away with many of the formalities of a marriage.   Even if the Augusta were not the prime mover in the matter of the Code, she gave her support to the man who broached the subject to the Emperor.   For in the government of that day such an undertaking was an affair of personal initiative, and it were sufficient to call the attention of Theodosius to the chaotic state of the law to ensure the appointment of a commission of enquiry and reform.   The cumbrous system of administration which referred everything to the Emperor's personal prerogative made the ship of state incredibly unwieldly.   The Emperor turned from the disposal of an army, or the convocation of a great Church Council, to issue some edict regulating the use of crosses on the pots in his subjects' kitchens. The fact which appealed most forcibly to Theodosius was the astonishing paucity of persons familiar with the civil law.   After all their labours, the most assiduous students from the great schools at Berytus had but an imperfect acquaintance with it.   The machinery of all state departments was greatly impeded and clogged by the tangle of red-tape; in the disputes of everyday life it was ruinous and ill worth while to go to law.   The Bishops who wielded magisterial powers, often allowed the obvious dictates of justice to cut the inextricable knot of legal difficulties.   But, on the other hand, there was no unravelling the maze of illegality and abuse with which a man's affairs might easily become involved in the hands of unscrupulous authorities.

The first commission appointed to deal with this problem, consisted of the President Antiochus, eight "Illustres," and a jurist styled the "vir disertissimus et scholasticus."   It began its labours just before the outbreak of the Nestorian troubles, and carried them on till the year 435, when a second commission, numbering sixteen members, brought them gradually to a successful conclusion.

The principle upon which the compilation was to be made considerably cleared the ground for the commissioners.   It decreed that only the enactments of the Christian Emperors should be included.   The President took as a model the collection of rescripts methodically arranged and published as codes, but without legislative authority, by Gregorianus and Hermogenianus.   These, however, beginning with the reign of Hadrian, did not reach the time of Constantine.   Theodosius directed that a digest should be made of all that Emperor's constitutions on the lines of these old codes, together with those enacted since, down to the current year. It was to take up the work of the two men above mentioned and bring it up to date from the time when the transference of Rome to the Bosphorus naturally "established a new form of civil [and military] administration."

After nine years' patient labour the commissioners were able to announce the completion of their herculean task. It received the imperial sanction, and the Theodosian Code was published at Constantinople in February, 438. From the kalends of January, 439, it stood as the sole source of imperial law in all the relationships of civil life.

The scene in the Senate House on this occasion was typical and curious. The august gathering of senators, commissioners, ministers, officials and grandees, the presence of the Emperor, and possibly of the Augusta, and the attendant throng of people in the Augustaeum without, marked an important event in the annals of the eastern Empire. It was however no magna charta being granted to a virile nation, no constitution being ceded to a clamorous people, only the autocrat of a servile state announcing that his ideas were set in order. The reception accorded it characterised his subjects. A series of adulatory salutations, addressed now to the Emperor, now to the ministers, and now to the Code itself reiterated with a strange monotony, through the audience hall. " Augusti Augustorum*," eight times repeated, " Maximi Augustorum," as often ; " Deus vos nobis dedit, Deus nos vobis servet," wailed, chanted or droned twenty-seven interminable times ; " Spes in vobis, salus in vobis," for twenty-six responses ; " Liberis cariores, parentibus cariores," sixteen times, and " Per vos honores, per vos patrimonia, per vos omnia " insisted upon more frequently than all the rest! Possibly these ejaculations encouraged speakers or punctuated ceremonies. They may have hailed the sixteen divisions of the Code, or declared the popular acceptance of its authority.

The work was presently adopted by Valentinian and authorised within his own dominions. Thus the time-honoured yoke of Roman law was once more imposed upon the restless nations, and at a moment when the Empire found itself upon the brink of ruin, it bequeathed to the world in Christian form this last effort of its genius.

The legislation of the reign of Theodosius II. illustrates, in a few typical directions, some interesting features of that early century.

In the year 437 the Emperor issued fresh edicts against the Jews, a people hated in the Byzantine Empire much as they are hated in Russia to-day. The bad harvests and severe winters †

---

* Translation : " Monarch of Monarchs : " " God has given thee to us, may He preserve thee to us ; " " Hope lives in thee, safety depends upon thee ; " " Dearer than our children, dearer than our fathers ; " " Honours spring from thee, patrimonies are derived from thee, all things flow from thee."

† Mr. W. G. Holmes, " Age of Justinian and Theodora " thus writes of the climate of Constantinople :—" It is very changeable, exposed as the city is to north winds chilled by transit over the Russian steppes, and to warm breezes which originate in the tropical expanses of Africa and Arabia. The temperature may range through twenty degrees in a single day, and winters of such Artic severity that the Golden Horn and even the Bosphoros are seen covered with ice, are not unknown to the inhabitants."

of the last few years were attributed by the people to the laxity with which the laws against pagans and the Jews had of late been enforced. To the modern who has not only a profound respect for the one ·time 'chosen people,' in virtue of their marvellous rôle in human history, but also a strong humanitarian sense which revolts at the sight of man's retribution overtaking the accursed nation,—to the modern, it is difficult to realise the state of hostility in which Jews and Christians lived in the first centuries after Christ. An anonymous article in the "Dublin Review" for April, 1867, on " St. Cyril and the Tumults of Alexandria," gives us a lively conception of that fierce state of things. The learned and authoritative writer offers a forceful summary of Jewish history, and of the tendencies of the dispossessed race during the first few Christian centuries. In the light of these terrific revelations, which read like the newspaper accounts of the Anti-Jewish riots in the cities of Czardom during the disturbances of 1905, no legislation could have been too emphatic. If ever a people could be shown to have outlived its providential mission, we are told, and to have died a moral death of incurable disease and wretched old age, that people was the race of Israel. "Had the Romans merely left them to themselves, they would have cut each other to pieces and sunk out of sight almost as soon as they did. But the hatred of pagan for Jew was still more intense than the sectarian animosity that one Jew felt for one another." When the Greeks and Romans became Christians (or pseudo-Christians, at least), this hatred was not one jot abated, and the Jews lived at daggers-drawn with the Gentile communities who baited them.

The Jews had not been severely fettered under Theodosius the Great or his successors. One of them, Gamaliel by name, had even risen in the imperial service to the rank of honorary Prefect. His power was only taken from him when St. Pulcheria assumed the direction of affairs, because he had abused it. By a law of the year 417 the Jews were allowed to retain their Christian slaves, (and even to claim their children), but were forbidden to acquire new ones, or to circumcise their Christian dependents. There was a large community of Jews in Constantinople, and although we do not hear of outbreaks in the capital itself like those which happened at Alexandria, the menace of their presence and the jealousy it caused, was a standing danger to the public peace. At Antioch a Christian child could be murdered in the savage fanaticism of a Jewish festival (A.D. 418); and St. Simeon Stylites once severely reproved the Emperor's tolerance of the building of new synagogues there, not indeed out of religious bigotry, but out of anxiety for the safety of the city.

False prophets constantly appeared among the Jews and led armies of their deluded co-religionists to destruction by fire and sword. Somewhere about this time (A.D. 432) a leader arose claiming to be that self-same Moses who delivered the nation long ago. He deceived a multitude of the people and led an immense following to a certain promontory in the island of Crete, commanding them to fling themselves into the sea and find a passage through it. Thousands obeyed—and were drowned. If Mr. Zangwill had gone further back than the sixteenth century for the first of his dreamers of the "dream that has not come true," he would have had to give some account (and how fine it would have been!) of the savage passions that seethed in the Jewries of the fourth and fifth centuries after Christ.

Under Theodosius II. laws against the Jews were framed in a spirit, harsh perhaps to the modern sense, but gentle for those times. They were designed not so much to persecute the people as to check the spread of Judaism. To Pulcheria and her brother, the grasping Jews of their great capital must have been a source of anxiety. The strong religious sense of the Augusta possibly prompted a disgust it was yet responsible for restraining. The repressive edicts of the period were comparatively clement.

Another very interesting story illustrating the times, is that of the great philanthropist Florentius. This nobleman was six times Prefect of the Orient before the year 449; he had been Prefect of Constantinople in 422, and Consul in 429. He was a fine character ; the only blemish on his career—which however Pulcheria could overlook—was his inclination to side with Eutyches in the terrible disturbances of a decade later. But, as Tillemont gently remarks, "it is difficult to be *in* the world and not a trifle *of* it." Florentius was a man in the world of his day, and he set himself to deal with one of its most heinous scandals. The status of women in the Empire was immeasurably raised when, at the instance of Florentius, Theodosius consented to forego the amount of revenue derived from the taxes imposed upon vice. Up to this time society had remained largely pagan, and that class of women whom the licentiousness of some of the old cults seemed to necessitate, was still widely spread and more than tolerated in the cities of the Empire. Thus the 'hetaira' was still a recognised ornament in society. But the Patrician Florentius offered the Emperor the whole of his estate, in order that the sanction given to this calling by taxing it in common with honest industries, might be withdrawn. Theodosius accepted this noble sacrifice, and paved the way for the philanthropies of Theodora. It was probably in the time of Theodosius II. that the foundations were laid for the conciliation of the Church and the theatre. In old Roman days no profession was held in less esteem than that of the actor ; and the actress ranked with the lowest women of the city, though often she led the brilliant existence of Mr. Kingsley's Pelagia.*

At last however, some degree of imperial and ecclesiastical countenance was destined to elevate a class whose performances were so

---

* "Hypatia."

indispensable to the people. Theodosius himself erected theatres in the city, and it is said that even Bishops sometimes bequeathed money for a similar purpose. St. Gregory Nazianzen had already written the first passion play,[*] and the heresiarch Arius had conceived the idea of establishing a theatre in his church, and of writing dramas for it. St. Chrysostom strongly disapproved of the stage and of this tendency to encourage it. "A contemporary music hall without its enforced decency would probably convey to a modern reader the most correct impression of the stage as maintained in Constantinople."[†] No woman could ever present herself in the auditorium of a fifth century theatre. The action of Florentius, its acceptation by the Emperor, and later the extraordinary moral conversion of the celebrated Empress Theodora, were however potent signs of improvement.

The institution of slavery still obtained among the Christian Romans of the fifth century. Society had readjusted its views but not its hierarchy. A slave was still an unpaid, unprivileged, servant but no longer the soulless chattel of his master. He had a certain value, and even a certain dignity of his own. But the manumission of slaves was becoming a far more common thing, and now took place so frequently as to create new social problems and dissatisfactions. "The Byzantines installed their new Consul every year with an imitation of the old republican function at Rome. The nominee, robed in a gorgeous mantle decorated with purple stripes and gold embroidery, grasping a sceptre surmounted by a figure of Victory, proceeded in state to the Hippodrome where he displayed his authority by manumitting a number of slaves provided for the purpose."[‡]

The division of Armenia in the year 437 added some small territory to the Empire of the Younger Theodosius, and as Gibbon remarks, reflected some lustre upon it.

Since the Emperor Jovian had been obliged to conclude a disastrous peace with Persia in 363, Persian influence had been paramount in a country whose native king was Christian. But in 384 Armenia was the subject of a treaty concluded between Theodosius the Great and Sapor III., by which it was divided into two portions, one passing under the suzerainty of Persia and the other under that of Rome. Theodosius and Sapor both confided the government of their respective territories to native Christian kings, and for thirty-six years Armenia ceased to trouble the wider politics of the east. On the death of the Roman feudatory King Arsaces, the succession was bitterly disputed by his sons, and

---

[*] The 'Christus Patiens' is a long tragedy with Christ, the Virgin Mary, S. Joseph, Mary Magdalen, Nicodemus, Pilate, as actors. It is to be found in a Latin version, in Migne's Patrology.

Mr. W. G. Holmes. "Age of Justinian and Theodora."

Ibid.

their quarrels once more threw their country on the mercy of the two great rival empires. The Romans suppressed the regal government in Roman Armenia and confided the province to the care of a "Count of the Armenian frontier." "The city of Theodosiopolis was built. . . and the dependant territories were ruled by five satraps whose dignity was marked by a peculiar habit of gold and purple."* A few years later on, Chrosroes, the Persian feudatory king, succeeded in uniting the two Armenias under his single rule, and would have again precipitated war between Rome and Persia but for the moderation of Theodosius who refused to receive his submission. Chrosroes' breach of faith with Persia subjected the Armenian Christians to fresh persecution and to Zoroastrian government. One result it will be remembered of the war of the year 421 had been to reseat a Christian king on the throne of Persian Armenia. But unfortunately the personal character of this monarch was bad. Another internal revolution threw the whole country under the Persian yoke, and the situation of A.D. 391 (when it had lain at the feet of Theodosius) was reversed. The usurpation was resented at Constantinople, and a fresh division of the distracted country seemed to be the only means whereby war might be averted. This was amicably effected; the Empire acquired fresh territory; the advantages to the Armenians gained by the peace of 422 were confirmed; and the government at Constantinople felt the stronger in that the Armenian question, in so far as it still survived, had taken on an aspect friendly to Rome.

* Gibbon.

CHAPTER XXII

UPON her return from Palestine in 439 the Empress Eudocia found the court much as she had left it. Her friend, the illustrious Cyrus, had atttained the dignity of Patrician, and was now Prefect of Constantinople. He had also been advanced further to the Prefecture of Illyria, and from the 21st of September stood for the consulship of the following year. Valerius and Genesius, Eudocia's brothers, who had long ago attained high rank in the Emperor's service, retained his favour through a cycle of offices. Paulinus still held the place he merited in Theodosius' confidence, although no longer Master of Offices ; the Patrician Anatolius was General of the Eastern forces ; Antiochus was covered with the glory of his recent great achievement, and a certain eunuch courtier, Chrysaphius, had begun to attract the esteem of his imperial master. The laborious annalist Tillemont notes the succession of officers and consuls with the punctiliousness of a Master of Ceremonies.

Who could have forseen that the last mentioned of all these well established men, should triumph over each in turn, and, by the ruin of first one and then another, aspire to the undoing of St. Pulcheria herself?

The rise of Chrysaphius dates from this period ; it was as sure and gradual as it was disastrous to all those who stood in its way. The Emperor Theodosius became more and more subject as time went on to the domination of successive favourites, retaining only sufficient self-assertion to resent a popularity greater than his own. In this he rather resembled the weak but conscientious Honorius than his entirely indolent father. St. Pulcheria's influence at court had already suffered some detriment for the discomfiture of the Nestorians to have cost her such an effort. But "I do not know," Tillemont avers, "who was then ruling in her place—since it must always be supposed that someone ruled under cover of Theodosius' name." The influence of the Patrician Antiochus already challenged that of the Augusta, when Chrysaphius appeared and asserted himself in spite of either. The compiler of the invaluable "Histoire des Empereurs" has drawn up a list of the grand chamberlains who served and governed by turns during the forty years of Theodosius' reign. The best of them held office under the regency of St. Pulcheria, but of Felix, Grand Chamberlain in 439 nothing ill was to be said.

Felix and Cyrus, as the Emperor's most authoritative ministers, were now inaugurating a policy of co-operation with the government of the west against the Vandals in Sicily and Africa, which might have proved successful but for the kaleidoscopic changes wrought by imperial caprice. Theodosius was falling under the most baneful influence that ever dominated his life and the success of Chrysaphius was marked by the failure of his rivals' plans. The Empress unconsciously played into the hands of this insidious plotter, and by some strange turn of fate precipitated the crisis which heralded her own disgrace.

Eudocia had come back from Jerusalem elated with the homage of the east. She now determined to claim in Constantinople, as in Antioch and elsewhere, the undivided attention and honour which had been accorded her, as Empress, throughout her brilliant "progresses" in Asia. She wished to assert herself in the imperial palace in place of the Augusta, and, as Empress indeed, and mother of an Empress, to take a more prominent place, not in the eyes of the world, since nothing had been left her to desire there, but in the conduct of affairs of state. If discordances had crept in between herself and St. Pulcheria in the past, the inharmonious elements of their respective rôles were now more strongly marked. Eudocia had outlived the graceful gratitude of Athenais, and came forward after all these years as Pulcheria's rival. She hoped, possibly, to attach the sympathies of the court to herself, or at least to revive the party spirit of 430 which had so nearly worsted the Augusta.

Chrysaphius, watchful and ambitions, was quick to see how this temper in the Empress could be turned to his own advantage. He was too astute a diplomat himself to fear Eudocia as a politician ; thus anything which made for the overthrow of St. Pulcheria would consolidate his growing power without substituting any very formidable obstacle. The later Byzantine historians have handed down some account, albeit confused and obscure, of an intrigue whereby Theodosius' evil genius aimed at dividing the imperial ladies in order to break the power of Pulcheria. All Chrysaphius had to do was to take advantage of Eudocia's sudden ambition. He recognised that the Augusta's influence was a greater check upon his own advancement than the presence at the Emperor's side of any number of excellent ministers and Prefects, of his cultivated wife and her literary friends. So the Chamberlain sought to ingratiate himself with Eudocia ; the theological opinions of his kinsman, a certain Abbot Eutyches, may have been discussed in her salons long before they attracted the notice of the Patriarch. Gregorovius thinks it not unlikely that the eunuch sought to win her over to some plot against Pulcheria, and that jealousy would have sufficently served as a handle for the base attempt.

Whatever these schemes may have been for the overthrow of the Emperor's sister, they seem to have miscarried, for it was Eudocia, and not Pulcheria, who fell a victim to them. The court was full of intrigue, and it has baffled truth and history to account for Athenais' fall. The story handed down by those who had little care for the reputation of the imperial ladies deserves to be remembered if only because it contains just that point of explanation which a dramatist, and not hagiographer, now needs, to bear out his characters, knit up his plot, and bring on the dénouement.

The scandal about the Augusta and Paulinus which had originated during the Nestorian ferment, was revived in another form. The Empress seems indeed to have felt some jealousy; she ceased to call the Marshal by the playful nickname of her 'paranymph,' and treated St. Pulcheria with an hauteur which we may be sure was elegant and imperial to the most exquisite degree. But the Emperor's jealousy was at last aroused, and his suspicion fastened rather on his wife than on his sister. The gentle unenthusiastic Prince whom Athenais married, had long ago fallen out of the most vivid part of his wife's existence. Christianity had made a sincere if not a revolutionary impression upon her, and Theodosius possibly exposed one who had all the capabilities of perfect Grecian womanhood, to a temptation she would never have entertained had her soul been impressed, like Pulcheria's, with the traditions of Christian asceticism, rather than with those of the pagan joy in life.

The third of the dramatis personæ was Paulinus, the courtly gentleman who had stood by the Emperor's side on Athenais' wedding-day, and ever after watched her mind and life with the sympathy that seems to constitute a right.

Fourthly, St. Pulcheria, of a totally different stamp: "A character at unity with itself; that performed what it intended, subdued every counteracting impulse, had no visions beyond the distinctly possible, was strong by its very negations."* Duty and self-sacrifice were her ideals; that she and the Empress presently ceased to appreciate each other was probably the fault of neither. The cultivated Greek must have known enough of human nature to be satisfied in her own heart of the severe Augusta's innocence. Intellectuality such as her own might foster passion with far more likelihood than Pulcheria's asceticism.

And lastly, Chrysaphius, the villain, seeking to undo all Melania had done; playing for his interest with the characters around him as a clever man plays chess.

The Emperor, so runs the tale, was going to church on the Feast of the Epiphany, when he met a peasant who presented him with a Phrygian apple of such enormous size, that he and all his following greatly marvelled at it. He rewarded the old man for his rustic

---

* "The Mill on the Floss," Geo. Eliot.

courtesy with a hundred and fifty pieces of gold, and sent the apple, a gift, to the Empress.

But Eudocia sent it to Paulinus, because he was sick,* and a great friend of the Emperor.

The Marshal, however, knowing nothing of the history of the apple, hastened to present so beautiful an object to the Emperor as he re-entered the Palace. "And Theodosius having received it, recognised it, and concealed it, and called his wife and questioned her saying,

"Where is the apple that I sent you?"

The Empress answered, with a tell-tale blush, "I have eaten it."

"Then he bade her swear by his salvation the truth, whether she had eaten it or sent it to someone. And Eudocia swore that she had sent it to no man but had herself eaten it.† Then the Emperor showed her the apple and was exceedingly wroth, suspecting that she was enamoured of Paulinus, and had sent it to him as a love gift for he was a very handsome man. On this account he put Paulinus to death, but he permitted Eudocia to go to the Holy Places to pray."

*   *   *   *   *   *

So much for the legend. The lees of historical truth that remain when all this wine of the imagination is poured off, are very small. They merely indicate that something serious had happened. "It would be useless," says Gregorovious, "to attempt to fathom the authenticity or the foundation of this story . . . Like many another in the life of Athenias, while it contains nothing altogether improbable, it may embody as much truth as there is in the famous account of the diamond necklace at the court of Louis XVI . . . " The tongue of slander and the Emperor's jealousy had turned from Pulcheria and fastened upon Athenais. Chrysaphius may have stirred up enmity between the imperial ladies, he may indeed have used Paulinus' name for such a purpose, but the plot ended differently to his intention. The execution of the Marshal—incidentally satisfactory as it may have been to Chrysaphius—seems to prove that some thoughtless word or act precipitated the catastrophe. The unfortunate Count fell a victim to someone's machinations, whether or not his own demeanour or that of the bright unaffected Empress lent any colour to them.

Theodosius ordered his execution, and one story has it that a murderous attack was made upon Paulinus that very night as he was leaving the imperial Palace. The would-be assassins sprang

---

* Gout is an unpoetic malady.

† The fifteenth century historian Cedrenus retails this incident in default of any better explanation of Eudocia's banishment, but makes her tell the truth and say " I have given the apple to our most faithful Paulinus."

upon him by a sombre stairway, but after a desperate scuffle he escaped with only the loss of his ears. Theodosius pretended to have known nothing of the affair, and Paulinus was banished, apparently to Cappadocia, until such time as a church which he was having built in Constantinople should be finished. His execution must have taken place some time between 440 and 444. The fall of this good and talented friend of Theodosius and Pulcheria was the first of a series of such tragedies by which Chrysaphius mounted step by step to the position he coveted. The historian Marcellinus mentions the death of Paulinus without attempting to account for it. His laconic silence makes it appear that even many years after the event a writer could shrink from casting aspersions on the memory of the Empress, who died after a long exile protesting her innocence to the last.

For, after an interval which might sufficiently dissociate her journey from the event of Paulinus' disgrace, Eudocia withdrew from court. When at last Chrysaphius applied the spark to the trail he had so wilily laid, and the Emperor's love was blasted, there flamed up in Theodosius an anger against Eudocia of which his mild nature might have been deemed incapable. If, however, he expelled her from the palace immediately upon Paulinus' banishment it would have branded her before the world with her husband's condemnation. Eudocia, stung to the quick of her proud and highly sensitive nature, mortified by the gossip of the court and city, and heart-broken for the fate of the Count, would have gladly shaken the golden dust of the palace from her feet and turned her back upon it.

But other counsels prevailed, and the lapse of a few years lent weight, later on, to the ex-Empress' dying protestation that neither she nor Paulinus had ever transgressed the bounds of friendship. Who but Pulcheria, Athenais' first protectress, against whom the exile nursed no shade of resentment, could have had the foresight and persuasiveness for this?

Even to the present day the lapse of four years between Paulinus' fall and Eudocia's second journey to Jerusalem is held to disconnect the two events. The disgrace of the Empress was in no way visited upon those numerous officials at court whom her favour had advanced, and even her brothers continued in the imperial employ. From such a fact only two inferences can be drawn—either that Eudocia was in no way the cause of the Marshal's downfall, or that some influence (probably the Augusta's) was exerted to save her name and fame. She departed from the capital in 444, attended by the train that became her rank.

She put the life which had ended in an impasse behind her.

A woman's heart is less fitted to bear the burden of accumulated wrong than a man's. She has not his fortitude in silence. But when she has exhausted her plea and defence, and finds either unavailing, to the original indignation is added a more painful weakness. If a woman can no longer appeal to the chivalry of the man who loved her, she feels that he is bereft of the qualities she had trusted in him. Her wrong pales before her disappointment, and with a shame like that of having exposed a bleeding breast to coldness or derision, she lapses into the sad silence that has no dignity. Athenais' fine Greek spirit must have suffered acutely before it reached this point. When first, reliance upon her power with her husband left her, and next, she came to doubt his magnanimity, she felt indeed her wrong to be beyond repair.

She suffered as Theodosius' wife what St. Pulcheria was to suffer as his sister. She now looked back upon her life at Constantinople with the indifference of one whose affection had been seared. She set her face towards Jerusalem, there to await her death and her justification.

The disgrace of Athenais was the saddest of the many dark events that began to crowd the closing years of Theodosius' reign. It must have had its own effect upon the Emperor. But if a weak nature allows itself to be embittered by the sorrows of its own making, it deteriorates and becomes the weaker. Theodosius fell more and more under the dominion of Chrysaphius ; and his blind favouritism was to work more dire harm than the wreck of his domestic happiness, before the end.

The Augusta sorrowed over the solution of her difficulties more than she had ever grieved to bear them. With the departure of Athenais went twenty years of her own life, twenty years of her solicitude for the Empire : no trace remained to her or Theodosius of all that time had brought forth. Athenais was gone, and her children too. Pulcheria looked back upon it all as a mother might look back upon the career of a daughter she had dearly loved—in childhood. It was the memory of the earlier years which softened that of the later.

If, as Augusta, Pulcheria had clung to her prerogatives, and defied Eudocia's pretensions, it had been for the sake of Theodosius and the Empire. She would, nevertheless, more willingly have seen the Empress usurp her place than have it stolen by such a man as Chrysaphius. The lovely Greek had never wielded much political influence ; it is curious to conjecture what the course of events would have been had the Empress, and not the eunuch, triumphed. In either case trouble was inevitable ; Eudocia would have plunged the Church into a greater ferment than that from which it had so recently emerged, but she would scarcely have blotted the record of her husband's reign so foully as Chrysaphius contrived to do. The alternative was removed from the anxious foresight of Pulcheria by the events narrated, but, for all that, there was a private grief in her heart which had nowhere a more sincere reflection than in Eudocia's own daughter.

The young wife of Valentinian III. must have heard with the utmost consternation and incredulity of the fate that had befallen

13

her mother. The Empress dowager, Placidia, would hardly have known what view to take of the extraordinary intelligence. She could neither credit it nor disbelieve it. The honour of her son was touched no less than the dignity of Theodosius, and she could not but sympathise with the grief of her daughter-in-law, even had her first impulse been less kindly. Eudocia the younger was now herself a mother. Soon after her arrival in Italy she had borne her husband twin daughters, Eudocia and Placidia. But since then there had been no child, and the young Empress may already have begun to taste unhappiness. She loved Valentinian most dearly to the last; his infidelities were a greater cause of sorrow than of anger to his wife. The news of Paulinus' fall and her mother's banishment came to Eudocia when she had had time to realise the difficulties of her own lot. Her heart, truly, had struck root in the west with her husband and children, but human nature, ever fundamentally the same, may tell us something of her relationship to Placidia. If at this juncture the young Empress felt that her imperial relations would have her forget her Greek blood, the proud Athenian strain would have made her heart beat the higher in defence of her mother. The two Eudocias never met after the marriage of 437. History has preserved few signs of what passed between them after Athenais' voluntary exile. It seems however that communication was carried on easily enough not only between Rome and Constantinople, but between Jerusalem and Ravenna, for the ex-Empress sent her daughter one of the chains of St. Peter; and at the time of the Eutychian controversy, much pressure was brought upon the exile by her imperial relations and her brothers to induce her to abandon her championship of the schismatics.

The sequel to the whole sad story has a note of fiercer tragedy. Eudocia was accompanied on her second pilgrimage—surely a chastened one!—by Severus, a priest of Constantinople, and a deacon John. These two members of her suite served her at Jerusalem as the dispensers of her abundant alms, with such devotion and assiduity that the Emperor, who kept a jealous watch upon her every movement found in this fact a new source of suspicion. Eudocia had taken up the thread of her former life in the Holy City, and, like many a humbler woman, was trying to forget the sorrows of her own life in the consolation of others, the relief of the poor and the beautifying of the Church. She entrusted Severus and John with large sums of money, which were represented to Theodosius in the light of gifts. The Emperor despatched Saturninus, Count of the Domestics, with orders to have the ecclesiastics executed forthwith. When this officer appeared before the Empress with the intelligence of his vindictive and wicked errand, the outraged woman flamed up in hotter anger than ever wrongs of her own had kindled. The magnificent indignation of her dauntless Greek blood burst Christian bounds, and in one flash Saturninus lay dead at her feet, and the hand of Athenais was the hand of an avenger!

She was summarily degraded from imperial rank. Her income was so far curtailed that she could no longer maintain any state ; the principal members of her retinue were recalled, and she was reduced to the level from which she had sprung.

Truly the star of the daughter of Leontius had set! It had arisen with pale beauty, had blazed with unrivalled splendour, and now was suddenly quenched in the blood of three good men.

CHAPTER XXIII

THE history of the reign of Theodosius began to darken from the year of Paulinus' disgrace. It is necessary to go back to 440 to pick up another thread in the narrative which serves no less than the story we have just pursued, to show how, in proportion as St. Pulcheria fades more and more into the background, as others are preferred before her, and as her influence tells less and less upon the counsels of state these approximate in character to the general Byzantine record. A craven policy in the face of dictatorial foes, disaster in the field, corruption in the administration, and dark schemes in the privy council chamber, mark the period when the Augusta could prevail no longer over the forces jealousy and ambition arrayed against her.

If the story of Pulcheria herself could be divorced from that of the Empire for whose integrity she had sacrificed all that a woman holds dearest in life, the next few years could be passed over in silence. If we could think that she took little interest in the sufferings of her country we need not delay to review the invasion of the Huns. But even in the darkest hours of the Augusta's failure, she remained no less an Empress than she had been in a happier day; and the vicissitudes of the war were of even greater moment to her than they would have been, had the selfish interests of her own position been affected by them.

In the year 440 it was decided at Constantinople to send a large force to co-operate with Valentinian's troops under Ætius, against the Vandal King Genseric. The Vandals had long been a thorn in the side of Italy, and had now become a menace to the entire Empire. They had, indeed, created a naval power and were attacking the Romans in an unprecedented manner. Carthage had just fallen into their hands after six centuries of Roman rule. From her historic ports warlike and marauding fleets were now setting out upon the Mediterranean and threatening the vast seaboard of the two astonished Empires.

In the year 441, then, an enormous armament set sail from the Bosphorus. It consisted of swift dromoi propelled by a single bank of oars, the warships of the period, and of innumerable transports. It was commanded by five men whose names would possibly have echoed through the ages had any action proved their skill or valour. Cyrus the Consul, a noble Egyptian, accompanied them, but a fate still more unkind than that which consigned Ansile and his fellow admirals to oblivion, was reserved for him. The Byzantine forces were ordered to unite in Sicily with those of Ætius and his barbarian allies, defend the island (the Vandals had already taken Lilybaeum, and the siege of Panormus was in process), and descend thence upon the shores of Africa.

But the gullibility, seconded by the jealousy, of Chrysaphius doomed the enterprise to failure.

The Grand Chamberlain Felix either went out of office or lost the Emperor's confidence to the ambitious eunuch. The latest favourite was now in the ascendant, and his counsels, aided by circumstance, necessitated the recall of the fleet before the distressed Sicilians had experienced anything but the burden of its useless presence in their harbours.

The astute Genseric "reserved his courage to encounter those dangers which his policy could not prevent or elude." He no sooner took stock of the danger that menaced him from the east than he sent off ambassadors to the Byzantine court. Their instructions were to open up specious negotiations with the Emperor during which the fleet would be diplomatically paralysed. These overtures were to be sufficiently prolonged and delayed, so as to allow Genseric in the meantime to communicate secretly with the Huns. He hoped to save himself, as on a previous occasion, by invoking the formidable interposition of Attila. While the Vandalic and the Hunnish kings devised a scheme whereby the Roman attack on Africa might be diverted, and an invasion of the Empire from the north be supported from the south, Chrysaphius at court was hoodwinked.

He listened to the Vandal embassy, attributing Genseric's professed desire for peace to the success of an alarm raised behind him. A certain son-in-law of the great Count Boniface, named Sebastian, who commanded a pirate crew in Theodosius' service, had made a descent upon Mauretania * in consequence of which Genseric abandoned his operations in Sicily. Chrysaphius was completely baffled by the Vandal's "artful delays, ambiguous promises and apparent concessions." Even before the conspiracy with Attila was ripe, the fleet was rendered useless. It rode idly in the Sicilian waters while the attention of the Senate was decoyed, and the Huns mustered beyond the Danube in preparation for a terrible irruption that should divert the attention of the east from the west.

With the rise of Chrysaphius, like a bird of ill-omen, all the enemies of the Empire came hovering around its borders. The wise heads at Byzantium had given place to those whose only

---

* Professor Bury, "Later Roman Empire," says that it is not clear how Sebastian's position menaced Genseric. Possibly it did not.

recommendation lay in a weak man's prejudice. Theodosius was surrounded by self-interested and incapable advisers when news came from every quarter of risings and of wars. The Huns chose the same moment as the Persians to invade his territory; ravaging tribes of Isaurians and other brigands seemed to concert their attacks with those of Vandalic pirates. The storm burst, like a cyclone, with amazing suddenness. All the sky was overcast and the whole world seemed in tempest.

The Huns had needed little urging to break faith with the Romans.

At this moment their brief "empire" had attained its highest and its fiercest reputation. Attila, the Hunnish king, was master of an enormous tract of continent stretching from the Don to Pannonia, including many barbaric nations with their subjugated kings. He was temperamentally full of vast designs, and proudly conscious of the pristine strength of his people as compared with enervated manhood of the Empire. He aspired to the devastation of every land, but his exploits were unable to establish as a nation a warlike and nomadic people who, without law and without literature, could neither preserve the fruit of these, nor impress themselves upon the civilized world. At one time the East Romans hoped Attila would have led his wild hordes against their hereditary rivals, the Persians, but the westerns pointed out that in case of his success the Empire would be encompassed on all sides by these awful Hunnish savages, whose boast it was that the grass never grew where the hoofs of their horse had passed.

During the reign of Arcadius some bands of adventurous Huns had ravaged the eastern provinces, but soon after the accession of Theodosius II. the Regent Anthemius greatly strengthened the northern defences of the Empire.

But later on, probably when harassed by the Persian campaign, the Emperor engaged to pay a yearly tribute to keep the Huns beyond the frontier; and the empty courtesy of a military title was bestowed upon their king. But both weak expedients failed in their object, for the Huns seldom scrupled to break faith with the Empire, and constantly ravaged the border provinces. The Romans were unable to extend their hospitality or protection to any barbarian nations who might attempt to throw off the Hunnish yoke, without finding themselves involved in war. A treaty of peace conclusive to some of these disturbances, was in process of negotiation in 433 when the death of Rugilas, the Hun king at that date, suspended his ambassador's instructions.

His two successors, Attila and Bleda, proceeded to dictate their own haughty terms, which, at the moment, the Byzantines seemed obliged to accept. The annual tribute was increased as the price of the short and arbitrary respite from anxiety which it suited Attila to grant the imperial government. The purchase of a fragile peace at an unreasonable cost showed "a strange debility

either in the courage or in the affairs " of the Empire. Attila
continued to insult it with impunity, and for some years levied a
sort of imperial blackmail against it. He required but the
slightest pretext at any time to sweep aside the diplomatic cobwebs
spun by the court eunuchs. When at the instigation of Genseric
in 441 this pretext became excusable, it was not hard to find.

The plot between the Vandals and the Huns ripened while
still the moments were propitious. The Byzantine fleet was
lying idle in the west, the best of the imperial generals had gone
east against the Persians, and the road to Constantinople was
practically open.

Attila condescended to allege a cause for his invasion. " Under
the faith of the Treaty of Margus (433) a free market was held on
the northern side of the Danube which was protected by a Roman
fortress named Constantia. A troop of barbarians violated the
commercial security; killed or dispersed the unsuspecting traders
and levelled the fortress with the ground. The Huns justified this
outrage as an act of reprisal; alleged that the Bishop of Margus
had entered their territories " and stolen secret treasure from the
tombs of their kings. "The refusal of the Byzantine court" to
surrender this prelate to their vengeance "was the signal of war;
and the Moesians at first applauded the generous firmness of their
sovereign."* Although the imperial government had hitherto
suffered the most ignominious indignities rather than precipitate a
war with the devastating and ferocious Huns, it was now obliged
to prosecute some sort of a campaign against them. The crisis
occurred at a most dangerous moment. Theodosius' ambassadors
were unable to induce Attila to abandon the siege he had already
laid to the town of Ratiaria ; their negotiations were all futile ; the
Hun crossed the frontier and speedily reduced several cities and
forts along the banks of the Danube.

Ratiaria was taken, then Viminiacum, Singidunum, Sirmium,
Margus and Naissus. The whole breadth of Europe as it extends
about five hundred miles from the Euxine to the Hadriatic was at
once invaded and occupied and desolated by the myriads of
barbarians whom Attila led into the field. The whirlwind host
swept through the narrow defiles of the Balkans south-eastwards
into Thrace leaving all the country behind blasted as by a swarm
of human locusts. Two towns in the neighbourhood of Constantinople fell before their onslaught, and a fort named Athyras, not
far from the Bosphorus itself, was taken.

Meanwhile the armies scattered east and west were hastily
recalled, and measures were adopted for raising a home force.
The fleet was ordered to return at once, whereupon Valentinian III.
was obliged to conclude peace with the Vandals. Genseric was
thus at liberty to co-operate with Attila by sea, and, too late,

Chrysaphius may have guessed the extent to which he had been duped. The officers of the Sicilian expedition, Cyrus the Consul amongst them, made all haste to reach Constantinople. The two Generals Anatolius and Aspar who had been sent against the Persians were also free to return. Bad weather and impassable roads had so impeded the invaders' advance that they failed to surprise the Romans as they had hoped, and finding themselves at a disadvantage, readily consented to make peace. The capital was placed under the protection of Zeno, General of the Armies of the East, and his powerful garrison of Isaurian troops. A military force was collected in Europe, formidable by their arms and numbers if the generals appointed in command had been equal to the vast emergency.

Theodosius himself had no thought of taking the field; battle was first offered the Huns by Arnegisele, " Magister militum " for Moesia and Thrace. The action was fought at the junction of the river Ute with the Danube, within sight of the walls of a city. No fault could be found with the Roman valour, but the day was lost owing possibly to the death of the Byzantine leader. His horse fell upon him, but he fought strenuously to the last.

The Emperor's troops met with nothing but defeat. For the next few years during which the war was carried on with intermittent intervals of peace as arbitrary as the will of Attila, the Hunnish king at the head of a hundred tributary peoples ravaged Illyria, the two Dacias, Moesia, Scythia and Thrace. Philippolis, Arcadiopolis, Constantia, Marcianopolis and all the cities in their path fell before them, excepting only Adrianople, Heraclia and the obscure but brave little township of Azimuntium. The Senate received news of the ruin and depopulation of more than seventy cities.

The chronology of the war is obscure, and the various historians ascribe conflicting dates to its chief events. Tillemont seems to divide it into ill-defined campaigns of which the most severe was that of the first year. Three heavy defeats were sustained by the Byzantines, but there seems to be no indication as to when exactly they were pressed backwards upon the Thracian Chersonesus where Attila extinguished the hope of further resistance.

Two men might have saved Constantinople from a fate that seemed impending over it like that which had befallen Rome thirty years before. But in the midst of disaster and disgrace Chrysaphius worked for nothing but his own advantage. He was profoundly jealous of the Prefect Cyrus and of the Isaurian General Zeno. It was not a difficult matter to fill the Emperor's mind with distrust of the latter, for Zeno was a pagan and his loyalty to the State might be doubted in the face of a pagan foe, and a very natural incident presently gave Chrysaphius the handle that he sought against the popular Consul.

The Patrician Cyrus owed his success in life to the patronage and appreciation of the Empress Eudocia. She had ranked him among her personal friends, and had esteemed his culture and literary gifts no less highly than those of the unfortunate Paulinus. His wife and daughter Alexandra were among the most welcome ladies at court. The noble Egyptian's leanings towards Hellenism caused him to be accused, afterwards, of paganism. Whether or no he had ever merited the charge it is difficult to say, for although the legislation of Theodosius' reign was inimical to classical cults and ceremonies, the atmosphere of his court was not illiberal. A pagan had full access to achievement and distinction so long as he made no public parade of idolatry. Cyrus, however, was a friend of St. Daniel, a Stylite near Constantinople, to whose prayers he attributed the deliverance of his wife and daughter from some strange possession. He was not only a man of letters and ideas but an officer of sterling merit. He was upright, prudent and successful. He greatly improved the nightly illumination of the city streets, and the great cincture of fortifications begun by Anthemius was completed during the Egyptian's Prefecture. In 442 it defended Constantinople on the northern side from the Propontis to the Euxine.

One day, early in the year, after the return of the fleet from Sicily, the people, feeling reassured by the presence of the Consul, cheered him enthusiastically in the circus. "Constantine founded the city," they shouted, "but Cyrus has renewed it!" The Emperor's face lowered, and had the popular hero glanced at the eager light in Chrysaphius' eye, he might have foreseen his fall. The many-throated roar was was not to be silenced; it came again and again "Constantine founded the city but Cyrus has renewed it!" The strong wine of the people's homage flushed the Egyptian's swarthy cheek. He was too proud at such a moment to fear the jealousy of the pale-faced Emperor or the malignity of the upstart eunuch.

But a few words from Chrysaphius, full of evil insight and timely address, removed a second obstacle in his upward path.

Neither the prayers of wife or daughter, nor the influence of the ex-Empress from her place of banishment, could avail to save the Consul. Cyrus was deposed, his goods were confiscated, and he himself sent into exile.

Shortly afterwards, before the June of 422, Theodosius withdrew from Constantinople, ostensibly to re-establish some of the decaying cities of Pontus. There must have been a temporary lull in the war, although it could not have lasted long, for Tillemont speaks of a peace concluded in 443, possibly during the Emperor's absence. He records also an incident on the road which lends some colour to the remark that Theodosius might have been a saint had he never worn the purple. One day, whilst journeying through Bythnia, he suffered much from the heat of the sun, and was all covered in sweat and dust. An officer in his Guards presented to him a beautiful goblet filled to overflowing with a most refreshing draught. Theodosius took the vessel in recognition of the service, but immediately returned it to the soldier without so much as moistening his lips. He desired to test his self-mastery, and preferred to suffer the inconveniences of travel like his followers than to accept a refreshment which they could not share. Such an anecdote reminds us of St. Louis the Crusader King. That Theodosius, however, should retain the mastery of his desires, and yield that of his will, was one of the contradictions in human nature which those who suffer from them most are the last to perceive.

During the winter the Constantinopolitans suffered terribly from the severity of the weather. Heavy snowstorms and bitter frosts killed hundreds of men and animals. The peace which the Government seems to have tried to negociate with Attila must have proceeded from the initiative of the Augusta, for Theodosius was still abroad. No details have survived as to its conditions, and it seems to have been abortive. After the final defeat of the Romans, Attila ravaged the country " without resistance and without mercy," from the Hellespont to the suburbs of the capital. When, however, five years later the war was really brought to a conclusion, Scotta, a Hunnish ambassador, was instructed to urge terms upon the imperial government, which it seems either Attila or the Byzantines had formerly rejected. This referred in all probability to the negotiations begun in 446, but it may cast some light on the obscure instance of this earlier effort. The terrible straits to which the people high and low were ultimately reduced in order to meet the Huns' demands may have justified Pulcheria in 443 for not yielding to them tamely. If indeed the Augusta or her advisers placed any limit to the pecuniary concessions the Empire was prepared to make, it showed that she at least would rather trust the fate of priests and Churches to their pagan defender Zeno than see the people dying of starvation in the streets, and the nobles hanging themselves for despair in the cold halls of their denuded palaces.

But Attila was in a position to play fast and loose with the Empire. He had recently become sole master of the Huns by the murder of his brother and colleague Bleda, and if for any short space he waged no active war against the Romans, he could force them to arms again without a moment's warning, or drain their treasury by threats. At his touch the fair-seeming fruit of the Empire crumbled into a mass of dry rot. Corruption, favouritism, and maladministration had eaten out its heart despite the Code, despite Florentius, despite the integrity of the Augusta. It only needed the ruthless shock of Attila's aggression to further reveal the hollowness of its prosperity. It only needed a few more years of Chrysaphius' domination to ruin the prestige of the imperial government, and to reduce the eastern Empire to a state from which, afterwards, it was Pulcheria's glory to redeem it.

CHAPTER XXIV

THE Eastern Empire was abandoned to "the Scourge of God."
The West apparently could do nothing but watch the progress of
Attila in helpless dismay. Valentinian had no quarrel with the
Huns; his most powerful general and minister, Ætius, was on a
friendly footing with their King, and the bond between the two
halves of the Roman world was not now so strong as to identify
their interests. Often as Theodosius had sent aid to the government
of Placidia, "the timid or selfish policy of the western Romans now
abandoned" * the Byzantines to their fate.

While all the provinces north of Constantinople were being
devastated, the people of the capital sheltered themselves behind its
massive walls, and apprehensively marked the machinations of
Chrysaphius. A period of misery and indetermination was
signalized in the year 444 by the fall of the man who then † filled
the office to which Theodosius' favourite aspired, and by the death
of the Princess Arcadia.

History has preserved no memories of the nun-like sisters who
shared Pulcheria's sacrifice, if not her burden. Their lives are
completely forgotten. But to Theodosius, who had lost wife and
children, upon whose head sorrows were beginning to accumulate,
some the deeper in that they were touched with remorse, the loss of
the Princess from the inner circle of imperial society must have
broken another link with the happier past. Those for whom the
drift of life has never repeated the success of its beginnings, feel
the break-up of an original circle with peculiar grief. But at this
moment the Emperor was filled with that absorbing jealousy of
power which has so often assailed kings when most it is threatened.
He began to fear for his throne and dignity when both were
practically lost. Chrysaphius had not yet attained the goal of his
ambition; he seized the opportunity of Theodusius' imperial alarm
and private sorrow to insinuate a charge of contemplated treason
against Antiochus the Chamberlain. The Empress, Paulinus, Cyrus,
all these had disappeared, yet Chrysaphius might have to spend

---

* The quotations throughout the chapter are from Gibbon's history of the Hunnish
war, ch. 34.

† The chronology is Theophanes'.

more time than he wished, idly strolling in the sunny cloisters of Eutyches', his kinsman's convent. Rivals yet remained to be thrown.

The man under whose presidency the celebrated Code had been compiled, was originally sent to Byzantium by the Persian king as one well versed in letters, who might serve Theodosius in some tutorial capacity. The friendship of Yezdegerd and Arcadius accounted for a courtesy which possibly lent colour to the report that the infant Emperor had been confided to the guardianship of Persia. Antiochus had previously been attached to a Count Narses, (possibly the Surenas in the campaign of 422) to whom he addressed a law in 416. Synesius spoke of him as one who wielded considerable power early in his career at court. He abused it apparently, for the Augusta Pulcheria deposed him so soon as she assumed the conduct of affairs. It seems that he returned to court later on, and was reinstated in imperial favour, for he became a Patrician and was entrusted with many high offices.

The historian Tillemont puts together these scrappy facts about Antiochus with the brevity of an annalist, and the scrupulosity that swamps facts in disputed dates. Even the identity of their subject may be confused, but notwithstanding all the drawbacks, another gorgeous figure is introduced into the tale, who jostles the throng around Theodosius' throne, and points the moral of a story.

As the President of the Law Commissions, Antiochus amply fulfilled his trust. If, however, he must be identified with the man whom St. Pulcheria originally dismissed from court, the Byzantine historians charge him with defects which account for her distrust. He is supposed to have been unjust, deceitful, and unreliable. The Augusta's foresight was overruled, and later on Antiochus' maladministration led to the triumph of a baser man. Chrysaphius forced the Chamberlain's ambition upon the notice of the Emperor, and accused him of casting covetous glances on the purple.

The same fate befel Antiochus that had overtaken Cyrus two years earlier. His goods were confiscated, he was degraded and reduced to the expedient of pleading for the priesthood. He was ordained, and attached to the Church of St. Euphemia at Calcedon, where he presently died. "Thus at one time prodigiously rich, he ended his life in the poverty in which it began." Chrysaphius had no more ruth for the latest than for the first of his victims. He now reigned supreme in the Emperor's counsels—but for the Augusta.

It must have been a serious thing for the Church that the punishment meted out to ministerial and political offenders was so frequently to force them into the ranks of her priesthood. When scandals have come and sullied her fair fame, the explanation—and sometimes indeed the exoneration—of them has often lain in some such fact as this. Cyrus the ex-Consul was no willing priest. He had recourse to the Church as an asylum, and was ordained in the hope of saving his life.   He even became a Bishop, and when forced by his derisive and inimical flock to preach one Christmas day, won their applause by the cleverness with which he sought exemption.   He simply said that since it was by the ear alone that the Word of God was conceived in the womb of the Blessed Virgin, so the birth of Jesus Christ our God and Saviour could best be honoured by silence.   He governed his diocese as conscientiously as he might, but was presently chased out of it by some resuscitated calumny.   If it were painful for laymen, men of the world worldly, to be thus forced into the Church by the tyrannical mercy of the Emperor, how far more harmful must it have been for her to admit them !   When at last Pulcheria, Byzantine Princess as she was, condemned Chrysaphius, she sent him to death rather than to the exalted service of the altar.

In the meantime the Huns overran the land from the Danube to the Bosphorus.   The year 446 or 447, opened ominously.   The famine of the winter was followed by one of those horrible plagues so often noted by the chroniclers.   The mortality was frighful among both men and beasts ; the air became tainted from the noisome purlieus of the city where the dead lay too long unburied among the crowded living.   These epidemics were of frequent occurrence not only in Constantinople but in Rome, and probably in all the cities of the Empire, though they attracted no such attention as the great plague of Justinian's time.   The 'medici' of the period probably did their best to cope with the fell emergency.   They tended the people of their district with assiduity and care ; the 'steps' of the city regions were blue with doctor's cloaks, but as the followers of Galen and the scoffers at Hippocrates, these preferred the philosophy of the situation to experiment.   There seems to have been no historian in 447 like Procopius, who, a century later, noted the progress and symptoms of the plague with the eyes of a physician.   The poor people had recourse to the druggists and the despised 'rhizotomi' or herb-gatherers.   Even the 'mendicamentarius,' the charlatan and poisoner, the man who traded in phials, refuse and credulity was not without his value at such a time.   The hospitals and alms-houses were crowded with the sick and indigent, but so great was the fear of the Huns and the impoverishment of the city, that there were few to tend their numbers and fewer to give the means.   The parabolani and the copiatae were incessantly occupied ; even the 'archiatri palati," the court physicians, found something more to do than prescribe for gouty Senators.   The Empress Flacilla, first wife of Theodosius the Great, had set an example which Pulcheria may well have copied, of visiting the public hospitals herself, attended by those who could diagnose and relieve the distresses of the sick.

If anything were wanting to fill up the measure of the people's misery, it were surely supplied by the frightful earthquake that shattered the city one Sunday morning at the end of January. The Byzantines received just so much warning as enabled them to fly from the pestilential streets and houses, and take refuge in the open country beyond. A portion of the great walls, with fifty-seven garrison towers, was toppled over like a heap of stones, and the lengthy western defence, the wall of the Chersonesus was thrown down here and there. The ground gaped, swallowing streets and palaces; fountains dried up in one place to burst out unexpectedly, with disastrous consequences elsewhere; trees were torn up and tossed, roots and all, into the air; the land reeled; myriads of dead fish were cast up by the angry sea, and ships were stranded on the hills. Whole islands disappeared, and all the Hellespont was craked and shaken. Bythnia and Phrygia suffered heavily, and the shock was felt far westward. But in Constantinople it was the most violent within the memory of living man. It wrought such havoc, and destroyed so many treasures, that the wonder is the city could so soon recover the splendour by which the Huns were dazzled in the course of the ensuing negotiations. The people no sooner recognised the dangerous import of the familiar earthquake presages, than every one, high and low, rich and poor, fled from the city. Only the plague-stricken remained. The Emperor and his sisters, the court and senate, the clergy, the military, and the common people wandered in the fields and spent whole nights in terrified prayer. By day the sleepless and exhausted crowds exaggerated the fearsomeness of the situation by delirious visions of fire in the air, and doubtless, many heard the thundering hoofs of the Hunnish cavalry. The Patriarch St. Proclus, and his priests were indefatigable in their endeavours to calm the distracted citizens. He voiced their terror and distress for them in prayer to God, and the people continually answered by the triple repetition of the cry, "Have mercy on us, O Lord!" A child—so the report ran—was taken up into the air and heard the Angels singing "Holy God, Holy Strong, Holy Immortal, have mercy on us," whereupon the prayer leapt to the lips of everyone, and shouted to Heaven by the whole mass of the people in extremis, was heard by the Angels' God. The reeling of the land grew less, the shuddering diminished, the sea poured back within its accustomed bounds, and little by little the awful visitation subsided. The great city lay, empty and shattered in the silence of death itself. The sun shone, as brilliantly as ever, on a scene of ruin. By the demolished heaps of masonry that had once been houses, lay smashed and mangled remains of human bodies. Broken columns, uptorn pavements, shattered statues obliterated the traces of the streets. The miasma of the plague slowly rose from the deserted slums, and fresh air blew through its foul haunts with the freedom of the daylight.

Gradually the people returned, finding the city a wilderness in its ruin. The prudence of the Augusta dictated that measures should immediately be taken to prevent excesses. The fear of the Huns might be requisitioned to inspire the manhood of the city to forget its griefs and losses in the immense work of repairing all the

LEAF OF A DYPTICH. CONSUL PRESIDING OVER THE GAMES
IN THE HIPPODROME ON THE OCCASION OF SETTING UP THE
OBELISK AFTER IT HAD BEEN THROWN DOWN BY AN EARTH-
QUAKE. INSCRIPTION, "LAMPADIORUM."

damage, rebuilding the wall, excavating its choked terraces, fortifying afresh the gates and towers, and clearing the public streets.

Terror reigned wild-eyed in Constantinople when it was bruited through its broken length and breadth that Attila indeed was at hand! So expeditiously was the work of reparation pushed forward that within a month or two the Prefect Constantine was free to turn his attention to the more ordinary business of his office. But in the meantime Theodosius was forced to sue for peace, and the Patrician Anatolius, with Theodulus, General of the Thracians and an interpreter, were despatched to the Hunnish camp to conclude a treaty on any terms. Thus began that extraordinary series of embassies of which the peace of 449 was the tardy and final outcome.

The Patriarch St. Proclus inserted the famous 'Trisagion,' the Angels' hymn at the earthquake, in the liturgy of the Church, and a day was set apart in the calendar for the yearly commemoration of that terrible event.

The result of the Imperial embassy was sufficiently appalling. The Hunnish King demanded the cession of all the territory he had conquered along the southern bank of the Danube from Singidunum to Novae and Naissus. Secondly, the annual subsidy first granted in 422 was to be increased to two thousand one hundred pounds of gold, and an immediate indemnity to be paid estimated at six thousand pounds. All prisoners taken by the Romans were to be released without delay or ransom, and all barbarian deserters to be restored to the standard of Attila. Those Romans who had escaped from their Hunnish captors were to be redeemed at twelve pounds a head. The King sent word to Theodosius that he would receive no further embassy until all refugees had been delivered up, and a promise made to harbour none in future. He was particularly desirous of regaining the persons of some Scythian princes who had thrown off their allegiance.

The Emperor was obliged to yield so far as the conditions went which made resistance possible. He sent the six thousand pounds of gold, and handed over those unwilling princes who preferred death at the hands of Attila to death at the hands of their friends. But the Treaty of Anatolius was inconclusive and imperfect. It humiliated the Byzantines without stopping the war. Theodosius refused to cede some points, and Attila still menaced him unless the citizens of Azimuntium could be persuaded "to comply with the conditions which their sovereign had accepted." The Azimuntines had offered the only successful resistance to the Huns, and now refused to deliver their Hunnish captives without obtaining the satisfaction they desired.

" It would have been strange indeed if Theodosius had purchased by the loss of honour a secure and solid tranquility ; " or if the

tameness of the Senate "had not invited the repetition of injuries."
The Hunnish envoys were instructed to press the execution of the
treaty and to inform the Byzantines that unless Attila received
complete satisfaction "it would be impossible for him . . . . to
check the resentment of his warlike tribes." But the negotiations
were wearisome and ineffectual. The Imperial government could
only pursue one servile and dilatory policy, to buy the good offices
of the Hun ambassadors and the neutrality of Attila's allies.
Money poured out of the Imperial treasury like water. "One
might imagine that Attila's pecuniary demand, which scarcely
equalled the measure of private wealth, would have been readily
discharged by the opulent Empire of the east. The public distress
affords a remarkable proof of the impoverished, or at least of the
disordered state of the finances. A large proportion of the
taxes . . . was detained and intercepted in its passage through the
foulest channels to the Imperial treasury. The immediate supplies
had been exhausted by the unforeseen expenditure upon the
ruined walls and by the military outlay of the past few years. A
personal contribution rigorously but capriciously imposed upon the
members of the senatorian order was the only expedient that could
disarm without loss of time the impatient avarice of Attila ; and
the poverty of the nobles compelled them to adopt the scandalous
resource of exposing to public auction the jewels of their wives and
the hereditary ornaments of their palaces." During a long series
of negotiations which it suited the Huns to protract, the nobles
were reduced to selling their furniture and valuables in order to
save the State, and to parting with everything rare and costly to
propitiate the greedy Hunnish envoys.

The poverty and distress that ensued can better be imagined
than described. St. Pulcheria, who had always been lavish with her
private fortune in favour of the poor and the Church, was probably
among the first of those to find themselves at the end of their resources.
She saw the wealth of the whole city flowing away to the enemy,
and knew that all funds must be diverted from the public hospitals
and charities. Even imperial munificence and saintly sacrifice
could do little to save the most helpless of Attila's victims.

"The barbarian monarch was flattered by the liberal reception
of his ministers: he computed with pleasure the value and
splendour of their gifts, rigorously exacted the performance of
every promise which would contribute to their private emolument,
and treated as an important business of state the marriage of his
secretary Constantius."

"This Gallic adventurer, who was recommended by Ætius to
the King of the Huns," had engaged to use all his influence with
Attila to make the proposed peace lasting, on condition that the
Byzantine Emperor would bestow upon him a rich and noble wife.

Chrysaphius suggested the sacrifice of a daughter of that Count
Saturninus who had met with his death at the hands of the ex-

Empress two years previously. The lady was accordingly immured in a castle, for it seems that many and ruthless were the plots against her maiden liberty. Before she could fall a victim to Constantius' greed, the Isaurian General Zeno, caring nothing for the honour or the pledge of his sovereign, wrested her from her guards and bestowed her upon Rufus, a follower of his own whom he wished to reward. Constantius complained loudly of his disappointment to Attila, and the Hun made a point of it on the occasion of the embassy of Maximinianus in 448. The Emperor, he demanded, should bring forward another lady with an equal dowry. It ill became him thus to break his word. Attila strongly suspected that Theodosius had consented· to this violence since he had not punished it. If it so happened that he was unable to command the obedience of his subjects Attila could lend him the arms and men whereby it might be forced.

Used as the Byzantine court might well be after the insults of five or six successive embassies, to the high tone of the Hun, the Emperor felt stung by this latest gibe. But he could do nothing to avenge it. The Isaurian of a truth had grown too powerful to molest. Theodosius might deprecate the indignation of Constantius and Attila by confiscating the goods of Saturninus' widow and making the bride of Rufinus penniless, and Chrysaphius, who hated Zeno, may well have suggested so expedient an injustice. But it failed to satisfy the ambassador. " He still demanded in the name of Attila an equivalent alliance, and after many ambiguous delays and excuses the Byzantine court was compelled to sacrifice to this insolent stranger the widow of Armatius, a lady whose birth, opulence, and beauty placed her in the most illustrious rank of the Roman matrons."

So low had the Empire sunk under the domination of Chrysaphius that it could neither protect its provinces nor the persons of its private subjects. The favourite was universally detested, but with the tenacity of inflexible purpose he continued to assert his influence over Theodosius. It belongs to another story to tell how in 447, or early in 448, the eunuch triumphed temporarily over the Augusta herself.

CHAPTER XXV

THE life of the Augusta Pulcheria might be more effectively written as a series of plays than as continuous history. It falls naturally into divisions which suggest them: in no single instance is the element of artistic finish lacking. Every plot has its own crisis and completion. No sooner is the curtain dropped upon one drama than another begins in which some of the former characters reappear while new ones are added to the caste. By the year 447 many who had played title rôles in scenes that are passed, such as the beautiful Athenian Empress or the heresiarch Nestorius, have disappeared, but others like Attila and Chrysaphius have come forward, and never for an instant is the stage thinned around the Byzantine throne. From 440 to 449 five separate dramas occupied it all at once. In the few foregoing chapters two of these have been distinguished ; it remains for this to tell the story of Honoria's wild betrothal, of Chrysaphius' triumph over the Augusta and of his plot against the Hun king's life. But while these things were attracting the attention of the people, the Church became involved in another fierce struggle with heresy, and by the middle of the century it became apparent that the gordian knot of trouble in the eastern empire was not to be unravelled.

Theodosius was obstinate in proportion to his weakness. Mere wax in the hands of an unscrupulous courtier, he yet had a certain doggedness. Weakness in character is too often confounded with the absence of distinctive traits. Yet it is also apparent when a man lacks the redeeming graces of his temperament. To be zealous without discretion, or purposeful without tact, is to be weak. Theodosius was faithful without reason to the friends he chose without judgment. He was weak in that he knew not how to admit a mistake, and latterly, seldom showed the graceful mind to remedy it. He maintained his faith in his evil genius with invulnerable prejudice, and sacrificed all who came in conflict with Chrysaphius at the latter's bidding. During the period of negotiation with the Huns the Grand Chamberlain had no policy but that of expediency to propose, and within a very short while the confusion, bound to follow on an arbitrary rule like this, robbed Theodosius of all respect and extinguished the earlier prestige of his reign.

The Peace of Anatolius was but the herald of three years of negotiation and humiliation. From 446 to 449 a series of embassies passed between the Byzantines and the Huns, of which the unfortunate Princess Honoria, in the obscurity of her enforced retirement, determined to take a desperate advantage. The history of these years involves the story of her wild bid for freedom.

Valentinian's unhappy sister had watched and chafed and waited through a long series of dreary years. Her restive spirit gave her no peace; she had profited nothing by imprisonment, but had prepared herself to trample down every instinct, every duty, every natural repugnance which might weaken a resolution that circumstances now suggested to her mind. The name of Attila was familiar at Constantinople, and perpetual intercourse was maintained between his camp and the imperial palace. The secret of much of his insolence was hidden in the breast of the desperate Princess. For "in the pursuit ... of revenge the daughter of Placidia .... offered to deliver her person into the arms of a barbarian of whose language she was ignorant, whose figure was scarcely human, and whose religion and manners she abhorred. By the ministry of a faithful eunuch, Honoria transmitted to Attila a ring, the pledge of her affection, and earnestly conjured him to claim her as a lawful spouse to whom he had been secretly betrothed."

Could she but succeed in inducing the Hunnish king to champion her forlorn cause under this grotesque excuse, Honoria might not only escape from durance, but pull down the house about the heads of those who held her. She had cast away more than the remembrance of her Roman and imperial blood. She was consumed with the desire for freedom, and once her ring was in the possession of Attila she must have waited with frantic anxiety for his answer. As the ambassadors came and went, every cladestine message fraught with the risk of detection and the agony of hope deferred, Honoria must have refined her dangerous tactics as only an ingenious and determined woman might. Possibly she sent again and again, for "her advances were met with coldness and disdain; Attila continued to multiply the number of his wives, until his 'chivalry' was awakened by the more forcible passions of ambition and avarice."

The poor Princess was too warped by the misfortunes of her life to weigh the consequences, either to herself or to the empire, of her rash plot. She could scarcely have been ignorant as to what manner of man Attila was, or as to what sort of life she herself would lead were she to be numbered among his wives. But, notwithstanding all that she heard on the return of Maximin and Priscus from the Hunnish capital, of Queen Cerca and Attila's harem, Honoria was in no mood to realise what it might cost her after a brief while to make way for another wife, to find her own level among these Hunnish women, to bear children whom the king scarce had leisure to distinguish from the rest. Honoria had too much time in which to reflect; the tediousness of her secret machinations enhanced the sweet illusions of revenge and freedom rather than broke a spirit whose rebelliousness had survived fourteen hopeless years.

Yet the lot for which she would so willingly have exchanged that of a Roman princess was truly no enviable one.

Attila himself was hideously ugly, typical in form and character of the savage Hunnish race. He was short and thickset, with skin so dark it was almost black, massive chest and shoulders, an enormous head, small eyes, coarse squat nose, a light coloured beard and some scanty white hair. A fitting mate for the descendant of the imperial Spaniard! The Hun, however, could match his pride with any Roman's. It appeared in his attitudes, his gestures, his walk, in the looks he cast on the right and on the left. Merely to see him, Jornandes tells us, was to be persuaded that he was born to inspire the earth with fear and to terrorise the nations. Moreover he added to his pride of kingship, the vanity of some wierd divinity. But he was destitute of religion in the Christian sense. The dispersion of so many captives, whom the imperial government was unable to redeem, among the Hunnish people prosecuted the work of evangelisation begun by St. Chrysostom on their behalf, and sowed the seeds of Christianity even in their untutored minds. But these missionaries were not allowed to approach the palace or the person of the King, and Attila continued to regard himself, or at least to desire that his subjects should regard him, as the favourite of some god of war. He was ruthless and cruel, a lover of power and might, but not altogether without weak, and better, points. He was susceptible to flattery, had some compassion for the poor and oppressed, especially of his own race, and never broke faith with those whom he might promise to protect.

Honoria, as the wife of this formidable man, would have shared the hardships of a nomadic and barbaric life. For a few brief years she might have ranked among the first of Attila's wives, and affected, in the mud and wattle capital of his empire, such state as Queen Cerca enjoyed. "A separate house was assigned to each of the numerous wives of Attila," and they enjoyed a certain degree of social state and liberty. When the Byzantine ambassador Maximin "offered his presents to the principal queen, he admired the singular architecture of her mansion, the height of the round columns, the size and beauty of the wood which was curiously shaped, or turned, or polished, or carved; and his attentive eye was able to distinguish some taste in the ornaments, and some regularity in the proportions. After passing through the guards who watched before the gate, the ambassadors were introduced into the private apartment of Cerca. The wife of Attila received their visit sitting, or rather lying, on a soft couch; the floor was covered with a carpet;

the domestics formed a circle round the queen, and her damsels
seated on the ground were employed in working the variegated
embroidery which adorned the dress of the barbaric warriors."
Attila himself lived with spartan simplicity; his clothing was
soldierly; he displayed in his footgear, his sword, and the trappings
of his charger a contempt for the decorations assumed by his
followers; he ate off wooden platters and took the long strong
draughts of the Huns, for they were great drinkers, out of wooden
cups.

There would have been no more imperial banquets for Honoria.
The Huns, accustomed to hunger, thirst, and want from earliest
childhood, were content with wild herbs for food, and to have
their meat uncooked. A certain degree of splendour marked the
barbaric feasts of Attila, but women, apparently, were excluded
from these gatherings of the chiefs and warriors. As a nation, the
people had no towns nor fixed abodes, they were perpetually on
horseback and in camp. The Roman Princess might have
languished, forgotten and neglected, among the women left behind
in the "royal village," while Attila and his hosts swept east or west
in their erratic wars, bringing back the spoils of either Empire, and
a selection of new queens. The Huns had no law but the will of
their king; no beliefs but in the sword of Mars and in the
superstitious rites of its worship; no use for money but for
ornament or gaming; no language but "a harsh and barren idiom"
which they aspired to exchange for Latin, or some Gothic tongue.
They had no clear sense of moral right or wrong; they were
perfidious and impulsive, and love among them was a savage passion
to be dreaded.

Such were the people over whom Honoria hoped to reign, to
whose lord she looked for succour and release.

But the calculating Hun cared nothing for the distress of
Valentinian's sister. Even though he seems to have carelessly
entertained her wild proposal, he thought of her less as a woman
than as a political puppet. The desperate recluse of thirty-two
made no appeal to his satiated fancy, though her cause might serve
his ambition and excuse his wars. The Princess waited vainly for
a chivalrous reply. Attila temporised, and held out just sufficient
hope to save her from despair, while he watched the success of his
embassies at Constantinople. And in the meantime her traitorous
overtures were discovered or betrayed. It was in vain to hope that
in a court riddled with spies, and corrupted by Chrysaphius, that
they could long remain secret. The Huns themselves, immeshed
in the Chamberlain's deceitful toils, probably revealed them.

Honoria was once more banished. The moment of her exposure
is difficult to determine, but it occurred most likely at the close of
the year 448. An object of fear and execration to the craven
Byzantines, the Princess was sent back to Italy. Her brother,
whose realm was threatened by her instigation of Attila no less

than that of Theodosius, spared her life, indeed, but in order to prevent the Hun from founding any claims upon her pledge, broke Honoria's wild troth, and married her to Herculanus, an obscure and nominal husband. The Empress Placidia received her daughter with implacable anger, and the scapegrace of the Empire was immured in a prison for the rest of her tragical life.

Attila was preoccupied, and raised no immediate protest. But Chrysaphius at Byzantium was uneasy, and conceived a plot to have him murdered. The eunuch knew the men with whom he had to deal, both Hun and Byzantine, also the temper of the Emperor whom he designed to serve. His way was clear, for recently he had compassed his aims against Pulcheria, and she was gone from court.

We must delay a moment to pick up this thread in the story.

St. Proclus the Patriarch, who had led the prayers of the people during the earthquake, died on October 24th, 447. Contrary to the secret hopes of the Archimandrite Eutyches, and of his powerful kinsman the Grand Chamberlain, a priest named Flavian, treasurer of St. Sophia, was recommended by the episcopal electors of the province for nomination to the vacant see.

The Augusta beheld in Flavian a worthy successor to the single-minded Churchmen who had filled the archiepiscopal throne since the expulsion of Nestorius. He was a priest of holy life and distinguished merit. His zeal for religion was of a different cast to the polemical, and it cost him an effort to overcome his natural gentleness of disposition when his conscientiousness demanded the exercise of his sterner priestly functions. He was not the man to mistake religious argumentativeness for spirituality of mind, and St. Pulcheria hoped that a Patriarch of this temperament would be so acceptable to her brother that the influence of Chrysaphius might wane. She exerted herself, accordingiy, to persuade the Emperor to confirm the election of Flavian. It lay within the rights of the sovereign to interfere in the nomination of a bishop, especially when it was deemed expedient to end a contest, or to foil an intrigue. Pulcheria suspected the intrigue of the Chamberlain to advance Eutyches, and whether she had any reason to distrust the latter or not, she feared to see Chrysaphius confirmed in power by the elevation of one who might become too easily his tool. She had foiled both the one and the other on the day when St. Flavian ascended the patriarchal throne of St. Sophia.

The Grand Chamberlain resolved to be revenged not only upon the Princess whom he had long hated, but upon Eutyches' successful rival. Never before had his ultimate object seemed so easy of attainment ; a scheme entered into his head whereby Flavian himself should assist at the undoing of Pulcheria.

Firstly the Patriarch must cross the Emperor, and incur the imperial displeasure, so that in the second instance he would know how to obey. Chrysaphius suggested to Theodosius that according to custom some present should be required of the Bishop in recognition of his promotion. St. Sophia, he represented, was an enormously wealthy church, no less so now than it had been in the days of Arcadius, when Nectarius was so great an ornament at court. Surely at such a moment, when the Emperor had pressing need of the wherewithal to satisfy the greed of the Huns, this Flavian should recognise his privilege and opportunity? The Count of the Sacred Largesses was allowed to intimate the fact to the Patriarch, but the latter's reply was unaccommodating. He sent a deputation of his clergy to the Imperial Palace, bearing the lowly offering of the 'eulogiae' or blessed bread, symbolic of bene-diction and communion. A remonstrance immediately followed, to which he replied that the wealth of the Church must not be appropriated for simonaical dealings, but expended in the service of God and relief of the poor. The upright priest could return nothing but a plain answer to the dictatorial insinuations of the ministers. Whereupon Theodosius was offended, and Chrysaphius played his second card.

Why should not the Augusta be made a deaconess of St. Sophia? The Emperor had ministers and soldiers to support his throne, surely he need submit no longer to the dictates of a woman? The new Archbishop entertained the very highest regard for the Princess, and would, doubtless, be only too glad to consecrate her to the service of his Church. At last so religious a lady would be graciously set free from the cares of state to follow the bent of her life-long inclinations. Theodosius had only to command the complaisance of the Patriarch.

The Emperor seems to have entertained the traitorous proposal, either deceived by Chrysaphius' specious argument, or willing to rid himself of the counsels and guidance of his sister. Weak man as he was, he had no mind to be torn any longer between the Augusta and the Chamberlain. Anger at the latest righteous rebuke he had suffered at the hands of Chrysaphius' opponents may have decided him to issue high-handed orders to the Patriarch to remove Pulcheria to another sphere. The Augusta was not consulted. Yet she who had refused to make way for the Empress, would scarcely cede to Chrysaphius. She resisted Theodosius' ingratitude, and flung herself with queenly confidence upon the protection of the man who was to act against her. No one, if not St. Flavian himself, could save her. The Bishop, nothing loath, firmly again refused to comply with the Emperor's demand, and advised the Augusta to retire from court. He declined to consecrate her against her will, and her own indignant protest possibly revealed to Theodosius and Chrysaphius that the Patriarch had betrayed to her their treacherous commands to him.

Pulcheria had taken a religious vow in 414 to which she had adhered with faultless fidelity for more than thirty years, and the diaconate could impose nothing further upon her. It could serve only to destroy the purpose of her patriotic life. The situation was critical for Flavian, for Theodosius refused to listen to his sister's case and only by flight could she disembarrass the Patriarch. Chrysaphius had made sure of the victory over one or the other of his two chief opponents. The Augusta saved both herself and the Archbishop by retiring from court, but the eunuch was well satisfied. It now only remained for him to again attempt the ruin of St. Flavian.

For thirty-three years St. Pulcheria had brought the power of her influence, no less than the patience of her long-suffering, to bear upon affairs of State and this was how the Emperor repaid her. She felt at last, or was obliged to feel, that the Empire lay no longer at the feet of Theodosius, but between the clutches of Chrysaphius and Attila. She departed not unwillingly from a court in which she could no longer maintain dignity or sway.

One of the imperial palaces, seven miles outside the city, served her in the brief season of her eclipse as a retreat or prison. Her heart broke, indeed, as every noble woman's must, when she realised that the end of her trust had come, that the brother to whom she had sacrificed herself without the last reserve of interest, could weigh her against an unworthy, base-souled upstart, and declare for him. Her love for Theodosius had been that selfless maternal passion which gives the right to depreciate anything less noble, less pure, than itself. She resented his indiscrimination even more than the pretension of the eunuch. But there comes a moment when the most long suffering must gather up the rags of a discarded pride and shivering beneath them, retire. The Augusta could stoop no more to dispute authority with Chrysaphius. She relinquished the struggle with so unworthy an adversary, and though it must have touched her to the quick to confess Theodosius' weakness and her own defeat, she gathered what fortitude she might from the thought of her brother's insensibility. The selfish and ungrateful cannot suffer like the loving. From the seclusion of her aslyum she watched the course of events at Constantinople with an unflagging sense of responsibility. It remained for St. Flavian to fight his battle with Chrysaphius, but the Chamberlain's last victory was the herald of a fearful nemesis.

* * * * * * * *

The embassy of the Patrician Maximin to the camp of Attila, which occupied some protracted months of the year 448, covered a plot of Chrysaphius' to have the Hun king murdered. It so happened that one of the Tartar's ambassadors named Edicon, with a colleague Orestes, had been entertained in Byzantium with such magnificence that his cupidity was greatly excited. The Roman interpreter, Vigilius, engaged to procure him a secret interview with the Grand Chamberlain, and "the eunuch who had not from his own feelings or experience imbibed any exalted notions of ministerial virtue, ventured to propose the death of Attila as an important service by which Edicon might deserve a liberal share of the wealth and luxury which he admired." Edicon professed his willingness to engage in the plot, and once Chrysaphius had obtained the consent of Theodosius, he elaborated its details. It was necessary to take into confidence Martial, the Master of Offices, since this functionary had charge of the couriers and linguists among the imperial retainers. The next move was to select an equally unscrupulous interpreter who might be trusted to keep the plot a secret from the heads of the embassy. Martial accordingly furnished Maximin and Priscus with Vigilius, and Theodosius' plenipotentiary set out on his weighty mission, little dreaming that, as the sequel went to show, his Emperor could so belie the eulogies he has passed upon him to the Persians in 422.

Orestes and Edicon accompanied the Byzantines, and the journey northwards was marked by many interesting incidents recorded by the historians Priscus and Cassiodorus. The ambassadors crossed the Danube and came presently into the neighbourhood of Attila, who then obliged them to undertake more weeks of travel in company with his own retinue, " in order that he might enjoy the proud satisfaction of receiving in the same camp the envoys of the eastern and western empires." For just about the same time Valentinian III. had sent representatives from Rome to propitiate the Hun.

Vigilius was turned back by Attila at the Danube with the peremptory demand of more complete restitution than Theodosius seemed prepared to grant. And in the interval Edicon turned traitor. Whether he quailed at the thought of the ghastly fate awaiting him were the murderous enterprise to fail, or whether from the outset he had more deeply schemed to betray the plotters by a counterplot, no sooner had Maximin arrived at the Hunnish capital than Edicon disclosed Chrysaphius' and Theodosius' perfidy. Attila perceived, apparently, that Maximin and Priscus knew nothing of the scheme, for he treated them with barbaric courtesy and kept his own counsel. When, however, Vigilius returned, accompanied by his son, and bearing " a weighty purse of gold which the favourite eunuch had furnished to satisfy the demands of Edicon and to corrupt Attila's guards, he found himself instantly arrested and dragged before the king. He protested his innocence until threatened with death, and then disclosed the whole of the nefarious scheme. Attila disdained to punish so menial a traitor; he merely demanded an enormous indemnity, and despatched two new ambassadors Eslaw and Orestes to the imperial court. " They boldly entered the presence of the Emperor, with the fatal purse hanging from the neck of Orestes who interrogated the eunuch Chrysaphius as he stood before the throne, whether he recognised the evidence of his guilt." At the same time Eslaw gravely reproved the Emperor and addressed him in a manner calculated to cover him with confusion. The Hun King's anger was majestic but it could be appeased by nothing less than the head of Chrysaphius.

Zeno, the Isaurian Commander of the Byzantine garrison, was scarcely less imperative in his demand for the execution of Chrysaphius. Deep jealousy had long existed between the two, and the soldier had reasons enough for his private enmity against the favourite. He seized the opportunity of this exposure to add his weight to the pressure exerted by Attila upon the distracted Theodosius. But Chrysaphius' ascendancy had been beyond the sphere of challenge from the moment of St. Pulcheria's eclipse. He could still dictate to the Emperor, and "a solemn embassy armed with full powers and magnificent gifts was hastily sent to deprecate the wrath of the Hun." It consisted, most adroitly, of a worthy man whose sincerity might not be questioned, and of one whose spendthrift liberality would better serve Chrysaphius' turn than any special pleading. Their exalted rank would gratify the Hunnish pride ; the " Prince of Patricians," Anatolius, now Grand Treasurer, was known to Attila as the Ambassador of 443, and Nonus or Nomius, the Master-General of the armies of the East, and personal friend of the Chamberlain, could make what impression he chose. He exerted himself in fact to some purpose. He dazzled the king with the magnificence of his bribes, and succeeded in obtaining from him more than Theodosius had dared to hope. Attila indeed could afford contempt where an Emperor would need revenge. His estimate of the imperial officers was so poor that he could be magnanimous. He condescended to pardon Theodosius, the eunuch, and the interpreter, and to re-open peace negotiations. Outstanding points of difference were waived, and a final treaty was signed. But this settlement was purchased at an enormous expense "and the subjects of the Empire were compelled to redeem the safety of a worthless favourite by oppressive taxes which they would more cheerfully have paid for his destruction."

St. Pulcheria, however, could no longer remain an inactive witness of these things. She chose a dangerous moment to return to court when St. Flavian was involved in trouble, when all those Bishops who might have defended her as he had done, had been overtaken by misfortune and disgrace, when Honoria's intrigue had just been discovered ; when Chrysaphius was all powerful. But the Augusta's holy indignation synchronised with Attila's scathing irony and Zeno's implacable hate. Nothing now stood between the Chamberlain and the retribution he deserved but the friendship of the weak and harassed Emperor.

The most critical moment of a man's life must assuredly be when, fighting desperately against the overwhelming odds which a tardy justice is piling up against him, he clenches all the powers of his clever and distorted soul to breast that tide ; when, black in the sight of God and man, black in the recesses of his heart, he defies the world to attain some vainglorious end.   In modern times examples of desperation of this sort are common enough when some gigantic financial, political, or social swindler turns at bay on the indignation of the world, and like a consummate actor poses still, until the moment when the iron-strung nerves and invulnerable mask can bear no more, and a scientific suicide ends the piece.   Chrysaphius had not the inexorable exposure of a modern court of law to dread, but wherever in the highways and byeways of that old Byzantine city, human indignation lent eloquence to some untutored orator, the burning resentment of the people found expression, and a savage cry went up for his head !   It was echoed in the garrison and in the Senate, in the hovels of the poor and the mansions of the rich, it reverberated through the Palace, and struck on no ear with more significance than on Pulcheria's.

CHAPTER XXVI

IF Chrysaphius hated St. Flavian for obtaining the position coveted by Eutyches and for detecting the plot against Pulcheria, he presently found food for fresh malignity against him in the series of happenings inaugurated by Bishop Eusebius' denunciation of the views of the Archimandrite. He found, moreover, in Dioscorus, Patriarch of Alexandria, a most powerful ally against St. Flavian, and in favour of his kinsman.

Eutyches, the superior of a populous monastery outside the walls of Constantinople, had spent practically the whole of his life in religion. He was now an old man, and the brilliant scarlet of his habit and the fillet in his thin white hair were faded from long hours of meditation in the sun.* He had kept the vows of his profession blamelessly, and like the holy Dalmatius, had only once set foot outside his convent. That was on the occasion of the great demonstration against Nestorius when all the kaloyers of the capital and its neighbourhood—a shabby but multi-coloured throng —had streamed in procession to the gates of the Emperor's Palace. Eutyches had followed the Nestorian controversy with the subtlety and passion of a fifth century theologian. Returning to his cell he had ruminated upon it to such an extent and pushed the orthodox arguments so far, and patched up so extraordinary a refutation from a thousand other arguments, as to originate or revive a heresy diametrically opposite to that of Nestorius. Bishop Theodoret had already written a work forestalling this danger, and called it "The Beggar," since monophytism begged its tenets from a variety of outworn heresies. Bishops Domnus of Antioch and Eusebius of Dorylaeum had apparently read this treatise, but Eutyches indeed deserved the reproach of ignorance if he had neglected to make himself acquainted with such a pronouncement on the views that interested him. The old abbot divided his attention between christological speculations and the secular career of his god-son Chrysaphius. It was delightful, when the courtier came to visit him, to pour into his ears the arguments with which the monks were sufficiently

---

* The clergy of the period wore no distinctive dress in ordinary life, but the monks and religious confraternities were distinguished by their "habits." One of these was scarlet, but the writer has no justification, beyond the picturesque, for attributing it to the order of Eutyches.

familiar, and to match his wits with those of one fresh from the world of men and things. Chrysaphius would scarcely have been a Byzantine had the darling theories of the old monk failed to interest him, but even as the abbot talked, the eunuch's multi-coloured thoughts busied themselves with plans for the furtherance of his ambition. If it had rested with Chrysaphius when St. Proclus died, Eutyches would certainly have succeeded to the archiepiscopal throne of St. Sophia.

The first intimation that the religious views of his kinsman might cause some stir, if not indeed some trouble, in the Church, was afforded Chrysaphius by a letter addressed to the Emperor on the subject by Bishop Domnus of Antioch. But the matter was allowed to drop.

In 448, however, the Emperor so far yielded to the heretical influences that, all unperceived, were being brought to bear upon him, as to depose a certain blameless Bishop Irenaeus at the instigation of some who held views like those of Eutyches. The Nestorian controversy still agitated men's minds, and the most vehement opponents of Nestorius' teaching, not content with the victory of St. Cyril, went so far beyond the mean, the orthodox position, as to accuse those who refused to think with them, of the original heresy. The orthodox became Nestorians according to the followers of Eutyches. When at last Bishop Eusebius of Dorylaeum, who had been at one time an intimate friend of the archimandrite, took up the matter and lodged a forcible complaint in the authoritative quarter, the light of day was let in upon the mischief, and Chrysaphius had to set his wits to work to make the opprobrium recoil upon St. Flavian.

The Archbishop was bound to take notice of Eusebius' letter. His office obliged him to sift accusations of heresy, however personally unwilling he might be to disturb an old and estimable monk. He seems to have feared to fasten deliberate fault on the self-opiniatedness of one who might have fallen a victim to nothing more widely dangerous than some self-conceit. It was a creditable thing to have lived so long and kept one's vows so well ; to have enjoyed the esteem of a large community ; and praiseworthy, at three score years and ten, to take a keen interest in subtle things when many a less aged man had yielded to the soporific influence of years and seclusion.

There was, at this date, a class of Councils peculiar to Constantinople, called permanent synods, which were presided over by the Patriarch and attended by all the bishops who chanced to be in the imperial city when there was occasion to hold them. St. Flavian referred this matter of the complaint against Eutyches to some such a meeting held in the Secretarium of the Archiepiscopal Palace. He tried to persuade Eusebius to have a private interview with the abbot, and ascertain exactly to what extent Eutyches' opinions were heretical, and how far they had obtained credence.

among the monks and people. He, the Patriarch, could scarcely believe the danger to be so serious as his brother of Dorylaeum would seem, by this deposition, to think. If, after a personal discussion, Eutyches were really to reveal himself a heretic, then it would be time enough to invite him to explain himself before the assembled Bishops in that place.

But Eusebius was insistent. He was anxious not only for the purity of the faith, but to justify his intervention, for at that time the measures taken against false accusers were exceedingly severe. He urged it upon the Patriarch that his accusation was not without foundation, that indeed it called for the attention of the Church.

" The facts," he afterwards wrote, are as follows :—

" I found that Eutyches, a presbyter and archimandrite in charge of a monastery in the city of Constantinople, was turning away many of his spiritual brethren from the faith of the orthodox, and maintaining opinions contrary to the determination of the Church. I thought that a very grave responsibility would lie upon me if I silently concealed so great and so serious a corruption. I approached the most religious Flavian, then bishop of the city of Constantinople, and the most religious bishops who at the time happened to be there present, with a formal charge drawn up in my own name, in which I accused Eutyches of rejecting the teaching and doctrine of our holy fathers, of complaining that all have erred alike from the right faith, and of putting forth doctrines contrary to the canons. I demanded his personal attendance at the religious consistory, to give satisfaction concerning these charges laid against him by me."

" You know the zeal of the accuser," said St. Flavian to the monks ; " fire itself seems cool in comparison with his passion for religion. God knows ! I besought him to yield and to desist ; as however he persisted what could I do ? Shall I scatter you and not rather gather ? To scatter is the work of enemies but it is the work of fathers to gather."

Accordingly a second sitting was held on November 12th, 448, four days after the first. The question of faith at issue was clearly defined, and an exposition was drawn up of the orthodox teaching as demonstrated at the Council of Ephesus. To this all the clergy present appended their signatures.

The proceedings were quiet and dignified. Chrysaphius watched them contemptuously. St. Flavian does not seem to have foreboded further trouble, but St. Pulcheria, who had known Eusebius of Dorylaeum as a layman and an official in her own household, knew better than anybody how this affair would turn to Chrysaphius' advantage if Theodosius hesitated as he had hesitated seventeen years ago.

When at the third Synod, a week later, St. Flavian's messengers to Eutyches announced that he refused to appear before it, and that his profession of faith seemed unsatisfactory, a second embassy was despatched to the monastery. Eutyches was again invited to present himself before the Archbishop, to hear what Bishop Eusebius preferred against him, and to clear himself of the charge. His excuse about clausura was not valid. It had been broken in the interests of the faith before; it could be broken for the same reason now, especially at the bidding of his superior.

In the meantime, the Archimandrite had done what weak men always do in such a situation—rushed to ink and paper, verbosity and self-justification. He had written an exposition of his views, and sent the 'tome' to all the monasteries of the city with a a request that the various superiors should subscribe it. One here and one there, did so, but for the most part the monks left the matter to its proper judges, and a certain slow and sure old man treated Eutyches' writing with the irrelevance so maddening to the self-important, and confessed he had not even read it!

A third summons, equally temperate but rather firmer in tone was now sent to the monk. He was citied to appear before the Bishops on Wednesday, November 17th. When the fourth session opened on the Tuesday, and messengers arrived from Eutyches full of excuses for his non-appearance, St. Flavian was still patient. He sent word back that if, indeed, the abbot were ill he should not be urged to come, that the Synod would wait, that he had no need to fear it. At last, however, the most long suffering must doubt. By this time it had become evident enough to the majority that Eutyches was imposing on St. Flavian. The last message sent him was to the effect that if he did not appear by November 22nd he would be degraded from the priesthood and deprived of his headship in the convent.

St. Flavian held a sixth consultation with his suffragans and clergy on the 20th, at which it was decided that Eutyches might be accompanied by as many friends as he wished. Theodosius sent a letter to the Synod stipulating for the presence of the Patrician Florentius: (The Emperors having assumed the right of convoking councils, were allowed to send their deputies invested with many privileges, as their representatives, in case they did not assist in person.) When the conclave opened the following Monday, Eutyches arrived before the doors escorted by the exalted Silentiary, Magnus (as Nestorius had been by Count Candidian,) and an enormous and motley following of monks, servants and soldiers.

Eutyches was confronted with Eusebius, and after the minutes had been read of all that had hitherto been done in the affair, the question of faith was battled out between them. Unlike Nestorius, who so insisted on the human nature of Our Blessed Lord, as to rather minimise the divine, Eutyches had arrived at the notion that His human body was so assimilated and deified by its association with divinity, as to no longer remain of the same substance as an ordinary human frame. The Archimandrite thus asserted the capability of suffering and death in God, and robbed the humanity of the Incarnate Christ of all its pathetic holiness and significance to man.

At the Synod, however, neither Eutyches nor Eusebius argued well. The monk was confused and obdurate, reiterating "I am not come to dispute but to say what I think," while the Bishop suddenly realised the force of the influential enmities he had incurred. The layman Florentius seems to have been a keener cross-questioner than St. Flavian. Often, when the Patriarch would have let a point pass, the Patrician caught up one or another of the speakers with consummate eclectical skill. He seems to have convicted Eutyches, when the old man's heat or obstinancy might still have deceived St. Flavian. When the test was applied to the schismatic, he failed to meet it. He consented to use the formula dictated to him by the Synod, but refused to anathematise views contrary to the faith it expressed. St. Flavian was dissatisfied. When the Imperial representative Florentius put the final question concerning the divine and human natures in the Saviour, Eutyches replied in the terms which afterwards became the standard of his heresy, "I confess that Our Lord was of two natures before union, but after the union I confess one nature." "As," said he, "a drop of water let fall into the ocean is quickly absorbed and disappears in the vast expanse, so also the human element, being infinitely less than the divine is entirely absorbed by the divinity." This view of the Incarnation was the exact reverse of Nestorianism, and equally obnoxious to the Church. The Synod could not recognise or accept Eutyches' confused confession. He had shown himself, as St. Leo afterwards said, to be "unskilled and ignorant," but it was not on this account that St. Flavian condemned him. He was intractable and a source of dissention and error. Eusebius of Dorylaeum was, unfortunately, justified. Perhaps the Patriarch scarcely knew how far Eutychianism had penetrated the court and the religious section of Constantinopolitan society, but the unsympathetic attitude of the Emperor and Florentius, showed him that all the influence of Chrysaphius was being exercised on Eutyches' behalf. St. Pulcheria at this moment in disgrace could do nothing to counteract the machinations of the Chamberlain.

Moreover, Bishop Dioscorus of Alexandria, who had already put himself at the head of the monophysite party, with the idea of exalting his See to the leadership of the Eastern, if not indeed of the whole Church, now entered into the affair. He had been unfriendly to St. Flavian from the outset of the latter's Patriarchal career, and had pointedly withheld from him the annual Paschal letters. In the year 448, St. Flavian's first Easter, the troubles were stirring in which both he and his predecessor Proclus had been opposed to Dioscorus, and later on, the Eutychian controversy rendered the relations of the two Patriarchs still more strained. At the close of the Constantinopolitan Synod, St. Flavian felt he must condemn Eutyches and his heresy not only in the spiritual but in the temporal interests of the Church. Thus he read the sentence :—

"Eutyches, a priest and Archimandrite, has by previous statements, and even now by his own confession shown himself to be entangled in the perversity of Valentinus and Apollinaris, without allowing himself to be won back to the genuine dogmas by our exhortation and instruction. Therefore we, bewailing his complete perversity, have decreed for the sake of Christ, Whom he has reviled, that he be deposed from every priestly office, expelled from our communion and deprived of his headship over the convent."

St. Flavian then wrote the formula "judicans subscripsi," and his signature at the foot of the document. All the assembled Bishops and twenty-three Archimandrites followed his example, but the latter wrote only "subscripsi," since, as Eutyches might have known, they had no right of judgment, simply of assent in such a matter.

Eutyches complained loudly of the finding of the Synod. As the assembly was breaking up, he told the Imperial representative that he meant to appeal to another Council, and Florentius communicated the fact to Flavian. The whole lamentable business now began to assume a more threatening aspect, and the graver fears of the Patriarch, St. Pulcheria and Bishop Eusebius seemed likely to be realised. The court party, swayed by Chrysaphius, was greatly incensed against St. Flavian, and the Chamberlain hastened to enlist the Patriarch of Alexandria in the interests of Eutyches. The abbot himself immediately wrote a budget of letters addressed to St. Leo at Rome (with whom he had already had some correspondence), St. Peter Chrysologus at Ravenna, and to Dioscorus among others, demanding justice at the hands of another Council. Theodosius also wrote to Rome to urge the intervention of the Pope.

St. Flavian, for his part, did not fail to convey the news of all that had happened, in the regular way, to the various provincial bishops, but for some considerable time no communication from his pen reached Rome. His letter to St. Leo was seriously delayed and the Pope wrote to him on the 18th of February the following year, nearly three months after Eutyches' condemnation, to ask the reason of his apparent neglect.

"Seeing that the most Christian Emperor in his zeal for the Catholic Church has written to us of the disturbed state of things with you," says this beautiful and forbearing letter, "we marvel, my brother, that you could remain silent, and neglect to send us, at the earliest opportunity your own account of the matter so as to free us from uncertainty as to what has taken place. For we have received a written statement (libellum) from Eutyches who complains that on the accusation of Bishop Eusebius he has been unjustly excommunicated, when yet he had presented himself before the Synod when summoned, and had offered a written statement of his belief, which statement the Synod refused to receive, so that he was obliged to post up bills in Constantinople protesting against the injustice which had been done him. Such being the case we do not understand as yet with what justice he has been excommunicated. But we desire to hear your account of what has been done, and to have the whole matter laid before us, since we, who would have the decisions of God's priests maturely arrived at, can form no judgment for either side, till we have heard a true statement of all the proceedings.

"Wherefore, my brother, inform us fully by a fit person, what new doctrine contrary to the ancient faith, hath arisen, which has deserved to be visited with so severe a punishment. For both the Church's moderation and the religious faith of the most pious Emperor bid us be careful of Christian peace, so that dissensions being cut off, the Catholic faith, may be preserved inviolate, and those who maintain error being reclaimed, those whose faith has been approved may be fortified by our authority. Nor can any difficulty arise in this instance since the aforesaid Presbyter has professed in his appeal, that he is prepared to amend anything that may be found worthy of blame in him. For in these cases this should especially be aimed at, that both charity should be preserved and truth vindicated without noise and contention. Wherefore, dearly beloved brother, as you see us to be necessarily solicitous in so grave a matter, lose no time in informing us of everything, as you ought to have done before, as fully and distinctly as possible, that we may run no risk of being deceived by party representations, and dissension fostered which ought to be crushed at its first beginning. For we are resolved, with God's help, that the determinations of the venerable Fathers, divinely confirmed, and pertaining to the soundness of the faith, shall not be violated by any man's perverse interpretation.

God preserve thee, dearest brother.*

February 18, 449. *The illustrious Asturius and Protogenes Consuls.*

To this St. Flavian replied at length, relating the intrigues going on at court, and begging for St. Leo's support. "The cause needs only your succour and defence," he wrote, "and by intimating your consent you may bring all to quietness and peace."

It must have been about this time that St. Pulcheria returned

---

* This letter is taken from the Rev. C. A, Heurtley's introduction to his translation of the famous "tome" of St. Leo (Parker & Co. 1885.) It is so full of apostolic grace and gentleness that I quite fail to see how the Rev. T. A. Lacey in his translation of St. Flavian's letters of appeal, (S.P.C.K., 1903) can say that it was "angry and suspicions." True it is that "like his predecessors St. Leo viewed with no favour the rise of Constantinople" to a too ambitious headship of the Church in the East, but he scarcely seems to have been so much concerned as to whether "this was an attempt of Flavian . . . . to decide an important question of faith without consulting the principal sees . . . . ," as to whether or not injustice had been done to Eutyches, formerly a zealous champion of the faith, as to whether or not a new heresy was started. It was for Dioscorus not St. Flavian to alarm Rome by arbitrary proceedings and unjustifiable pretensions.

to court, summoned thither by her anxiety about the Patriarch no less than by her indignation on account of the plot against Attila. She had, however, nothing but her fears to add to those of St. Flavian and Eusebius, who both dreaded the prospect of a further council. No one could have forseen better than the Augusta the lengths to which Chrysaphius would go to secure the triumph of the abbot and the disgrace of her protector. The Chamberlain was in fact, at that very moment planning an outrage beside which his attempt against the Hun King fades into insignificance. Loaded with the execration of the people who groaned under the taxes imposed upon them for the liquidation of Attila's indemnity, Chrysaphius seemed reckless of the public hate. But the interposition of Pulcheria was not even now, without effect. Theodosius had several interviews with Eutyches in which he made some attempt to dissuade the old man from his heresy. He found himself again on the horns of a dilemma, torn between the Augusta and the Chamberlain. He desired, perhaps sincerely, to prevent a schism in the Church, but was unwilling or unable to abandon the cause of the schismatic. Equally ineffectual as theologian or diplomat he failed to get a profession of faith from the abbot's lips which would satisfy the bishops, as he failed to withstand Chrysaphius. The duel was unequal; Theodosius was worsted, and prevailed upon to inaugurate a series of enquiries designed to throw discredit on St. Flavian and the recent Synod. The Patriarch was charged with having prejudiced the case and falsified the minutes. But prior to the gathering of this ecclesiastical commission the Chamberlain had accomplished his greater purpose. Bent upon the ruin of the Patriarch and the foiling of Pulcheria, he employed all his craft and power to save Eutyches.

With this object in view he wrote to Dioscorus, Patriarch of Alexandria, urging him to undertake the vindication of the deposed abbot, and promising him every support for his own ambitious designs if he would but press upon the Emperor the necessity of another Council. Dioscorus, a man of violent actions and rash presumption, was nothing loath to come forward as the monophysite champion and as arbitrator in the affairs of a rival see. He was himself no less inimical than Chrysaphius to St. Flavian and St. Pulcheria. Both men beheld in the Augusta the ultimate obstacle to their several ends. So long as she retained a shred of influence, of power, neither the rival Patriarch nor the upstart eunuch could succeed in their plans for self-aggrandisement. Her downfall would materially assist the assertion of Chrysaphius in the State, and of Dioscorus in the Church. Thus this theological embroglio presented itself to the one as to the other in the light of a handle against St. Flavian and the Augusta, as an opportunity for the furtherance of every worldly scheme.

Theodosius was easily duped, and in March, 449, an order was issued in the name of the co-adjutant Emperors for an Œcumenical

Council to assemble from East and West at Ephesus by the August following.

St. Pulcheria had turned her attention to the more immediate prospect. It must be in part attributed to the support of her favour and assurance that the commission of enquiry resulted in a favourable verdict for St. Flavian. In April that assembly met before whom the Patriarch was impeached and by which the proceedings of the original council were to be examined. It consisted of about thirty bishops the minority of whom had sat in the recent Synod, and it condemned the Archimandrite. St. Flavian being on trial, Thalassius, Bishop of Caesarea, presided in his place. However eagerly Eutyches may have counted on the new elements in the Synod to reverse the verdict of the first, however much Chrysaphius may have hoped for the discomfiture of the Patriarch, both men were deeply disappointed. At the very time when Theodosius' letters of convocation were speeding on their way to all the prelates of the East, the justice of St. Flavian's attitude was made abundantly manifest. The result of the insult put upon the Patriarch by this inquisitorial conclave was wholly contrary to the expectations of his enemies. He approached the Emperor with a profession of faith entirely satisfactory to the Church. The charge of Nestorianism urged against him was shown to have no foundation but in the exaggerations of Eutyches. The monophysites were far too prone thus to wound the good name of the orthodox. The Patriarch and his adherents must have taken heart of grace from the happy termination of this Synod, but it was too late to cancel the arrangements set afoot for the Œcumenical Council, and Chrysaphius and Dioscorus strained every nerve in the interval to secure a prejudiced assembly. For them everything depended on St. Flavian's defeat, and they hesitated at nothing to ensure this end.

St. Leo received the imperial summons on the thirteenth of May. A few days later he wrote to say that in his judgment the matter was too clear to call for synodical treatment, but that if this were really necessary, the Council should be held not at Ephesus, amid the heat and factions of the East, but in Italy. As time went on and it became impossible to stop the preparations, the Pope chose three representative legates and despatched them to Constantinople bearing his famous dogmatic epistle to St. Flavian among other important letters.

It would be an undertaking out of all proportion with the pretensions of this book to enter into the merits of the Eutychian controversy. It is only necessary to sketch the history of that agitation in order to include the great Council of Chalcedon which subsequently formed not only its antidote and sequel, but the monumental event of Pulcheria's brief reign. Ecclesiastical historians like Bishop Hefele (" History of the Christian Councils ") supply a circumstantial background for the one particular note in it all which it is our purpose to accentuate. The subject would be tedious for any but the theologian or the specialist. The biographer of St. Pulcheria dares approach it from one side alone. In the correspondence which passed between St. Leo at Rome and the Byzantine Princess on the subject of this controversy, we have the only original material which remains for any portion of her story. The letters are not numerous. Although they scarcely strike the personal note, it would be so invaluable to catch, they bring us into closer touch with the Augusta than anything we have yet related. Hitherto St. Pulcheria has been hidden all too much. It almost seems as though any story but hers has been told. For only in connection with Athenais, Honoria, Antiochus and the rest has it been possible to discern her influence or describe her presence. Thus the peculiar value of the Eutychian controversy in this connection is, that however wide a digression it might seem to occasion in a narrative too full of digressions, it nevertheless enshrines a portion of the actual correspondence of the Byzantine Princess, and brings her forward as a salient character.

CHAPTER XXVII

A MARTYR FOR THE FAITH AND ROME

DIOSCORUS received Eutyches back into communion, and moreover reinstated him in his priestly and abbatial dignities, contrary to all canonical regulations, and notwithstanding the fact that as Patriarch of Alexandria he had no shadow of jurisdiction in St. Flavian's diocese.

The Emperor invited Chrysaphius' powerful ally to preside at Ephesus, and directed him to come to the Council accompanied by ten Egyptian metropolitans, and ten other bishops. The mandates issued in the name of Theodosius were dictated by the wile of one who knew every move in the game. Dioscorus was assured that Theodoret of Cyzicus should not be admitted unless with the consent of the Counsel; the champion of the faith was actually forbidden to leave his see. A Syrian abbot Barsumus, was specially invited, as the representative of that large body of Egyptian monks known to be inclined to the monophysite party. Other letters committed to Dioscorus, Juvenal of Jerusalem and Thalassius of Cæsarea, the effective control of the Council.

Once again Constantinople was invaded by churchmen from every part of the Empire, and once again the courtesies of the Patriarchæon were refused when tendered by a Bishop in disgrace with the Grand Chamberlain.

St. Leo declined to leave Rome for more than one reason, but he sent four representatives to Ephesus, Bishop Julius of Pozzuolo, a priest Renatus, who died on the journey, Hilarius a deacon, and a secretary Dulcitius. These legates bore letters to the Archimandrites of Constantinople, the members of the Synod, the Emperor, the Augusta, and some high dignitaries, and among them a theological treatise to St. Flavian, which was afterwards incorporated with a similar letter to the Council, and became known and venerated as the "tome of St. Leo." This "masterly, profound and clear analysis of the orthodox doctrine of two natures in one Person" is only comparable for simplicity and depth, beauty and solidity, to the Gospels themselves. It would be difficult to exaggerate its spirituality and reasonableness; difficult to convey the wonderful spirit which informs its maturely meditated truths in any words but those of the great Pope himself. Perhaps in the whole history of Christianity no other controversial document has attained the level, at once argumentative and devotional, of the celebrated tome of St. Leo.

" . . . what can be more iniquitous," he asks, "than to be wise towards impiety and to refuse to yield to those who are wiser and more learned? But some men fall into this folly when, on being prevented by some obscurity from becoming acquainted with the truth, they have recourse not to the writings of the Prophets, not to the Epistles of the Apostles, not to the authority of the Gospels, but to themselves, and thus become teachers of error because they have not been disciples of truth. For what instruction has he gained from the sacred pages of New and Old Testament who does not comprehend the first words even of the Creed?

" The Son of God coming down from His heavenly throne, and yet not departing from the glory of his Father, enters this lower world, born after a new order by a new mode of birth : born after a new order forasmuch as, invisible in His own nature, He became visible in ours; incomprehensible He willed to be comprehended ; being ever before time He began to be in time ; the Lord of the Universe He took upon Him the form of a servant; throwing a veil over His infinite majesty, God impassible, He did not disdain to become passible man ; immortal to be subject to the laws of death : born by a new mode of birth, forasmuch as virginity inviolate which knew not concupiscence ministered the substance of flesh. From the Mother of the Lord was received nature not sin . . . He who is very God is also very man . . . for as the God is not changed by compassion, so the man is not consumed by dignity. For each nature in union with the other performs the actions which are proper to it . . . the one is resplendent with miracles, the other succumbs to injuries . . . As therefore it belongs not to the same nature to weep with pity for a dead friend, and with a command to raise the same restored to life . . . so it does not belong to the same nature to say ' I and my Father are one,' and to say ' the Father is greater than I ' . . . ' What indeed is [in the words of St. John] to ' disunite Jesus ' but to separate His human [or in modern days, His divine] nature from Him and to make void the mystery by which alone we have been saved ? "

The letter goes on to show how, that if the Lord's body had been unreal, so too had the Cross and His Passion "since the denial of very flesh is the denial of bodily suffering." St. Leo concludes by recommending Eutyches to every mercy in the event of his recantation "for our Lord the true and good Shepherd ' who laid down His life for His sheep,' and who came to save men's souls not to destroy, would have us to imitate His clemency, that those who sin, justice should restrain, but those who repent, mercy should not repel. For then is the true faith most effectually depended when a false opinion is condemned also by its upholders."

The Council at Ephesus was formally opened August 8th, 449,

in the very Church where the last great Synod, on Nestorianism, had been held. It consisted of one hundred and thirty Bishops, or their deputies, from Egypt and the East, and Illyricum alone ; only the Roman legates came from farther west. The Count Elpidius and the tribune Eulogius represented the Emperor, and Proclus the pro-consul of Asia was directed to supply them with an armed force for the police of the Council. Eutyches was present, also St. Flavian, and a number of those who had sat in the original Constantinopolitan conclave.

From the acts of the Council it is impossible to say whether its proceedings occupied one or more days. These acts themselves are only preserved in the minutes of the subsequent Council of Chalcedon, and require far more explanation than their own fragmentary character supplies. Moreover, Dioscorus falsified them ; they were read in 451 with passionate interruptions and recriminations from those who had been present at Ephesus. The Patriarch of Alexandria had not allowed any but his own notaries to take minutes—nothing less dishonest would have suited Chrysaphius—with brutal violence he had destroyed those written by men employed by St. Flavian and Stephen of Ephesus. " If," says Mr. Lacey, " we judge Dioscorus by his demeanour at Chalcedon, where he was standing on his defence, already a beaten man, we shall not easily imagine him smooth and conciliatory at Ephesus in his day of power. The taunts and gibes which he flung fearlessly" at his triumphant opponents would not ring less fiercely when he had the power of the Chamberlain at his back and the Emperor's soldiers at his call.

The sitting opened apparently with the reading of the various letters of convocation. Thalassius moved that the Council should proceed at once to the consideration of the theological question, and he was seconded by Bishop Julius, anxious to bring in St. Leo's letter. But Dioscorus deftly turned the attention of the Fathers ; it would ill suit Eutyches to speak after the tome. The overbearing Egyptian had also taken care that the Roman legates should experience the greatest difficulty in communicating with any who might be favourable to Flavian. As Nestorius had withheld St. Cyril's letters from the the Emperor, so now Dioscorus hoped to prevent St. Leo's letters reaching St. Pulcheria. His myrmidons outside the Council were to intercept the papal missives, as he himself, within it, contrived to postpone the reading of the tome. But the deacon Hilarius succeeded in getting St. Leo's letter to the Augusta transmitted to Constantinople, and no doubt can be cast on Pulcheria's attitude towards the controversy.

After some account had been rendered of all that had happened since Eusebius of Dorylæum first denounced Eutyches to Flavian, the abbot stepped forward with his profession of faith and his speech in self-justification. A petition from the monks of the monastery was read ; " there was a short wrangle about the asserted falsification of the acts [of the Constantinopolitian synod] and Dioscorus promptly asked for the judgment of the Council."

From this moment the true character of Chrysaphius' packed assembly declared itself. St. Flavian was not allowed to protest, Dioscorus ruled aside the reading of St. Leo's letter, Eutyches' monks were restored to communion, their abbot himself declared blameless, and Dioscorus proceeded to secure the condemnation of St. Flavian. The Pope's envoys were shouted down or chased out of the church. Everything was carried by violence and open faction. The imperial officers did nothing to restrain the tumultuousness of the soldiery and the monks. Questions were settled by party cries within and by riotous mobs without. Ferocious threats were breathed against Eusebius and Flavian. It was a scene "unparalleled in the history of the Church." The story was told afterwards at Chalcedon, where bishop after bishop rose, and recounted how he had been coerced and terrified, recounted his own treachery and shame. Dioscorus sprang to his feet to read the condemnation of St. Flavian but a number of the fathers fell on their knees imploring him to carry the outrageous affair no further. Upon this Dioscorus called loudly for Elpidius and Eulogius, who without more ado, ordered the doors to be flung open. A band of soldiers under Proclus, burst in upon the uproar, followed by a dangerous crowd of rudely armed citizens and monks. This intrusion still further terrified the bishops, and when the president called for their subscription to the interrupted sentence, few save the Roman deacon had the courage to refuse. Shouting 'contradicitur' Hilarius sprang to St. Flavian's side, and the Patriarch dashed down in writing some feverish lines of appeal to the Pope, which he thrust into the legate's hand. This was the crowning moment. In a second the Patriarch was down upon the ground, and Dioscorus, Barsumus and others of their party fell upon him in ruffianly rage. While St. Flavian was being kicked and mauled within an inch of his life, Hilarius fled from the riot and contrived his escape to Rome.

*   *   *   *   *   *   *   *

The historians of the Latrocinale, or Robber Synod, as St. Leo dubbed the Council, were baffled for many years to supply the missing link in the tale, of this appeal of St. Flavian. Those hastily scribbled lines to St. Leo were all important to the subject, but they had been, apparently, destroyed or lost. Mr. Lacey has published a booklet (1903) under the auspices of the Church Historical Society, which gives the history of one of the most important and interesting literary discoveries of modern times.

"The letter of St. Flavian," he tells us was unearthed in 1874, by Professor Amelli in the Ambrosian Library, and "was accompanied by another document, the existence of which had not been even suspected, viz. : a similar appeal on the part of Eusebius of Dorylaeum.

"We seem to feel the breathless haste in which they were

delivered.   I picture Flavian in his closely watched retreat, rapidly
dictating his complaint—there was no lack of shorthand writers—
and handing the copy to Hilarius" who waited in hot indignation
and keen anxiety.

" Flavian to the most religious and holy Father and Archbishop Leo
—" thus runs Mr. Lacey's translation, "greeting in the Lord.

" With good cause at the present time I purpose a further reference to
your holiness, by way of apostolic appeal, that you may visit the East and
rescue in its imminent peril the godly faith of our holy fathers, which they
with laborious defence have handed down to us.   For lo, all is confounded ;
the laws of the Church are broken ; the faith is destroyed ; godly souls
are bewildered by controversy ; the doctrine of the fathers is now no
longer called the faith, but, by the authority of Dioscorus the bishop of
the Alexandrine church and those who hold with him, the teaching of
Eutyches is now extolled and called the faith.   This he has established by
his own decree and by the suffrages of bishops giving a forced consent.
All the circumstances it is impossible for me at this moment to report to
your blessedness, but I will briefly explain what has happened :
"We arrived at the city of Ephesus, according to the goodly writ of
the Emperors . . . and met the representatives of your Holiness. . . .
We spent ten days [waiting] in the city of Ephesus, finding almost all the
assembled bishops in agreement with us except the company of the bishop
of Alexandria, who from the day that I was ordained bishop, has, without
any cause, pursued me with implacable enmity. . . . "

The letter goes on to describe the opening of the Council, the
course of its proceedings, and the declaration of Eutychianism,
until it comes to the point when

"all wrongs, so to say, were suddenly packed into one day, riot, the
restoration of the condemned, the condemnation of the innocent—of
me who have never in any way thought of transgressing against the
authority of the fathers.   And since all was going unjustly against me, as
if by a settled agreement, after the iniquitous proposal which, of his own
motion, he levelled at me, on my appealing to the throne of the Apostolic
See of Peter, the Prince of the Apostles, and to the holy council in general
which meets under your holiness, a crowd of soldiers at once surrounds
me, prevents me from taking refuge at the holy altar, as I desired, and
tried to drag me out of the church.   Then amid the utmost tumult I barely
succeeded in reaching a certain part of the church, and there hid myself
with my companions, not without being watched, however, to prevent my
reporting to you all the wrongs which have been done me.

" I therefore beseech your holiness not to let things rest in regard to
this mad plot . . . but to rise up in the cause of our right faith . . . and
instructing with suitable letters our faithful and Christian Emperor," and
many others, * bring to nothing that "which has now been effected evilly
and by a sort of gamester's trick."

* Mr. Lacey thinks that some corruption in the text of the letter accounts for the
absence of Pulcheria's name, but that certain words "survive from a description of her
person."

The appeal of Eusebius gives substantially the same account, although the Bishop of Dorylaeum was uncanonically excluded from the deliberations of the Council. St. Flavian desired his presence, but Dioscorus refused to admit him. He was held prisoner by the Imperial commissioners and saw more of the rioting without the assembly than of the violence within it. "Wherefore," says Eusebius, "entangled in toils from which there is no escape, afflicted and in the last extremity of trouble, I fly to the only refuge left me under God, eagerly seeking deliverance from the evils into which I am fallen."

*   *   *   *   *   *   *

St. Flavian died within a few days after the conclusion of the Conncil,—died of his grief and injuries at Hypaepa, a city about forty miles distant from Ephesus and situated on the route of his exile.

If any proof were yet wanting of the brazen wickedness of Chrysaphius and his confederates, as of the criminal weakness of the "most religious" Emperor, the sequel supplies it. Dioscorus concluded by excommunicating St. Leo himself, the most outrageous act yet done by any rival bishop. Theodosius confirmed the Acts of the Council and deliberately rent Christendom. All Egypt, Thrace, and Palestine, went over to monophysite heresy, while Syria, Pontus, and Asia remained faithful to the Church.

CHAPTER XXVIII

Upon the death of St. Flavian, the monophysite Bishops raised one of their own party to the vacant see of Constantinople.

St. Leo immediately wrote to the Emperor that the Acts of the infamous Council just held were to be regarded as null and void, and that everything was to remain as it had been before August until another and properly constituted gathering could be called. Theodoret of Cyzicus wrote most earnestly to the Pope begging him to take every interest in the affairs of the Eastern Church, and to convene another council to quash the enactments of Dioscorus. The zealous historian prelate, who always chafed at his exile from the centres of life and activity, wrote also to a high official in Constantinople imploring him to obtain the Emperor's permission, for him, Theodoret, to assist at the next Council.

Theodosius, however, had no intention of calling one. Eutyches had been reinstated in his convent, his faith had been declared orthodox and his monks had been restored to communion. Anything which might tend to reverse the enactments of Dioscorus and Chrysaphius must be discountenanced by the Emperor who had sanctioned them.

St. Leo, however, would not yield to such base adversaries. The man who could confront the barbarian invaders of his country, armed only by the majesty of a faith they did not profess, was not the man to be dismayed by a Disocorus or Chrysaphius. The atrocious death of St. Flavian banished any hesitation St. Leo may have felt about a second council. He had been too solicitous for the welfare of his people, too apprehensive of the dangers of the time to present himself at Ephesus, but when devotion chanced to bring the Emperor Valentinian, his wife and mother to the Eternal City early the following year, the Pope embraced such an opportunity to urge upon them the necessity of a remedial council. It was his desire that this should be held in Italy, far removed from the prejudicial influences of the East, where he himself could attend without setting any precedent derogatory to his pre-eminent dignity. Valentinian wrote at once urging these views upon his father-in-law, as also did Eudocia. The Pope himself wrote to Byzantium, and the following is extracted from his letter to the Emperor's sister :—

"To my Most Glorious and Most Clement Daughter,
Pulcheria, always
Augusta,
Leo, Bishop, and the Council at Rome assembled.

"If the letters which were sent by the hands of the Clerics had been delivered to you, it is certain that with the Lord's assistance, you would have been able to intervene and remedy those things which have been done contrary to the faith. For when have you gone back from the clergy or from the Christian faith and religion? But since the messengers were unable to reach your humanity, so that but one of them a deacon, Hilarius by name, barely escaping by flight returned, we have deemed it right to repeat the letters, and that our prayers may be effective, we here present a copy of what was written to your humanity, imploring you by the most instant supplication, that in proportion as the deeds, against which for the Roman faith we have to contend, have been more atrocious, with so much the more glory, for which you are renowned, you should foster religion, lest the integrity of the Catholic faith through any cause or human contention be infringed."

The Pope briefly recapitulated the shocking news that had reached him, urged Pulcheria to second his desire with the Emperor of holding a Council in Italy. The letter well shows St. Leo's recognition of the Augusta's constancy and influence:

"And that this may obtain, let the piety of your faith most approved by me, which has ever borne a part in the labours of the Church, vouchsafe to manifest to the most clement Emperor, as if by special commission from the most blessed Peter, our supplication, that ere this civil and destructive war gather force within the Church, he may, God helping, grant means to restore unity, knowing as he does that whatever by kindly act he confers on the liberty of the Church, will redound to his own empire's strength."

The letter of the Empress Galla Placidia has an interest all its own:—

"The most Pious and most illustrious Galla Placidia always
Augusta
to her Daughter the most Pious Ælia Pulcheria always
Augusta.

"It is religion chiefly that prompts us to make frequent visits to Rome, so also the desire to inspect the city, that we may be present in the sanctuaries of God's saints, for it is a certain truth that placed as they are for their virtues in heaven, they still do not contemn what is here below. We then regard it as a kind of sacrilege if we reject the order of sacred things. When therefore we had betaken ourselves to [the Church of] the holy Apostle St. Peter, there the most revered Leo amid a throng of priests, was the first in accordance with his dignity to approach us, but because sobs of grief choked his utterance, he could scarcely give expression to his desire. Nevertheless the fortitude of the bishop gaining the upper hand, he was able for a while to restrain his tears and to bring forward as its champion the cause of truth which had been outraged. In this discourse we learned that in our days the Catholic faith has been disturbed, which our forebears since our father Constantine, have hitherto preserved. For agreeably to the will of a certain individual, evil has been wrought against the Bishop of Constantinople. We have learned then that in the Ephesine Council which maintained no order of the priesthood, no, nor moderation, insolence and injustice went so far as to usurp power for the condemnation of sundry proceedings that appear dreadful in our times. Faith then, my most holy Lady and venerable daughter and Empress, ought specially to prevail. Therefore let your clemency according to the Catholic faith vouchsafe, as it hath done always, so now likewise, to combine with us, that whatever was enacted in that tumultuous and wretched council may with all courage be annulled, and all things remaining intact, let the cause of the episcopacy be referred to the Apostolic See, in which the first of the Apostles, blessed Peter, receiving the keys of heaven, adorned and governed the princedom of the priesthood. For we must in all things attribute the primacy to the eternal city which by its valour gained the dominion of the world and entrusted it to our Empire to be governed and preserved."

Theodosius' daughter also wrote to him in the same strain. It is interesting, from the personal point of view, to reproduce her letter.

" To the illustrious Lord and Father Theodosius always
Augustus,
his most dutiful Daughter Eudoxia always
Augusta.

"It is known to all men that your mildness fosters and cares for Christians and the Catholic truth so far as to order that nothing to its detriment should be done. Learn then that when we happily entered the City of Rome and reached the threshold of the Basilica of the Holy Apostles Peter and Paul, Leo the most blessed Bishop of the Roman City, in company with many more bishops presented to us a petition saying that all religious belief throughout the East had become disturbed, and it had come about that the whole faith of Christians was being brought to a state of confusion. For he mourned over the expulsion of Flavian Bishop of the Church of Constantinople, through the enmity of the Bishop of Alexandria, and this with the other bishops he begged of me, appealing to me by the worship due to the venerable sanctuaries and by the safety of our mildness, that I should address letters concerning these matters to you my most holy Lord, Father and venerable Emperor. Saluting you therefore I ask for justice, and that your mildness would vouchsafe to give heed to these letters, and order that what has been foully done should be set right, and what has been defined having been cancelled, the cause of faith and the Christian religion, which has been disturbed, should be once more enquired into by a Council assembled in Italy. For it has been written here that the whole storm was raised for the purpose of getting rid of the Bishop Flavian."

Theodosius replied to St. Leo's letter about Easter time, refusing his requests, and profferring the arguments dictated by Chrysaphius. But to his daughter he wrote in a rather different tone.

"We always indeed rejoice in the letters of you, beloved. We embrace them with the sweetness of our soul, and we are wont to accede with pleasure to all your petitions, lady and daughter, most sacred and venerable Augusta. But in regard to the present cause of Flavian, who was bishop, what has been the sequel our perfect mildness has made known to the most reverend Archbishop Leo. But to you, Sweetness, we approve that this only should be intimated that the above-mentioned Flavian has been taken from human affairs by the divine judgment, so that the dispute concerning the whole matter in doubt is removed from the sacred Churches, and nothing further can now be defined since these matters have been once decided."

It would take up too much space to give Theodosius' answers to Placida and Valentinian, but we can only regret that St. Pulcheria's letter to the Pope is lost. She wrote, apparently, in entire accordance with her correspondent's expectations, and laid the foundations of that great esteem and confidence which St. Leo afterwards expressed in her. It seems that, altogether, only four letters of the Augusta's have been preserved; namely one of her replies to the twelve or more epistles addressed to her by the Pope, a letter to the Governor of Bythnia, and two more to some heretically inclined monks and nuns in Ælia (Jerusalem.) Such as they are, these stilted and official missives, form invaluable material in St. Pulcheria's biography, and such as it is, our account of the Eutychian controversy must be written round them.

History has preserved much of the correspondence that was carried on between Rome and Constantinople, and indeed all over the ecclesiastical world, at the time of the great Council of Chalcedon. In the various collections of St. Leo's letters, and of the acts of the Councils, numerous epistles are to be found addressed by the Pope to the Augusta, by the Emperor to the Pope, but the letters of the members of the imperial families to each other have an interest all their own, an interest distinct from that of the subject matter. But it needs some knowledge of the history of epistolary styles, official and private, imperial and familiar, business-like and personal, ancient and modern, to appraise these relics at their proper value. The stilted language and absurd titles which rob them of individual character, also throw an artificial air about the sentiments of the writers. St. Leo's letters alone are fine and unaffected, full of the great Pope's goodness of heart, gentleness of judgment and zeal of soul. It is a disappointment that Eudocia, Placidia, and Pulcheria are as stereotyped in their writings as on their coins, but it is much that these fragments, embedded in an obscure, forgotten, and bulky correspondence, should have owed their very preservation to the importance of their context.*

Whether the Pope suggested that Valentinian should follow up these epistolary overtures by a visit to Constantinople, or whether that Emperor took sufficiently keen an interest in the matter to conceive the idea himself, we do not know. The husband of Athenais' sorrowful daughter was one of those men who would try to deceive their own uneasy consciences by making a public act of devotion atone or compensate for private sins. Thus Valentinian a profligate, patronised the Church, issued many an edict in her favour, and listened to St. Leo in 449. Apart from his relationship to Theodosius, so insignificant a man would have had little weight in the councils of the Eastern government. St. Leo might have chosen an abler delegate from the humblest ranks of his clergy. But in order to summon an Œcumenical Council it was necessary to obtain the consent of both Emperors; possibly Valentinian might win that of his co-adjutor.

Hostilities had not yet broken out between the western empire and its many threatening foes. Valentinian's ambassadors were returning unmolested from the camp of Attila, and Italy might as well be left to the guardianship of Ætius in 450, as it had been fourteen or fifteen years ago. The thoughts of all who were not absorbed, like the great Vandal minister, in military cares and preparations, turned upon the threatening pretensions of Dioscorus, and the martyrdom of St. Flavian.

The deacon Hilarius wrote to St. Pulcheria after his return to Rome, to explain how it had happened that he had failed to see her after the Robber Synod. His letter well expresses the righteous indignation that filled every justice-loving heart.

"Inasmuch," he says "as it was a most manifest necessity that compelled me to send by the Tabellarius [postman] the letter addressed to your Clemency by the most blessed Pope, I need not say that I was most eager after the Council of Ephesus to proceed to Constantinople, that I might in person pay as I ought to you and the most invincible and Christian prince the debt of my reverence. But I was prevented from carrying out this my resolve by that hindrance, which is hostile to all the good and the common cause of sorrow to all Christians, to wit, the Bishop of Alexandria, most potent in the condemnation of the innocent. For after I was unable to take part in his unjust will and decision, he tried to force me by menaces and trickery to attend that council; with the design of compelling me by cajolery to assent, which God forbid, to the condemnation of the most innocent Flavian, or else if I refused to hold me a

* Although the writer has, in the Preface, acknowledged her indebtedness to the Rev. Father Elphege Power, O.S.B., of Margate, for his translation of these various letters, she feels she has not sufficiently emphasized her appreciation of the promptitude, the interest, the unfailing readiness with which he always replied to her calls upon his valuable time. Whatever there may be of worth in these next few chapters she owes entirely to him.

prisoner and so deprive me of liberty to appear before your piety in the city of Constantinople, or to return to the Roman Church. Nevertheless, trusting to the assistance of Christ our God, I preserved myself innocent and free from the condemnation of that most reverend and holy man, albeit no scourges and no torments could have made me agree to their unjust sentence; but abandoning everything I departed from thence and by untried and trackless regions I reached Rome, that all the acts done at Ephesus might be suitably narrated to the most reverend Pope. Be it known to your venerable Clemency, that the Pope with the whole council of the West, condemns all that was done at Ephesus contrary to the canons by tumult and worldly rancour, by the Bishop Dioscorus; nor can those acts in any wise be here received which by the influence of the aforesaid, not without harm to the faith, have been perpetrated to the prejudice of that holy and innocent man. But what was done by myself with unwavering and intrepid authority hand to hand in defence of the faith, has been already narrated and it were superfluous to recount. For all this you will learn from the letter of the most reverend Pope. Wherefore, most splendid and most clement Empress, may your worshipful piety, which ought not to abandon what hath been begun, with the religious zeal of sincere faith, and constant mind, take your resolve."

The imperial visit to Constantinople was of short duration. It does not seem to have affected the situation, for none of the ecclesiastical historians attribute any importance to it. Disappointed by his inability to make an impression on Theodosius, and finding his every effort foiled by the Chamberlain, Valentinian's self-confidence quickly vanished. His wife was filled with sadness at the changes that had befallen her old home; the only one who derived some stay and consolation from their coming was the Augusta. St. Pulcheria had many a conference with her nephew, and Valentinian little thought at the time how this circumstance redeemed the apparent failure of his mission. He could only return to Rome as speedily as he might, bearing her assurances to St Leo. If indeed Eudocia too, took as keen an interest in the Eutychian struggle as Pulcheria and Placidia, she must have been no less ready than her husband to leave Constantinople where nothing could be done. Eleven years were to pass before she set foot once more upon the shores of the Bosphorus. The remembrance of this present visit would then be far more poignant to her, than she now found the memory of her wedding-day.

*   *   *   *   *   *   *   *

It was in the height of summer 450. Heat reigned intolerably even in the languorous stillness of the palace. Awnings could shade and darken, softly waving fans could stir, plashing water could cool but not dispel the oppressive air. The marbles and ivories of the imperial apartments were warm like their mellow hues. Flowers fainted in the garlands that hung like a cornice from column to column through the spacious vistas, or floated with recovered vigour in the shallow impluvia below. Everything was still and silent. Only the clicking and whirring of the cicalas in the gardens, only the poising of a hawk or two against the unfathomable blue, disturbed the trance of the general siesta.

The blazing brilliance of the sea was pitiless as the dazzle of the sun-smitten city. Across the straits the hills of Asia shimmered in an ague of heat. The blinding whiteness of the forenoon gave place, as the hours wore on, to the golden suffusion of a summer day's decline. The ardent heavens shone like palest amber shot with an indescribable rosiness, and the palms and cypresses of the Golden Horn, the woods of Sycae and the white domes of the city stood out against it clear as cameos.

The Emperor Theodosius was worn and jaded. The deadlock of polemical affairs oppressed him like the bright interminable day. The futile brooding into which his mind had sunk was troubled by some superstitious dread. He had one day gone to Ephesus to pray at the tomb of St. John, and ever since was haunted with the premonition of a speedy death. He was filled with the cares that had ennobled his father's end, and possibly with regret that nothing now could " bend his past out of its eternal shape." Only Pulcheria could remedy the mistakes of his reign, but Pulcheria was now an elderly lady.

Of late years Theodosius had taken little exercise or recreation save on horseback. A gallop on the polo field had ever more charm for him than a lordly 'progress' behind his 'sacred' Cappadocians. The Via Egnatia had seen his charger proudly caracolling to the Campus Martius without the Golden Gate far oftener than the Agustaeum had cheered his lumbrous chariot. It occurred to him this sad and airless day, like an inspiration from some happier time, to escape from the palace and his thoughts and go a hunting on the morrow in the country. The woods that lined the shores of the Bosphorus were full of boar, and a chase through dappled glades and shady hills in the freshness of the morning would dispel his cares and forebodings.

Thus one radiant summer morn, nearer fifteen than fourteen hundred years ago, the Emperor rode out of the Miletus Gate of the great Byzantine Palace, accompanied by a retinue of courtiers, guards, and huntsmen, with a pack of noble dogs. The citizens saw them go—a flaunting cavalcade—scowled to recognise the Chamberlain, and turned with a shrug of the shoulders to the business or pleasure of the day.

A coppersmith, sitting in his cavernous booth in the Brass Market, hammered arguments with a neighbouring melon seller, as ceaselessly as he did his metal, thinking no more of the Emperor, until it occurred to him afterwards that he had remarked a thousand times how there had been something ominous in Theodosius' mien that morning! Senators pacing up and down the shady arcades of the forum remembered how they had commented on the import of last night's comet; and the busy crowds swarming round the unlading cornships down by the waterside recalled a hundred presages in this and that.

For suddenly tidings had sped through the city that the hunting party was returning; that the Emperor was hurt, or killed, or dying. The cavalcade came in sight with a litter in its midst and a horse, bleeding and mud-bespattered, limping and stumbling behind. Swift messengers preceded the ominous procession to the palace, and the litter was borne out of the ken of the crowd, as if none cared to tell the people what it hid.

The injured man was carried to his own apartments and laid upon the "sacred" bed; and as the day waned and died, the Augusta watched beside it. The moon shone with limpid radiance through the night, and the great vault of heaven, purple as the dying Emperor's richest robes, was strewn with the eternal stars.

The verdict of history is gentle with Theodosius, as a man of insignificance. His virtues were not those of an Emperor, and his crimes were not his own. In the beginning of his record of this reign, the laborious Tillemont devotes some chapters to a criticism of the Prince. He remarks truly enough that even the solicitude and love of the Augusta could do no more than cultivate such character as her brother already possessed. In many aspects it was thoroughly unkingly, but in none was it vicious and bad. The only comment that seems to suit the occasion of Theodosius' death is the charitable pronouncement of the annalist. "This Prince," says Tillemont, "as we have depicted him, was possessed of every quality that might have made him a saint in private life." He was unfitted for absolutism, for publicity, for the imperial rôle, and the evils of his reign were rather the consequences of his false position than of his personal defects. "Theodosius," says Gibbon, "was chaste, temperate, liberal and merciful," but these are qualities which can only be called virtues in an Emperor when they are supported by courage, regulated by discretion, and secured by a certain noble self-sufficiency. Theodosius' worst aspect was his favouritism. He was no judge of character, and mistook obstinacy for fidelity. Had the Emperor been content to recognise in his sister his most disinterested friend, his reign had been without reproach. In a state such as the Byzantine, and a century such as the fifth, history is a curious compound of the political and the domestic. Thus the alienation brought about between the Emperor and the high-souled Augusta, by base intriguers and unfounded claims, was responsible for the equivocal nature of the imperial administration from the time when Chrysaphius first intruded himself into its councils. It is part of the story of the times to recount that the Emperor's shaken trust reverted to Pulcheria before he died. It is the devoted Augusta's due to describe her in his death-chamber.

During the long hours of that night the thoughts of both had travelled over the vanished years. And before the dawn lightened over the green-tinged roof of St. Sophia the Emperor had made his peace with God and man.

There was a solemn gathering of the ministers, senators, officers and clergy in the anteroom of the "hieros koiton," the imperial bedchamber. Presently they found themselves summoned into the presence of the dying Emperor. The moment had precipitately arrived when Theodosius must commend his realm to the guardianship of one among them, and that guardian to the countenance of the rest. So suddenly had the crisis occurred against which court intrigues and cabals may have long been concerting plans, that these were all undone.

Theodosius turned to the Augusta, and asked for her the loyalty of the Army and the Senate. The name of Marcian, as her co-adjutor and protector, was understood to fall from his dying lips, and in the silence of consent and awe, the ministers withdrew.

As St. Pulcheria knelt in that hushed chamber of death, reinstated in all her dignities, raised above all her foes, and clothed with a weightier majesty than before, her thoughts turned on the Providence of God, the welfare of her people and the succour of the Church.

LEAF OF A DYPTICH, FOURTH OR FIFTH CENTURY,
REPRESENTING THEODOSIUS THE GREAT, OR POSSIBLY
THE EMPEROR MARCIAN.

[Face p. 245.

CHAPTER XXIX

As soon as the death of the Emperor became generally known, the Augusta Pulcheria was unanimously proclaimed Empress of the East, "and the Romans for the first time submitted to a female reign."

The right of female succession obtained no recognition in the Empire, even though the recent example of the Empress Galla Placidia in the West, seemed to set some precedent for the elevation of Pulcheria to the vacant throne of the East. Had it really done so, Eudocia, wife of Valentinian III., should have asserted her claim above that of her aunt. The natural instinct which led the Emperors to desire that the members of their own family should succeed them, caused them to adopt the plan of nominating a successor during their lifetime and securing his recognition as Cæsar or Augustus by the army and the senate. By this expedient the sovereign could virtually found a dynasty without violating the theory that nomination to the purple was elective.* Theodosius II. had not been unmindful of the Empire's need, or of the Augusta's fitness to supply it. He commended her to the senate to succeed him, and it had only remained to provide her with a co-adjutor who would at once protect her and the state. He doubtless consulted her wisdom and her inclinations, for the Princess declared, a month later, at the Hebdomon, that she herself had chosen Marcian. The dynasty of Theodosius was threatened with extinction. The wife of Valentinian had borne only daughters, mere children at this date, and the Augusta Pulcheria was a consecrated virgin. It was, moreover, understood that the Patrician Marcian was to share the labours and the dignities of the Empress, her husband in name alone. St. Pulcheria chose this noble veteran to fill so strange a position with a judgment not only worthy of herself, but sufficiently appreciative of his merits. She saw in this senator and soldier, a man in every essential worthy of her trust and honour; one who would prove acceptable to the army, the senate, and the people; a helpmeet for herself, who would respect her religious vow, second her efforts to aid the church, and support her charitable enterprises. His sterling

* Cf. Chapter VI.

Catholicity recommended him to her no less than his other splendid qualities. Cultivated woman as she was, Pulcheria sought no dispositions in her husband save those best calculated to serve the Church and State. She sought neither conventional courtliness nor erudition; but chose Marcian as one in whom the responsibility and seriousness of life had ripened a manly character, a generous sympathy, and a devout belief. Baronius doubts if there had been any among all the Emperors who had reigned in Constantinople since the time of its founder, to compare with the one whom Pulcheria invested with the purple. Marcian had every practical qualification for statemanship, and so well did he right the labouring ship of Theodosius' distracted realm that his reign was called contemporaneously the "golden age." From the death of Arcadius to the accession of Justinian," Mr. Finlay tells us, "the power of the Emperor was never more unlimited, but it was never more systematically exercised." To some extent Pulcheria the stateswoman had encouraged and organised a systematic administration. "It is probable," continues the historian of the Greek nation, "that Marcian was one of those senators who had supported the systematic policy by which Pulcheria endeavoured to restore the strength of the Empire; a policy which sought to limit the arbitrary exercise of . . . despotic power . . . by fixed institutions, well-regulated forms of procedure, and an educated and organised body of civil officials."* That gravity and punctiliousness which had made the Augusta, as a young girl, anxious to train the bearing and gestures of the Emperor, helped her to this wise estimate of the value of forms and ceremonies; and enabled her, at the close of her life to discern in Marcian, not indeed a courtier, but one who would respect the constitution such as she had been able to conceive it.

Those elements of romance, picturesque and chimerical, which have marked the lives of so many characters in these pages, are not wanting to the story of Theodosius' successor.

Marcian was a Thracian of humble birth. He was fifty-eight in the year 450, having been born towards the close of the reign of Theodosius the Great. He was educated in the profession of arms, and so little is known of his life that any of the stories retailed by the various historians is worth repeating for lack of better material.

"Throughout the Empire," we are told † "it was the usual practice for sons of the free peasantry to abandon agricultural penury, and without a change of clothing, provided only with a wallet containing a few days' provisions, to betake themselves on foot to the capital in the hope of chancing on better fortune. Thus," for example, "about the year 470, when Leo the Thracian

---

*Finlay " History of Greece."

† " The Age of Justinian and Theodra," W. G. Holmes.

had succeeded" Marcian on the throne, "a young herdsman of Bederiana . . . resolved on this enterprise and arrived at Constantinople with two companions whose lot was similar to his own. There they presented themselves for enlistment in the army, and as the three youths were distinguished by a fine physique, they were gladly accepted and enrolled among the Palace Guards. Two of them are lost to our view for ever afterwards, in the obscurity of a private soldier's life, but Justin, though wholly illiterate, entered on a successful career." He attained, in fact, to the purple, and is ever remembered in history as the uncle and predecessor of the great Justinian.

The lot of Marcian as a youth was no more inspiring than that of Justin. He was "sorely exercised by poverty and misfortune," says Gibbon, "since his only resource when he first arrived in Constantinople consisted of two hundred pieces of gold which he had borrowed from a friend." He entered into the military service of the powerful General Aspar and of Ardaburius, his son.

One day, so the first story runs, as Marcian was setting out to join his detachment, he came across the body of a murdered man lying by the roadside. A natural impulse of compassion made him stop and consider how he best might render the dishonoured corpse a decent burial. He was seen in the act of carrying out his Christian purpose, and being mistaken for the assassin, was seized, dragged before the magistrates of the nearest town, and thrown into prison. Notwithstanding his vehement protestations of innocence and ignorance, circumstantial evidence seems to have been so strong against him that he was on the point of being condemned to death, when the real culprit, who had also been arrested, confessed to the crime, and thus saved Marcian's life.

It was hardly to be expected that all sorts of curious prophecies and portents should not have been remembered—afterwards— which from an early date in his career pointed to the remarkable future in store for the Thracian legionary. It is related of his journey with the army into Persia, during the campaign of 422, that he fell ill, and was billeted upon two brothers remarkable for their prophetic wisdom. These men could not conceal from their chance guest that a glorious fate was in store for him, and eagerly enquired how would he reward their foresight, when as Emperor he should confess its truth? Marcian laughed and humoured his hosts,

"I will dub you Patricians," he replied.

"Fare you well," returned the brothers, with impressive eastern solemnity, "work out your destiny and remember us."

Strangely enough the prophecy came true and the Emperor fulfilled the soldier's word.

Marcian accompanied the Italian expedition of 423, which placed Placidia and Valentinian in possession of the western throne, and went with Ardaburius to Africa a decade later. The story of the Vandal king and the Byzantine legionary may possibly be an African version of the Persian legend. Marcian seems to have met with milder treatment at the hands of Genseric's officers than that meted out to the generality of Roman prisoners during the disastrous campaign. He was one day resting in the open air beneath the sunny sky, when Genseric himself came up and saw a hovering eagle casting the shadow of its wings upon the face of the sleeping captive. The king noted the omen, woke Marcian and restored him to freedom, on condition that when Emperor he should abstain from war against the Vandals.

Again a coincidence would verify the prophecy, for it so happened that in 457 the Emperor was on the very eve of these hostilities when his death prevented them. "Truth," Tillemont remarks, "eternally prefers the religious observance of a vow to the conquest of the world."

Later in his career, Marcian obtained through the influence of his Illustrious superiors, the honourable rank at Constantinople of tribune and senator. He married, and his daughter Euphemia Flavia Marciana doubtless learnt at court all unconsciously to prepare herself for a rôle as brilliant and as unexpected as that which fell to her father.

"The austerity of Marcian's unpolished manners," writes M. Amedée Thierry, "his disinterestedness, his just and open character, recall the ancient Roman type, lost in the corruption of town life, but which still flourished under the soldier's tent, protected by the discipline of the camp. He was comparatively unlettered, but renowned for splendid common sense and personal bravery."

It would be interesting, in the pursuance of this type through the decadent ages, to draw some parallel between the Emperors Marcian and Nicephorus. The devout, half-fanatical and rugged character of the latter is portrayed in Mr. Frederick Harrison's "Theophano." Nicephorus, like Marcian, was first a soldier, a reformer, and secondly an Emperor. In his case, however, a dramatic interior struggle between the religious ideal of life and the love of a wicked woman brought his public work to nought. In the case of Marcian, reverence for a saint confirmed his personal excellence and redeemed the Empire.

We hardly ask whether the Augusta loved the widowed Senator. A woman does not outlive the possibility of love, but she had outlived the thought of self. It were unworthy of the theme of her steadfast life to throw a gratuitous atmosphere of romance around its closing years. Both Pulcheria and Marcian had passed the meridian of the mortal span. As the Empress herself declared, she sought a colleague, not a husband. Thirty-four years ago she had dedicated her virginity to God, and had since kept her vow against all the seductions of the Byzantine court, to preserve it through the last the most victorious phase of her private and public life. Moderns may scoff, but St. Pulcheria's own subjects, corrupt in practice and sceptical in theory as they were, could glory in the virtue of their virgin Empress no less than they had marvelled at her initial sacrifice.

St. Pulcheria's choice of a consort was unanimously approved by all who had a voice in the matter. Neither Aspar nor Ardaburius could aspire to the purple since they were both staunch Arians, and that heresy was still detested in the capital above all others. They were however influential (and cruel) men, who, if they themselves might not rule, hoped to rule an Emperor who had once held command below them. But they had no shadow of success with Marcian, and it does not belong to this story to recount what happened later on in the century when another of their officers, Leo, was elevated to the soon vacant throne.

The Empress did not wait to solemnise her marriage before she "indulged the popular resentment," against the hated eunuch Chrysaphius by an act of public justice. The whole city detested him, and there was scarcely a party or an individual who had not cause to feel avenged by the advent of this tardy retribution. The Empress must have felt that no justice would be done to the memory of the late Emperor until Chrysaphius were removed from men's fears and thoughts. Without legal trial he was condemned to death, and the execution of the sentence was entrusted to the son of one of his countless victims.* In 441 a noble Vandal, named John, had retired to Constantinople and ingratiated him-self with Theodosius. Chrysaphius easily persuaded the General Arnegiscle that at such a moment this intimacy was highly dangerous, and that all things are fair in love and war. The Vandal was treacherously assassinated, but the General fell in his first engagement, and the crime was finally avenged when in 450 St Pulcheria ordered Jourdain, the son of John, to conduct Chrysaphius to death without the city gates. In this instance no pardon overtook the prisoner on his fateful way, nothing in the breast of the Augusta nor in the temper of the crowds could prompt this not infrequent act. A certain fierce satisfaction sat in Jourdain's countenance which it would have been dangerous to baulk.

Thus the most mischievous and malignant figure in the story passed away, burnt or hewn to death without the walls, and abandoned to the dogs for sepulture.

Theodosius was laid to rest in the Church of the Holy Apostles, and all Constantinople streamed in black behind the imperial bier. But the period of mourning was interrupted, or cut short, by the wedding and proclamation of Marcian and Pulcheria on August 24th, as Emperor and Empress. The ceremony took place at the Palace of the Hebdomon. The hands of the bride and bridegroom

---

* It was not however carried out before the lapse of thirty days, according to the celebrated law enacted by Theodosius after hfs impulsive anger had resulted in the massacre of Thessalonica

were bound together with white and red fillets after the benediction
of the Patriarch, and the consecrated virgin became, in the eyes
of the world, a wife.   As the nuptial procession reached the
Augustaeum on its return to the Sacred Palace, Marcian dis-
mounted from his charger, and according to a custom which had
hailed Trajan, Constantine and Theodosius successors of Julius
and Augustus, was himself now raised upon an immense shield,
upborne by the greatest officers of state, and acclaimed by the
thronging populace.   St. Pulcheria, gorgeously robed as became
her state, bore her part in the public ceremonies with new grace.
Her diadem was crowned with sprays of jewels which flashed in
the blazing sunlight, and laden with strings of pearls falling in
priceless cascades about her neck and shoulders.   The broad hem
of her purple mantle was laden with embroideries in silk and gold.
Her dress beneath it was beyond description rich and beautiful;
on her feet were golden slippers, and her hands were cased in
jewelled gloves.   Her chariot traversed the city from end to end,
amid groves of myrtle, ivy, rosemary and flowers; the air was
filled with the odour of incense and the sound of singing choirs.
From every balcony and portico hung flaunting lengths of
multicoloured fabrics; flags fluttered from the masts; and the
golden rain of the imperial largesses fell on the motley throngs.

Neither the Senate nor the Emperor-elect had delayed these
celebrations to await the approbation of Valentinian III.   The
moment had been critical and decisive.   Shortly afterwards, however, the Patrician Maximin was despatched on an embassy to
Rome to fulfil all the requirements of diplomacy and of imperial
etiquette.   He bore in his train the customary portrait busts, (the
"labrata" or "clypei") of Pulcheria and Marcian, and was
graciously received by the western Emperor at the close of March
in the following year.

The succession of Marcian to the throne of Theodosius was
solemnly ratified by his colleague in the purple, and Valentinian
confirmed the imperial elevation of one who, thirty years ago, had
been among the obscurer instruments of his own success.

COIN OF THE EMPEROR MARCIAN, ENLARGED.

[Face p. 251.

CHAPTER XXX

EMPEROR AND EMPRESS

Hymn written by Anatolius Archbishop of Constantinople and translated by the Rev. J. M. Neale, "Some Hymns of the Holy Eastern Church."

> "Fierce was the wild billow,
>   Dark was the night ;
>   Oars laboured heavily,
>   Foam glimmered white ;
>   Mariners trembled ;
>   Peril was nigh
>   Then saith the God of God
>   'Peace ! it is I !'
>
> "Ridge of the mountain wave
>   Lower thy crest,
>   Wail of Euroclydon
>   Be thou at rest ;
>   Peril can none be,
>   Sorrow must fly,
>   Where saith the Light of Light
>   'Peace ! it is I !'
>
> "Jesus Deliverer
>   Come Thou to me !
>   Soothe Thou my voyaging
>   Over life's sea !
>   Thou when the storm of Death
>   Roars sweeping by,
>   Whisper, O Truth of Truth,
>   'Peace ! it is I.'"

The Failure of the Theodosian Dynasty.

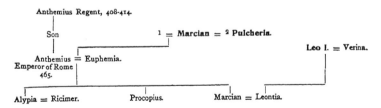

The reign of the Emperor Marcian was short, but energetic and profoundly salutary to a state which for the last sixty years had suffered, under his immediate predecessors, all the initial stages of decay. He was no sooner seated on the throne beside the Empress than he assumed the honours of the Consulate for the succeeding year and entered into a correspondence with St. Leo.

"By the providence of God," he wrote, "by the election of the most excellent Senate and of the whole army, we have reached the height of Empire. Whence for the sake of the reverend Catholic religion and Christian faith by whose aid we trust that the power of our authority is governed, we deem it right at the outset to address sacred letters to your Holiness, possessing as you do, the principality of divine faith; inviting and requesting your Holiness to implore the eternal Deity for the firmness and welfare of our Empire; inasmuch as we have this resolve and desire that every impious error being removed by the Council which, at your instance, is to be convened, the greatest peace, untainted and pure, should prevail touching all the Bishops of the Catholic faith."

The tide of disaster which had inundated the Church seemed to have turned at last! Marcian's letters, like those of Pope Leo themselves have the impress of a manly personality behind them. They are short, to the point, and very energetic.

Within a few weeks of the imperial marriage, an embassy arrived at Constantinople from the Pope asking particulars of St. Pulcheria, as to the dispositions of the new Patriarch Anatolius, and requesting her consent for the convocation of that Council against which Theodosius had so resolutely set his face. He sent by four legates a profession of faith to guide the Empress's judgment, but forebore to load his letter with the "protracted disputations" of which the faithful Pulcheria had no need. It was possibly by way of reply to this embassy that Marcian sent the above letter to Rome.

"I rejoice at the faith of your clemency," wrote St. Leo, "that you worthily devote your religious zeal to renew the peace of the Church, which through the dissensions of some seems to have suffered disturbance. For it is specially owing to your glory that by the removal of all the scandals which the enemy hath raised up against the Catholic Faith, the confession of the truth should, throughout the whole world, be one and the same, and the truth will be more easily and more certainly restored, if no seeds and no trace be left of heretical opinions. But that which is my duty nevertheless I cannot neglect, namely that I should ask to be informed of the sentiments of the Bishop of Constantinople touching the incarnation of the Son of God, for especially as troublous times or incidents had preceded his ordination he ought to have transmitted to us such writings as would evidently prove him untainted with the contagion of this new-born error. Desiring then to have secure concord with him and to bestow upon him the grace of fraternal charity, I have deferred writing to him, not withholding from him my love, but awaiting the manifestation of Catholic truth. For what I demand of him is simple and unconditional, that he should, put aside the toil of protracted disputations, acquiesce in the Epistle of Cyril Bishop of Alexandria to Nestorius, in which he confuted the Nestorian heresy and expounded the faith of the Nicene confession; or else agree with my letter addressed to Flavian of holy memory. Having then carefully examined these documents let the Bishop of Constantinople at once understand that he must repudiate what ignorant folly contrary to the pure and one faith had ventured to define. For touching the incarnation of the Lord, ·my confession and that of the Holy Fathers is in all respects identical and the same. And if any man should think that this should not be followed, he has (thereby) cut himself adrift from the bond of Catholic unity, although it be our wish that all things should be wholly restored. To obtain more speedily the effect of these wholesome dispositions, I have sent my brothers and fellow bishops, Abundius and Asterius, as also Basil and Senator priests, most trusted men, to present to your clemency the formula of faith, which we preach in agreement with the doctrine of the venerable Fathers we preach, and putting aside all circumlocutions by which faith is obscured, to show what doctrine has been upheld by approved priests throughout the world, concerning the incarnation of the Son of God, and it is meet that these should be assisted after the favour of heaven, by the holy aid of your piety lest an ill-advised intention cause the disturbance of the whole Church, for when correction hath been applied, all should return to the concord of the one Confession. If any should dissent therefrom, let it be enjoined with the consent of your clemency, that a universal council of the Bishops be held in Italy, in which with all sincerity, it may after profounder discussion be at length made clear what disciplinary and what remedial measures should be adopted.

Given on the seventeenth day before the Kalends of August (July 16) in the seventh consulship of Valentinian and of Avienus.*

To this epistle St. Pulcheria returned the following reply :—

" To the Most Reverend Leo, Bishop of the glorious city of Rome, the most venerable Pulcheria Augusta.†

The letters of your blessedness we have received, with all the reverence due to a Bishop ; by which we know that your faith is pure and such as ought with holiness to be held forth in the sacred Church. But I equally with my lord, the most serene emperor, my spouse, have ever abode and do still abide therein, turning away from all perverseness, defilement and evil-doing. The most holy Bishop, therefore, of glorious Constantinople, hath continued in the same faith and worship, and embraces the confession of your apostolic letters, putting away that error arisen from some, which from his own letters, also your holiness will be able to perceive, and he hath without delay of any kind subscribed the letter likewise of Catholic faith which your blessedness addressed to the Bishop Flavian of holy memory. And accordingly, let your reverence deign in whatever way you

* Ep lxx Migne's Patrology.
† Ep lxxvii Migne's Patrology.

see good to signify to all Bishops, even of the whole East, of Thrace and Illyrium, as also it hath pleased our Lord the most pious Emperor, my spouse, that they may be able quickly to muster from the western parts and meet in one city, and there having formed a council, let them at your invitation proceed to decree about the Catholic confession and concerning those bishops who previously held aloof, as the faith and Christian piety may require. Moreover let your holiness know, that by the command of our lord and most serene prince, my spouse, the body of Flavian of holy memory has been brought to the most glorious city of Constantinople, and has been duly placed in the basilica of the Apostles in which his predecessors were wont to be buried. And likewise, by the authority of his decree he has ordered those bishops to return who for the same cause of having agreed with the most holy Flavian in the concord of Catholic faith had been sent into exile, in order that by the sanction of the Council and the decree of the Bishops assembled they may be enabled to recover the episcopate and their own churches."

Anatolius had indeed held a Synod in conjunction with St. Leo's envoys, at which the celebrated epistle to St. Flavian was ratified, and generally subscribed. Eutyches was once again degraded from the priesthood and deprived of the office of archimandrite, while those Bishops who had been exiled from their sees for upholding Flavian, were recalled. As the Empress relates, the body of the martyred Patriarch was brought home to the capital, and interred with fitting solemnity and honour in the great mausoleum of the Eastern Empire, the Church of the Holy Apostles, where St. Chrysostom also lay. But her letter omits the very sufficient reasons for which it was proposed to hold the forthcoming Council not in Italy but in the East. St. Leo, however, acquiesced, when these were represented to him, and his letter of thanks to St. Pulcheria comes fittingly towards the close of her life as its most valuable criticism and authoritative eulogy.

"Leo, Bishop of the city of Rome, to Pulcheria Empress*

"What we have always presumed concerning the holy mind of your piety, that most fully by experience we have learned that the Catholic faith though it be assailed by sundry devices of the wicked cannot, while you are at hand raised up by the Lord for its defence, suffer any disturbance. For God will neither forsake the sacrament of his mercy nor the merit of your toil, by which long since you ejected from the very bowels of the Church the crafty enemy of holy religion, for the Nestorian impiety could not uphold its heresy since it did not lead astray the handmaid and disciple of the truth, however much the poison might be poured into the simple by the specious lies of that loquacious man. And from this conflict of your virtues this has been the result, that those evils which the devil by means of Eutyches endeavoured to compass, have not remained concealed, and they who chose to sustain a part in a similar impiety have been defeated by the virtue alone of the Catholic faith. This then is

* Ep lxxix in Migne's Patrology.

the second victory you have gained over the error now crushed, of Eutyches which, had he possessed any sound principles, he might easily have avoided (since long ago it had been overthrown and confuted in its very authors), without endeavouring from buried ashes to fan the fire into a flame once more, to the end that the most glorious Empress, whose example he might have followed, might side with them. It pleases me now to exult with gladness, and to offer my prayers for the due prosperity of your clemency to God, Who on thee through all the parts of the world, in which the Gospel of the Lord is preached, has now bestowed a twofold palm and crown.

"Let your clemency, then, learn that the whole Roman Church exceedingly congratulates you on the works of your faith; whether in that you have aided our embassy with pious affection in all matters, brought back to their several churches the Catholic Bishops who by unjust sentence had been expelled, or in that you have caused the remains of Flavian of holy memory, the innocent and Catholic Bishop, to be with fitting honour restored to his Church. In all which indeed the increase of your glory is multiplied, inasmuch as you venerate the saints according to their merits, and desire that from the Lord's vineyard thorns and briars should be plucked up. But that some Bishops of those who had given consent to impious doings seek for reconciliation and long for Catholic communion, I have learned both from the relation of my own messengers and from that of my brother and fellow Bishop Anatolius, to whom you deign to bear testimony. We give effect to their desires as follows:—that when they have been corrected, and on their condemning by their own subscription what has been evilly done, the favour of peace be conceded to them, by the united care of those whom we have sent and of the above-mentioned Bishop Anatolius, for both these courses befit Christian devotion, that just truth should coerce the obstinate, and charity not repel the penitent.

"But because we are acquainted with your clemency's great solicitude for the welfare of Catholic bishops we have had it intimated to you that our brother and fellow bishop, Eusebius, is here at Rome with us, and admitted to our communion. His church we commend to you, for report goes that it is being laid waste by one who is asserted to be intruded into his see. This also we ask of your piety which we doubt not you will readily perform unasked, to cherish with fitting favour my brother Julian, as also the clergy of Constantinople, who by faithful service clung to Flavian of blessed memory. But we have informed your piety by means of our ambassador respecting all that we wish to be done or arranged.

"Given on the Ides of April (Ap. 13th.) in the consulship of Adelfius."

From the above letter of St. Leo, it looks as though the worst evils of the late rupture were now overcome, and that the need of another Council was less apparent. The Robber Synod was meeting naturally with general rejection, but there were still some outstanding difficulties to be met. Eusebius had not yet been restored to Dorylaeum, and Dioscorus and his immediate followers went still unpunished. "All this," says the Protestant historian "was far enough removed from the vigorous action for which St. Flavian had appealed. . . ." "But the position was full of peril." Dioscorus had fought for the supremacy of his see, and had possibly hoped that an acute schism would end by placing him in "the undisputed headship of the East, and eventually of the whole church. Leo, while certainly not careless of the dignity and honour of his See, had a wider and more generous outlook." He acted with the firmness of a bishop but the gentleness of a father, and in dealing with the backslidings of men who had been rather weak than bad, he displayed the considerate tactfulness of a woman. It would be, however, absurd to suppose that so long as no imposing protest on the part of the Catholic Church were entered against the ecclesiastical presumption and heretical championships of Dioscorus, St. Leo would have waived the project of the Council. He waived indeed his own wishes, and discouraged any impulsive haste. He had little trust in the virtue of argument and rancour, and preferred to see the storm calm down naturally.

The convocation of the great Œcumenical Council of Chalcedon must be attributed to St. Pulcheria's readiness to co-operate with the Pope.

The objection to Italy as the scene of the deliberations was well founded on the weariness and impoverishment of the eastern bishops, many of whom had lost more money and time travelling from Synod to Synod of late than their dioceses could afford. None of the western bishops could allege those inconveniences since only the Papal Legates had gone to Ephesus. Moreover Ætius and Valentinian were now threatened by Attila, who, hovering upon the borders of the Empire, hesitated whether to descend upon the East or West. The indications pointed to the West.

Nicaea, accordingly, was chosen as the spot where the Council should assemble, but the irruption of a Hunnish horde rendered that plan abortive. The Emperor Marcian begged the bishops to postpone their business until such time as he himself might be present to assist. He further proposed Chalcedon as their haven, a place within easy reach of the capital, which latter he could not leave. Thus, altogether, little more than a year rolled away in which Marcian had time to vindicate the trust Pulcheria reposed in him, and during which St. Leo's temperate wisdom gained the day.

It was the opinion of the new Emperor "that war should be avoided so long as it is possible to preserve a secure and honourable peace; but . . . . that peace cannot be honourable or secure if the sovereign betrays a pusillanimous aversion to war." Marcian had been brought up in the camp, not in the enervating atmosphere of a court; the manly exercise of his own judgment, decision and ingenuity, had not been constantly forestalled by a host of self-interested counsellors, nor had his personal activity and self-reliance been smothered under the ineffectual aid of others. At sixty years of age this clear-headed soldier was little likely to change the habits of a lifetime and to be corrupted by the pride of the purple. His initial acts were a sufficient guarantee of his practicality and value. Unlike the noble Avitus, who, as a subject, commanded the esteem of the Western Romans, but, as their Emperor, incurred nothing but contempt, Marcian justified the estimates formed from his private life. He immediately engaged in a scheme of financial reform, which might redeem the shame and ruin of the last few years; he winnowed out the administration; filled the higher offices of state with reputable men; recalled a host of exiles ecclesiastical and lay, and laboured day and night to restore the public confidence. His "temperate courage" dictated a spirited reply to Attila, "who insolently pressed the payment of the annual tribute." The Emperor signified to the barbarians that they must no longer insult the majesty of Rome by the mention of a tribute; that he was disposed to reward with becoming liberality the faithful friendship of his allies, but that if they presumed to violate the public peace they should feel that he possessed troops and arms and resolution to repel their attacks. The same language even in the camp of the Huns was used by his ambassador Apollonius, whose bold refusal to deliver the presents till he had been admitted to a personal interview, displayed a sense of dignity and contempt of danger "no less surprising to Attila than inspiriting to the Byzantines themselves." The government was nerved at last to shake off the shameful Hunnish yoke.

Marcian appointed Ardaburius to the generalship of the Armies of the East, and the Hunnish invasion of 451 was repelled without difficulty. Henceforth only the most insignificant of wars broke the tranquility of the reign; a Saracen rebellion was crushed, and the rising of a tribe in Palestine put down. This state of comparative inactivity seems to have had a dangerous effect on Ardaburius. For three generations the Eastern forces had been commanded by members of this powerful Alan family; their barbarian guards formed a military force which overawed the Palace and the capital, and the liberal distribution of their immense wealth went some way with the Constantinopolitans to overcome the popular prejudice against the heretics. Marcian, unlike his successor, proved strong enough to hold this military family in check, and no political strife marred the brief period of his reign.

In 452 he effected an alliance with the Emperor of the West, which gave great satisfaction to the entire Empire, and material assistance to Ætius in his struggle with the Huns.

The most noble lady Euphemia, daughter of Marcian, was of marriagable age, and in uniting her to Anthemius (a grandson of the great Prefect who had sustained the government from the death of Arcadius to the majority of St. Pulcheria), both the Emperor and Empress may have hoped for an heir to their throne. Anthemius was generally regarded as the best educated man of his time, and might himself have succeeded to the purple in 457 unless, as

17

Tillemont suggests, he was still considered too young. Marcian could hardly have foreseen his own speedy death, nor perhaps have provided against the jealousy of his generals and the consequent prejudice of the army. Euphemia bore indeed, three children, Alypia, Procopius, and Marcian, but neither St. Pulcheria nor the Emperor lived long enough to see in this St. Martin's summer a revival of the hopes that had died with the departure of Athenais.

CHAPTER XXXI

A MONUMENT TO ST. PULCHERIA

This chapter, or at least that part of it which deals with the Council of Chalcedon, is based on Hefele's "History of the Christian Councils." The letters of St. Pulcheria in this and in the following chapter are taken from the "Sacrosancta Concilia" of the Jesuit compilers Labbé and Gossaert, vol. 4, paragraphs 872-876.

THE Council of Chalcedon was the one monumental event of the reign of St. Pulcheria and Marcian. It was essentially their work, for however ardently St. Leo had originally desired its convocation by the year 451, he no longer perceived any particular necessity to hold it. He had already written to the Empress entreating her to have Eutyches removed from the neighbourhood of Constantinople, and to see that a Catholic abbot was appointed to rule the monastery in his stead, and now considered that the question as to orthodoxy being settled, nothing more remained to be done than to arrange for the reconciliation and pardon of those bishops and monks who had gone astray over the Eutychian question.

The Emperor however issued his summons before he had received the representations of St. Leo to the contrary effect. Had Marcian been more accurately acquainted with the latest views of the Pope on the subject, he might have been induced to desist from his purpose; as it was, he believed, in accordance with the previous anxiety of St. Leo, that he was only doing what he wished. "It is probable," says one of the Pope's biographers, "that the still divided condition of the Church in the East aroused in the Emperor [no less than in the Empress] the desire to assemble an Œcumenical Council, and thereby conclusively and thoroughly to put an end to the disturbances, embarrassments and dissentions which, in spite of all the pains which had been taken on the subject, were not yet over." It was like the decisive and reforming Emperor.

St. Leo yielded with his customary grace and statesmanship. "Since from love to the Catholic faith," he magnanimously wrote, "you wish this assembly to be held now, in order to offer no impediment to your pious will, I have chosen as my representative my fellow-bishop Paschasinus . . . . whose province appears to be less disquieted by war, and have joined with him the priest Boniface. These two, together with the previous Legates (at

Constantinople), the bishops Lucretius, and the presbyter Basil, and Julian of Cos, shall form the representatives of the Papal see at the Synod, and in particular, Paschasinus shall there preside in my place."

St. Leo's chief fear, and one of his first reasons for having desired that the Syond should be held in the West, was that the uncertain eastern bishops would take advantage of the rejection of Eutychianism and originate a new discussion tending to revive the Nestorian heresy. In order to remove this danger he impressed it upon Marcian and Pulcheria that the faith must in nowise again be called in question at the Synod. He seemed, in allowing the Emperor and Empress to do as they desired, to rely upon them and their sincerity for the safe conduct of the Council. His trust was justified: only in one particular did Byzantium make a mistake, and that was quickly recognised.

St. Pulcheria wrote to the Governor of Bythnia, in whose province the Bishops were to assemble, that, as many of them had already arrived at Nicaea, and as she herself soon hoped to be able to appear in person, he should in the meantime remove from the city those clerics, monks, and laymen who were neither summoned thither by the court, nor brought by the Fathers, but appeared to have come of their own accord to excite disorder. She was naturally anxious to avoid any repetition of the late scenes at Ephesus, and determined to take every precaution to ensure the seemliness of the proceedings in a Council the responsibility of which rested so largely upon her own and her husband's shoulders. It is interesting to reproduce her letter as one of the very few that have been preserved.

"It is the will of our Tranquility that before civil causes, the holy Churches of Christ, and those addicted to them, should be in peace and the othordox faith, which as we believe maintains our empire, should by every class of men be preserved undisturbed and unshaken. Hence, not long since, some slight discord having appeared, we had much care that a multitude of holy Bishops should be gathered from all sides at Nicæa, in order that by the agreement of all, all disturbance should be removed, and for the time to come the venerable faith should prevail firm and immovable. Since with our approval all the most reverend Bishops have indeed assembled, awaiting the presence of our Power, which, with God's help, will shortly arrive; and inasmuch as some, as we are aware, are wont to disturb and upset the discipline well-pleasing unto God,—clerics and monks as well as laymen arriving at Nicæa endeavour to cause disorder, contending without those safeguards which we have sanctioned, we therefore needs must address these pious letters to your Renown, that you proceed with much strictness to expel from the city and its neighbourhood all those of the clergy who without our summons or the permission of their own Bishops are staying there, or any belonging to that order, or any removed by their Bishops, or monks or laymen whom no reason calls to the Council, that the holy Synod sitting with all discipline, without broils or disturbance, the truths revealed by Christ the Lord may be by all generally reinforced. For know that if any disorderly person be for the future found dwelling there either before our arrival or certainly after our coming, he does so with imminent risk to himself.

As we have seen, however, the Emperor was unable to present himself at Nicæa. At the instance of his own convenience, at the prayer of the bishops to whom a long delay was a misfortune, and since without him the Papal envoys refused to appear, Marcian transferred the Council to Chalcedon.

The Fathers, to the number of about six hundred, met in the church of St. Euphemia the Martyr, a beautiful edifice situated in front of the town on the Bosphorus, only two stadia (about twelve hundred paces) distant, on a gentle slope opposite Constantinople, having a magnificent view over the sea and the surrounding fields. The Council opened on October 8th, 451, and closed on the first of the following month. It numbered sixteen sessions, all held within three weeks, and accomplished its many tasks with the utmost expedition and decorum.

The Imperial commissioners consisted of the Patrician and former Consul Anatolius, the Prefect of the Pretorians, Palladius, the Prefect of Constantinople Tatian, the Master of Offices Vincomalus, the Count of the Domestics ; Sparacius, and the Count of the Privy Purse, Genethius. Eleven noblemen represented the Senate, and together with the commissioners had their places near the centre of the church before the altar rails ; next to them, on the left side, sat the representatives of Rome.

The commissioners merely managed the official arrangements of the Council ; they took the votes, consented to this or that being brought forward, closed the sessions, and generally discharged those functions which belong to the conduct of a large assembly. They had nothing whatever to do with the matter of the conference, but it was owing to their presence that when, at the close, the Emperor asked the Council whether or not they had enjoyed perfect freedom of debate and suffrage, the assembled Fathers returned an affirmative reply.

At the head of the Synod itself, in the proper sense, stood the representatives of St. Leo. Near, and after them, came Bishops Anatolius of Constantinople, Maximus of Antioch, Thalassius of Cæsarea, Stephen of Ephesus, &c., &c., and on the other side to the right sat Dioscorus of Alexandria, Juvenal of Jerusalem, Peter of Corinth, &c., &c., in the midst of all being the book of the holy Gospels.

At the first sitting of this imposing assembly on October 8th, the proceedings of the Robber Synod were annulled, the orthodoxy of St Flavian was affirmed, and Dioscorus, after vainly seeking to extenuate his share in the violence perpetrated at Ephesus was deposed, together with many other bishops who had taken part in his violence at Ephesus. Night had come on before the business had proceeded thus far, and the latter part of the Acts of Ephesus were read by candlelight. The Imperial commissioners pronounced the depositions, and then Ætius, Archdeacon of Constantinople, as first notary of the Synod, declared the Session ended.

The second session, October 10th, was occupied in reading the Nicene Creed, two dogmatic letters of St. Cyril, and St. Leo's famous tome, all of which were greeted by loyal and enthusiastic cheers. "When the session was about to terminate, some bishops took advantage of the moment to intercede for the heads of the Robber Synod. "We petition for the Fathers," they cried, "that they may be again allowed to enter the Synod. The Emperor and Empress should hear of this petition!"

The third session, October 13th, was held for the formal trial of Dioscorus on various charges of avarice, injustice, and immorality.

The imperial commissioners and the Senators purposely remained away, in order, probably, to avoid the appearance of the royal authority having influenced the sentence. Bishop Eusebius of Dorylaeum was at length able to appeal to the Council, as he had appealed to the Pope on that fatal day at Ephesus. Dioscorus was thrice cited to appear but he refused to do so by one excuse and another, even after his guards had been ordered to release him. He was accordingly unfrocked, deposed, and deprived of all spiritual functions. He was afterwards banished by the Emperor to Gangra in Paphlagonia, where he died three years later. The Synod sent a copy of the minutes of this session to the Emperors Valentinian and Marcian, and also a letter to St. Pulcheria which closes with the assumption of her approval, and the assurance that one who is so zealous for the cause of God as her august self, cannot miss the divine reward.

The fourth (Oct. 17th) and fifth (Oct. 22nd) sessions were devoted to the work of adopting a confession of the Catholic faith, which, based on the Nicene Creed, should provide at one and the same time against both Nestorianism and Eutychianism. The concord of the Fathers was confirmed by the anathemas on dissentient views without which no affirmation of the truth was then thought valid.

The formal ratification of this amended creed was made at the sixth Session on October 25th in the presence of the Emperor and Empress who came to Chalcedon, accompanied by a splendid retinue, for that express purpose. Marcian formally opened the proceedings with a speech in Latin which was translated into Greek and followed by the reading of the creed. This ran as follows:—

"Following therefore the Holy Fathers, we all, with one voice, declare that we ought to acknowledge one and the same (Son) our Lord Jesus Christ, the same perfect in Godhead, perfect in manhood, truly God and truly man; the same composed of a reasonable soul and body; consubstantial with the Father in respect of the Godhead, and consubstantial with us in respect of the manhood; like to us in all things, yet without sin; begotten of the Father before all ages in respect of the Godhead, and the same in these last days, born of Mary the Virgin, Mother of God, in respect of the manhood, for our sake and for our salvation; one and the same Christ, Son, Lord, Only-begotten, in two natures, without confusion, change, division, separation; the difference of the natures being in nowise taken away by the union; on the contrary, the property of each is preserved, and concurs into one person and one Hypostasis; so that He is not parted nor divided into two persons, but He, one and the same, is Son and Only-begotten, God the Word, our Lord Jesus Christ."

The Emperor then asked whether the view of all was expresed in this formula and the bishops answered, unanimously, yes. "Prosperity to Marcian the new Constantine, the new Paul, the new David! You are the peace of the word! . . . You have strengthened the orthodox faith! Many years to the Empress! You are the lights of the orthodox faith by which peace everywhere prevails! Marcian is the new Constantine, Pulcheria the new Helena!" The Session closed with more loyal vociferations. "Thou art priest and Emperor together, conqueror in war, and teacher of the faith!"

With this enthusiastic sitting ended the principal work of the Synod of Chalcedon. The bishops remained in the city a few days longer, at the express desire of the Emperor, but what was further done was only of secondary importance.

The remaining sessions, making sixteen in all, were occupied with various matters of jurisdiction and order and by the enactment of thirty canons. Three of these were suggested to the Fathers by the Emperor as lying within the province of ecclesiastical rather than of civil legislation. It was in the celebrated twenty-eighth canon that the Council made its great mistake and incurred the displeasure of St. Leo.

After the retirement for the day of the Papal legates and the imperial commissioners, under the presidency of the Patriarch Anatolius, the bishops of the Council, or so many of them as remained, passed a canon which elevated Constantinople to a rank second only to Rome.

The eastern Fathers considered that as Rome was the imperial city, St. Peter therefore made it the capital of the new world-wide faith, and that he gave a second and third place to Alexandria and Antioch as being the second and third cities of the Empire. "They would have urged with some reason that the disposition with regard to these latter cities, which was universally attributed to St. Peter, would have been altered by the Apostle had he lived in the fourth century,"—namely that St. Peter would have ranked Constantinople at least second to Rome. "The western Fathers saw however three Petrine sees, of which one had inherited all St. Peter's primacy, while the other two (Alexandria and Antioch) had a reflection of it." Even so the latter ranked before other apostolic sees. "In themselves the two doctrines are one, but the points of view are different, and their divergence first became apparent when Constantine moved the capital to Byzantium.*

"It did not strike the Easterns as possible to move to Constantinople the primacy left by Peter to Rome; but to a large number of them it seemed obvious that the new metropolis of the world must have a Patriarchate, and must rank above Alexandria and Antioch. The first attempt to get its authority regularised was made in the Council of Constantinople in 381. . . . . ." when it was declared that "the Bishop of Constantinople shall hold the first rank after the Bishop of Rome, because Constantinople is New Rome." But a subsequent council held by Pope Damasus entered an "imposing protest" against this assumption. In 451, however, circumstances favoured a second attempt to aggrandise the imperial see. "The Patriarch of Alexandria had just been convicted of heresy. . . . . . the Patriarch of Antioch had been deposed the year before. . . . . . and was now allowed only lay communion. His successor was in a doubtful position. . ." Consequently the twenty-eighth Canon was framed by the Bishops at Chalcedon, which again asserted the precedence of Constantinople.

"But the day after the passing of the canon the legates made their protest. . . ." The Fathers, however, sent to St. Leo the Acts of the Council just closed, having "no idea that their doctrine of the coincidence of ecclesiastical with secular jurisdiction could be in any way contrary to the prerogatives of Rome." "Soon afterwards the Emperor and Anatolius both wrote to ask the Pope to accept the canon, the confirmation of which had been expressly reserved to him. The replies of St. Leo were in his gravest and most fatherly style. He spoke of the dangers of ambition, and pointed out that Anatolius should have been satisfied with the generosity shown by the Apostolic See in passing over the irregularity of his election. He did not detect anything in the canon inconsistent with the respect due to Rome, but insisted upon the principle that the rank of the great sees was from Peter and not from their secular importance. . ." On the same day St. Leo wrote to St. Pulcheria condemning the ambition of Anatolius. "Anatolius," he said, "should consider whose successor he is and imitate Flavian in faith, in modesty, in humility. . . As for the resolution of the bishops [the 28th canon]. . . . in union with the piety of your faith I declare it to be invalid, and annul it by the

---

* The exposition of this point in ecclesiastical precedence is taken from the refutation of Bishop Gore by the Rev. Father Chapman, o.s.b. (Bishop Gore and Catholic Claims), and seems, to the writer, to put the matter in a nutshell.

authority of the holy Apostle Peter. You will however, restrain my brother Bishop, Anatolius, within the limits which are wholesome for him."

Anatolius presently gave way, and so, we presume did the Emperor and Empress, for St. Leo's correspondence with them received no check and maintained its cordiality.

The canon was not copied into the western collections of the Acts of the Councils, nor did the Greeks themselves for some considerable time make any further reference to it. It was not inserted among the decrees (with the signatures of the attending bishops appended) which were sent to the faithful of the various dioceses in the form of synodical letters.

Under St. Pulcheria and Marcian the tendency to schism which the East had always exhibited was checked as soon as detected, but the divergence between East and West in regard to the point of view from which they regarded the privileges of the see of Rome could not be disguised under less Roman and Catholic minded sovereigns. The ecclesiastical pretensions of Constantinople revived during subsequent reigns, and, favoured by the Emperors, led directly to that 'cæsarpapism' which destroyed and enslaved the Church in the East. It must be ranked as one of the glories of St. Pulcheria, the second St. Helena, that this point was ceded to the Pope when raised by the Council she summoned.

*   *   *   *   *   *   *

But the story draws rapidly to a close: within the next few years the deaths occurred, one after another, of nearly all the characters who have played any part in it. The Empress Galla Placidia died in Rome on November 27th, 450. Her body was embalmed and taken back to Ravenna, the city she had so loved and adorned. Arrayed in the richest of imperial robes and seated in a chair of cypress wood she was enclosed in a tomb of Greek marble in one of her own churches. Her brother Honorius had been laid to rest in the right transept of SS. Nazarus and Celsus, and Constantius, her second husband, in the left, and close to either Placidia now remained, regal and impassive throughout hundreds of succeeding years. If the rich mosaics of the walls and vaults can still recall the Church the Empress knew and loved, how much more strangely must the sight of that fifth century Queen, as she sat in her airless tomb, have bridged the centuries for those who might still behold her, up to a few years ago! Mr Augustus Hare, in his "Cities of Italy," tells us how in a moment of thoughtless mischief some children destroyed this extraordinary relic. They thrust a taper into the tomb to see its weird occupant more clearly, and in a second the ashy semblance of the once beautiful Placidia, was reduced to the handful of dust which represents mortality: "Memento homo quia pulvis es, et in pulverem revetetur!"

Two years had not elapsed since the Council of Chalcedon

when the Empire in the East sustained the loss of St. Pulcheria. She died at the age of fifty-four, on September 11th, 453, and as Baronius devoutly says, "passed to Heaven to receive her crown among the virgins." The great work of her life was accomplished when peace was restored to the Church and a new era of prestige inaugurated for the State. She survived her brother Theodosius long enough to confide the rectification of his errors to her husband, and seems latterly to have retained little but the honours of an empress. She was interred amidst the other members of the Theodosian house in the Church of the Holy Apostles. The ceremony of her funeral was no less magnificent and impressive than befitted the wife of the Emperor, but no king's ransom in gold and jewels was lavished on Pulcheria's tomb. She left the whole of her personal estate to the poor, and Marican executed her will with the most scrupulous exactitude. "If anyone," says Sozomen,* "should doubt my statements† and desire to enquire into their truth. . . . . let him examine the registers kept by the treasurers of the Princess."

The body of the virgin Empress was borne through the city accompanied by throngs of the sorrowing people, carrying torches and branches of palm and olive, and crying that the dead Augusta was a saint. It was received at the doors of the basilica by the Patriarch Anatolius whose funeral oration was punctuated by the cries of the grieving crowd. Her death made a profound impression on the volatile Byzantines who had been accustomed for half a century to hold their Empress up to the admiration of the world, to look upon her as the ornament of their city, and to trust in her for the protection of the Church. Her name was acclaimed with an extraordinary access of enthusiasm when it occurred during the canon of the Mass, and the whole Empire rang with her praise.

St. Leo had written to her, " As touching the robustness of your faith, by which you offer to God an unceasing sacrifice of praise, I cannot find words to express what fervent thanks I give to God that the princes of our days possess not only regal power but priestly learning in addition." No more fitting eulogy could be passed upon St. Pulcheria than that of the epithet the great Pope himself applied to her. He called her the Ornament of the Catholic Faith.

Lastly, her epitaph reflects the esteem of her contemporaries.

" Commemoratio sanctae Pulcheriae Reginae, in pace quiesceiitis : Haec fuit soror Theodosii Junioris, conjux Marcian pietate praestantissimi Imperatoris ; quae cum virginitatem ipsam ad senectutem usque servavet, multaque praeclara opera in templorum et hospitalium domorum aedificia contulisset, et sanctae Chalcedonensis Synodi Patres adjuvasset, in pace quievit."

---

* Ecc. Hist. Bohn's trans.

† As to her charity and munificence, &c.

In memory of the holy Augusta Pulcheria, who lies [here] in peace. She was a sister of Theodosius the Younger, and wife of the most pious Emperor now reigning; she preserved her virginity into old age, and wrought many eminent good works in founding churches and hospitals, and in assisting the Fathers of the Holy Synod of Chalcedon : she lies in peace.

CHAPTER XXXII

THE ex-Empress Athenais, in exile at Jerusalem, took a profound interest in the Eutychian controversy. Some writers suppose that after the lapse of a few years Eudocia returned to Constantinople and played no inconsiderable part in the events of 449. The eunuch Chrysaphius found in her a tool against St. Flavian and the Augusta. And she only returned once more to Jerusalem after the death of her husband.

But such an hypothesis is not necessary to account for Athenais' interest in Eutychianism. She had very possibly heard Chrysaphius discuss the theological speculations of his venerable kinsman long before the death of St. Proclus occasioned that series of animosities which came to so terrible a head at the Robber Synod. Moreover, Eudocia was living a life so full of literary and philanthropic interests in Jerusalem that she would have felt little inclination, and no need, to return home. Her relations with St. Pulcheria, far from growing still more strained and painful, seem to have regained much of their early sweetness. The two ladies kept up some correspondence, and Athenais sent the Empress presents.

The author of " The Daughter of Leontius " supposes that the greater part of Eudocia's literary work was accomplished during this season of exile and leisure. But from the year 444 to the time of her death the ex-Empress was as much occupied with the topics of the day as ever she had been during her prosperity. Her love of poetry and interest in literature characterised not only the concluding portion but the whole of her life.

The poem written to commemorate the campaign of 422 against the Persians was the only secular theme to which she turned her attention : all the rest were religious. Photius, an historian of the ninth century, praises the Empress's Octateuch—her paraphrase in hexameters, divided into eight books, of Moses, Joshua, Judges and Ruth, and marvels at such studies being pursued amid the distractions of court life. He tells us that Eudocia carefully observed the rules of her art and fidelity to the text of her original. She also turned the Prophets Zacharias and Daniel into verse, and wrote a poem in three books on SS. Cyprian and Justina. Zonaras mentions another work, the Homerian Cento, composed of Homerian verses, and a poetic Life of Christ. This last may well have been written in Jerusalem. It was undertaken to complete the work of another, possibly Paulinus or Cyrus. Some slight doubt has been thrown upon the athorship of the whole Cento, but since the other writer to whom they might be attributed was a pagan, it seems more likely that they issued from Eudocia's pen.

M. Thierry writes of the Empress' love of letters and of her circle of intimates in the imperial Palace as he might have written of any of the salons of the literary women of the seventeenth century in France. Of the famous Legend of SS. Cyprian and Justina— conceived in 438, and written, possibly, at a time of great mental anguish—he says: "On croirait lire parfois des pages de Milton ou de Tasse, et il y a là tels passages assurement que n'eut pas renié l'auteur du Paradis Perdu."

Gregorovius has rendered it into German. He thinks that iambic verse suits the philosophic theme even better than the heroics of the original Greek. He detects in Cyprian and Justina the beginnings of the Faust legend, but this critisism is more qualified than that of M. Thierry. "As Hellenic philosophy had outlived itself, so had the poetic power of the Greek now vanished. It shared the fate of the other arts ; the Attic tongue still lived, but no longer in its purity. The poetry of the fifth century was but an echo, a rhetorical and philological memory of what had been . . . . Such fragments as have been preserved of the sacred subjects treated by Athenais show no trace of a creative talent, but reveal, at least, as gifted an artist as the age could produce." Christian poetry was at this period gradually throwing off the bondage of classical metres and originating styles of its own. Eudocia treated new thoughts in old modes. In his introduction to the "Hymns of the Holy Eastern Church" the Rev. J. M. Neale passes over St Gregory Nazienzen and St. Sophronius (as he would have passed over Eudocia had she written hymns) as mere imitators of the Greek models. Their poetry remained in literature, but unlike the Syriac verses of St. Ephrem and the Armenian songs of St. Maruthas, none of it passed into use in the Church. The attempt of Athenais to deal with Christian subjects in a classic style was characteristic of the peculiar significance of her own romantic personalty. She connected two spheres of high intellectuality. She lived in a transitional age, and had herself passed through many experiences and changes. No one was better qualified than she to "marry Christianity and classicism;" to infuse a new spirituality into the old forms of thought and speculation. Though Gregorovius— whose whole book is rather dirge-like—speaks of the "pedantic mosaic" of her versification, Eudocia won the praise and approval of her own contemporaries. In the magician Cyprian we have a representation of the idolatry and dæmonology of the time, the neo-platonic theurgy and magic against which even Hypatia was not proof, and Eudocia must have studied the travels of Apollonius of Tyana, one in whom the pagan world would have discerned a philosophic counterpart to Christ, in order to conceive her lover convert and martyr.

"I have explored what breeds corruption in the human breast," confesses Cyprian, "what in plants ferments the sap of flowers; what harms the tired body as sickliness creeps on; and what the mottled serpent Prince of the World, full of evil craft, creates to contest the decrees of the eternal God. . . ." "So learnt I to know the manifold nature of matter, the art of metals and stones, the secret writings of the world, myths of the Cosmos, and all characters. . . .   To Memphis I went where I learned. . . . the power of knowledge, memory, the art of deception, fear, forgetfulness, . . . then to the region where spirits themselves coin clearly the vice of the earth. . . the lie I saw there, most versatile, . . . hate unmerciful without heart or bowels, vindictiveness utterly consumed with hollow rage. . . gluttony with mouths fore and aft swallowing flintstones and hard earth, . . . idolatry with broad dense wings. . . hypocrisy with wasting sickness, . . . hellish calumny long of tongue. . .   Oh how inane that bombast with which Greek wisdom would deceive mankind!"

The confession carries Cyprian on with marvellous descriptive force through all the years of his life and vain researches.   It is the self-examination of a Paracelsus.   At last he comes to Antioch and undertakes by diabolic arts to overcome the firmness of a Christian maid who refuses the love of Aglaidas.   "She showed me how vain my arts, and many a sleepless night I too lay awake consumed with the fever of love."   The fortitude of Justina through incessant trouble and Job-like temptations at last wrought the conversion not only of the pagan youth but of the magician Cyprian.   Astonished at the might of the sign of the Cross he breaks out into a magnificent denunciation of the defeated and deceiving demon.

"I know at last the value of your lie!   You corrupted my heart and my hope; my breast swarms with care, the foundations of my life are destroyed, and the pillars of my nature are snapped.   I gave my soul to you!   Science brought me no profit nor the knowledge for which I delved in old books.   I squandered all my inheritance on your behests—Oh, had sufferers and the poor but consumed that wealth, then a drop of mercy might perchance still flow to me! . . .   With my gold I dug my very grave and saw not the abyss.

But now I must invoke the pious servants of God. . . . and embracing Justina's precious knees beseech her to take my soul into her care."

This resolve infuriates the demon, who hurls himself upon Cyprian, gripping him by the throat.   But like a flash the magician imitates Justina, signs his writhing body with the cross, and is free. The devil flees, howling execrations and threats, and at his blasphemies "desperation seized me."

The poem breaks off suddenly as Cyprian concludes his terrible story and asks for the intercession, the advice, of those who have heard his confession.

It would be impossible to exaggerate its power. The Empress makes no mere superstitious use of the sign of the cross such as would carry no conviction and maim her story with an irresponsible trick. She produces on her reader an effect like that of the moment when Mephistopheles, confronted by the cross of the sword hilts, cowers unnerved and terrified before that impalpable power, and betrays himself. The holy thrill of undaunted spiritual confidence is actually conveyed by Eudocia's spirited poem.

It is curious to reflect that the Empress, upon whom Christianity had made so stirring an impression, fell into the two successive heresies of her time, first into Nestorianism and then into its exact opposite, Eutychianism.

Bishop Juvenal of Jerusalem, himself a monophysite, must have been largely responsible for the spread of that heresy in his diocese, and for its capture of Eudocia.* He had taken a prominent part in the Robber Synod on the side of Dioscorus. When, however, on the close of the Council of Chalcedon, a certain monk, Theodosius by name, hurried off to Jerusalem with the report that Juvenal had recanted, and signed its revolutionary decrees, there was an indignant uproar in the city. The garrison proved too small to quell the riots and disturbance. The partisans of Eutyches and Dioscorus took possession of the church of the Holy Sepulchre and refused, when the bishop arrived, to allow him to cross the threshold unless he repudiated his late recantation. Juvenal fled to Constantinople, and Theodosius being made bishop in his stead, a persecution broke out against the orthodox, and for two years Jerusalem remained at the mercy of a violent party of schismatics supported and countenanced by the Athenian exile. Eudocia was a sincere Eutychian, and neither the exhortations of St. Leo nor the remonstrances of St. Pulcheria, with those of her own brothers and daughter, could induce her to give up the cause of Theodosius. After the fall of Eutyches and Dioscorus, the whole monophysite party in the East looked to Athenais as its head. The monks of Jerusalem addressed some insolent epistles to the Empress Pulcheria, but she wrote two letters in reply, one to them, and one to the Abbess of a schismatically inclined community of nuns, which produced a marked effect.

> "To Bassa, the Superior of the Monastery in Ælia, the Empress Pulcheria.

" . . . . . Since through the benignity and kindness of our Lord and Saviour Jesus Christ, the inhabitants of the City of Ælia have learned of the true and orthodox faith of my serenity, and of the most religious

---

* In the fifth century the prerogative of preaching belonged to the Bishop alone, or to his immediate delegates.

Lord of the earth my husband, they have embraced it, and with many praises have extolled our Lord and Saviour and our authority . . . . and respecting them indeed, my most sacred and pious lord and husband, with his usual clemency showed himself of such a character as befitted his piety.   But our serenity . . . . . fearing lest [Theodosius] should circumvent any of the more simple religious women . . . . . direct these our sacred letters unto you, by which we declare to you the faith received from our fathers, and we wish it to become known through you to all women consecrated to God that we keep the faith "according to the Creed of Nicaea."   Wherefore . . . . let your reverence be zealous to pray assiduously for ourselves and our Empire."

The Pope was so pleased with this effort, that, although Pulcheria had not addressed herself to him or involved him in the correspondence, he wrote to thank her for it.   But no sterner measures were taken for a while to restore order in Jerusalem.   Neither Rome nor Byzantium cared to persecute the ex-Empress Athenais.

After the death of St. Pulcheria, however, the Emperor Marcian determined to suppress the revolt.   He issued orders to his troops in Palestine to advance upon Ælia, but Athenais encouraged the people to bid them defiance and to bar the gates. The city prepared to withstand a siege, but the Roman general first tried the effect of pacific overtures before proceeding to extremities.   His parleys proved successful, and a revolution took place in the state of ecclesiastical affairs which practically solved the problem.   Bishop Juvenal was reinstated and Theodosius retired to a cloister on Mount Sinai.

The Imperial exile, however, yet persisted in that heresy.   At last, in 455, when she learnt the terrible news of Valentinian's death, and of the misfortunes of her daughter, she determined to accept the moral of all this strange experience and grief.   She listened to her brother, to Olybrius, the broken-hearted fiancé of her granddaughter, and made up her mind to submit her case to the judgment of St. Simeon Stylites.   With the self-distrust that is one of the noblest effects of a soul-stirring blow, Athenais fell at the feet of the saint.   The Stylite of Antioch was the man to whom all turned about this time when in doubt or distress. Eudocia's poor husband had himself once sought the pillar saint's advice.

"There was something wonderful," says Father Dalgairns,* "in the apparition of this man with beautiful face and bright hair, raised up on high night and day adoring God.   With a tendency to error in the race from which he sprang one would have expected to find marks of fanaticism about him.   Yet no one had less of the arrogance or obstinacy of delusion.   He came down from his pillar at a word of advice from the neighbouring monks.   He cast away his chain that bound him at the suggestion of a visitor."   On

* History of Holy Communion.

one occasion the Emperor Marcian was among the many great
ones of the age who went in disguise to see and hear the stylite.
The story goes that the General Ardaburius, who accompanied
him, drew down upon himself a saint's rebuke to scepticism. The
Arian, full of contempt for the monk, readily granted one of his
officers, Julian by name, permission to drag him from the column.
On the unaccountable failure of this attempt—it must have been
made at night—Ardaburius himself fitted an arrow to his bow and
took aim at the strange devoted figure, whereupon his arm was
momentarily paralysed and he only succeeded in wounding his
own palm. "Above all, the good which St. Simeon effected
marked him out as an apostle. Not in the desert, but in the
vicinity of vast wicked Antioch, he stood on his pillar and preached.
Once he grew weary of the streams of people who were continually
flocking from all parts of the world, even from distant Britain, to
hear him ; he bade the monks shut up the enclosure round his
column because he wished to be alone with God. At night a
troop of angels came and threatened him for quitting the post
assigned him by God. He began again at once his weary work.
For thirty-seven years his sleepless eyes looked down with pity
and compassion on the crowds who came to consult him. Cheerfully, and with temper unruffled by the burning heat, or the
pitiless pelting of the mountain storms, he listened to all and
consoled them. From three o'clock in the afternoon till set of sun
he preached to the most motley congregation ever assembled to
hear the word of God. Wild Bedouin Arabs, mountaineers from
the highlands of Armenia, and from the cedars of Lebanon,
banditti from the Isaurian hills, blacks from Ethiopia were mingled
there with the perfumed counts of the East, and prefects of
Antioch with Romanised Gauls and Spaniards. Even the objects
of St. Chrysostom's indignant eloquence, the ladies of Antioch,
who never deigned to set their embroidered slippers on the
pavement of the city, quitted the bazaar and their gilded
palanquins to toil up the mountains to catch a glimpse of the
saint outside the enclosure within which no woman entered.
Wicked women looked from a distance on that strange figure,
high in air, with hands lifted up to heaven, and body bowing down
with fear of God ; and they burst into an agony of tears, and
renounced their sins for ever. Thousands of heathens were
converted by his preaching; and an Arab chief, himself a pagan,
ascribed it to him that under their tents there were Christian
bishops and priests. The savage persecution of the Christians in
Persia was stopped by respect for his name. Many a wrong did
he redress, for tyrants trembled at his threats; many a sorrow did
he soothe. A wonderful sight was that long, painful life of
suffering and supernatural prayer in the midst of that vast
corrupt and effeminate East . . . From the height of his column
St. Simeon could see the glory fading from the degenerate East,

18

and God set him up on high in that strange guise to be its last chance of repentance. Such was St. Simeon.

To this man then Eudocia turned for counsel. She sent him a couple of messengers bearing an autograph letter in which she set forth all her religious doubts and difficulties, in which she explained her position. St. Simeon Stylites thus replied :—

"Be it known to thee, O my daughter, that the devil who is cognisant of thy many virtues is tempting thee in order to test their genuinenss. The wretched Theodosius who is the cause of all this mischief has flooded thy God-fearing mind with darkness, and brought upon thee this spiritual perplexity. Be trustful, however, for thy faith shall triumph. But I marvel greatly thou hast come so far in search of water seeing that a living fountain is springing at thy door without thy knowledge. I mean the God-like man Euthymius. Follow his instructions and thou shalt be delivered."

There is nothing so powerful for good in an hour of abasement as a word of cheer and trust. Eudocia received St. Simeon's letter with most grateful reverence, and acted with child-like promptitude and obedience on his advice. She must have often heard of Euthymius, an holy anchorite living in an obscure laura in the desert of Ruba. No woman was allowed to venture there, and the ex-Empress was a little puzzled to know how she could possibly obtain an interview with the saint. Some priestly messenger resolved the difficulty, and Euthymius met Eudocia on a little hill in the wilderness some four miles south of the city, where his celebrated penitent had caused a wooden tower to be erected for the purpose of their conference. The result was wholly comforting to the perplexed and sorrowing woman. She submitted meekly to the Church, and enjoyed before her ensuing death that peace of mind which is such pure and holy compensation for the loss of earthly happiness and fame.

She affirmed with her dying breath that her friendship with the Patrician Paulinus had been irreproachable. Her defection and her loss dealt a heavy blow to the monophysite party in the East. She died a peaceful but lonely death in the year 456,* and was buried in the Church of St. Stephen outside the walls of Jerusalem, a beautiful edifice which she herself had caused to be built, and at the consecration of which she had assisted only a few months previously.

Athenais fades from the pages of the story as in the peaceful twilight which so often succeeds a day of storm. She outlived all the principal characters who figured at the Byzantine court in her time ; only her daughter, the third of the famous Eudocias remained to suffer wrongs still more grievous than those of her beautiful and gifted mother.

---

* Or. 460.

In the year 450—to wind up another thread in the tale—a variety of circumstances seemed to give Attila, King of the Huns, the excuse he and his restless nation sought, for once again sweeping down upon the Empire. When in 449 the ambassadors of Theodosius II. had hoped to have conducted negotiations with the Huns just beyond the Danube, they found themselves obliged to continue their arduous journey into the recesses of Dacia in order that Attila might have the proud satisfaction of beholding the emissaries of both halves of the Roman world suing at his feet together. Maximin and Priscus met Count Romulus, and the Governor of Noricum at Attila's barbaric board. For the relations of the Huns with the Western government had already been declining in cordiality, and were, in 450 as threatening as those with the East. Four or five distinct considerations determined Attila to descend upon Italy rather than upon Thrace, especially as the unlooked-for attitude of the new Emperor at Byzantium indicated the realms of Valentinian as lying in the line of least resistance.

Firstly, the Western ambassadors declined to agree with Attila's demand for the restoration of certain sacred vessels. As a Christian, Valentinian was in a difficulty which the Hun had neither the instinct nor the will to appreciate. For in the siege of Sirmich, during one of the Hunnish wars, the Bishop of the place had confided the sacred vessels of his Church to the care of Constantius, Attila's Gaulish secretary. They were to serve as ransom for the Bishop, or for any of the members of his flock, in case the city should fall and its inhabitants be taken prisoners. Whatever befell Sirmich and its bishop, it seems that the sacred vessels remained on the Secretary's hands, for he afterwards made them over to a certain official in Rome, named Silvanus. This man not daring to put them to any profane use, presently sold them back to the Church. Attila traced the booty with punctilious greed and was extremely incensed that it should thus have escaped his clutches. He had Constantius crucified and sent a peremptory order for the surrender of Silvanus as a thief. Valentinian could no more consent to the sacred vessels falling into Hunnish hands than he could abandon an innocent man to Hunnish vengeance. Thus he despatched this embassy to offer Attila an equivalent in money for the treasure he had lost, and to return a firm if a very careful refusal to either demand. The King, however, pressed the point with uncompromising obstinacy: he was determined to have the vessels, or Silvanus, and would listen to no remonstrance. The only alternative was war.

At the same time the Huns were preparing to espouse the cause of two other nations, the Vandals and the Franks, against the Western Empire. Valentinian was allied with Theodoric, King of Visigoths, whose daughter had been given in marriage to the son of Genseric. When this jealous tyrant " suspected that his son's wife had conspired to poison him, the supposed crime was punished by the amputation of her nose and ears, and the unhappy daughter of Theodoric was ignominiously returned to the court of Thoulouse in that deformed and mutilated condition . . . Theodoric was urged . . . to revenge such irreparable injuries. The Imperial ministers, who always cherished discord between the barbarians, would have supplied the Goths with arms and ships and treasures for the African war, and the cruelty of Genseric might have been fatal to himself, if the artful Vandal had not [once again] armed in in his cause the formidable power of the Huns. His rich gifts and pressing solicitations inflamed the ambition of Attila."

Yet another invitation seemed to demand a Hunnish invasion of the West. The death of Clodion, king of the Franks, exposed his realm about this time, "to the discord and ambition of his two sons. Meroveus, the younger, was persuaded to implore the protection of Rome; he was received at the Imperial court as the ally of Valentinian, and the adopted son of the Patrician Ætius; and dismissed to his native country with splendid gifts and the strongest assurances of friendship and support. During his absence his elder brother, Claudeband, had solicited with equal ardour the formidable aid of Attila . . ."

It would hardly seem that the Hun king need have mocked the misery of the Princess Honoria by seeking in her cause yet another reason for invading Roman territory. If in her forlorn despair Herculanus' obscure wife or widow heard any echoes of the warlike tidings founded on the King's demand for her hand, they could scarcely at this belated date kindle any flicker of the old hope and passion in that quenched spirit. Attila, however, availed himself of the plea of Honoria's betrothal to demand a large share of the Imperial patrimony. Thus by embracing a variety of causes he found the pretext for plunging headlong into another ferocious war. Valentinian communicated feeble remonstrances and feeble refusals to all these assumptions and demands. Honoria's poor ring was returned to her "Scythian lover," (who had sent it to the indignant Emperor in proof of her pledge) with the announcement of her "indissoluble engagements," and with the advent of summer, 450, Attila opened hostilities against both halves of the Roman Empire.

He sent two Gothic ambassadors, one to Valentinian at Ravenna and one to Theodosius at Byzantium with the same insolent declaration. "Attila, my lord and thy lord, commands thee to provide a palace for his immediate reception." "But," says the historian of the "Decline and Fall," "as the barbarian despised, or affected to despise the Romans of the East, whom he had so often vanquished, he soon declared his resolution of suspending the easy conquest until he had achieved the more glorious and important enterprise." An ingenious face to put upon his discomfiture by Marcian!

The story of Attila's invasion of Gaul and of his extraordinary progress, arrested here and there by · the interposition of a St. Agnan or a St. Geneviève, does not belong to the history of the Eastern empire. Baronius thinks, however, that Attila revenged himself in person on Illyria for his great defeat at Chalons. But when the Huns swept down on Italy it seemed that Honoria's revenge had also come at last!

Ætius alone was incapable of fear, but his power and prestige were being sapped, and he could do nothing more effectual than harass the invader. The barbarian allies who had defended Gaul refused to succour Italy, and the aid promised by the Eastern Emperor was very distant. Valentinian fled from Rome to Ravenna, as Honorius had fled at the approach of Alaric, and like his predecessor, thought of abandoning the country. The Scourge of God was checked, however, not by the men of war but by the man of peace. St. Leo, the noble and intrepid bishop of Rome headed an embassy sent by the Senate to Attila's camp. He made so profound an impression on the savage King that the tide of war was effectually stemmed.

" The deliverance of Italy was purchased by the immense ransom or dowry of the Princess Honoria." It seems that the prisoner was indeed at length to be set free since " Attila threatened to return more dreadful and more implacable if his bride . . . were not delivered to his ambassadors within the term stipulated by the treaty." The unhappy Augusta's marriage with Herculanus could have been but nominal, a mere political ruse whereby to counteract any possible claim of Attila, or St. Leo could not have countenanced the treaty.

Fate interposed once again. Attila had retired to his timber palace beyond the Danube, and was in the midst of fresh wedding festivities when his terrified German bride, Ildico, saw him struggling in a gush of drunken blood upon his pallet. An artery had burst and he was quickly dead. " The Teutons whispered among themselves that the girl had slain her tyrant. One longs," says Professor Kingsley, " to know what became of her." The world was delivered from this terror, and "it was reported at Constantinople that on the fortunate night when he expired, Marcian beheld in a dream the bow of Attila broken asunder."

This happened in 453, and Honoria did not long survive the shock. The cup had been at her very lips when it was again dashed aside, and hopeless woman as she was, the bitter disappointment killed her. She died the following year, and the tide of disaster in the West rushed headlong over her forgotten woes.

Everyone doubtless supposed that the western Empire, delivered from Attila and Thorismond, would now enjoy a season of repose, but another tragedy of jealousy and mistrust precipitated its inevitable ruin.

There was a curious similarity between the careers of Stilicho and Ætius, the two successive ministers of the West. Both men were virtually its rulers under their respective sovereigns; both cherished the same political and domestic ambitions, both suffered an ungrateful fall. General Ætius had hereto figured as the defence and stay of Valentinian's government. He had been raised to the highest and noblest offices of the state, and had thrice worn the palmata vestis of the Consulate. It is not surprising that so feeble a Prince as Honorius' nephew became uneasy sooner or later at Ætius popularity and power. Something salient must have occurred in 454, or about that time, to unsettle the Emperor's trust, for only a short while previously mutual assurances of fidelity had passed between the sovereign and his general. A marriage had been arranged between Gaudentius, Ætius' elder son, and Eudocia, Valentinian's daughter. This pledge was, however, as unavailing as the rest to preserve a friendship cancered by mistrust and jealousy. Moreover, the eunuch Heraclius, played just such a part in Ravenna, as Chrysaphius had played at Byzantium. He managed so to insinuate himself into the confidence of his contemptible master, by rendering him a hundred disreputable services, as to become possessed of indisputable power. He undermined Valentinian's belief in Ætius and at last persuaded him that his only safety lay in condemning the general to death.

Ætius lent some appearance of truth to Heraclius' misrepresentations. He displayed great eagerness about the marriage of the Princess and his son. Although the witness of many historians would sufficiently prove that for the most part the calumnies of Heraclius were groundless, Ætius' attitude in the past towards Count Boniface and others, indicate that he was not incapable of sacrificing honour and conscience for his personal advancement. His ambition was fanned by his wife, who longed to see Gaudentius in the purple. This lady discovered, by means of superstitious rites and haruspices, that Majorien, one of her husband's officers, would one day fill the office she so coveted for her son, and accordingly obliged Ætius to dismiss him since she could not obtain his condemnation to death. If the general would not clear the way for Gaudentius at the sacrifice of a soldier's life, neither could he have nourished plans of regicide. He was so greatly beloved and trusted by his troops and personal friends, that when danger was discerned ahead, and they were bribed by Ætius' enemies to desert him, they all stood firm. Even the father of Majorien, Ætius' master of finance, refused to desert the general.

"The luxury of Rome seems to have attracted the long and frequent visits of the Emperor, who was consequently more despised there than in any other part of his dominions." His residence in the eternal city was injurious to the peace and honour of innumerable noble families, and some of Ætius' chief enemies at court were the men who longed to see him removed merely in order to revenge themselves on the man whom his presence protected. They instigated Heraclius to defame the general, and at last when Ætius was summoned in disgrace before the Emperor none rushed forward to parry the treacherous thrust, and Ætius fell by his sovereign's own hand. His friends without were despatched singly by the Palace Guard.

But his death was speedily avenged. The murderous and ungrateful Emperor supposing no men capable of fine resentment, had the folly to admit Majorien and others of the late general's followers into his corps d'élite. The vengeful nobles found no difficulty in arranging with these for the assassination of the licentious tyrant.

The story which would most sensationally account for Maximus' share in the death of Valentinian is now discredited, but whether the Emperor had done this senator the foulest wrong one man can do another or not, certain it is that the latter had some cause to rejoice, even if he did not assist, at Valentinian's end. When on March 16, 455, as the Emperor was witnessing some sports in the Campus Martius at Rome, Majorien and the rest sprang upon him with naked swords and bore him to the ground; not one of his numerous train raised a hand in his defence. The Senator Petronius Maximus saw the bleeding corpse of the enemy of his entire order at his feet, and heard himself saluted Emperor by the unanimous voice of the Senate and people.

When the grief-stricken widow of Valentinian found herself forced into a speedy marriage with the senator she indeed felt doubly outraged. The union of his son Palladius with Eudocia, lately betrothed to Gaudentius, might tend to establish the hereditary succession of the noble Anician family, "but the violence" offered to herself "could only proceed from the blind impulse of lust or revenge. His own wife had been removed by death," and Athenais' widowed daughter "was compelled to violate her decent mourning" and marry a man whom she suspected as the prime mover in the plot against her murdered husband.

These suspicions were soon confirmed by the indiscreet confession of the Emperor himself, who declared that he had conspired against Valentinian solely for love of his reluctant bride. But when he saw that Eudocia was further incensed against him by this vain assertion, and not to be cajoled by his vile endearments, he wantonly provoked her hatred; "while his hours were disturbed by guilt, remorse and terror, and his recently acquired throne was shaken by ever-recurring seditions."

Eudocia still retained something of her mother's spirit. At little over thirty she was yet young enough to feel that if life had been robbed of all its possibilities of happiness, its peace was worth an effort. Life with Maximus was intolerable! From the East she could look for no assistance. Her father and her aunt

Pulcheria were dead, and the sceptre of Constantinople was now wielded by a stranger. Her mother languished in exile at the head of a schismatical party, and only by a hazard as desperate as Honoria's might the indignant Empress hope to burst her bonds.

She sent to Genseric, King of the African Vandals, imploring him to come to Italy and avenge her husband's murder and her own disgrace.

Three days before the barbarian entered Rome, filled with the lust of sack and booty, Maximus in ignominious flight had been overwhelmed with a shower of stones, and torn limb from limb in the streets. His dishonoured corpse was flung derisively into the river; his son Palladius met with a similar end, and Eudocia's daughter was a widow like her mother. Pope Leo went forth from the gates of the distracted city to intercede with Genseric, as he had already turned Attila aside. His intervention mitigated the ruthlessness of the Vandal's intentions, and although Genseric's promises of moderation were neither sincerely given, nor his orders strictly obeyed, St. Leo's intervention was glorious to himself, and to some degree providential for the Romans. Eudocia met her supposed deliverer at the gates in royal robes and jewels. He stripped her of her heirloom treasures on the spot and sacked the city; "and that was her reward." Rome and its inhabitants were delivered to the Vandals and Moors "whose blind passions revenged the injuries of Carthage." The pillage lasted fourteen days and nights, and the mistress of the world was robbed of all the riches it had taken her twelve centuries to amass. When Genseric and his host regained their ships at Ostia they were overladen with the spoil.

The Empress found the protection she had invoked more terrible than the affronts it was to have avenged. She herself, together with her two daughters and Ætius' son, Gaudentius, was carried off to Africa with a host of other captives. The charity of Deogratias, the celebrated Bishop of Carthage, who like Acacius of Amida, sold the gold and silver of his Church to alleviate their sufferings, was no less welcome to the Imperial prisoners in their fallen estate than to the humblest of the Roman sufferers. "By his order two spacious churches were converted into hospitals, the sick were distributed in convenient beds and liberally supplied with food and medicines." The unhappy Eudocia must have suffered most of all during the hardships and the mental anguish of that passage from Italy to Africa.

She was held prisoner by the Vandal king despite many Imperial remonstrances from Constantinople for the weary term of six years. During that interval the Emperor Marcian died at Constantinople and the house of Theodosius became extinct in the East.

Marcian had legally become head of the entire Empire on the

death of Valentinian, but like Theodosius in 423, he judged it best to admit a co-adjutor in the West, and accordingly returned a friendly reply to the embassy sent him by Avitus, the successor of Maximus The death of Attila naturally relieved the Byzantines of one of their greatest fears, and the Emperor hoped to garrison the Empire against any further inroads of the Huns by granting large tracts of territory to many of those barbaric nations who revolted from their allegiance to that people. He sent an embassy to Genseric in 455 to remonstrate against the Italian expedition which had resulted in the sack of Rome, and the capture of the Empress and her daughters. But it was entirely without avail, and on the failure of a second mission headed specially by an Arian Bishop, Bleda, Marcian began to prepare for war. He had, however, already been ill for some months. On the 26th of January, 457, he took part in some religious procession outside Constantinople, and died very shortly afterwards. The historian Zonaras seems to indicate that he was possibly poisoned by the ambitious Aspar. His reign had lasted just long enough to restore order and security in the Empire, and comparative peace in the Church, but with its sudden termination the Theodosian epoch abruptly closes.

Only by one frail thread was the East still linked to the West. The ex-Empress Eudocia was yet in bondage, and she could only look to Constantinople for release. Her elder daughter Eudocia, the seventeen-year-old widow of Palladius had been early forced into a marriage with Hunneric, Genseric's eldest son. She became the mother of Hilderic, the king who afterwards gave peace to the persecuted Church in Africa.

When at last, in 462, the Byzantine Emperor Leo succeeded in persuading Genseric to send the ex-Empress and her younger daughter back to Constantinople, Hunneric's unhappy wife decided to escape. Some ten years elapsed before she was able to effect her purpose. At last, however, aided by a certain Curcus and his sons, whom she gratefully remembered on her deathbed, Eudocia fled from Hunneric and Africa and found a refuge at Jerusalem. She meant to spend the remainder of her life in religious retirement, but died within a few days of her arrival in that city. She was laid to rest beside her mother's mother; of all the Eudocias none had led a sadder life than she.

The ex-Empress of the West resumed some rank in Constantinople, and lived there in honoured and religious widowhood. She greatly revered St. Daniel the Stylite, he who had been the Prefect Cyrus' friend, and at one time hoped he would have accepted a "solitude" of one of her numerous estates. The Saint praised her devotion, thanked her for her affection, but declared his determination of remaining where Almighty God had placed him.

The rapid changes of the next few years tended to rob Eudocia of her Imperial prestige. With the deaths of Theodosius, Pulcheria and Marcian, the memory of that family passed away, and within a short cycle history was made afresh in the East. In the West, however, the dynasty of Theodosius the Great lingered on a few years longer.

Valentinian's second daughter, the young Placidia, had been affianced to Olybrius, one of the noblest scions of the great Anician family, and a Senator of Rome, before the sacking of that city by the Vandals. But for this fact, or for some reason of greater weight, Genseric might have bestowed her upon his younger son Gento, with as little consideration as he displayed for her sister. As it was, the lovers lost each other, and for six years Placidia had to call to her aid what fortitude, what constancy, what patience, and hope, a loving woman in desperate circumstances may. She was twenty-three when release came at last. She met Olybrius again in Constantinople whither he had fled in 455. Neither had he married nor forgotten in the interval. It was easy to obtain the Emperor's sanction, and Placidia and Olybrius were shortly united. In the meantime, however, two transitory Emperors had occupied the throne of the Western Empire, and for the last few years discord had been fomenting between Anthemius, a third, and the powerful Patrician Ricimer. In 472 an extraordinary civil war in Italy caused this "king-maker" to disclaim all allegiance to the Greek Emperor nominated from Constantinople, and to espouse the cause of another candidate. Olybrius, as the husband of an Imperial princess, might esteem himself the lawful heir of her father's long lost throne, and the King of the Vandals himself was disposed to support the claim of one who had entered into an alliance with Hunneric, his son. "Thus when Ricimer meditated the ruin of the Emperor Anthemius, he tempted with the offer of a diadem the candidate who could justify his rebellion by an illustrious name and a royal alliance." Olybrius and Placidia left Constantinople in 479, and with the help of the Emperor Leo and of Genseric the Vandal, proceeded without hindrance to Italy and Ricimer, in whose camp they were received as sovereigns of the Western world.

But Fortune spun her wheel with incredible caprice in these years of the fall of Rome.

No sooner had Valentinian's death and the miseries of his widow been apparently avenged by the restoration of their daughter to their dishonoured throne, than "all the principal actors in this great revolution were removed from the stage; and the whole reign of Olybrius . . . . was included within the term of seven months." He left one daughter, the Princess Julia Anicia, the offspring of his marriage with the younger Placidia, who consoled herself in the midst of fluctuating fortunes by the study of medicine. There is, in one of the Italian museums to this day, the celebrated manuscript which Dioscorides executed at her orders. The family of the great Theodosius transplanted from

Spain to the Imperial cities of the East and West was propagated in the female line as far as the eighth generation. But with the deaths of Placidia and Olybrius, which apparently took place last of all of the deaths it concerns us to chronicle, the story of St. Pulcheria draws to an obscure close.

The history of the fourth century is full of crisis, and in the story of each of its salient personalities there is climax and anti-climax. With the attenuation of the Theodosian line the tale grows confused and crowded. New figures belonging rather to the fateful coming time than to the years which they link with the past, crowd the familiar scenes and open up new history. St. Pulcheria and her attendant throng are swept aside by the onrushing stream which presently engulfs the Empire. And now

> " Over the waters in the vaporous West
> The sun goes down as in a sphere of gold
> Behind the arm of her city, which between,
> With all that length of domes and minarets,
> Athwart the splendour, black and crooked runs
> Like a Turk verse along a scimitar ! " *

Browning * Paracelsus.

W. JOLLY & SONS, PRINTERS, BRIDGE STREET, ABERDEEN.

INDEX

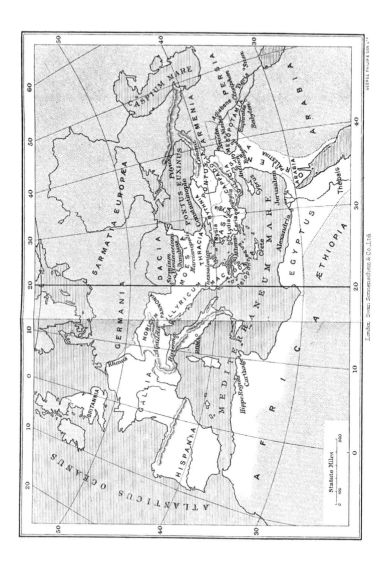

Sketch Map of the Roman Empire, as divided under the sons of Theodosius the Great, A.D. 395. Arcadius (and his son, Theodosius ii.), reigned over the provinces extending from the Danube to the confines of Persia and Æthiopia; Honorius assumed the government of Italy, Africa. Gaul, Spain and Britain. The martial prefecture of Illyricum was divided between the two princes. The eastern half of the Empire (divided approximately from the western by the meridian 20) was regarded as even more important than the portion ruled from Ravenna, and in 395 fell to the share of the elder son.

27453752R00182

Made in the USA
Lexington, KY
10 November 2013